"Steeler Nation"
History of the Pittsburgh Steelers

To order go to https://stevesfootballbible.com/paperback-bookstore/

Table of Contents

Brief History of the Pittsburgh Steelers

Founded in 1933, the Steelers are the seventh-oldest franchise in the NFL, and the oldest franchise in the AFC. In contrast with their status as perennial also-rans in the pre-merger NFL, where they were the oldest team never to have won a league championship, the Steelers of the post-merger (modern) era are among the most successful NFL franchises. The team is tied with the New England Patriots for the most Super Bowl titles at six, and they have both played in (sixteen times) and hosted (eleven times) more conference championship games than any other team in the NFL. The Steelers have also won eight AFC championships, tied with the Denver Broncos, but behind the Patriots' record eleven AFC championships. The team is tied with the Broncos and Dallas Cowboys for the second-most Super Bowl appearances with eight. They lost their most recent championship appearance, Super Bowl XLV, on February 6, 2011.

The Steelers, whose history may be traced to a regional pro team that was established in the early 1920s, joined the NFL as the Pittsburgh Pirates on July 8, 1933. The team was owned by Art Rooney and took its original name from the baseball team of the same name, as was common practice for NFL teams at the time. To distinguish them from the baseball team, local media took to calling the football team the Rooneymen, an unofficial nickname that persisted for decades after the team had adopted its current nickname. The ownership of the Steelers has remained within the Rooney family since the organization's founding. Art Rooney's son, Dan Rooney, owned the team from 1988 until his death in 2017. Much control of the franchise has been given to Dan Rooney's son, Art Rooney II.

The Steelers enjoy a large, widespread fanbase nicknamed Steeler Nation. They currently play their home games at Heinz Field on Pittsburgh's North Side in the North Shore neighborhood, which also hosts the University of Pittsburgh Panthers. Built in 2001, the stadium replaced Three Rivers Stadium, which had hosted the Steelers for 31 seasons. Prior to Three Rivers, the Steelers had played their games in Pitt Stadium and at Forbes Field.

The Pittsburgh Steelers of the NFL first took to the field as the Pittsburgh Pirates on September 20, 1933, losing 23–2 to the New York Giants. Through the 1930s, the Pirates never finished higher than second place in their division, or with a record better than .500 (1936). Pittsburgh did make history in 1938 by signing Byron White, a future Justice of the U.S. Supreme Court, to what was at the time the biggest contract in NFL history, but he played only one year with the Pirates before signing with the Detroit Lions. Prior to the 1940 season, the Pirates renamed themselves the Steelers. During World War II, the Steelers experienced player shortages. They twice merged with other NFL franchises to field a team. During the 1943 season, they merged with the Philadelphia Eagles forming the "Phil-Pitt Eagles" and were known as the "Steagles". This team went 5–4–1. In 1944, they merged with the Chicago Cardinals and were known as Card-Pitt (or, mockingly, as the "Carpets"). This team finished 0–10, marking the only winless team in franchise history.

The Steelers made the playoffs for the first time in 1947, tying for first place in the division at 8–4 with the Philadelphia Eagles. This forced a tie-breaking playoff game at Forbes Field, which the Steelers lost 21–0. That would be Pittsburgh's only playoff game in the pre-merger era; they did qualify for a "Playoff Bowl" in 1962 as the second-best team in their conference, but this was not considered an official playoff. In 1970, the year they moved into Three Rivers Stadium and the year of the AFL–NFL merger, the Pittsburgh Steelers were one of three old-guard NFL teams to switch to the newly formed American Football Conference (the others being the Cleveland Browns and the Baltimore Colts), in order to equalize the number of teams in the two conferences of the newly merged league. The Steelers also received a $3 million ($20 million today) relocation fee, which was a windfall for them; for years they rarely had enough to build a true contending team.

Logo and uniforms

The Steelers have used black and gold as their colors since the
club's inception, the lone exception being the 1943 season when they
merged with the Philadelphia Eagles and formed the "Steagles"; the
team's colors at that time were green and white because of wearing
Eagles uniforms. Originally, the team wore solid gold-colored helmets
and black jerseys. The Steelers' black and gold colors are now shared
by all major professional teams in the city, including the Pittsburgh

Pirates in baseball and the Pittsburgh Penguins in ice hockey. The shade of gold differs slightly among
teams: the Penguins have previously used "Vegas Gold", a color like metallic gold, and the Pirates' gold is
a darker mustard yellow gold, while the Steelers "gold" is more of a bright canary yellow. Black and gold
are also the colors of the city's official flag.

The Steelers logo was introduced in 1962 and is based on the "Steelmark", originally designed by
Pittsburgh's U.S. Steel, and now owned by the American Iron and Steel Institute (AISI). In fact, it
was Cleveland-based Republic Steel that suggested the Steelers adopt the industry logo. It consists of the
word "Steelers" surrounded by three astroids (hypocycloids of four cusps). The original meanings behind
the astroids were, "Steel lightens your work, brightens your leisure, and widens your world." Later, the
colors came to represent the ingredients used in the steel-making process: yellow for coal, red for iron ore,
and blue for scrap steel. While the formal Steelmark logo contains only the word "Steel", the team was
given permission to add "ers" in 1963 after a petition to AISI.

The Steelers are the only NFL team that puts its logo on only one side of the helmet (the right
side). Longtime field and equipment manager Jack Hart was instructed to do this by Art Rooney as a test
to see how the logo appeared on the gold helmets; however, its popularity led the team to leave it that way
permanently. A year after introducing the logo, they switched to black helmets to make it stand out more.
The Steelers, along with the New York Giants, are one of only two teams in the National Football
League to have the players' uniform numbers on both the front and back of the helmets.

The current uniform designs were introduced in 1968. The design
consists of gold pants and either black jerseys or white jerseys, except for
the 1970 and 1971 seasons when the Steelers wore white pants with their
white jerseys. In 1997, the team switched to rounded numbers on the jersey
to match the number font (Futura Condensed) on the helmets, and a Steelers
logo was added to the left side of the jersey.
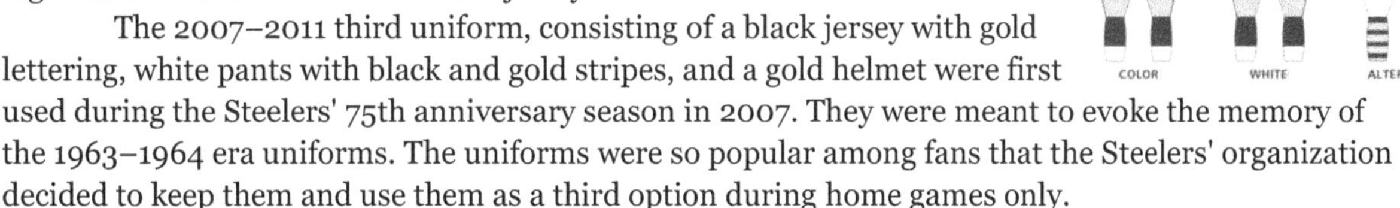

The 2007–2011 third uniform, consisting of a black jersey with gold
lettering, white pants with black and gold stripes, and a gold helmet were first
used during the Steelers' 75th anniversary season in 2007. They were meant to evoke the memory of
the 1963–1964 era uniforms. The uniforms were so popular among fans that the Steelers' organization
decided to keep them and use them as a third option during home games only.

In 2012, the Steelers introduced a new third uniform, consisting of a yellow jersey with black
horizontal lines (making a bumble bee like pattern) with black lettering and black numbers placed inside a
white box, to represent the jerseys worn by the Steelers in their 1934 season. The rest of the uniform
consists of beige pants, yellow with black horizontal stripped socks, and the Steelers regular black helmet.
The uniforms were used for the Steelers' 80th anniversary season. Much like the previous alternate these
jerseys were so popular that they were used up through the 2016 season. The jerseys were nicknamed the
"bumblebee jerseys" due to looking like the pattern of a bumblebee. The jerseys were retired after the
2016 season.

In 2018, the Steelers unveiled a third uniform based on those worn by the Steel Curtain teams of
the 1970s. It is like the current uniforms but without the Steelers logo on the left chest and uses block
lettering and numbers in place of Futura Condensed. In 1979, the team owners were approached by then-
Iowa Hawkeyes Head Coach Hayden Fry about designing his fading college team's uniforms in the image

of the Steelers. Three days later, the owners sent Fry the reproduction jerseys (home and away versions) of then quarterback Terry Bradshaw. Today, the Hawkeyes still retain the 1979 Steelers uniforms as their home, and away colors.

Stadiums

Forbes Field {1933-1963}

Forbes Field was a baseball park in the Oakland neighborhood of Pittsburgh, Pennsylvania, from 1909 to June 28, 1970. It was the third home of the Pittsburgh Pirates Major League Baseball (MLB) team, and the first home of the Pittsburgh Steelers, the city's National Football League (NFL) franchise. The stadium also served as the home football field for the University of Pittsburgh "Pitt" Panthers from 1909 to 1924. The stadium was named after its adjacent street, Forbes Ave., itself named for British general John Forbes, who fought in the French and Indian War and named the city in 1758.

The US$1 million ($28.8 million today) project was initiated by Pittsburgh Pirates' owner Barney Dreyfuss, with the goal of replacing his franchise's then-current home, Exposition Park. The stadium was made of concrete and steel, the first such stadium in the National League and third in Major League Baseball, in order to increase its lifespan. The Pirates opened Forbes Field on June 30, 1909, against the Chicago Cubs, and played the final game against the Cubs on June 28, 1970. The field itself featured a large playing surface, with the batting cage placed in the deepest part of center field during games. Seating was altered multiple times throughout the stadium's life; at times fans were permitted to sit on the grass in the outfield during overflow crowds. The Pirates won three World Series while at Forbes Field and the other original tenant, the Pittsburgh Panthers football team had five undefeated seasons before moving in 1924. Indeed, it was the late-fifties resurgence of its long-dormant baseball franchise, rather than any intrinsic properties of the stadium itself, that led broadcaster Bob Prince to dub Forbes Field "The House of Thrills" in 1958.

A Pittsburgh native, Art Rooney founded his NFL team under the name the Pittsburgh Pirates, on July 8, 1933, for $2,500 ($49,981 in present-day terms). The franchise's first game, against the New York Giants, was held on September 20, 1933, at Forbes Field. The Giants won the game 23–2 in front of 25,000 people. Rooney wrote of the game, "The Giants won. Our team looks terrible. The fans didn't get their money's worth." The Pirates rebounded to gain their first ever franchise victory a week later at Forbes Field, against the Chicago Cardinals. The NFL's Pirates were renamed the Steelers in 1940, and otherwise struggled during much of their three-decades of tenancy at Forbes. The club achieved its first winning record in 1942; its tenth season of existence. On November 30, 1952, the Steelers met the New York Giants at Forbes Field for a snowy afternoon game. Pittsburgh entered the game with a 3–6 record, but went on to set multiple team records, including scoring nine touchdowns, to win the game 63–7. Excited by their team's play, the 15,140 spectators ran onto the field and began to tear the field goal posts out of the ground. The University of Pittsburgh's acquisition of Forbes Field in 1958 gave the Steelers some options, and they began transferring some of their home games to the much larger Pitt Stadium that year. The Steelers played their final game at Forbes Field on December 1, 1963. The franchise moved to Pitt Stadium exclusively the following season.

Pitt Stadium {1958-1969}

Pitt Stadium was an outdoor athletic stadium in the eastern United States, located on the campus of the University of Pittsburgh in the Oakland neighborhood of Pittsburgh, Pennsylvania. Opened in 1925, it served primarily as the home of the university's Pittsburgh Panthers football team through 1999. It was also used for other sporting events, including basketball, soccer, baseball, track and field, rifle, and gymnastics. Designed by University of Pittsburgh graduate W. S.

Hindman, the $2.1 million stadium was built after the seating capacity of the Panthers' previous home, Forbes Field, was deemed inadequate considering the growing popularity of college football. Pitt Stadium also served as the second home of the Pittsburgh Steelers, the city's National Football League (NFL) franchise. After demolition, the Pittsburgh Panthers football team played home games at Three Rivers Stadium in 2000, before moving to the new Heinz Field in 2001, where the Panthers have played their home games ever since.

The NFL's Steelers played home games at Forbes Field from their 1933 inception to 1957. They first played at Pitt Stadium in 1942, in an exhibition match for U.S.O. charity against the Fort Knox "Armoraiders" on November 15. From 1958 to 1963, the Steelers split home games between Forbes Field and Pitt Stadium. Fans were able to purchase season ticket packages for one site or the other. In 1964, the Steelers began to play home games exclusively at Pitt Stadium, which they continued until moving to the new Three Rivers Stadium in 1970. Of historic note, the iconic photo of New York Giants quarterback Y. A. Tittle, helmetless, bloodied and kneeling, was taken at Pitt Stadium in 1964 following a Giants' loss to the Steelers on September 20. The photo, taken by Pittsburgh Post-Gazette photographer Morris Berman, now hangs in the Pro Football Hall of Fame.

Three Rivers Stadium {1970-2000}

Three Rivers Stadium was a multi-purpose stadium located in Pittsburgh, Pennsylvania, from 1970 to 2000. It was home to the Pittsburgh Pirates of Major League Baseball (MLB) and the Pittsburgh Steelers of the National Football League (NFL). Built as a replacement for Forbes Field, which opened in 1909, the US$55 million ($388.1 million today) multi-purpose facility was designed to maximize efficiency. Ground was broken in April 1968 and an oft behind-schedule construction plan lasted for 29 months. The stadium opened on July 16, 1970, when the Pirates played their first game there. In the 1971 World Series, Three Rivers Stadium hosted the first World Series game played at night. The following year, the stadium was the site of the Immaculate Reception. The final game in the stadium was won by the Steelers on December 16, 2000. Three Rivers Stadium also hosted the Pittsburgh Maulers of the United States Football League and the University of Pittsburgh Panthers football team for a single season each. After its closing, Three Rivers Stadium was imploded in 2001.

Three Rivers Stadium was a multi-purpose stadium located in Pittsburgh, Pennsylvania, from 1970 to 2000. It was home to the Pittsburgh Pirates of Major League Baseball (MLB) and the Pittsburgh Steelers of the National Football League (NFL). Built as a replacement for Forbes Field, which opened in 1909, the US$55 million ($388.1 million today) multi-purpose facility was designed to maximize efficiency. Ground was broken in April 1968 and an oft behind-schedule construction plan lasted for 29 months.[6] The stadium opened on July 16, 1970, when the Pirates played their first game there. In the 1971 World Series, Three Rivers Stadium hosted the first World Series game played at night. The following year, the stadium was the site of the Immaculate Reception. The final game in the stadium was won by the Steelers on December 16, 2000. Three Rivers Stadium also hosted the Pittsburgh Maulers of the United States Football League and the University of Pittsburgh Panthers football team for a single season each. After its closing, Three Rivers Stadium was imploded in 2001.

Heinz Field {2001-Present}

Heinz Field is a football stadium located in the North Shore neighborhood of Pittsburgh, Pennsylvania, United States. It primarily serves as the home of the Pittsburgh Steelers of the National Football League (NFL) and the Pittsburgh Panthers of the University of Pittsburgh. The stadium opened in 2001, after the controlled implosion of both teams' previous home, Three Rivers Stadium, and is named for the locally based H. J. Heinz Company, which purchased the naming rights in 2001. In February of 2022, the naming rights for the stadium expired, leaving the stadium's name for the 2022 season uncertain. Funded in conjunction with PNC Park and the David L. Lawrence Convention Center, the $281 million (equivalent to $410.7 million in 2020) stadium stands along the Ohio River, on the Northside of Pittsburgh in the North Shore neighborhood. The stadium was designed with the city of Pittsburgh's history of steel production in mind, which led to the inclusion of 12,000 tons of steel into construction. The ground for the stadium was broken in June 1999, and the first football game was hosted in September 2001. The stadium's natural grass surface has been criticized throughout its history, but Steelers ownership has kept the grass after lobbying from players and coaches. Attendance for the 68,400-seat stadium has sold out for every Steelers home game, a streak which dates to 1972. A collection of memorabilia from the Steelers and Panthers of the past can be found in the Great Hall.

Prior to the Steelers regular season schedule, the team played a pre-season game against the Detroit Lions on August 25, 2001. Pittsburgh won the stadium's unofficial opening game 20–7, with 57,829 spectators in attendance. The first official football game played in the stadium was between the Pittsburgh Panthers and East Tennessee State, on September 1. The Panthers won the game 31–0, with quarterback David Priestley scoring the first touchdown on an 85-yard run. The Steelers were scheduled to open the regular season play at Heinz Field on September 16 against the Cleveland Browns; however, due to the September 11 attacks, all NFL games of the week were postponed, thus moving the stadium's premiere to October 7, against the Cincinnati Bengals. Prior to the game, a speech from US President George W. Bush, ordering attacks on Taliban-controlled Afghanistan, was shown live on the stadium's JumboTron. The speech was met with much applause and support from the spectators in attendance. Pittsburgh defeated the Bengals, 16–7. Steelers kicker Kris Brown scored the first NFL points in the stadium on a 26-yard field goal, and quarterback Kordell Stewart scored the first touchdown on an eight-yard run.

Retired uniform numbers

No.	Player	Position	Seasons	Retired
32	Franco Harris	RB	1972-1983	December 24, 2022
70	Ernie Stautner	DT	1950–1963	October 25, 1964
75	Joe Greene	DT	1969–1981	November 2, 2014

The Steelers retired Stautner's #70 in 1964 before creating a 50-year tradition of not retiring numbers. The team retired Greene's #75 in 2014 and left the possibility open that they would retire other players' jersey numbers at later dates. However, several numbers have not been reissued since the retirement of the players who wore them, including:

1	Gary Anderson
7	Ben Roethlisberger
12	Terry Bradshaw
36	Jerome Bettis
43	Troy Polamalu
47	Mel Blount
52	Mike Webster
58	Jack Lambert
59	Jack Ham
63	Dermontti Dawson
86	Hines Ward

Pro Football Hall-of-Famers

No.	Name	Inducted	Position(s)	Years w/ Steelers
35	"Bullet" Bill Dudley	1966	RB	1942, 1945–1946
35	Walt Kiesling	1966	G/Line coach/Head coach/Aide	1937–1944 1949–1961
70	Ernie Stautner	1969	DT	1950–1963
35	John Henry Johnson	1987	RB	1960–1965
75	"Mean" Joe Greene	1987	DT	1969–1981
59	Jack Ham	1988	LB	1971–1982
47	Mel Blount	1989	CB	1970–1983
12	Terry Bradshaw	1989	QB	1970–1983
32	Franco Harris	1990	RB	1972–1983
58	Jack Lambert	1990	LB	1974–1984
52	"Iron" Mike Webster	1997	C	1974–1988
88	Lynn Swann	2001	WR	1974–1982
82	John Stallworth	2002	WR	1974–1987
26	Rod Woodson	2009	CB	1987–1996
80	Jack Butler	2012	CB	1951–1959
63	Dermontti Dawson	2012	C	1988–2000
36	"The Bus" Jerome Bettis	2015	RB	1996–2005
91	Kevin Greene	2016	LB	1993–1996
43	Troy Polamalu	2020	S	2003–2014
31	Donnie Shell	2020	S	1974–1987
66	Alan Faneca	2021	G	1998–2007

Coaches and Contributors

Name	Inducted	Position(s)	Years w/ Steelers
"The Chief" Art Rooney	1964	Founder, Owner	1933–1988
Chuck Noll	1993	Head coach	1969–1991
Dan Rooney	2000	Executive, Owner	1975–2017
Bill Cowher	2020	Head coach	1992–2006
Bill Nunn	2021	Scout/Assistant Director Player Personnel/Senior Scout	1968–2014

Steelers Hall-of-Honor

#	Name	Position	Years With Club	Inducted
36	Jerome Bettis	RB	1996–2005	2017
20	Rocky Bleier	RB	1968, 1970–80	2018
47	Mel Blount	CB	1970–83	2017
12	Terry Bradshaw	QB	1970–83	2017
87/79	Larry Brown	TE/OT	1971–76/1977–84	2019
80	Jack Butler	CB	1951–59	2017
—	Bill Cowher	Coach	1992–2006	2019
63	Dermontti Dawson	C	1988–2000	2017
84	Buddy Dial	WR	1959–63	2018
35	Bill Dudley	HB	1942, 1945–46	2017
66	Alan Faneca	G	1998–2007	2018
51	James Farrior	LB	2002–11	2020
75	Joe Greene	DT	1969–81	2017
91	Kevin Greene	LB	1993–95	2017
68	L.C. Greenwood	DE	1969–81	2017
59	Jack Ham	LB	1971–82	2017
32	Franco Harris	RB	1972–83	2017
42	Dick Hoak	RB/Coach	1961–70/1972–2006	2017
62	Tunch Ilkin	OT	1980–92	2021
35	John Henry Johnson	FB	1960–65	2017
35	Walt Kiesling	G/Coach	1937–39 1939–44, 1954–56	2017
55	Jon Kolb	OT	1969–81	2021
37	Carnell Lake	S/CB	1989–98	2021
58	Jack Lambert	LB	1974–84	2017
22	Bobby Layne	QB	1958–62	2017
83	Louis Lipps	WR	1984–91	2021
95	Greg Lloyd	LB	1988–97	2020
15	Johnny "Blood" McNally	FB/Coach	1934, 1937–39 1937–39	2017
81	Elbie Nickel	TE	1947–57	2019
—	Chuck Noll	Coach	1969–91	2017
—	Bill Nunn	Scout/Assistant Director Player Personnel/Senior Scout	1968–2014	2018

43	Troy Polamalu	S	2003–14	2020
—	Art Rooney, Jr.	Personnel Director/Vice President	1965–86 1987–present	2018
—	Art Rooney, Sr.	Founder/President/Chairman of the Board	1933–88	2017
—	Dan Rooney, Sr.	President/Chairman	1955–2017	2017
34	Andy Russell	LB	1963, 1966–76	2017
31	Donnie Shell	S	1974–87	2017
82	John Stallworth	WR	1974–87	2017
70	Ernie Stautner	DT	1950–63	2017
88	Lynn Swann	WR	1974–82	2017
23	Mike Wagner	S	1971–80	2020
86	Hines Ward	WR	1998–2011	2019
52	Mike Webster	C	1974–88	2017
78	Dwight White	DE	1971–80	2020
26	Rod Woodson	CB	1987–96	2017
---	Myron Cope	Broadcaster	1970-2004	2022
57	Sam Davis	G	1967-1979	2022
83	Heath Miller	TE	2005-2015	2022
25	Ray Matthews	RB	1951-1959	2022
92	James Harrison	LB	2002—2012, 2014-17	2023
72	Gerry Mullins	G	1971-1979	2023
56	Ray Mansfield	C	1964-1976	2023
91	Aaron Smith	DE	1999-2011	2023
92	Jason Gildon	LB	1994-2003	2024
98	Casey Hampton	NT	2001-2012	2024
---	Dick LeBeau	DB Coach/DB Coordinator	1992-1996/2004-2014	2024
39	Willie Parker	RB	2004-2009	2024

Tribute to Franco Harris

Harris was born in Fort Dix, New Jersey. His father, Cad Harris, a Black soldier, served in World War II and was stationed in Italy during the war. His mother, Gina Parenti Harris, was a native Italian and became a "war bride", who moved with her husband when he returned to the United States after the end of the war. Harris graduated from Rancocas Valley Regional High School in Mount Holly Township, New Jersey, in 1968. He then attended Penn State University, where he played on the Nittany Lions football team. Although he was primarily a blocker for the running back during his first year at Penn State, he amassed a career total of 2,002 yards rushing with 24 touchdowns and averaged over 5 yards per carry, while also catching 28 passes for 352 yards and another touchdown. He led the team in scoring in 1970. After playing college football for the Penn State Nittany Lions, Harris was selected by the Steelers in the first round of the 1972 NFL Draft, the 13th overall pick. He played his first 12 seasons with the Steelers and his last with the Seattle Seahawks. He was inducted into the Pro Football Hall of Fame in 1990.

Harris was selected 13th overall in the first round of the 1972 NFL Draft by the Pittsburgh Steelers despite assistant personnel director Bill Nunn and head coach Chuck Noll preferring Robert Newhouse. In his first season with the Steelers (1972), Harris was named the NFL Rookie of the Year by The Sporting News and NFL Offensive Rookie of the Year by the Associated Press. In that season he gained 1,055 yards on 188 carries, with a 5.6 yards per carry average. He also rushed for 10 touchdowns and caught one touchdown pass. He was popular with Pittsburgh's large Italian American population: his fans, including "Brigadier General" Frank Sinatra, dubbed themselves "Franco's Italian Army" and wore army helmets with his number on them. During his rookie season, Harris was a key player in one of professional football's most famous plays, dubbed the "Immaculate Reception" by Pittsburgh sportscaster Myron Cope. In the first round of the playoffs, the Oakland Raiders were leading the Steelers 7–6 with 22 seconds to play when a Terry Bradshaw pass was deflected away from intended receiver John "Frenchy" Fuqua as defender Jack Tatum arrived to tackle him. Harris snatched the ball just before it hit the ground and ran it into the endzone, resulting in the Steelers' first playoff win. Harris was chosen for nine consecutive Pro Bowls (1972–1980) and was All-Pro in 1977. Harris rushed for more than 1,000 yards in eight seasons, breaking a record set by Jim Brown. The running back tandem of Harris and Rocky Bleier combined with a strong defense to win four Super Bowls following the 1974, 1975, 1978, and 1979 seasons. On January 12, 1975, he was the Most Valuable Player of Super Bowl IX; in that game he rushed for 158 yards and a touchdown on 34 carries for a 16–6 win over the Minnesota Vikings. Harris was the first African American as well as the first Italian American to be named Super Bowl MVP. Harris was a major contributor for the Steelers in all their first four Super Bowl wins. His Super Bowl career totals of 101 carries for 354 yards are records and his four career rushing touchdowns are tied for the second-most in Super Bowl history. Harris claimed that he extended his career and thus his contribution to the team's objectives (including four Super Bowl victories) by avoiding unnecessary contact. In his 13 professional seasons, Harris gained 12,120 yards (3rd all-time) on 2,949 carries, a 4.1 yards per carry average, and scored 91 rushing touchdowns (then also 3rd). He caught 307 passes for 2,287 yards, a 7.4 yards per reception average, and nine receiving touchdowns. Harris's 12,120 career rushing yards rank him 12th all-time in the NFL, while his 91 career rushing touchdowns rank him 10th all-time, tied with Jerome Bettis.

Harris died in his sleep at his home in Sewickley, Pennsylvania on December 20, 2022 at age 72, three days before the 50th anniversary of the "Immaculate Reception". Harris' death was considered sudden, as he had been active on social media just days before his death and had spoken to visitors at the Heinz History Center the day before his death including a live interview with KDKA-TV from the Heinz History Center. He was set to attend a ceremony at halftime during a Steelers game against the Las Vegas Raiders on December 24, 2022, to retire his jersey number. Hours before his death, Harris recorded an interview with Steelers defensive end Cameron Heyward for his podcast in what would be his last public interview, during which he ironically commented about how he was "feeling good" and happy to have made it to the 50th anniversary of the "Immaculate Reception".

R.I.P. Franco

Head Coaches

#	Name	Term	Regular season					Playoffs			
			GC	W	L	T	Win %	GC	W	L	Win%
1	Forrest Douds*	1933*	11	3	6	2	.333	—			
2	Luby DiMeolo*	1934*	12	2	10	0	.167	—			
3	Joe Bach*	1935–1936*	24	10	14	0	.416	—			
4	John McNally ‡*	1937–1939*	25	6	19	0	.240	—			
5	Walt Kiesling ‡*	1939–1940*	19	3	13	3	.188	—			
6	Bert Bell ^	1941	2	0	2	0	.000	—			
7	Aldo Donelli	1941	5	0	5	0	.000	—			
—	Walt Kiesling ‡*	1941–1944*	35	13	20	2	.394	—			
8	Jim Leonard*	1945*	10	2	8	0	.200	—			
9	Jock Sutherland	1946–1947	23	13	9	1	.591	1	0	1	.000
10	John Michelosen*	1948–1951*	48	20	26	2	.435	—			
—	Joe Bach*	1952–1953*	24	11	13	0	.485	—			
—	Walt Kiesling ‡*	1954–1956*	36	14	22	0	.389	—			
11	Buddy Parker	1957–1964	104	51	47	6	.520	—			
12	Mike Nixon	1965	14	2	12	0	.143	—			
13	Bill Austin	1966–1968	42	11	28	3	.282	—			
14	Chuck Noll †*	1969–1991*	342	193	148	1	.566	24	16	8	.667
15	Bill Cowher†*	1992–2006*	240	149	90	1	.623	21	12	9	.571
16	Mike Tomlin+*	2007–2025	309	193	114	2	.628	16	8	8	.500

The Chuck Noll era

    The Steelers' history of bad luck changed with the hiring of coach Chuck Noll from the NFL champion Baltimore Colts for the 1969 season. Noll's most remarkable talent was in his draft selections, taking Hall of Famers "Mean" Joe Greene in 1969, Terry Bradshaw and Mel Blount in 1970, Jack Ham in 1971, Franco Harris in 1972, and finally, in 1974, pulling off the incredible feat of selecting four Hall of Famers in one draft year, Lynn Swann, Jack Lambert, John Stallworth, and Mike Webster. The Pittsburgh Steelers' 1974 draft was their best; no other team has ever drafted four future Hall of Famers in one year, and only very few (including the 1970 Steelers) have drafted two or more in one year. The players drafted in the early 1970s formed the base of an NFL dynasty, making the playoffs in eight seasons and becoming the only team in NFL history to win four Super Bowls in six years, as well as the first to win more than two. They also enjoyed a regular-season streak of 49 consecutive wins (1971–1979) against teams that would finish with a losing record that year.

    The Steelers suffered a rash of injuries in the 1980 season and missed the playoffs with a 9–7 record. The 1981 season was no better, with an 8–8 showing. The team was then hit with the retirements of all their key players from the Super Bowl years. "Mean" Joe Greene retired after the 1981 season, Lynn Swann and Jack Ham after 1982's playoff berth, Terry Bradshaw and Mel Blount after 1983's divisional championship, and Jack Lambert after 1984's AFC Championship Game appearance. After those retirements, the franchise skidded to its first losing seasons since 1971. Though still competitive, the Steelers would not finish above .500 in 1985, 1986, and 1988. In 1987, the year of the players' strike, the Steelers finished with a record of 8–7 but missed the playoffs. In 1989, they would reach the second round of the playoffs on the strength of Merrill Hoge and Rod Woodson before narrowly missing the playoffs in each of the next two seasons, Noll's last seasons. Noll's career record with Pittsburgh was 209–156–1.

The Bill Cowher era

In 1992, Chuck Noll retired and was succeeded by Kansas City Chiefs defensive coordinator Bill Cowher, a native of the Pittsburgh suburb of Crafton. Cowher led the Steelers to the playoffs in each of his first six seasons, a feat that had been accomplished only by legendary coach Paul Brown of the Cleveland Browns. In those first six seasons, Cowher coached them as deep as the AFC Championship Game three times and following the 1995 season an appearance in Super Bowl XXX on the strength of the "Blitzburgh" defense. However, the Steelers lost to the Dallas Cowboys in Super Bowl XXX, two weeks after a thrilling AFC Championship victory over the Indianapolis Colts. Cowher produced the franchise's record-tying fifth Super Bowl win in Super Bowl XL over the NFC champion Seattle Seahawks ten years later. With that victory, the Steelers became the third team to win five Super Bowls, and the first sixth-seeded playoff team to reach and win the Super Bowl since the NFL expanded to a 12-team post-season tournament in 1990. He coached through the 2006 season which ended with an 8–8 record, just short of the playoffs. Overall Cowher's teams reached the playoffs 10 of 15 seasons with six AFC Championship Games, two Super Bowl berths and a championship. Cowher's career record with Pittsburgh was 149–90–1 in the regular season and 161–99–1 overall, including playoff games.

The Mike Tomlin era

On January 7, 2007, Cowher resigned from coaching the Steelers, citing a need to spend more time with his family. He did not use the term "retire", leaving open a possible return to the NFL as coach of another team. A three-man committee consisting of Art Rooney II, Dan Rooney, and Kevin Colbert was set up to conduct interviews for the head coaching vacancy. On January 22, 2007, Minnesota Vikings defensive coordinator Mike Tomlin was announced as Cowher's successor as head coach. Tomlin is the first African American to be named head coach of the team in its 75-year history. Tomlin became the third consecutive Steelers Head Coach to go to the Super Bowl, equaling the Dallas Cowboys (Tom Landry, Jimmy Johnson and Barry Switzer) in this achievement. He was named the Motorola 2008 Coach of the Year. On February 1, 2009, Tomlin led the Steelers to their second Super Bowl of this decade and went on to win 27–23 against the Arizona Cardinals. At age 36, he was the youngest head coach to ever win the Super Bowl, and he is only the second African American coach to ever win the Super Bowl (Tony Dungy was the first). The 2010 season made Tomlin the only coach to reach the Super Bowl twice before the age of 40 as he took the team to Super Bowl XLV on February 6, 2011. However, the Steelers were defeated by the Green Bay Packers, 31–25. The Steelers recorded their 400th victory in 2012 after defeating the Washington Redskins. Through the end of the 2020 season, Tomlin's record is 153–86–1 (.640), including playoffs. He is the first Pittsburgh coach to never post a losing season. The 2013–17 seasons were noted for record performances from the "Killer B's". This trio consisted of Antonio Brown, Ben Roethlisberger, and Le'Veon Bell. Occasionally, the "Killer B's" has also included kicker Chris Boswell due to his ability to hit game-winning field goals.

NFL Award Winners

NFL MVP Award Winners

Season	Player	Position
1946	Bill Dudley	HB
1978	Terry Bradshaw	QB

NFL Defensive Rookie of the Year

Season	Player	Position
1969	Joe Greene	DT
1974	Jack Lambert	LB
2001	Kendrell Bell	LB

NFL Defensive Player of the Year

Season	Player	Position
1972	Joe Greene	DT
1974	Joe Greene	DT
1975	Mel Blount	CB
1976	Jack Lambert	LB
1993	Rod Woodson	DB
2008	James Harrison	LB
2010	Troy Polamalu	S
2021	T. J. Watt	LB

Super Bowl MVP Award Winners

Super Bowl	Player	Position
IX	Franco Harris	RB
X	Lynn Swann	WR
XIII	Terry Bradshaw	QB
XIV	Terry Bradshaw	QB
XL	Hines Ward	WR
XLIII	Santonio Holmes	WR

NFL Offensive Rookie of the Year

Season	Player	Position
1972	Franco Harris	RB
1984	Louis Lipps	WR/RS
2004	Ben Roethlisberger	QB

1933 Pittsburgh Pirates

The 1933 Pittsburgh Pirates was the debut season of the team that eventually became the Pittsburgh Steelers. The team was founded after Pennsylvania relaxed its blue laws that, prior to 1933, prohibited sporting events from taking place on Sundays, when most NFL games took place. The new squad was composed largely of local semi-pro players, many of whom played for sports promoter Art Rooney. Rooney became the Pirates owner, paying the NFL a $2,500 fee to join the league. Except for a brief period in 1940 and '41, Rooney would remain the franchise's principal owner until his death in 1988. The Rooney family has retained a controlling interest ever since. The team took the field for the first time on September 20 against the New York Giants at Forbes Field, losing 23–2. The following week, the team got its first win, defeating the Chicago Cardinals at home 14–13. The team finished 3–6–2 for the season.

Tony Holm led the team in passing with 407 yards. Angelo Brovelli led the team in rushing with 236 yards. Ray Tesser led the team in receptions with 14. Paul Moss led the team with 283 yards receiving.

PITTSBURGH			1933			3-6-2	Game Highlights
9/20/1933		vs	NEW YORK GIANTS	2	23	L	**Oehler blocks punt out of end zone for safety**
9/27/1933		vs	CHICAGO CARDINALS	14	13	W	**Kottler 99-yard INT return TD**
10/4/1933	WED	vs	BOSTON REDSKINS	6	21	L	Brovelli scores lone TD for Pirates
10/11/1933	WED	vs	CINCINNATI REDS	17	3	W	Westfall & Vaughn score TDs for Pirates
10/15/1933		@	Green Bay	0	47	L	Pirates give up 7 touchdowns to Packers
10/22/1933		@	Cincinnati Reds	0	0	T	Snoozefest-Neither team can score
10/29/1933		@	Boston Redskins	16	14	W	Westfall 60-yard TD reception from Holm
11/5/1933		@	Brooklyn Dodgers	3	3	T	Kelsch kicks FG for Pirates only score
11/12/1933		vs	BROOKLYN DODGERS	0	32	L	Shipwreck Kelly runs wild over the Pirates
11/19/1933		@	Philadelphia	6	25	L	Brovelli scores lone Pirate TD
12/3/1933		@	New York Giants	3	27	L	Kelsch kicks FG for Pirates only score

Schedule courtesy of Steve's Football Bible LLC

1933 NFL Eastern Division	W	L	T	PCT	DIV	PF	PA
New York Giants	11	3	0	.786	7–1	244	101
Brooklyn Dodgers	5	4	1	.556	2–2–1	93	54
Boston Redskins	5	5	2	.500	2–3	103	97
Philadelphia Eagles	3	5	1	.375	1–2	77	158
Pittsburgh Pirates	**3**	**6**	**2**	**.333**	**1–5–1**	**67**	**208**

Pennsylvania Blue Laws

The state had "blue laws" designed to enforce religious practices on Sundays. The Sabbath was set aside as a day of rest and had restrictions on just about everything from shopping to restaurants to athletic events. Because the blue laws would not be voted on until November, the first four games of the maiden 1933 season were home games played on Wednesday nights followed by four road games. The first Sunday contest was played on November 12, 1933, in a 32-0 loss to the Brooklyn Dodgers before just over 12,000 patrons. The final two games were both road games.

1934 Pittsburgh Pirates

The 1934 Pirates (later renamed in 1940) began the season with a new coach, Luby DiMeolo, but again found themselves finishing in 5th place in the Eastern Division. The Pirates suffered a miserable 2–10 season, in which they were shut out in 6 games and only scored more than 10 points in 2 games. One point of interest of the season was the arrival of All-Pro and future Hall of Famer John McNally for one season from the Green Bay Packers. However, he did not have much of an impact for the Pirates before returning to the Packers the next season. This Pirates team also introduced their "jailbird" uniforms. While these uniforms were worn by the Steelers as throwbacks from 2012 to 2016 (albeit with the current colors, making them "bumblebee" uniforms), this was the only year they were used as the team was constantly made fun of for looking like convicts.

Warren Heller led the team in passing with 511 yards. Heller also led the team in rushing with 528 yards. Ben Smith led the team with 14 receptions. Joe Skladany led with 222 yards receiving.

PITTSBURGH			1934			2-10	Game Highlights
9/19/1934		vs	CINCINNATI REDS	13	0	W	Clark rush TD/Kelsch & Nicolai FG each
9/16/1934		vs	BOSTON REDSKINS	0	7	L	Pirates lose on touchdown pass
9/26/1934	WED	vs	PHILADELPHIA	0	7	L	Pirates shutout again/Hanson runs wild for Eagles
10/3/1934	WED	vs	NEW YORK GIANTS	12	14	L	Heller TD pass to Skladany/Heller rush TD
10/7/1934		@	Philadelphia	9	7	W	Brovelli rush TD/Nicolai FG
10/10/1934	WED	vs	CHICAGO	0	28	L	Pirates allow Feathers over 100 rush yads
10/14/1934		@	Boston Redskins	0	39	L	Pirates get blown out
10/21/1934		@	New York Giants	7	17	L	Vaughn TD pass to Sortet
10/28/1934		@	Brooklyn Dodgers	3	21	L	Nicolai kicks 50-yard FG
11/4/1934		@	Detroit	7	40	L	Vaughn 62-yard TD pass to Skladany
11/11/1934		@	St. Louis Gunners	0	6	L	Gunners kick 2 FGs to beat Pirates
11/18/1934		@	Brooklyn Dodgers	0	10	L	Kercheval scores all Dodgers points as Pirates lose

Schedule courtesy of Steve's Football Bible LLC

1934 NFL Eastern Division	W	L	T	PCT	DIV	PF	PA
New York Giants	8	5	0	.615	7–1	147	107
Boston Redskins	6	6	0	.500	5–3	107	94
Brooklyn Dodgers	4	7	0	.364	4–4	61	153
Philadelphia Eagles	4	7	0	.364	3–5	127	85
Pittsburgh Pirates	**2**	**10**	**0**	**.167**	**1–7**	**51**	**206**

1935 Pittsburgh Pirates

The 1935 Pirates fired former coach Luby DiMeolo after completing the '34 season with a 2–10 record. They brought in Duquesne head coach, Joe Bach, who improved their record to 4-8, and stayed until the next season before returning to coach in college.

Johnny Gildea led the team in passing with 529 yards and threw 2 touchdown passes. Warren Heller led the team with 112 rushing yards. Art Strutt and Jim Levey led the team in receptions with 7 each and 112 receiving yards each.

In Week 2 vs the Giants, New York head coach Steve Owen admits in 1935 that he "shaved" the game, ordering his Giants to fumble 3 times inside the 10 & didn't call a pass play in the 4th quarter, the world's first public admission of game fixing.

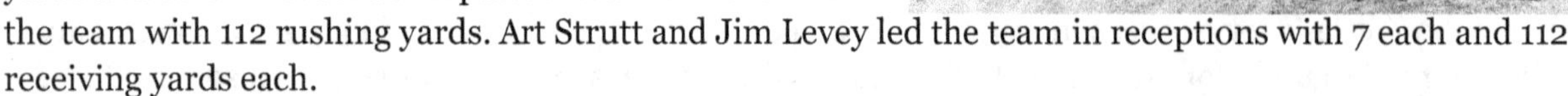

PITTSBURGH			1935			4-8	Game Highlights
9/13/1935	FR	@	Philadelphia	17	7	W	**Ribble blocked punt recovery for TD**
9/22/1935		vs	NEW YORK GIANTS	7	42	L	Gildea TD pass to Wisenbuagh
9/29/1935		vs	CHICAGO	7	23	L	Casper scores lone TD for Pirates
10/6/1935		@	Green Bay	0	27	L	Pirates get lit up by Packers Hutson
10/9/1935	WED	vs	PHILADELPHIA	6	17	L	Doehring TD pass to Wisenbuagh
10/20/1935		vs	CHICAGO CARDINALS	17	13	W	**Strutt INT return TD**/Doehring TD reception
10/27/1935		vs	BOSTON REDSKINS	6	0	W	Nicolai 2 FGs in Pirates win
11/3/1935		vs	BROOKLYN DODGERS	7	13	L	Wetzel rush TD for Pirates lone score
11/10/1935		@	Brooklyn Dodgers	16	7	W	Levey rush TD and TD reception
11/24/1935		vs	GREEN BAY	14	34	L	Levey rush TD and TD reception
12/1/1935		@	Boston Redskins	3	13	L	Nicolai FG for lone Pirates points
12/8/1935		@	Brooklyn Dodgers	0	13	L	Pirates shutout to end season

Schedule courtesy of Steve's Football Bible LLC

1935 NFL Eastern Division	W	L	T	PCT	DIV	PF	PA
New York Giants	9	3	0	.750	8–0	180	96
Brooklyn Dodgers	5	6	1	.455	3–4–1	90	141
Pittsburgh Pirates	**4**	**8**	**0**	**.333**	**3–5**	**100**	**209**
Boston Redskins	2	8	1	.200	2–4–1	65	123
Philadelphia Eagles	2	9	0	.182	2–5	60	179

NATIONAL LEAGUE FOOTBALL
Philadelphia Eagles vs Pittsburgh Pirates
SEPTEMBER 13th, 1935

1936 Pittsburgh Pirates

The team welcomed back head coach, Joe Bach who served his last year at the position (until returning in 1952). His team finished the season with the franchise's best record yet, at 6-6. The Pirates played all their home games at Forbes Field in Pittsburgh, Pennsylvania, except for one that was played at Point Stadium in Johnstown, Pennsylvania. George Rado {G} was selected to various first team All-Pro teams.

Ed Matesic led the team in passing with 850 yards and threw 4 touchdown passes. Warren Heller led the team in rushing with 332 yards. Bill Sortet led the team with 14 receptions for 197 yards.

PITTSBURGH		1936		6-6		Game Highlights
9/13/1936	vs	BOSTON REDSKINS	10	0	W	**Kakasic fumble return TD** and FG
9/23/1936	@	Brooklyn Dodgers	10	6	W	Strutt rush TD/Nicolai FG
9/27/1936	vs	NEW YORK GIANTS	10	7	W	Matesic TD pass to Sortet/Nicolai FG
10/4/1936	vs	CHICAGO	9	27	L	Gildea TD pass to Heller
10/14/1936	vs	PHILADELPHIA	17	0	W	Matesic 2 TD pass/Kakasic FG
10/18/1936	@	Chicago	7	26	L	Zaninelli rush TD
10/25/1936	@	Green Bay	10	38	L	Karcis rush TD/Nicolai FG
11/1/1936	vs	BROOKLYN DODGERS	10	7	W	Karcis rush TD/Nicolai FG
11/5/1936	vs	vs Philadelphia	6	0	W	Nicolai 2 FGs
11/8/1936	@	Detroit	3	28	L	Nicolai FG for only Pirates points
11/15/1936	@	Chicago Cardinals	6	14	L	Matesic TD pass to Heller
11/29/1936	@	Boston Redskins	0	30	L	Pirates give up INT return TD-fumble recovery TD

Schedule courtesy of Steve's Football Bible LLC

1936 NFL Eastern Division	W	L	T	PCT	DIV	PF	PA
Boston Redskins	7	5	0	.583	6–2	149	110
Pittsburgh Pirates	**6**	**6**	**0**	**.500**	**6–1**	**98**	**187**
New York Giants	5	6	1	.455	3–3–1	115	163
Brooklyn Dodgers	3	8	1	.273	2–5–1	92	161
Philadelphia Eagles	1	11	0	.083	1–7	51	206

1936 NFL Draft

Round	Choice	Overall	Player	Position	College
1	3	3	Bill Shakespeare	Halfback	Notre Dame
2	3	12	Len Barnum	Quarterback	West Virginia Wesleyan
3	3	21	Bobby Grayson	Fullback	Stanford
4	3	30	Truman Spain	Tackle	Southern Methodist University
5	3	39	Wayne Sandefur	Fullback	Purdue University
6	3	48	Maurice Orr	Tackle	Southern Methodist University
7	3	57	Marty Peters	Defensive End	Notre Dame
8	3	66	Ed Karpowich	Tackle	Catholic University
9	3	75	Joe Meglen	Back	Georgetown University

1937 Pittsburgh Pirates

The team hired John McNally as head coach after John Bach stepped down during the offseason. McNally was a former player, who played halfback for the Pirates during the 1934 season. His team finished with another 4–7 record however, McNally was welcomed back the next season. Mike Basrak {C} was selected to various first team All-Pro teams.

Max Fiske led the team in passing with 318 yards and threw 4 touchdown passes. Bill Karcis led the team in rushing with 513 yards and 4 rushing touchdowns. Johnny Blood led the team in receptions with 10 and had 4 TD receptions. Bill Davidson led the team with 169 receiving yards.

PITTSBURGH			1937			4-7	Game Highlights
9/5/1937		vs	PHILADELPHIA	27	14	W	**Blood kickoff return TD**-TD reception
9/19/1937		@	Brooklyn Dodgers	21	0	W	Fiske TD pass to Blood/Karcis+Gildea TDs
9/26/1937		vs	NEW YORK GIANTS	7	10	L	Karcis rush TD/Pirates held to 117 total yds
10/4/1937	MON	vs	CHICAGO	0	7	L	Pirates shutout by Bears
10/10/1937		@	Detroit	3	7	L	Nicolai FG
10/17/1937		@	Washington Redskins	20	34	L	Blood 2 TD receptions-TD pass
10/24/1937		vs	CHICAGO CARDINALS	7	13	L	Fiske TD pass to Davidson
10/31/1937		vs	PHILADELPHIA	16	7	W	**Davidson INT return TD**
11/7/1937		@	New York Giants	0	17	L	Pirates get shutout at Polo Grounds
11/14/1937		vs	WASHINGTON REDSKINS	21	13	W	Davidson & Karcis Rush TDs/Nicolai 2 FG
11/21/1937		vs	BROOKLYN DODGERS	0	23	L	Pirates can't control Ace Parker

Schedule courtesy of Steve's Football Bible LLC

1937 NFL Eastern Division	W	L	T	PCT	DIV	PF	PA
Washington Redskins	8	3	0	.727	6–2	195	120
New York Giants	6	3	2	.667	5–2–1	128	109
Pittsburgh Pirates	**4**	**7**	**0**	**.364**	**4–4**	**122**	**145**
Brooklyn Dodgers	3	7	1	.300	2–5–1	82	174
Philadelphia Eagles	2	8	1	.200	2–6	86	177

1937 NFL Draft

Round	Pick	Player	Position	College
1	5	Mike Basrak	C	Duquesne
2	15	Bob Finley	B	SMU
3	25	Bill Breeden	B	Oklahoma
4	35	Elmo "Bo" Hewes	B	Oklahoma
5	45	Jack Frye	B	Missouri
6	55	Walt Roach	E	TCU
7	65	Byron Haines	HB	Washington
8	75	Marty Kordich	G	Saint Mary's (CA)
9	85	Matt Patanelli	E	Michigan
10	95	Stan Nevers	T	Kentucky

1938 Pittsburgh Pirates

The '38 Pirates welcomed back John McNally as head coach after finishing with a 4-10 record the previous year. McNally coached the team's second 2-win season in 3 years, as they placed last in the NFL Eastern Division. The '38 team welcomed one of the Steelers' best players during their tenure as "the Pirates" (1933-1940). Art Rooney signed college phenom Byron "Whizzer" White for one season and was given a huge contract. White led the league in rushing that year and became the first player to do so whilst playing for a losing team. He left the team the next year to pursue his studies overseas, he did however return as a Lion in 1940. White {TB} and Byron Gentry {G} were selected to various first team All-Pro teams.

Whizzer White led the team in passing with 393 yards. White led the team in rushing with 567 yards and 4 rushing touchdowns. Bill Davidson led the team in receptions with 12 for 229 yards.

PITTSBURGH			1938			2-9	Game Highlights
9/9/1938	FR	@	Detroit	7	16	L	Whizzer White rush TD
9/11/1938		vs	NEW YORK GIANTS	14	27	L	White rush TD/Manske TD reception
9/16/1938	FR	vs	PHILADELPHIA	7	27	L	White rush TD
9/23/1938	FR	@	Brooklyn Dodgers	17	3	W	**Manske fumble return TD**/Nicolai FG
10/3/1938	MON	@	New York Giants	13	10	W	Filchock 2 TD pass to Sortet
10/9/1938		vs	BROOKLYN DODGERS	7	17	L	White TD pass to Sortet
10/23/1938		@	Green Bay	0	20	L	Pirates shutout at City Stadium
11/6/1938		vs	WASHINGTON REDSKINS	0	7	L	Pirates 178 rush yards/0 pass yards
11/20/1938		@	Philadelphia	7	14	L	White 133 rush yards/rush TD
11/27/1938		@	Washington Redskins	0	15	L	Pirates 180 pass yards-still get shutout
12/4/1938		vs	Cleveland Rams (New Orleans)	7	13	L	White TD pass to Sortet

Schedule courtesy of Steve's Football Bible LLC

1938 NFL Eastern Division	W	L	T	PCT	DIV	PF	PA
New York Giants	8	2	1	.800	5–2–1	194	79
Washington Redskins	6	3	2	.667	4–2–2	148	154
Brooklyn Dodgers	4	4	3	.500	3–2–3	131	161
Philadelphia Eagles	5	6	0	.455	3–5	154	164
Pittsburgh Pirates	**2**	**9**	**0**	**.182**	**2–6**	**79**	**169**

1938 NFL Draft

Round	Choice	Overall	Player	Position	College
1	4	4	Byron White	Back	Colorado
2	4	14	Frank Filchock	Back	Indiana
3	4	19	Hugh Wolfe	Back	Texas
4	4	29	Tony Matisi	Tackle	Pittsburgh
5	4	34	Lou Midler	Tackle	Minnesota
6	4	44	George Platukis	End	Duquesne
7	4	54	Ray King	End	Minnesota
8	4	64	Tom Burnette	Halfback	North Carolina
9	4	74	Paul McDonough	End	Utah
10	4	84	Paul McCarty	Center	Notre Dame
11	4	94	Bill Krause	Guard	Baldwin–Wallace
12	4	104	Joe Kuharich	Guard	Notre Dame

Byron "Whizzer" White

1939 Pittsburgh Pirates

The Pirates brought John McNally back for his third year, however, after finishing with a 2–9 record, Owner Art Rooney provided him with support by signing Walt Kiesling during the offseason. Despite this, the Pirates experienced their worst season yet, placing last in the league with a 1–9–1 record. The team just barely tallied a number in the win column, but during Week 11, they beat the Philadelphia Eagles. It was their first win at home in 9 games at Forbes Field (Week 10, 1937). It was also the final season for the franchise before becoming the "Steelers" the following season. Byron Gentry {G} was selected to various first team All-Pro teams.

Hugh McCullough led the team in passing with 443 yards. Boyd Brumbaugh led the team in rushing with 282 yards. Sam Boyd led the team in receptions with 21 for 423 yards.

PITTSBURGH			1939			1-9-1	Game Highlights
9/14/1939	TH	@	Brooklyn Dodgers	7	12	L	Platukis TD pass to Wheeler
9/24/1939		vs	CHICAGO CARDINALS	0	10	L	Pirates rush for 287 yards-can't crack EZ
10/2/1939	MON	vs	CHICAGO	0	32	L	Pirates held to 39 total yards/2 turnovers
10/8/1939		vs	NEW YORK GIANTS	7	14	L	Swede Johnston rush TD
10/15/1939		@	Washington Redskins	14	44	L	Tomasetti TD pass to McDonough
10/22/1939		vs	WASHINGTON REDSKINS	14	21	L	McDonough 2 pass TDs-175 pass yards
10/29/1939		@	Cleveland Rams	14	14	T	McCullough rush TD-TD pass to Boyd
11/6/1939	MON	@	Brooklyn Dodgers	13	17	L	McCullough TD pass to Sortet/Nicolai FG
11/19/1939		@	New York Giants	7	24	L	Brumbaugh rush TD
11/23/1939	TH	@	Philadelphia	14	17	L	Brumbaugh rush TD-TD pass to Platukis
11/26/1939		vs	PHILADELPHIA	24	12	W	Johnston & Tomasetti rush TD/Nicolai FG

Schedule courtesy of Steve's Football Bible LLC

1939 NFL Eastern Division	W	L	T	PCT	DIV	PF	PA
New York Giants	9	1	1	.900	7–0–1	168	85
Washington Redskins	8	2	1	.800	6–1–1	242	94
Brooklyn Dodgers	4	6	1	.400	3–4–1	108	219
Pittsburgh Pirates	**1**	**9**	**1**	**.100**	**1–7**	**114**	**216**
Philadelphia Eagles	1	9	1	.100	1–6–1	105	200

1939 NFL Draft

Draft order			Player name	Position	College
Round	Choice	Overall			
1	2	2	Sidney "Sid" Luckman	Quarterback	Columbia
2	1	11	Clarence "Pug" Manders	Fullback	Drake
3	2	17	Billy Patterson	Back	Baylor
4	1	26	Hugh McCullough	Defensive Back	Pittsburgh
5	2	32	Ernie Wheeler	Back	North Dakota State
6	1	41	Sam Boyd	End	Baylor
7	2	52	Eddie Palumbo	Back	Detroit
8	1	61	Ole Nelson	End	Michigan State
9	2	72	Steve Petro	Guard	Pittsburgh
10	1	81	Jack Lee	Back	Carnegie-Mellon
11	2	92	Lou Tomasetti	Back	Buckwell
12	1	101	Denny Cochran	Back	St. Louis
13	2	112	Fabian Hoffman	End	Pittsburgh
14	1	121	Ed Clary	Back	South Carolina
15	2	132	John Tosi	Center	Niagara
16	1	141	Al Lezouski	Guard	Pittsburgh
17	2	152	Ed Longhi	Center	Notre Dame
18	1	161	Dave Shirk	End	Kansas
19	2	172	Frank Peters	End	Washington
20	1	181	Tom Sheldrake	End	Washington

1940 Pittsburgh Steelers

It was also the first season in which the team was known as the Pittsburgh Steelers, and not the copycat "Pirates" moniker. The 1940 team was led by head coach Walt Kiesling in his first full season as the head coach. Kiesling's assistant coaches were Wilbur "Bill" Sortet and Hank Bruder, who both also played. They held training camp at St. Francis College in Loretto, Pennsylvania.

Billy Patterson led the team in passing with 529 yards and threw 3 touchdown passes. Lou Tomasetti led the team in rushing with 246 yards. George Platukis led the team with 15 receptions for 290 yards and 2 TD receptions.

PITTSBURGH			1940			2-7-2	Game Highlights
9/8/1940		vs	CHICAGO CARDINALS	7	7	T	Patterson TD pass to Platukis
9/15/1940		vs	NEW YORK GIANTS	10	10	T	Patterson TD pass to Tomasetti/Nicolai FG
9/22/1940		@	Detroit	10	7	W	Tomasetti rush TD/Nicolai FG
9/29/1940		vs	BROOKLYN DODGERS	3	10	L	Nicolai FG/Steelers 188 total yards
10/6/1940		vs	WASHINGTON REDSKINS	10	40	L	Thompson TD pass to Condit/Nicolai FG
10/13/1940		@	Brooklyn Dodgers	0	21	L	Steelers 213 total yards/commit 3 turnovers
10/20/1940		@	New York Giants	0	12	L	Steelers manage only 148 yards total offense
10/27/1940		@	Green Bay	3	24	L	Nicolai FG/Steelers held to 95 total yards
11/3/1940		@	Washington Redskins	10	37	L	Patterson TD pass to Platukis/Nicolai FG
11/10/1940		vs	PHILADELPHIA	7	3	W	McDonough rush TD
11/28/1940	TH	@	Philadelphia	0	7	L	Steelers held to 130 total yards of offense

Schedule courtesy of Steve's Football Bible LLC

1940 NFL Eastern Division	W	L	T	PCT	DIV	PF	PA
Washington Redskins	9	2	0	.818	6–2	245	142
Brooklyn Dodgers	8	3	0	.727	6–2	186	120
New York Giants	6	4	1	.600	5–2–1	131	133
Pittsburgh Steelers	**2**	**7**	**2**	**.222**	**1–6–1**	**60**	**178**
Philadelphia Eagles	1	10	0	.091	1–7	111	211

1940 NFL Draft

Round	Choice	Player	Position	College
1	3	Kay Eakin	Halfback	Arkansas
2	12	Ralph Wenzel	End	Tulane
3	18	George Kiick	Back	Bucknell
4	27	Frank "Pop" Ivy	End	Oklahoma
5	33	Clark Goff	Tackle	Florida
6	42	Frank Bykowski	Guard	Purdue
7	53	Pete Cignetti	Back	Boston College
8	62	Carl Nery	Guard	Duquesne
9	73	Dick Boisseau	Tackle	Washington & Lee
10	82	Paul Shu	Back	VMI
11	93	Cary Cox	Center	Alabama
12	102	Rocco Piro	Back	Catholic U
13	113	John Noppenburg	Back	Miami-FL
14	122	Nick Stublar	Tackle	Santa Clara
15	133	Ray McCarthy	Back	Santa Clara
16	142	Leon Gajecki	Guard	Penn State
17	153	Mickey Sullivan	End	NC State
18	162	Seaton Daly	Tackle	Gonzaga
19	173	Thad Harvey	Tackle	Notre Dame
20	182	Marvin Katzenstein	Tackle	Colorado Mines

1941 Pittsburgh Steelers

In the offseason, the team had been sold and then re-acquired (more or less) in a bizarre series of transactions which has come to be referred to as the "Pennsylvania Polka". The roster consisted of many players who had played for the Philadelphia Eagles the previous year, who joined the Steelers because of the moves. Bert Bell became half-owner of the team, and he named himself the head coach. After starting the season with two straight losses, Aldo "Buff" Donelli was brought in. Donelli was acting concurrently as head coach at Duquesne University, and when the team's schedules prevented him from fulfilling both roles, he stepped down as the Steelers' coach in favor of Walt Kiesling. The team held training camp in Hershey, Pennsylvania.

Boyd Brumbaugh led the team in passing with 260 yards. Dick Riffle led the team in rushing with 388 yards. Don Looney led the team in receptions with 10 for 186 yards.

PITTSBURGH		1941			1-9-1	Game Highlights
9/7/1941	@	Cleveland Rams (Akron, OH)	14	17	L	Hackney & Jones rush TD each
9/21/1941	vs	PHILADELPHIA	7	10	L	Brumbaugh rush TD
10/5/1941	vs	NEW YORK GIANTS	10	37	L	Brumbaugh TD pass to Kichefski/Nicolai FG
10/12/1941	vs	WASHINGTON REDSKINS	20	24	L	Riffle TD catch/Jones TD catch/Brumbaugh TD
10/19/1941	@	New York Giants	7	28	L	Brumbaugh TD pass to Looney
10/26/1941	@	Chicago	7	34	L	Riffle TD pass to Hoague
11/2/1941	@	Washington Redskins	3	23	L	Steelers held to 47 total yards/Nicolai FG
11/9/1941	@	Philadelphia	7	7	T	Jones rush TD/Steelers 155 yards offense
11/16/1941	vs	BROOKLYN DODGERS	14	7	W	Riffle & Jones rush TD/Defense force 3 turnovers
11/23/1941	vs	GREEN BAY	7	54	L	Hoague rush TD/Steelers score first-give up 54 straight
11/30/1941	@	Brooklyn Dodgers	7	35	L	Jones rush TD/Steelers held to 112 total yards

Schedule courtesy of Steve's Football Bible LLC

1941 NFL Eastern Division	W	L	T	PCT	DIV	PF	PA
New York Giants	8	3	0	.727	6–2	238	114
Brooklyn Dodgers	7	4	0	.636	6–2	158	127
Washington Redskins	6	5	0	.545	5–3	176	174
Philadelphia Eagles	2	8	1	.200	1–6–1	119	218
Pittsburgh Steelers	**1**	**9**	**1**	**.100**	**1–6–1**	**103**	**276**

1941 NFL Draft

Round	Choice	Player	Position	College
2	12	Chet Gladchuck	Center	Boston College
3	18	Johnny Knolla	Back	Creighton
4	27	Jim Ringgold	Back	Wake Forest
5	33	Vic Sears	Tackle	Oregon State
6	42	Bob Suffridge	Guard	Tennessee
7	53	Jim Roberts	Center	Marshall
9	73	Ervin "Buddy" Elrod	End	Mississippi State
10	82	Ralph Fritz	Guard	Michigan
11	93	Emil Uremovich	Tackle	Indiana
12	102	Paul Severin	End	North Carolina
13	113	Russ Cotton	Back	Texas-El Paso
14	122	J.W. Goree	Guard	LSU
15	133	John Eibner	Tackle	Kentucky
16	142	Wes McAfee	Back	Duke
17	153	Terry Fox	Back	Miami-FL
18	162	Bill Cornwall	Tackle	Furman
19	173	George Kerr	Guard	Boston College
20	182	Bob Bjorklund	Back	Minnesota
21	193	Jim Castiglia	Back	Georgetown
22	202	Mort Landsberg	Back	Cornell

1942 Pittsburgh Steelers

The team improved on their previous season result of 1–9–1 with a record of 7–4–0, which was good enough for 2nd place in the NFL East. This was the franchise's first ever winning record. For the second straight year, the team held training camp in Hershey, Pennsylvania. The 1942 Steeler Team was the best team the club had up to that point. For the first time in 10 seasons, the Steelers had a 4-game winning streak. Bill Dudley {TB} and Milt Simington {G} were selected to various first team All-Pro teams.

Bill Dudley led the team in passing with 438 yards. Dudley led the team in rushing with 696 yards and 5 rushing touchdowns. Walt Kichefski led the team in receptions with 15 for 189 yards.

PITTSBURGH		1942			7-4	**Game Highlights**
9/13/1942	**vs**	PHILADELPHIA	14	24	L	Dudley TD pass to Looney/rush TD
9/20/1942	@	Washington Redskins	14	28	L	**Dudley kickoff return TD**/Riffle rush TD
10/4/1942	**vs**	NEW YORK GIANTS	13	10	W	Hoague & Sandig rush TD each
10/11/1942	@	Brooklyn Dodgers	7	0	W	Dudley rush TD/Steeler offense 0 pass yards
10/18/1942	@	Philadelphia	14	0	W	Riffle & Sandig rush TD each
10/25/1942	**vs**	WASHINGTON REDSKINS	0	14	L	Steelers 247 yards offense but fail to score
11/1/1942	@	New York Giants	17	9	W	**Sandig punt return TD**/Dudley 135 rush yds- TD
11/8/1942	@	Detroit	35	7	W	**Lamas fumble return TD**/Steelers 267 rush yards
11/22/1942	**vs**	CHICAGO CARDINALS	19	3	W	Riffle & Gonda rush TDs/Nicolai 2 FGs
11/29/1942	**vs**	BROOKLYN DODGERS	13	0	W	**Tomasic punt return TD**/Gonda 68 yd rush TD
12/6/1942	@	Green Bay	21	24	L	Martin-Riddick-Dudley rush TDs each

Schedule courtesy of Steve's Football Bible LLC

1942 NFL Eastern Division	W	L	T	PCT	DIV	PF	PA
Washington Redskins	10	1	0	.909	7–1	227	102
Pittsburgh Steelers	**7**	**4**	**0**	**.636**	**5–3**	**167**	**119**
New York Giants	5	5	1	.500	4–4	155	139
Brooklyn Dodgers	3	8	0	.273	2–6	100	168
Philadelphia Eagles	2	9	0	.182	2–6	134	239

1942 NFL Draft

Round	Choice	Player	Position	College
1	1	Bill Dudley	Back	Virginia
2	11	Vern Martin	Back	Texas
3	16	Ken Casanega	Back	Santa Clara
4	26	Malcolm Kutner	End	Texas
5	31	Curt Sandig	Back	St. Mary's (TX)
6	41	Charley Greene	Tackle	Tulsa
7	51	Johnny Butler	Back	Tennessee
8	61	Floyd Spendlove	Tackle	Utah
9	71	Rayburn Chase	Back	Missouri
10	81	Ernie Steele	Back	Washington
11	91	Thornley Wood	Back	Columbia
12	101	Bill Roach	End	TCU
13	111	Wayne Holt	Guard	Tulsa
14	121	Clure Mosher	Center	Louisville
15	131	Hubbard Law	Back	Sam Houston State
16	141	Andy Tomasic	Back	Temple
17	151	Garth Chamberlain	Tackle	BYU
18	161	John Rokisky	End	Duquesne
19	171	Ray Jenkins	Back	Colorado
20	181	Frank Kapriva	Guard	Wake Forest

1943 Steagles

The Steagles were the team created by the temporary merger of Pennsylvania's two National Football League (NFL) teams, the Pittsburgh Steelers, and the Philadelphia Eagles, during the 1943 season. The teams were forced to merge because both had lost many players to military service  during World War II. The league's official record book refers to the team as "Phil-Pitt Combine", but the unofficial "Steagles", despite never being registered by the NFL, has become the enduring moniker.

Even with these deferments, NFL rosters were hurting. The Cleveland Rams suspended operations, and the Pittsburgh Steelers had only six men left under contract while the Philadelphia Eagles had only sixteen. The 1943 NFL Draft did not help much. Most players drafted went off to the war instead of joining NFL teams. Further exacerbating the issue was the continued insistence of George Preston Marshall and other NFL owners on continuing the ten-year-old ban on black players, which disqualified potential replacement players such as Kenny Washington. The league nearly ceased operations before the 1943 season, but it continued. Steelers' owner Art Rooney knew that the league needed at least eight teams to survive. Rooney's idea was to merge the Steelers with the Eagles. This idea came quickly to him for two years earlier he thought about combining the two teams into the Pennsylvania Keystoners. Eagles' owner Alexis Thompson, who was serving in the US Army as a corporal, was not as keen on the plan since he at least had 16 players under contract. However, Thompson remembered how Rooney in 1941 swapped cities with him which allowed him to keep the Eagles in Philadelphia close to his New York City home. This led to an agreement on combining the teams. The league approved the merger by a vote of 5–4. However, several owners expressed fears that the merger would produce a team with an unfair advantage. The merger had a slight lean in favor of Philadelphia based on stipulations imposed by Thompson. The team would be known as the Philadelphia Eagles and be based in Philadelphia. Rooney had very little leverage, bringing only six players to the table. However, he was successful in landing two home games in Pittsburgh, while Philadelphia would host four. The team was also to wear the Eagles' green and white colors instead of Pittsburgh's black and gold. This event officially marked the only time in the Steelers history (other than in 1941 when green and white were used as well as black and gold) that the team colors were something other than black and gold.

Ray Zimmerman led the team in passing with 846 yards and threw 9 touchdown passes. Jack Hinkle led the team in rushing with 571 yards. Tony Bova led the team in receiving with 17 for 419 yards and 5 TD receptions.

STEAGLES			1943			5-4-1	Game Highlights
10/2/1943	SAT	vs	BROOKLYN DODGERS	17	10	W	Butler & Steele rush TD each/Zimmerman FG
10/9/1943	SAT	vs	NEW YORK GIANTS	28	14	W	Zimmerman 2 TD pass/Steele & Sherman TDs
10/17/1943		@	Chicago	21	48	L	Zimmerman 2 TD pass/Steele & Bova TDs
10/24/1943		@	New York Giants	14	42	L	**Wukits fumble return TD**/Sherman TD pass
10/31/1943		vs	CHICAGO CARDINALS	34	13	W	**Kish INT return TD**/Zimmerman 2 TD pass
11/7/1943		vs	WASHINGTON REDSKINS	14	14	T	**Cabrelli INT return TD**/Steele TD catch
11/14/1943		@	Brooklyn Dodgers	7	13	L	Thurbon rush TD/Steagles 197 rush yards
11/21/1943		vs	DETROIT	35	34	W	Zimmerman rush TD-TD pass to Cabrelli
11/28/1943		@	Washington Redskins	27	14	W	Thurbon 2 rush TD/Steagles 308 rush yards
12/5/1943		vs	GREEN BAY	28	38	L	Zimmerman 2 TD pass to Bova

Schedule courtesy of Steve's Football Bible LLC

1943 NFL Eastern Division	W	L	T	PCT	DIV	PF	PA
Washington Redskins	6	3	1	.667	2–3–1	229	137
New York Giants	6	3	1	.667	5–1	197	170
Phil-Pitt	**5**	**4**	**1**	**.556**	**3–2–1**	**225**	**230**
Brooklyn Dodgers	2	8	0	.200	1–5	65	234

1943 NFL Draft

Round	Choice	Player	Position	College
1	7	Bill Daley	Fullback	Minnesota
3	22	Jack Russell	End	Baylor
5	37	Harry Connolly	Back	Boston College
6	47	Lou Sossoman	Center	South Carolina
7	57	Al Ratto	Center	St. Mary's (CA)
8	67	Ray Curry	End	St. Mary's (CA)
9	77	Ed Murphy	End	Holy Cross
10	87	Dick Dwelle	Back	Rice
11	97	Al Wukits	Center	Duquesne
12	107	Joe Repko	Tackle	Boston College
13	117	Pete Boltrek	Tackle	NC State
14	127	Mort Sheikman	Guard	Pennsylvania
15	137	Milt Crain	Back	Baylor
16	147	Max Kielbasa	Back	Duquesne
17	157	Nick Skorich	Guard	Cincinnati
18	167	Jackie Field	Back	Texas
19	177	Felix Bucek	Guard	Texas A&M
20	187	Johnny Welsh	Back	Pennsylvania
21	197	Tony Compagno	Back	St. Mary's (CA)
22	207	Willie Zapalac	Back	Texas A&M
23	217	George Bain	Tackle	Oregon State
24	227	Harry Wynne	Tackle	Arkansas
25	237	Joe Ciibulas	Tackle	Duquesne
26	247	Bill Yambrick	Center	Western Michigan
27	257	Jack Freeman	Guard	Texas
28	267	Joe Goode	Back	Duquesne
29	277	Jack Durishan	Tackle	Pittsburgh
30	287	Fritz Lobpries	Guard	Texas
31	292	Art Jones	Back	Haverford
32	297	Bob Ruman	Back	Arizona

1944 Card-Pitt

Card-Pitt was the team created by the temporary merger of two National Football League (NFL) teams, the Pittsburgh Steelers, and the Chicago Cardinals, during the 1944 season. It was the second such merger for the Steelers, who had combined with the Philadelphia Eagles in 1943 to form the "Steagles". The arrangement was made necessary by the loss of numerous players to World War II military service and was dissolved upon completion of the season. The war ended before the start of the 1945 season, and both teams resumed normal operations. Card-Pitt finished with a 0–10 record in the Western Division, which led sportswriters to derisively label the team the "Car-Pitts", or "carpets".

Card-Pitt opened the regular season portion of its schedule in front of 21,000 spectators at Forbes Field on September 24, 1944, against a Cleveland Rams team led by former Steelers head coach Aldo Donelli. Card-Pitt came back from a 16–0 deficit to take the lead, but a bad punt late in the fourth quarter allowed Cleveland to score the winning touchdown for a final score of 28–23. The team won an exhibition game the next week at Forbes Field, 17–16 over the New York Giants. Quarterback Coley McDonough was drafted into the U.S. Army two days before the team's second regular season game, a contest against Green Bay. The Pittsburgh Press gave the team little chance to defeat the Packers, who would go on to win that game 34–7. However, John McCarthy, a rookie out of Saint Francis University in Loretto, Pennsylvania, performed well as McDonough's replacement.

Card-Pitt then met the Chicago Bears, a team missing MVP quarterback Sid Luckman and coach George Halas among a roster that had been depleted by the war and injuries, in the third game of the season. The Pittsburgh Post-Gazette called Card-Pitt's effort against the Bears "pitiful", and the coaching staff became so irate that they fined Johnny Butler, John Grigas and Eberle Schultz $200 apiece for "indifferent play". Upset with the coaches' strict, dictatorial style, the team refused to practice until the fined players received a fair hearing. The players then met with Rooney, and Grigas and Schultz agreed to pay their fines and return to practice. Butler was suspended indefinitely, before being placed on waivers and later claimed by Brooklyn. Rooney eventually rescinded the fines, except for Butler's.

Pittsburgh Post-Gazette sports Editor Al Abrams then quoted a disgusted fan as having written, "Why don't they call themselves the Car-Pits? I think it's very appropriate as every team in the league walks over them." The team lost a rematch against the Giants. Midway through their next game against the Washington Redskins, a brawl between the two teams erupted and had to be broken up by police. Coaches Kiesling and Handler were in the middle of the fight, while Rooney, a former boxer, ran to join his team, until he realized that it would be a breach of protocol for an NFL owner to get into a fight with opposing players. The Redskins would go on to win the game, 42–20. Card-Pitt's Cliff Duggan was fined $200 for his role in the fight; however, Rooney paid his fine.

Losses then ensued against the Rams, Packers and Lions, and Grigas left the team to return home to Massachusetts. He had twice won the league rushing title but had grown tired of losing and retired. Despite his sudden departure, he was named to the New York Daily News All-Pro team, and finished the season with 610 yards rushing, an average of 3.3 yards per carry. His departure was followed by a 49–7 loss to the Bears. The team's 0–10 season tied the Brooklyn Tigers for the league's worst record. The merger of the Chicago Cardinals and the Pittsburgh Steelers was dissolved the day after the season ended.

The Card-Pitt punters averaged 32.7 yards per attempt, which as of 2021 is still the worst mark in NFL history. The team was 0–2 in field goal attempts, while Conway Baker missed four of his 15 extra point tries. Card-Pitt passers had a 31% completion rate and threw for just eight touchdowns; their total of 41 interceptions is still the third highest number in NFL history, even more remarkable given the season was incrementally lengthened to 12, 14, 16, and currently 17 games (the 1944 season had 10). McCarthy threw 13 interceptions, had no touchdown passes, and finished with a quarterback rating of 3.0. Card-Pitt also had the worst run defense in the league and were outscored 328–108 by opponents.

John Grigas led the team in passing with 690 yards and threw 6 touchdown passes. Grigas led the team in rushing with 610 yards. Ed Rucinski led the team with 22 receptions. Tony Bova led with 287 reception yards.

CARD-PITT		1944		0-10		Game Highlights
9/24/1944	vs	CLEVELAND RAMS	28	30	L	McDonough 2 TD pass/Schultz kickoff return TD
10/8/1944	@	Green Bay	7	34	L	Grigas TD pass to Butler/QBs threw 4 INTs
10/15/1944	@	Chicago	7	42	L	Thurbon rush TD/Card-Pitt 26 passing yards
10/22/1944	@	New York Giants	0	23	L	Offense commits 7 turnovers
10/29/1944	@	Washington Redskins	20	42	L	Grigas 100 rush yards-2 rush TDs-TD pass to Currivan
11/5/1944	vs	DETROIT	6	27	L	Grigas 117 rush yards-TD pass to Bova
11/12/1944	@	Detroit	7	21	L	Thurbon rush TD/Grigas 123 rush yards
11/19/1944	@	Cleveland Rams	6	33	L	Grigas TD pass to Bova
11/26/1944	vs	GREEN BAY	20	35	L	Thurbon 2 rush TD/Grigas TD pass to Currivan
12/3/1944	vs	CHICAGO	7	49	L	Thurbon rush TD/Offense held to 96 total yards

Schedule courtesy of Steve's Football Bible LLC

1944 NFL Western Division	W	L	T	PCT	DIV	PF	PA
Green Bay Packers	8	2	0	.800	7–1	238	141
Chicago Bears	6	3	1	.667	4–3–1	258	172
Detroit Lions	6	3	1	.667	4–3–1	216	151
Cleveland Rams	4	6	0	.400	4–4	188	224
Card-Pitt	**0**	**10**	**0**	**.000**	**0–8**	**108**	**328**

1944 NFL Draft

Round	Choice	Player	Position	College
1	10	Johnny Podesto	Halfback	St. Mary's (CA)
2	15	Bo Odell	End	Pennsylvania
3	25	Bob Gantt	End	Duke
4	31	Art McCaffray	Tackle	Pacific
5	41	George Own	Guard	Wake Forest
6	47	Dan Savage	Back	Brown
7	63	Jesse Freitas	Back	Santa Clara
8	69	George Titus	Center	Holy Cross
9	85	Ed Stofko	Back	St. Francis (PA)
10	91	Val Jansante	End	Duquesne
11	107	Carl Buda	Guard	Tulsa
12	113	Sam Gray	End	Tulsa
13	129	Bob Longacre	Back	William & Mary
14	135	Les Zetty	End	Muhlenberg
15	151	Jim Myers	Guard	Tennessee
16	157	Joe Gottlieb	Back	Duquesne
17	173	Hugh Davis	Back	Michigan State
18	179	Bill Sullivan	End	Villanova
19	195	Jimmy Woodside	Center	Temple
20	201	Bill Miller	Back	Pennsylvania
21	217	Bob Lawson	End	Holy Cross
22	223	Hank Caver	Back	Presbyterian
23	239	Paul Carter	Tackle	Michigan State
24	245	Dick Holben	Tackle	Muhlenberg
25	261	Howard Tippee	Back	Iowa State
26	267	Charley Malmberg	Tackle	Rice
27	283	Russ Ashbaugh	Back	Notre Dame
28	289	Pat Petroski	Guard	Miami-FL
29	305	Joe Tosti	End	Scranton
30	311	Len Seelinger	Back	Wisconsin

1945 Pittsburgh Steelers

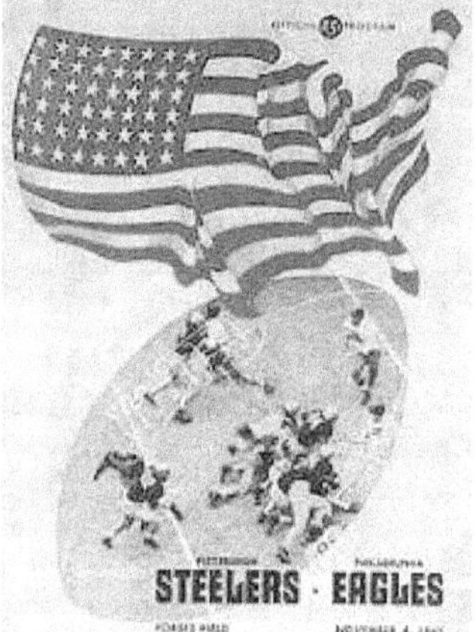

The team finished the season with a record of 2–8. This season marked the first and only season played with Jim Leonard as head coach. They played their home games at Forbes Field.

Buss Warren led the team in passing with 368 yards. Warren also led the team in rushing with 292 yards. Tony Bova led the team in receiving with 15 receptions for 215 yards.

PITTSBURGH			1945			2-8	Game Highlights
9/26/1945	WED	@	Boston Yanks	7	28	L	Jarvi TD pass to Lucente
10/7/1945		vs	NEW YORK GIANTS	6	34	L	Duhart rush TD/Steelers held to 134 yards
10/14/1945		vs	WASHINGTON REDSKINS	0	14	L	Steelers held to 119 yards total offense
10/21/1945		@	New York Giants	21	7	W	**Doyle INT return TD**/Defense force 3 TO's
10/28/1945		vs	BOSTON YANKS	6	10	L	Agajanian 2 FGs/Steelers commit 5 turnovers
11/4/1945		vs	PHILADELPHIA	3	45	L	Agajanian FG/Steelers held to 141 yards
11/11/1945		vs	CHICAGO CARDINALS	23	0	W	Dudley 2 rush TDs/Agajanian FG
11/18/1945		@	Philadelphia	6	30	L	Kiick rush TD/Steelers held to 52 pass yards
11/25/1945		@	Chicago	7	28	L	Dudley rush TD/Steelers held to 9 pass yds
12/2/1945		@	Washington Redskins	0	24	L	Steelers held to 156 yards

Schedule courtesy of Steve's Football Bible LLC

1945 NFL Eastern Division	W	L	T	PCT	DIV	PF	PA
Washington Redskins	8	2	0	.800	6–2	209	121
Philadelphia Eagles	7	3	0	.700	5–2	272	133
Yanks	3	6	1	.333	3–2–1	123	211
New York Giants	3	6	1	.333	2–4–1	179	198
Pittsburgh Steelers	**2**	**8**	**0**	**.200**	**1–7**	**79**	**220**

1945 NFL Draft

Round	Choice	Player	Position	School
1	2	Paul Duhart	Back	Florida
2	12	Jack Dugger	End	Ohio State
3	19	Bill Dellastatious	Back	Missouri
4	29	Roger Adams	Center	Florida
5	33	Chuck Mehelich	End	Duquesne
6	46	Greg Browning	End	Denver
7	56	Mike Wolak	Back	Duquesne
8	66	Tom Hughes	Tackle	Missouri
9	79	Leon Pense	Back	Arkansas
10	89	Art Brandau	Center	Tennessee
11	99	Ray Ball	Back	Holy Cross
12	112	Frank Basilone	Back	Duquesne
13	122	John Monahan	End	Dartmouth
14	132	Mel Odelli	Back	Duquesne
15	145	George Connor	Tackle	Notre Dame
16	155	Jim Ungles	Back	Kansas State
17	165	John Itzel	Back	Pittsburgh
18	178	Alex Wizbicki	Back	Holy Cross
19	188	Jim Landrigan	Tackle	Dartmouth
20	198	Bill Lilienthal	Tackle	Villanova
21	211	Art Price	Back	Rutgers
22	221	Don Malmberg	Back	UCLA
23	231	Everett Hartwell	End	Auburn
24	244	Ed Cain	Back	Rice
25	254	Angelo Carlaccini	Back	Pittsburgh
26	264	Ed Burns	Back	Boston College
27	277	Glen Stough	Tackle	Duke
28	287	Jim Marsh	Tackle	Oklahoma State
29	297	Ralph Grant	Back	Bucknell
30	310	John Kondria	Tackle	St. Vincent

1946 Pittsburgh Steelers

The team finished the season with a record of 5–5–1. This season marked the first of two seasons played with Jock Sutherland as head coach. When the 1945 season ended, Jock Sutherland returned from service in World War II and signed a head coaching contract with team owner Art Rooney, Sr. on December 29, 1945, in front of local reporters. Sutherland's fame as a college coach caused a great deal of excitement among Steelers fans and ticket sales for the 1946 season set records. Additionally, fan favorite Bill Dudley was set to return for his first full season since serving in World War II. Dudley had only played in 4 games in 1945. By the end of the season, **Dudley's play was so exceptional, he was named the NFL's Most Valuable Player.** Dudley was selected to various first team All-Pro teams.

Dudley led the team in passing with 452 yards. Dudley also led the team in rushing with 604 yards. Val Jansante and Bill Mehelich led the team with 10 receptions. Tony Bova led the team with 171 yards receiving.

PITTSBURGH		1946			5-5-1	Game Highlights
9/29/1946	vs	CHICAGO CARDINALS	14	7	W	Dudley TD pass to Seabright/Compagno rush TD
10/6/1946	@	Washington Redskins	14	14	T	Clement TD pass to Jansante/Dudley rush TD
10/13/1946	vs	NEW YORK GIANTS	14	17	L	Dudley TD pass to Garnaas/Clement rush TD
10/20/1946	vs	BOSTON YANKS	16	7	W	Lach 2 rush TD/Dudley FG/Steelers 217 rush yds
10/27/1946	@	Green Bay	7	17	L	Dudley rush TD/Steelers 59 pass yards
11/3/1946	@	Boston Yanks	33	7	W	**Davis fumble return TD**/Dudley Td catch
11/10/1946	vs	WASHINGTON REDSKINS	14	7	W	**Dudley INT return TD**/Defense force 5 turnovers
11/17/1946	@	Detroit	7	17	L	Dutton rush TD/Steelers held to 28 rush yards
11/24/1946	vs	PHILADELPHIA	10	7	W	Lach rush TD/Dudley FG/Defense force 5 TO's
12/1/1946	@	New York Giants	0	7	L	Steelers held to 139 yards/commit 3 turnovers
12/8/1946	@	Philadelphia	7	10	L	Lach rush TD/Steelers commit 5 turnovers

Schedule courtesy of Steve's Football Bible LLC

1946 NFL Eastern Division	W	L	T	PCT	DIV	PF	PA
New York Giants	7	3	1	.700	5–2–1	236	162
Philadelphia Eagles	6	5	0	.545	5–3	231	220
Pittsburgh Steelers	**5**	**5**	**1**	**.500**	**4–3–1**	**136**	**117**
Washington Redskins	5	5	1	.500	4–3–1	171	191
Boston Yanks	2	8	1	.200	0–7–1	189	273

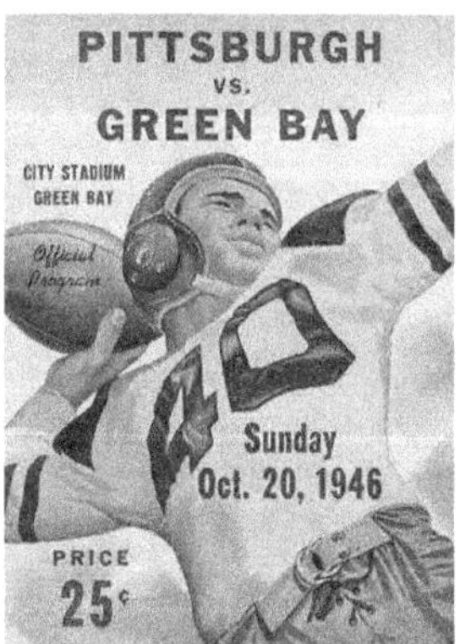

1946 NFL Draft

Round	Choice	Player	Position	School
1	3	Felix (Doc) Blanchard	Back	Army
2	13	George Clark	Back	Duke
3	18	Harmon Rowe	Back	San Francisco
4	28	Joe Tepsic	Back	Penn State
5	33	Jack Seiferling	Back	Utah State
6	43	Marion Woods	Guard	Clemson
7	53	Tom Reinhardt	Tackle	Minnesota
8	63	Joe Ponsetto	Back	Michigan
9	73	Bob Evans	Back	Pennsylvania
10	83	Mel Bonwell	Back	Central (IA)
11	93	Doc Holloway	Guard	William & Mary
12	103	Carroll Owen	Back	Catawba
13	113	George Poppin	Tackle	New Mexico
14	123	Bob McCain	End	Mississippi
15	133	Tom Tallchief	Tackle	Oklahoma
16	143	Al Perl	Back	Youngstown State
17	153	Russ Lopez	Center	West Virginia
18	163	Charles (Buck) Garrison	Guard	Wake Forest
19	173	Bill Cloud	Tackle	Temple
20	183	Mike Garbinski	Back	Penn State
21	193	Charley Loiacano	Center	Lafayette
22	203	George Johnson	Tackle	Pittsburgh
23	213	Bill Leitheiser	Guard	Duke
24	223	Roger Adams	Center	Florida
25	233	Bob Verkins	Back	Tulsa
26	243	Clarence Castle	Back	Mississippi
27	253	Marchi Marino	Tackle	Penn State
28	263	Bob Hansen	End	UCLA
29	273	Larry Graves	Tackle	Newberry
30	283	Gail Bruce	End	Washington

1947 Pittsburgh Steelers

The team improved on its 1946 record by winning eight games and losing four. This record tied for the lead in the Eastern Division and qualified the Steelers for the franchise's first playoff berth. It was the Steelers' only postseason appearance before 1972. It was Jock Sutherland's second and final year as head coach; he died the following April after being found wandering around in a field in Kentucky. Once flown back to Pittsburgh, he was diagnosed as having two brain tumors. He only lived a few more days. The 1947 team was the most successful team in club history to date. It was the Steelers' first playoff appearance, the first time winning more than four games consecutively, and the club posted a franchise-best 8–4 record. Though the Steelers lost the playoffs, fans and players were excited for their future.

Val Jasnsante {E} and Charley Mohelivich {DE} were selected to various first team All-Pro teams. Johnny Clement led the team in passing with 1,004 yards and threw 7 touchdown passes. Clement also led the team in rushing with 670 yards. Steve Lach led with 8 rushing touchdowns. Val Jansante led the team in receiving with 35 receptions for 599 yards and 5 TD receptions.

PITTSBURGH			1947			8-5	Game Highlights
9/21/1947		vs	DETROIT	17	10	W	**Repko fumble return TD**/Glamp FG
9/29/1947	MON	vs	LOS ANGELES RAMS	7	48	L	Lach rush TD/Steelers held to 149 yards
10/5/1947		@	Washington Redskins	26	27	L	Compagno INT return TD
10/12/1947		@	Boston Yanks	30	14	W	Lach 2 rush TD/Steelers 276 rush yards
10/19/1947		vs	PHILADELPHIA	35	24	W	Clement 2 rush TD-2 Pass TD
10/26/1947		@	New York Giants	38	21	W	**Sinkovitz INT return TD**/Lach 2 rush TD
11/2/1947		@	Green Bay	18	17	W	**Compagno INT return TD**
11/9/1947		vs	WASHINGTON REDSKINS	21	14	W	Lach-Compagno-Clement rush TD each
11/16/1947		vs	NEW YORK GIANTS	24	7	W	**Seabright INT return TD**
11/23/1947		@	Chicago	7	49	L	Morales TD pass to Jansante
11/30/1947		@	Philadelphia	0	21	L	Steelers held to 120 yards total offense
12/7/1947		vs	BOSTON YANKS	17	7	W	Mastrangelo fumble return TD
12/21/1947		vs	**PHILADELPHIA**	**0**	**21**	**L**	Steelers held to 154 yards total offense

Schedule courtesy of Steve's Football Bible LLC

1947 NFL Eastern Division	W	L	T	PCT	DIV	PF	PA
Philadelphia Eagles	8	4	0	.667	6–2	308	242
Pittsburgh Steelers	**8**	**4**	**0**	**.667**	**6–2**	**240**	**259**
Boston Yanks	4	7	1	.364	3–4–1	168	256
Washington Redskins	4	8	0	.333	3–5	295	367
New York Giants	2	8	2	.200	1–6–1	190	309

1947 NFL Draft

Round	Pick	Player	Position	College
1	5	Hub Bechtol	E	Texas
3	16	John Mastrangelo	T	Notre Dame
5	29	Frank Wydo	T	Cornell
6	38	Frank Aschenbrenner	RB	Northwestern
7	49	Bryant Meeks	C	South Carolina
8	58	Jerry Shipkey *	LB	UCLA
9	69	Bert Vander Clute	G	Wesleyan
10	78	Paul Gibson	E	NC State
11	89	Jack Medd	C	Wesleyan
12	98	Jack Fitch	B	North Carolina
13	109	Ara Parseghian	HB	Miami (OH)
14	118	Red Moore	G	Penn State
15	129	Larry Bruno	B	Geneva
16	138	Ralph Jenkins	C	Clemson
17	149	Elbie Nickel *	E	Cincinnati
18	158	Bill Cregar	G	Holy Cross
19	169	Jerry Mulready	E	North Dakota State
20	178	Warren Smith	T	Kansas Wesleyan
21	189	Fred Hamilton	T	Vanderbilt
22	198	Fred Taylor	E	TCU
23	209	Binks Bushmiaer	B	Vanderbilt
24	218	Paul Davis	FB	Otterbein
25	229	Tommy Kalmanir	HB	Nevada
26	238	Don Mohr	E	Baldwin Wallace
27	249	Art Young	G	Dartmouth
28	258	Ralph Sazio	T	William & Mary
29	269	Dick Pitzer	E	Army
30	278	Tom Stalloni	T	Delaware
31	287	Vince DiFrancesca	G	Northwestern
32	294	Warren Lahr *	DB	Case Western Reserve

1947 Eastern Conference Playoff Game

The 1947 National Football League season resulted in a tie for the Eastern Division title between the Philadelphia Eagles and Pittsburgh Steelers; both finished the regular season at 8–4, requiring a one-game playoff. They had split their two-game series in the season, with the home teams prevailing; the Steelers won by eleven on October 19, while the Eagles carded a 21–0 shutout on November 30 at Shibe Park.

The Steelers and Detroit Lions opened their seasons a week before the rest of the ten-team league on September 21 and completed their schedules on December 7. Philadelphia needed a win over the visiting Green Bay Packers on December 14 to force a playoff the following week and won by fourteen points.

This division playoff game, the Steelers' sole postseason appearance until 1972, was played on December 21 at Forbes Field in Pittsburgh. Scoring touchdowns in each of the first three quarters, the Eagles posted another 21–0 shutout to win the East title and advanced to the championship game in Chicago.

12/21/1947	1	2	3	4	Final
Philadelphia Eagles	7	7	7	0	21
Pittsburgh Steelers	0	0	0	0	0

Scoring

Team	
Eagles	Steve Van Buren 15 yard pass from Tommy Thompson (Cliff Patton kick)
Eagles	Jack Ferrante 28 yard pass from Tommy Thompson (Cliff Patton kick)
Eagles	Bosh Pritchard 79 yard punt return (Cliff Patton kick)

1948 Pittsburgh Steelers

The team finished the season with a record of 4–8, failing to qualify for the playoffs. This season marked the first played with John Michelosen as head coach. Jack Wiley {T} was selected to various first team All-Pro teams.

Ray Evans led the team in passing with 947 yards and threw 5 touchdown passes. Bob Cifers led the team in rushing with 361 yards. Val Jansante led the team in receiving with 39 receptions for 623 yards and 3 TD receptions.

PITTSBURGH		1948			4-8	Game Highlights
9/26/1948	@	Washington Redskins	14	17	L	Clement rush TD-TD pass to Glamp
10/3/1948	vs	BOSTON YANKS	24	14	W	Clement 2 TD pass/Mosely rush TD/Glamp FG
10/10/1948	vs	WASHINGTON REDSKINS	10	7	W	Clement rush TD/Glamp FG/Defense 6 turnovers
10/17/1948	@	Boston Yanks	7	13	L	Shipkey rush TD/Offense commits 7 turnovers
10/24/1948	@	New York Giants	27	34	L	Evans 2 TD pass to Jansante/Shipkey 2 rush TD
10/31/1948	vs	PHILADELPHIA	7	34	L	Shipkey rush TD/Evans 138 pass yards-3 INTs
11/7/1948	vs	GREEN BAY	38	7	W	**Compagno INT return TD**/Evans rush TD & pass
11/14/1948	vs	CHICAGO CARDINALS	7	24	L	Shipkey rush TD/Offense commits 5 turnovers
11/21/1948	@	Detroit	14	17	L	Shipkey & Papach rush TD/5 turnovers by Pitt
11/28/1948	@	Philadelphia	0	17	L	Steelers held to 87 rush yards/defense force 5 TO's
12/5/1948	vs	NEW YORK GIANTS	38	28	W	**Morales fumble return TD**/Papach 148 rush yards
12/12/1948	@	Los Angeles Rams	14	31	L	Papach rush TD-TD catch/Evans 166 pass yards

Schedule courtesy of Steve's Football Bible LLC

1948 NFL Eastern Division	W	L	T	PCT	DIV	PF	PA
Philadelphia Eagles	9	2	1	.818	7–1	376	156
Washington Redskins	7	5	0	.583	5–3	291	287
New York Giants	4	8	0	.333	3–5	297	388
Pittsburgh Steelers	**4**	**8**	**0**	**.333**	**3–5**	**200**	**243**
Boston Yanks	3	9	0	.250	2–6	174	372

1948 NFL Draft

Round	Choice	Player	Position	School
1	9	Dan Edwards	End	Georgia
3	20	Jerry Nuzum	Back	New Mexico State
5	34	John Wozniak	Guard	Alabama
6	43	Joe Gasparella	Back	Notre Dame
6	45	Phil O'Reilly	Tackle	Purdue
7	52	Bill Luongo	Back	Pennsylvania
8	64	Jim Cooper	Center	North Texas State
9	73	Ed Ryan	End	St. Mary's (CA)
10	82	Dick Deranek	Back	Indiana
11	94	Paul Redfield	Tackle	Colgate
12	103	George Papach	Back	Purdue
13	112	Tom Finical	End	Princeton
14	124	Clayton Lane	Tackle	New Hampshire
15	133	Dick Mazuca	Guard	Canisius
16	142	Bill McPeak	End	Pittsburgh
17	154	Frank Messoline	Back	Scranton
18	163	Tom Lane	Tackle	Muhlenberg
19	172	Pete Barbolak	Tackle	Purdue
20	184	Fred Folger	Back	Duke
21	193	Charley Snyder	Tackle	Marshall
22	202	Tally Stevens	End	Utah
23	214	Dike Norman	Center	Washington & Lee
24	223	Floyd Simmons	Back	Notre Dame
25	232	Paul Hausser	Tackle	Wichita State
26	244	Bob Ramsey	Back	Southern Methodist
27	253	Felton Whitlow	Tackle	North Texas State
28	262	Dinky Bowen	Back	Georgia Tech
29	274	Abe Gibron	Guard	Purdue
30	283	Bruce Hilkene	Tackle	Michigan
31	290	Ted Zuchowski	Tackle	Toledo
32	299	Tony DeMattea	Back	Pittsburgh

Bill Moore

Jack Wiley

1949 Pittsburgh Steelers

It was the franchise's 17th in the National Football League, and the second season with John Michelosen as head coach. The team finished the season with a record of 6–5-1, improving slightly from the previous season record of 4-8, but again failing to qualify for the playoffs. Darrell Hogan {LB} was selected to various first team All-Pro teams.

Joe Geri led the team in passing with 554 yards and threw 5 touchdown passes. Jerry Nuzum led the team in rushing with 611 yards and 5 rushing touchdowns. Val Jansante led the team in receiving with 29 receptions for 445 yards and 4 TD receptions.

PITTSBURGH			1949			6-5-1	Game Highlights
9/25/1949	SAT	vs	NEW YORK GIANTS	28	7	W	Steelers 223 rush yards-4 rush TDs
10/3/1949	MON	vs	WASHINGTON REDSKINS	14	27	L	Shipkey & Nuzum rush TDs
10/8/1949	SAT	vs	DETROIT	14	7	W	Shipkey 2 rush TDs/Steelers 206 rush yds
10/16/1949		@	New York Giants	21	17	W	**Samuelson fumble return TD**
10/23/1949		vs	NEW YORK BULLDOGS	24	13	W	Nuzum 117 rush yards-2 rush TDs
10/30/1949		vs	PHILADELPHIA	7	38	L	Finks TD pass to Jansante-115 pass yards
11/6/1949		@	Washington Redskins	14	27	L	Finks & Shipkey rush TDs
11/13/1949		vs	LOS ANGELES RAMS	7	7	T	Geri rush TD/Defense forces 3 turnovers
11/20/1949		@	Green Bay	30	7	W	Geri 2 pass TD-123 pass yards-98 rush yds
11/27/1949		@	Philadelphia	17	34	L	Geri TD pass to Nuzum/Geri FG
12/4/1949		@	Chicago	21	30	L	Gage 87 rush yards-2 rush TD
12/11/1949		@	New York Bulldogs	27	0	W	Geri 108 pass yds-TD pass-78 rush yds-TD

Schedule courtesy of Steve's Football Bible LLC

1949 NFL Eastern Division	W	L	T	PCT	DIV	PF	PA
Philadelphia Eagles	11	1	0	.917	8–0	364	134
Pittsburgh Steelers	6	5	1	.545	4–4	224	214
New York Giants	6	6	0	.500	3–5	287	298
Washington Redskins	4	7	1	.364	3–4–1	268	339
New York Bulldogs	1	10	1	.091	1–6–1	153	368

1949 NFL Draft

Round	Choice	Player	Position	School
1	6	Bobby Gage	Back	Clemson
2	16	Harper Davis	Back	Mississippi State
3	26	Bill Walsh	Center	Notre Dame
4	36	Joe Geri	Back	Georgia
5	45	Bill Long	End	Oklahoma State
6	56	Doug Brightwell	Center	Texas Christian
7	65	Bill Talarico	Back	Pennsylvania
8	76	George Brown	Guard	Texas Christian
9	85	Tom Brennan	Tackle	Boston College
10	96	Bob Hood	End	Alabama
11	105	Al Sanders	Center	Southern Mississippi
12	116	Jim Finks	QB	Tulsa
13	125	R.R. Walston	Guard	North Texas State
14	136	Dave Moon	Back	Southern Methodist
15	145	Ed Sobczak	End	Michigan
16	156	Denvard Snell	Tackle	Auburn
17	165	Veto Kissell	Back	Holy Cross
18	176	Clint Shipman	Tackle	East Texas State
19	185	Jack McBride	End	Rice
20	196	Ben Mann	Guard	Mississippi
21	205	Joe Jackura	Center	Georgia
22	216	Lloyd Johnson	Back	West Texas State
23	225	Jim Owens	End	Oklahoma
24	236	Ivan Snowden	Tackle	Texas A&I
25	245	Bobby Gaff	Back	Texas A&M

Johnny Clement

Forbes Field vs Chicago Cardinals

1950 Pittsburgh Steelers

It was the team's third season under head coach John Michelosen who had led the team to a combined 10–13–1 record over the previous two years. Despite finishing last in the league in scoring, the team compiled a 6–6 record which left them tied for third place among the six teams in the NFL's American Conference. The Steelers were the league's only team that employed the single wing; most of the league's other franchises had switched to the T formation. Joe Geri {TB} was selected to various first team All-Pro teams.

Joe Geri led the team in passing with 866 yards and threw 6 touchdown passes. Geri also led the team in rushing with 705 yards. Val Jansante led the team with 26 receptions. Elbie Nickel led the team with 527 receiving yards and 4 TD receptions.

PITTSBURGH			1950			6-6	Game Highlights
9/17/1950		vs	NEW YORK GIANTS	7	18	L	Shipkey rush TD/Steelers commit 9 turnovers
9/24/1950		@	Detroit	7	10	L	Gage TD pass to Nickel/110 pass yards
10/1/1950		@	Washington Redskins	26	7	W	Geri pass TD to Nickel/Gage & Rogel TDs
10/7/1950	SAT	vs	CLEVELAND BROWNS	17	30	L	Geri TD pass to Seabright-122 pass yards
10/15/1950		@	New York Giants	17	6	W	Geri TD pass to Nickel-159 pass yards
10/22/1950		vs	PHILADELPHIA	10	17	L	Geri TD pass to Rogel-144 pass yards-FG
10/29/1950		@	Cleveland Browns	7	45	L	Gasparella TD pass to Gage-QBs 6 INTs
11/5/1950		@	Philadelphia	9	7	W	Geri 113 rush yards/3 FGs
11/12/1950		vs	BALTIMORE COLTS	17	7	W	Rogel and Gage rush TD/Geri FG
11/23/1950	TH	@	Chicago Cardinals	28	17	W	Geri 101 rush yards-2 rush TDs
12/3/1950		vs	WASHINGTON REDSKINS	7	24	L	Geri TD pass to Nickel-103 pass yards
12/10/1950		vs	CHICAGO CARDINALS	28	7	W	Gasparella 2 pass TD-111 pass yards

Schedule courtesy of Steve's Football Bible LLC

1950 NFL American Conference	W	L	T	PCT	CONF	PF	PA
Cleveland Browns	10	2	0	.833	8–2	310	144
New York Giants	10	2	0	.833	8–2	268	150
Pittsburgh Steelers	**6**	**6**	**0**	**.500**	**5–5**	**180**	**195**
Philadelphia Eagles	6	6	0	.500	4–6	254	141
Chicago Cardinals	5	7	0	.417	3–6	233	287
Washington Redskins	3	9	0	.250	1–8	232	326

1950 NFL Draft

Round	Choice	Player	Position	School
1	8	Lynn Chandois	Back	Michigan State
2	22	Ernie Stautner	DT	Boston College
3	34	George Hughes	Guard	William & Mary
5	56	Tom Rowe	End	Dartmouth
5	60	Lou Allen	Tackle	Duke
6	74	Ed Mattson	Back	Trinity (TX)
7	86	Truett Smith	Back	Mississippi State
8	100	Fran Rogel	Back	Penn State
9	112	Max Drue	Tackle	Tulane
11	138	Charley Williams	End	Sam Houston State
13	164	Negley Norton	Tackle	Penn State
14	178	Jim Kynes	Center	Florida
15	190	Harry Russell	Back	San Jose State
16	204	Bernie Barkouskie	Guard	Pittsburgh
17	216	Al Bodine	Back	Georgia
18	230	Kenneth Powell	End	North Carolina
19	242	Frank Gaul	Tackle	Notre Dame
20	256	Mike DeNoia	Back	Scranton
21	268	Dick Tomlinson	Guard	Kansas
22	282	Stan Burak	Back	George Washington
23	294	Walt Kerulis	End	Illinois
24	308	John Weaver	Guard	Miami (OH)
25	320	Bob Numbers	Center	Lehigh
26	334	Nick Vaccaro	Back	Florida
27	346	Elmer Kreiser	End	Bloomsburg
28	360	Jerry Diehl	Back	Idaho
29	372	Carl DePasqua	Back	Pittsburgh
30	386	Ed Hudak	Tackle	Notre Dame

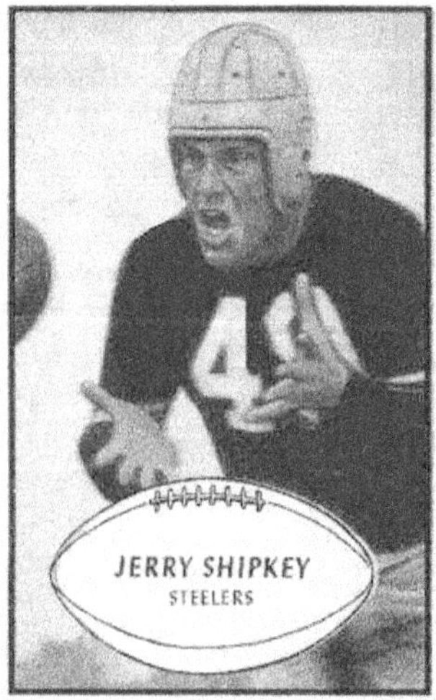

1951 Pittsburgh Steelers

It was the team's 4th season under head coach John Michelosen who had led the team to a combined 16–19–1 record over the previous three years. The Steelers ended the 1951 season with a record of 4 wins and 7 losses and 1 tie, finishing fourth in the NFL's American Division. Jerry Shipkey {LB} was selected to various first team All-Pro teams.

Chuck Ortmann led the team in passing with 671 yards. Fran Rogel led the team in rushing with 385 yards. Henry Minarik led the team in receiving with 35 receptions for 459 yards.

PITTSBURGH			1951			4-7-1	Game Highlights
10/1/1951	MON	vs	NEW YORK GIANTS	13	13	T	Geri rush TD-2 FGs-102 pass yards
10/7/1951		@	Green Bay	33	35	L	**Finks INT return TD**/Chandnois 2 TDs
10/14/1951		vs	SAN FRANCISCO	24	28	L	Nickel 5 catch-149 yards-2 TD reception
10/21/1951		@	Cleveland Browns	0	17	L	Matthews 111 pass yards/4 turnovers
10/28/1951		@	Chicago Cardinals	28	14	W	**Butler INT return TD**/Geri TD catch
11/4/1951		vs	PHILADELPHIA	13	34	L	**Shipkey INT return TD**/Geri 2 FGs
11/11/1951		vs	GREEN BAY	28	7	W	Chandnois rush TD-TD pass to Minarik
11/18/1951		vs	WASHINGTON REDSKINS	7	22	L	**Matthews punt return TD**/126 total yards
11/25/1951		@	Philadelphia	17	13	W	Ortmann 108 pass yards-TD pass
12/2/1951		@	New York Giants	0	14	L	Giants score on 2 defensive touchdowns
12/9/1951		vs	CLEVELAND BROWNS	0	28	L	Steelers commit 5 turnovers in loss
12/16/1951		@	Washington Redskins	20	10	W	Finks 201 pass yds-TD pass to Chandnois

Schedule courtesy of Steve's Football Bible LLC

1951 NFL American Conference	W	L	T	PCT	CONF	PF	PA
Cleveland Browns	11	1	0	.917	9–0	331	152
New York Giants	9	2	1	.818	7–2–1	254	161
Washington Redskins	5	7	0	.417	4–5	183	296
Pittsburgh Steelers	**4**	**7**	**1**	**.364**	**3–5–1**	**183**	**235**
Philadelphia Eagles	4	8	0	.333	3–6	234	264
Chicago Cardinals	3	9	0	.250	0–8	210	287

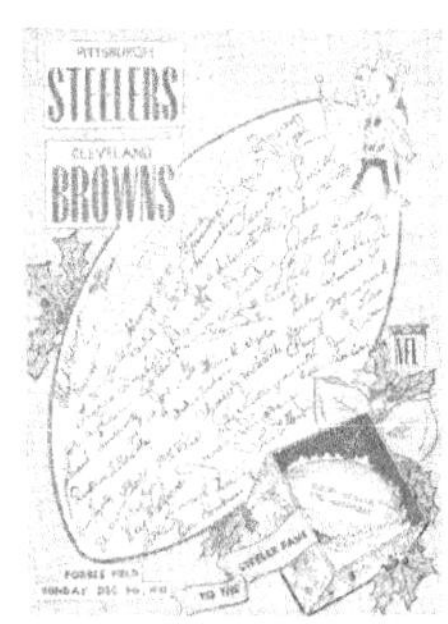

1951 NFL Draft

Round	Choice	Player	Position	School
1	9	Clarence (Butch) Avinger	Back	Alabama
2	20	Chuck Ortmann	Back	Michigan
3	31	George Sulima	End	Boston University
4	45	Barry (Bear) French	Tackle	Purdue
5	56	Floyd Sampson	Back	McMurry
6	67	Dale Dodrill	Guard	Colorado State
7	81	Ray Mathews	Back	Clemson
8	92	Hank Minarik	End	Michigan State
9	103	John (Bull) Schweder	Guard	Pennsylvania
10	118	Paul Salata	End	USC
11	129	Joe McCutcheon	Center	Washington & Lee
12	140	Jim (Popcorn) Brandt	Back	St. Thomas (MN)
13	154	Bill Szabo	Tackle	Bucknell
14	165	Mike Mizerany	Guard	Alabama
15	176	Clay Webb	Back	Kentucky
16	190	Lambert Oberg	Center	Trinity (CT)
17	201	Ted Gehlmann	Tackle	William & Mary
18	212	Pat Field	Back	Georgia
19	226	Bill Pavlikowski	Back	Boston University
20	237	Tom (Tex) Donnelly	Tackle	Holy Cross
21	248	Ernie Cheatam	Tackle	Loyola (CA)
22	262	Dick Hendley	Back	Clemson
23	273	Joe Minor	End	John Carroll
24	284	Art Alois	Center	San Francisco
25	298	Tommy Calvin	Back	Alabama
26	309	Bill (Pug) Pearman	Guard	Tennessee
27	320	Bob Radcliffe	Back	Wisconsin
28	334	Howie Hansen	Back	UCLA
29	345	Fred Smith	End	Tulsa
30	356	John Gruble	End	Tennessee

1952 Pittsburgh Steelers

    The 1952 Pittsburgh Steelers, coached by Joe Bach, missed the playoffs after finishing the NFL regular season in 4th place in the American Conference with a 5-7 record. Bach returned to the organization replacing John Michelosen. The season was notable in that it was the last year the Steelers used the single-wing formation on offense, switching to the T formation the following year. The Steelers were the last NFL team to use the single wing as their primary offensive formation. Bill Walsh {C} and Jerry Shipkey {LB} were selected to various first team All-Pro teams.

    Jim Finks led the team in passing with a then franchise record if 2,307 yards and threw 20 touchdown passes, also a franchise record. Ray Matthews led the team in rushing with 315 yards. Elbie Nickel led the team in receiving with 55 receptions for 884 yards and 9 TD receptions, all franchise records. **Lynn Chandnois set a team record by returning 2 kickoff returns for a touchdown. Ray Matthews set a team record with 2 punt returns for touchdowns.**

PITTSBURGH			1952			5-7	Game Highlights
9/28/1952		vs	PHILADELPHIA	25	31	L	Finks 235 pass yards-2 rush TD-TD pass
10/4/1952	SAT	vs	CLEVELAND BROWNS	20	21	L	Finks 203 pass yards-2 TD pass to Nickel
10/12/1952		@	Philadelphia	21	26	L	**Chandnois kickoff return TD**/Finks 2 TDs
10/19/1952		vs	WASHINGTON REDSKINS	24	28	L	**Hays INT return TD**/Nickel 2 TD catch
10/26/1952		@	Chicago Cardinals	34	28	W	**Matthews punt return TD**/Ferry fumble TD
11/2/1952		@	Washington Redskins	24	23	W	**Dodrill blocked FG return TD**
11/9/1952		vs	DETROIT	6	31	L	Rogel rush TD/Finks 209 pass yards
11/16/1952		@	Cleveland Browns	28	29	L	Finks 306 pass yards-4 pass TD
11/23/1952		vs	CHICAGO CARDINALS	17	14	W	Modzewlewski & Finks rush TD
11/30/1952		vs	NEW YORK GIANTS	63	7	W	**Chandnois kickoff return TD**-Finks 4 TD pass
12/7/1952		@	San Francisco	24	7	W	Finks rush TD-TD pass to Chandnois
12/14/1952		@	Los Angeles Rams	14	28	L	**Hogan INT return TD**/Nickel TD catch

Schedule courtesy of Steve's Football Bible LLC

1952 NFL American Conference	W	L	T	PCT	CONF	PF	PA
Cleveland Browns	8	4	0	.667	7–3	310	213
Philadelphia Eagles	7	5	0	.583	6–4	252	271
New York Giants	7	5	0	.583	5–4	234	231
Pittsburgh Steelers	**5**	**7**	**0**	**.417**	**4–5**	**300**	**273**
Chicago Cardinals	4	8	0	.333	3–7	172	221
Washington Redskins	4	8	0	.333	4–6	240	287

1952 NFL Draft

Round	Choice	Player	Position	School
1	6	Ed Modzelewski	Back	Maryland
2	18	George Tarasovic	Center	LSU
3	30	Steve Wadiak	Back	South Carolina
4	42	Jack Gearding	Tackle	Xavier
7	78	Claude Hipps	Back	Georgia
9	102	Hal (Herky) Payne	Back	Tennessee
10	114	George Gilmartin	Back	Xavier
11	126	Jack Spinks	Back	Alcorn State
12	138	Marv McFadden	Tackle	Michigan State
13	150	Dave Flood	Back	Notre Dame
14	162	June Davis	Guard	Texas
15	174	Dick Pivirotto	Back	Princeton
16	186	Pete Ladygo	Guard	Maryland
17	198	Pat Smithwick	End	St. Norbert
18	210	Andy MacDonald	Back	Central Michigan
19	222	Gary Kerkorian	QB	Stanford
20	234	Dan Simeone	Tackle	Villanova
21	246	Harry Babcock	End	Georgia
22	258	Bob Byrne	Back	Montana State
23	270	Vic Pollock	Back	Army
24	282	Bob Bestwick	Back	Pittsburgh
25	294	Bill Robinson	Back	Lincoln (MO)
26	306	Bobby Wilson	Back	Alabama
27	318	Dick (Skippy) Doyle	Back	Ohio State
28	330	Jerry Hanifan	Back	St. Bonaventure
29	342	Chris Warriner	End	Pittsburgh
30	354	Ed Kissell	Back	Wake Forest

1953 Pittsburgh Steelers

The 1953 Pittsburgh Steelers, coached by Joe Bach, missed the playoffs after finishing the NFL regular season in 4th place in the Eastern Conference with a 6-6 record. The Steelers average over 26,000 fans at home. They played at Forbes Field. Dale Dodrill {MG} was selected to various first team All-Pro teams.

Jim Finks led the team in passing with 1,484 yards and threw 8 touchdown passes. Fran Rogel led the team in rushing with 527 yards. Elbie Nickel led the team in receiving with 62 receptions, setting a new franchise record, for 743 yards and 4 TD receptions.

PITTSBURGH			1953			6-6	Game Highlights
9/27/1953		@	Detroit	21	38	L	**Matthews fumble return TD**/Nickel 2 TDs
10/3/1953	SAT	vs	NEW YORK GIANTS	24	14	W	**Chandnois kickoff return TD**
10/11/1953		vs	CHICAGO CARDINALS	31	28	W	Steelers rally from 21 down/Rogel 2 rush TD
10/17/1953	SAT	@	Philadelphia	7	23	L	Finks 138 pass yards-TD pass to Matthews
10/24/1953	SAT	vs	GREEN BAY	31	14	W	Rogel 168 rush yards-Brandt 2 rush TDs
11/1/1953		vs	PHILADELPHIA	7	35	L	Finks 224 pass yards-TD pass to Matthews
11/8/1953		@	Cleveland Browns	16	34	L	Finks 219 pass yards-TD pass to Matthews
11/15/1953		@	New York Giants	14	10	W	**Dodrill fumble return TD**/Butler TD catch
11/22/1953		vs	CLEVELAND BROWNS	16	20	L	Finks & Matthews rush TDs
11/29/1953		vs	WASHINGTON REDSKINS	9	17	L	Mackrides 238 pass yds/Chandnois rush TD
12/6/1953		@	Chicago Cardinals	21	17	W	Mackrides rush TD-TD pass to Nickel
12/13/1953		@	Washington Redskins	14	13	W	**Butler INT return TD**/Chandnois rush TD

Schedule courtesy of Steve's Football Bible LLC

1953 NFL Eastern Conference	W	L	T	PCT	CONF	PF	PA
Cleveland Browns	11	1	0	.917	9–1	348	162
Philadelphia Eagles	7	4	1	.636	6–3–1	352	215
Washington Redskins	6	5	1	.545	6–3–1	208	215
Pittsburgh Steelers	**6**	**6**	**0**	**.500**	**5–5**	**211**	**263**
New York Giants	3	9	0	.250	3–7	179	277
Chicago Cardinals	1	10	1	.091	0–10	190	337

1953 NFL Draft

Round	Choice	Player	Position	School
1	5	Ted Marchibroda	QB	Detroit
2	18	John Henry Johnson	RB	Arizona State
3	29	Marv Matuszak	Tackle	Tulsa
4	42	Lloyd Colteryahnn	End	Maryland
5	53	Bob Gaona	Tackle	Wake Forest
6	66	Tom Barton	Guard	Clemson
7	77	John Alderton	End	Maryland
8	90	Lowell Perry	End	Michigan
9	101	Pat Sarnese	Tackle	Temple
10	114	Frank Holohan	Tackle	Tennessee
12	138	Jerry Robertson	Back	Kansas
13	149	Leo Davis	End	Bradley
14	162	Charley Montgomery	Tackle	Mississippi
15	173	Bob O'Neil	End	Notre Dame
16	186	John Zachary	Back	Miami (OH)
17	197	Reed Quinn	Back	Florida
18	210	Carl Holben	Tackle	Duke
19	221	Jim Williams	Back	Louisville
20	234	Will Lee Hayley	End	Auburn
21	245	Don Earley	Guard	South Carolina
22	258	Ed O'Connor	Tackle	Maryland
23	269	Ray Correll	Guard	Kentucky
24	282	Bob Schneidenbach	Back	Miami (FL)
25	293	Vic Hampel	End	Houston
26	306	Jack (Goose) McClairen	End	Bethune-Cookman
27	317	Jack Delaney	Back	Cincinnati
28	330	Joe Cimini	Tackle	Mississippi State
29	341	Art Massaro	Back	Washington & Jefferson
30	354	Lou Tepe	Center	Duke

1954 Pittsburgh Steelers

  The 1954 Pittsburgh Steelers, coached by Walt Kiesling, missed the playoffs after finishing the NFL regular season in 4th place in the Eastern Conference with a 5-7 record. Bill Walsh {C} and Dale Dodrill {MG} were selected to various first team All-Pro teams.

  Jim Finks led the team in passing with 2,003 yards and threw 14 touchdown passes. Fran Rogel led the team in rushing with 415 yards. Johnny Lattner led the team with 5 rushing touchdowns. Ray Matthews led the team in receiving with 44 receptions for 652 yards and 6 TD receptions.

PITTSBURGH			1954			5-7	Game Highlights
9/26/1954		@	Green Bay	21	20	W	Finks 327 pass yards- 3 pass TDs
10/2/1954	SAT	vs	WASHINGTON REDSKINS	37	7	W	Finks & Held 277 pass yards-2 pass TDs
10/9/1954	SAT	@	Philadelphia	22	24	L	**Butler INT return TD**/Held 2 FGs
10/17/1954		vs	CLEVELAND BROWNS	55	27	W	**Butler & Craft INT return TDs**/Finks 4 pass TD
10/23/1954	SAT	vs	PHILADELPHIA	17	7	W	Finks 171 pass yards-TD pass to Nickel
10/31/1954		@	Chicago Cardinals	14	17	L	Finks 206 pass yards-TD pass to Nickel
11/7/1954		vs	NEW YORK GIANTS	6	30	L	Finks 187 pass yards/Lattner rush TD
11/14/1954		@	Washington Redskins	14	17	L	Finks 196 pass yards-2 pass TD
11/20/1954	SAT	vs	SAN FRANCISCO	3	31	L	Steelers 202 total yards/commit 3 turnovers
11/28/1954		vs	CHICAGO CARDINALS	20	17	W	Matthews rush TD and TD catch
12/5/1954		@	New York Giants	3	24	L	Steelers 177 total yards/commit 8 turnovers
12/12/1954		@	Cleveland Browns	7	42	L	Steelers 171 total yards/commit 6 turnovers

Schedule courtesy of Steve's Football Bible LLC

1954 NFL Eastern Conference	W	L	T	PCT	CONF	PF	PA
Cleveland Browns	9	3	0	.750	8–2	336	162
Philadelphia Eagles	7	4	1	.636	7–3	284	230
New York Giants	7	5	0	.583	7–3	293	184
Pittsburgh Steelers	**5**	**7**	**0**	**.417**	**4–6**	**219**	**263**
Washington Redskins	3	9	0	.250	2–8	207	432
Chicago Cardinals	2	10	0	.167	2–8	183	347

1954 NFL Draft

Round	Choice	Player	Position	School
1	7	John Lattner	RB	Notre Dame
2	19	Pat Stark	Back	Syracuse
3	31	Tom Miner	End	Tulsa
6	67	Laurin Pepper	Back	Southern Mississippi
7	79	Jack O'Brien	Back	Florida
8	91	Paul Cameron	Back	UCLA
9	103	Joe Zombek	End	Pittsburgh
10	115	Bob Fisher	Tackle	Tennessee
11	127	Lou Cimarolli	Back	Pittsburgh
12	139	Don Fritz	End	Cincinnati
13	151	Charley Lattimer	Center	Maryland
14	163	Roger Bradford	End	Waynesburg
15	175	Tom Drake	Guard	Tennessee-Chattanooga
16	187	Cas Krol	Tackle	Detroit
17	199	Joe Fulwyler	Center	Oregon State
18	211	Don Penze	End	Notre Dame
19	223	Don Rydalch	Back	Utah
20	235	Fred Prender	Back	West Chester
21	247	Dan Tassotti	Tackle	Miami (FL)
22	259	John Lapsley	Guard	Northeastern
23	271	Joe Pascarella	Tackle	Penn State
24	283	Jack Flanagan	End	Detroit
25	295	Jim Barron	Tackle	Mississipi State
26	307	Joe Varaitis	Back	Pennsylvania
27	319	Tom Yewcic	QB	Michigan State
28	331	Joe Bush	Guard	Notre Dame
29	343	Joe Fagan	Tackle	John Carroll
30	355	Juel Sweatte	Back	Oklahoma

1955 Pittsburgh Steelers

The 1955 Pittsburgh Steelers, coached by Walt Kiesling, missed the playoffs after finishing the NFL regular season in 6th place in the Eastern Conference with a 4-8 record. Dale Dodrill {MG} and Ernie Stautner {G} were selected to various first team All-Pro teams.

Jim Finks led the team in passing with 2,270 yards and threw 10 touchdown passes. Fran Rogel led the team in rushing with 588 yards. Lynn Chadnois led with 5 rushing touchdowns. Ray Matthews led the team in receiving with 42 receptions for 762 yards and 6 TD receptions.

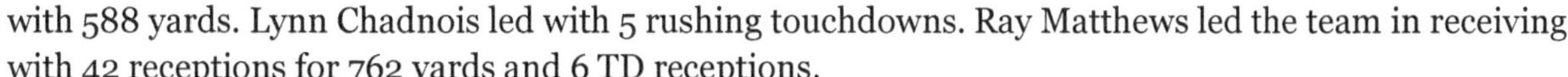

PITTSBURGH			1955			4-8	Game Highlights
9/26/1955	MON	vs	CHICAGO CARDINALS	14	7	W	Finks 245 pass yards-2 pass TD
10/2/1955		@	Los Angeles Rams	26	27	L	**McCabe fumble return TD**/Chandnois 2 TD
10/9/1955		vs	NEW YORK GIANTS	30	23	W	Finks 297 pass yards-2 TD pass-rush TD
10/15/1955	SAT	vs	PHILADELPHIA	13	7	W	Finks & Chandnois tush TDs
10/23/1955		@	New York Giants	19	17	W	Matthews-Finks-Chandnois rush TD each
10/30/1955		@	Philadelphia	0	24	L	Steelers 176 total yards/commit 3 turnovers
11/5/1955	SAT	@	Chicago Cardinals	13	27	L	Finks 337 pass yards-3 INT/Weed 2 FGs
11/13/1955		vs	DETROIT	28	31	L	Finks 246 pass yards-TD pass to O'Brien
11/20/1955		@	Cleveland Browns	14	41	L	Nickel 4 catch/76 yards/2 TD catch
11/27/1955		vs	WASHINGTON REDSKINS	14	23	L	Finks 262 pass yards-2 pass TD
12/4/1955		vs	CLEVELAND BROWNS	7	30	L	**O'Malley fumble return TD**
12/11/1955		@	Washington Redskins	17	28	L	Matthews 170 pass yards-TD pass to Matthews

Schedule courtesy of Steve's Football Bible LLC

1955 NFL Eastern Conference	W	L	T	PCT	CONF	PF	PA
Cleveland Browns	9	2	1	.818	7–2–1	349	218
Washington Redskins	8	4	0	.667	6–4	246	222
New York Giants	6	5	1	.545	4–5–1	267	223
Philadelphia Eagles	4	7	1	.364	4–5–1	248	231
Chicago Cardinals	4	7	1	.364	3–6–1	224	252
Pittsburgh Steelers	**4**	**8**	**0**	**.333**	**4–6**	**195**	**285**

1955 NFL Draft

Round	Choice	Player	Position	School
1	6	Frank Varrichione	Tackle	Notre Dame
3	30	Ed Bernet	End	Southern Methodist
4	42	Fred Broussard	Center	Northwestern State (LA)
5	54	George Mason	Tackle	Alabama
6	66	Lem Harkey	Back	Emporia State
7	78	Hal Reeve	Tackle	Oregon
9	102	Johnny Unitas	QB	Louisville
10	114	Terry Boyle	Tackle	Cincinnati
11	126	Vic Eaton	Back	Missouri
12	138	Jim Cooke	End	Lincoln (PA)
13	150	Jim Whitmer	Back	Purdue
14	162	John (Buck) Byrne	Guard	John Carroll
15	174	Ellis Duckett	Back	Michigan State
16	186	Frank Vincent	Center	Glenville State
17	198	Ed Merchant	Back	Miami (OH)
18	210	Albie Maier	Guard	Marshall
19	222	Ed Smith	Back	Texas Southern
20	234	Lou Matykiewicz	End	Iowa
21	246	Rees Phenix	Tackle	Georgia Tech
22	258	Richie McCabe	Back	Pittsburgh
23	270	Gordy Holz	Tackle	Minnesota
24	282	Mike Mayock	End	Villanova
25	294	Charlie Bull	Guard	Missouri
26	306	Jim Soltau	End	Minnesota
27	318	Bill Sanford	Back	Hofstra
28	330	Dave Williams	Guard	Ohio State
29	342	Bernie Sinclair	End	Texas A&M
30	353	Jim Caruzzi	Back	Marquette

1956 Pittsburgh Steelers

The 1956 Pittsburgh Steelers, coached by Walt Kiesling, missed the playoffs after finishing the NFL regular season in 5th place in the Eastern Conference with a 5-7 record. Ernie Stautner {DT} was selected to various first team All-Pro teams. Ted Marchibroda led the team in passing with 1,585 yards and threw 12 touchdown passes. Fran Rogel led the team in rushing with 476 yards. Ray Matthews led the team in receiving with 31 receptions for 540 yards and 5 TD receptions.

PITTSBURGH			1956			5-7	Game Highlights
9/30/1956		vs	WASHINGTON REDSKINS	30	13	W	Chandnois 2 rush TD-TD catch
10/6/1956	SAT	vs	CLEVELAND BROWNS	10	14	L	Marchibroda 153 pass yds/Chandnois rush TD
10/14/1956		vs	PHILADELPHIA	21	35	L	Marchibroda 276 pass yards-3 TD pass
10/21/1956		@	New York Giants	38	10	L	Marchibroda TD pass to Nickel
10/28/1956		@	Cleveland Browns	24	16	W	Marchibroda 227 pass yards-2 TD pass
11/4/1956		vs	NEW YORK GIANTS	14	17	L	Watson 2 rush TD/Marchibroda 142 pass yards
11/11/1956		@	Philadelphia	7	14	L	Steelers held to 149 total yards
11/18/1956		vs	CHICAGO CARDINALS	14	7	W	**Butler fumble return TD**/Rogel rush TD
11/25/1956		@	Chicago Cardinals	27	38	L	Marchibroda 174 pass yards-2 pass TD-3 INTs
12/2/1956		vs	LOS ANGELES RAMS	30	13	W	Scarbath 117 pass yards-2 TD pass to Nickel
12/9/1956		@	Detroit	7	45	L	Steelers held to 129 total yards/Watson rush TD
12/16/1956		@	Washington Redskins	23	0	W	Marchibroda 177 pass yards-2 pass TD

Schedule courtesy of Steve's Football Bible LLC

1956 NFL Eastern Conference	W	L	T	PCT	CONF	PF	PA
New York Giants	8	3	1	.727	7–3	264	197
Chicago Cardinals	7	5	0	.583	7–3	240	182
Washington Redskins	6	6	0	.500	5–5	183	225
Cleveland Browns	5	7	0	.417	4–6	167	177
Pittsburgh Steelers	**5**	**7**	**0**	**.417**	**4–6**	**217**	**250**
Philadelphia Eagles	3	8	1	.273	3–7	143	215

1956 NFL Draft

Round	Pick	Player	Position	College
1	1	Gary Glick	DB	Colorado A&M
1	5	Art Davis	DB	Mississippi State
2	17	Joe Krupa *	DT	Purdue
3	29	Jim Taylor	C	Baylor
4	39	Dick Murley	T	Purdue
5	52	Bill Murakowski	B	Purdue
6	63	Ray Taylor	B	TCU
7	76	Dick Gaspari	C	George Washington
8	87	Vere Wellmen	G	Wichita
9	100	Wayne Edmonds	G	Notre Dame
10	111	Lou Baldacci	HB	Michigan
10	118	Bob Nolan	E	Miami (FL)
12	135	Phil Tarasovic	E	Yale
13	148	Weldon Holley	B	Baylor
14	159	Jim Emmons	T	Alabama
16	183	Lionel Reed	B	Central State (OK)
17	196	Bill Schmitt	G	Pittsburgh
18	207	John Stephans	QB	Holy Cross
19	220	Jerry Jacobs	G	Florida State
20	231	Fred Glatz	E	Pittsburgh
21	244	Gene Martell	T	Notre Dame
22	255	Ray DiPasquale	B	Pittsburgh
23	268	Pete Neft	QB	Pittsburgh
24	279	Bryan Engram	E	TCU
25	292	Bill O'Dell	B	Clemson
26	303	Frank Sweeney	G	Xavier
27	316	Buddy Benson	B	Arkansas
28	327	Bill DeGraaf	B	Cornell
29	340	Wes Thompson	T	Alabama

1957 Pittsburgh Steelers

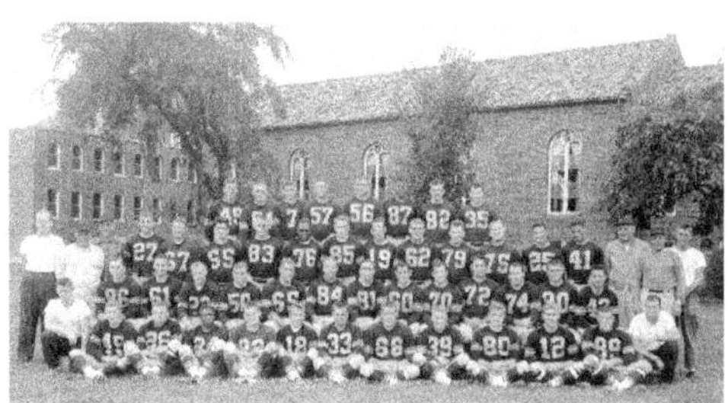

The 1957 Pittsburgh Steelers, coached by Buddy Parker, missed the playoffs after finishing the NFL regular season in 3rd place in the Eastern Conference with a 6-6 record. For the first time, the Steelers' yellow helmets sported uniform numbers. Pittsburgh would use these uniforms through the 1961 season. Jack Butler {S} was selected to various first team All-Pro teams.

Earl Morrall led the team in passing with 1,900 yards and threw 11 touchdown passes. Billy Wells led the team in rushing with 532 yards. Jack McClairen led the team in receiving with 46 receptions for 630 yards.

PITTSBURGH			1957			6-6	Game Highlights
9/29/1957		vs	WASHINGTON REDSKINS	28	7	W	Morrall 249 pass yards-3 TD pass/Girard 2 TDs
10/5/1957	SAT	vs	CLEVELAND BROWNS	12	23	L	Morrall 255 pass yards-2 TD pass to Girard
10/13/1957		vs	CHICAGO CARDINALS	29	20	W	**Wells kickoff return TD/O'Neil blocked punt Td**
10/20/1957		@	New York Giants	0	35	L	Steelers held to 172 yards-commit 4 turnovers
10/27/1957		vs	PHILADELPHIA	6	0	W	Defense hold Eagles to 70 yards/Matthews TD
11/3/1957		@	Baltimore Colts	19	13	W	Morrall 270 pass yards-2 TD pass to Matthews
11/10/1957		@	Cleveland Browns	0	24	L	Morrall 193 pass yards/Steelers commit 4 TO's
11/24/1957		vs	GREEN BAY	10	27	L	Morrall 149 pass yards-TD pass to McClairen
12/1/1957		@	Philadelphia	6	7	L	Glick 2 FGs/Steelers 171 rush yards
12/7/1957	SAT	vs	NEW YORK GIANTS	21	10	W	**Reger fumble return TD**/Nickel TD catch
12/15/1957		@	Washington Redskins	3	10	L	Steelers held to 158 yards/Glick FG
12/22/1957		@	Chicago Cardinals	27	2	W	Morrall 161 pass yards-TD pass to McClairen

Schedule courtesy of Steve's Football Bible LLC

1957 NFL Eastern Conference	W	L	T	PCT	CONF	PF	PA
Cleveland Browns	9	2	1	.818	8–1–1	269	172
New York Giants	7	5	0	.583	6–4	254	211
Pittsburgh Steelers	**6**	**6**	**0**	**.500**	**5–5**	**161**	**178**
Washington Redskins	5	6	1	.455	4–5–1	251	230
Philadelphia Eagles	4	8	0	.333	4–6	173	230
Chicago Cardinals	3	9	0	.250	2–8	200	299

1957 NFL Draft

Round	Choice	Player	Position	School
1	5	Len Dawson	QB	Purdue
2	16	Bill Michael	Tackle	Ohio State
3	30	Don Owens	Tackle	Southern Mississippi
5	55	Perry Richards	End	Detroit
6	66	George Volkert	Back	Georgia Tech
7	77	Curley Johnson	Back	Houston
9	102	Charley Hutchings	Tackle	Miami (FL)
10	113	Ralph Jelic	Back	Pittsburgh
11	127	Dick Hughes	Back	Tulsa
12	138	Vern Ellison	Guard	Oregon State
13	149	Dwaine Underwood	Tackle	Oklahoma State
14	163	Jim Crawford	Back	Wyoming
15	174	Herman Canil	Tackle	Pittsburgh
17	199	Corny Salvaterra	QB	Pittsburgh
18	210	Len Bigbee	End	East Texas State
19	221	Phil Bennett	End	Miami (FL)
20	235	John Szuehan	Tackle	North Carolina State
21	246	Gene Cichowski	QB	Indiana
22	257	Aurelius Thomas	Guard	Ohio State
23	271	Bob Pollock	Tackle	Pittsburgh
24	282	Gary Francis	End	Illinois
25	293	Jim Hinesley	End	Michigan State
26	307	Bob Swann	Tackle	Vanderbilt
27	318	Bob Konkoly	Back	Xavier
28	329	Frank Kilinsky	Tackle	Tennessee
29	343	Tom Ramage	Guard	Utah State
30	353	Don Serier	End	Arkansas State

1958 Pittsburgh Steelers

The 1958 Pittsburgh Steelers, coached by Buddy Parker, missed the playoffs after finishing the NFL regular season in 3rd place in the Eastern Conference with a 7-4-1 record. After the second game of the season, Steelers coach Buddy Parker, formerly in Detroit, arranged a trade on October 6 that sent quarterback Earl Morrall and two draft picks to the Detroit Lions for quarterback Bobby Layne, a future hall of famer. Jack Butler {S} and Ernie Stautner {DE} were selected to various first team All-Pro teams.

Bobby Lane led the team in passing with 2,339 yards and threw 13 touchdown passes. Tom Tracy led the team in rushing with 714 yards and 5 rushing touchdowns. Jimmy Orr led the team in receiving with 33 receptions for 910 yards and 7 TD receptions.

PITTSBURGH			1958			7-4-1	Game Highlights
9/28/1958		@	San Francisco	20	23	L	Morrall 117 pass yards-TD pass to Matthews
10/5/1958		vs	CLEVELAND BROWNS	12	45	L	Morrall 158 pass yards-4 INTs/Tracy rush TD
10/12/1958		vs	PHILADELPHIA	24	3	W	Tracy 88 rush yards-2 rush TDs
10/19/1958		@	Cleveland Browns	10	27	L	Tracy TD pass to Matthews/Miner FG
10/26/1958		@	New York Giants	6	17	L	Steelers commit 4 turnovers/Miner 2 FGs
11/2/1958		vs	WASHINGTON REDSKINS	24	16	W	Layne 265 pass yards-2 TD pass
11/9/1958		@	Philadelphia	31	24	W	Layne 225 pass yards-4 TD pass/Tracy 3 TDs
11/16/1958		vs	NEW YORK GIANTS	31	10	W	**Glick fumble return TD**/Layne 2 rush TD
11/23/1958		@	Chicago Cardinals	27	20	W	Layne 352 pass yards-TD pass to Orr
11/30/1958		vs	CHICAGO	24	10	W	Tracy 156 rush yards-2 rush TD/Miner FG
12/7/1958		@	Washington Redskins	14	14	T	Layne 309 pass yards-2 TD pass-3 INTs
12/13/1958	SAT	vs	CHICAGO CARDINALS	38	21	W	Orr 6 catch-205 yds-3 TD catch/Layne 409 yds

Schedule courtesy of Steve's Football Bible LLC

1958 NFL Eastern Conference	W	L	T	PCT	CONF	PF	PA
New York Giants	9	3	0	.750	7–3	246	183
Cleveland Browns	9	3	0	.750	8–2	302	217
Pittsburgh Steelers	**7**	**4**	**1**	**.636**	**6–3–1**	**261**	**230**
Washington Redskins	4	7	1	.364	3–6–1	214	268
Chicago Cardinals	2	9	1	.182	2–7–1	261	356
Philadelphia Eagles	2	9	1	.182	2–7–1	235	306

1958 NFL Draft

Round	Choice	Player	Position	School
2	20	Larry Krutko	Back	West Virginia
3	32	Bill Krisher	Guard	Oklahoma
6	68	Dick Lasse	End	Syracuse
9	100	Mike Henry	Tackle	USC
10	116	Dick Campbell	Center	Marquette
11	127	Larry Aldrich	End	Idaho
12	140	Leroy Reed	Back	Mississippi
14	164	Doyle Jennings	Tackle	Oklahoma
15	175	Ed Sears	Back	Florida
16	188	John Perkins	Tackle	Southern Mississippi
17	199	Joe Lewis	Tackle	Compton J.C.
19	223	Gene Keady	Back	Kansas State
20	236	George Johnson	Tackle	Wake Forest
21	247	Everett Jones	Guard	Utah
22	260	Bill Thompson	End	Duke
23	271	Ken Trowbridge	Back	North Carolina State
24	284	Norm Roberts	End	East Texas State
25	295	Bill Groce	Back	North Texas State
26	308	Jon Evans	End	Oklahoma State
27	319	Flyd Dellinger	Back	Texas Tech
28	332	Dean Akin	End	Jacksonville State
29	343	Mert Fuquay	End	Baylor
30	355	Dick Scherer	End	Pittsburgh

1959 Pittsburgh Steelers

The 1959 Pittsburgh Steelers, coached by Buddy Parker, missed the playoffs after finishing the NFL regular season in 4th place in the Eastern Conference with a 6-5-1 record. Jack Butler {S}, Dean Derby {DB} and Ernie Stautner {DE} were selected to various first team All-Pro teams.

Bobby Lane led the team in passing with 1,986 yards and threw 20 touchdown passes. Tom Tracy led the team in rushing with 794 yards. Jimmy Orr led the team in receiving with 35 receptions for 604 yards and 5 TD receptions.

PITTSBURGH			1959			6-5-1	Game Highlights
9/26/1959	SAT	vs	CLEVELAND BROWNS	17	7	W	Layne 209 pass yards-2 TD pass
10/4/1959		vs	WASHINGTON REDSKINS	17	23	L	Layne 226 pass yards-TD pass to Brewster
10/11/1959		@	Philadelphia	24	28	L	Layne 2 TD pass-rush TD-FG
10/18/1959		@	Washington Redskins	27	6	W	**Tarasovic fumble return TD**/Krutko 2 rush TD
10/25/1959		@	New York Giants	16	21	L	Dial 4 catch-146 yards-TC catch/Layne 3 FGs
11/1/1959		@	Chicago Cardinals	24	45	L	Dawson TD pass to Barnett/Barnett rush TD
11/8/1959		vs	DETROIT	10	10	T	Layne 181 pass yards-TD pass to Tracy
11/15/1959		@	New York Giants	14	9	W	Layne 190 pass yards-2 TD pass
11/22/1959		@	Cleveland Browns	21	20	W	Tracy 99 rush yards-2 rush TD
11/29/1959		vs	PHILADELPHIA	31	0	W	Layne 182 pass yards-4 TD pass
12/6/1959		@	Chicago	21	27	L	Tracy 109 rush yards-rush TD/Krutko rush TD
12/13/1959		vs	CHICAGO CARDINALS	35	20	W	Layne 201 pass yards-4 TD pass/Dial 2 TDs

Schedule courtesy of Steve's Football Bible LLC

1959 NFL Eastern Conference	W	L	T	PCT	CONF	PF	PA
New York Giants	10	2	0	.833	8–2	284	170
Philadelphia Eagles	7	5	0	.583	6–4	268	278
Cleveland Browns	7	5	0	.583	6–4	270	214
Pittsburgh Steelers	**6**	**5**	**1**	**.545**	**6–4**	**257**	**216**
Washington Redskins	3	9	0	.250	2–8	185	350
Chicago Cardinals	2	10	0	.167	2–8	234	324

1959 NFL Draft

Round	Choice	Player	Position	School
8	91	Tom Barnett	Back	Purdue
9	103	Hal Davis	Guard	Houston
10	115	Riley Gunnels	Tackle	Georgia
11	127	Overton Curtis	Back	Utah State
12	139	Bill Pavliska	Back	Baylor
13	151	Dewey Bohling	Back	Hardin-Simmons
14	163	John Peppercorn	End	Kansas
15	175	J.W. (Red) Brodnax	Back	LSU
16	187	Bill Carrico	Guard	North Texas State
17	199	Bill Leeka	Tackle	UCLA
18	211	John Seinturier	Tackle	USC
19	223	Dave Kocourek	WR	Wisconsin
20	235	Rudy Hayes	Back	Clemson
21	247	Johnny Green	QB	Tennessee-Chattanooga
22	259	Burley Polk	Tackle	Hardin-Simmons
23	271	Emye Davis	Back	McMurry
24	283	Wayne Farmer	Tackle	Purdue
25	295	Ron Miller	End	Vanderbilt
26	307	John Scott	Tackle	Ohio State
27	319	Charley Tolar	Back	Northwestern State (LA)
28	331	Ronnie Hall	Back	Missouri Valley
29	343	Dick Loncar	Tackle	Notre Dame
30	355	Willus Fjerstad	Back	Minnesota

1960 Pittsburgh Steelers

The 1960 Pittsburgh Steelers, coached by Buddy Parker, missed the playoffs after finishing the NFL regular season in 5th place in the Eastern Conference with a 5-6-1 record. Among the Steelers' preseason games in 1960 was an exhibition match with the Toronto Argonauts of the Canadian Football League; the Steelers won handily, 43–16.

Bobby Lane led the team in passing with 1,814 yards and threw 13 touchdown passes. Tom Tracy led the team in rushing with 680 yards and 5 rushing touchdowns. Buddy Dial led the team in receiving with 40 receptions for 972 yards and 9 TD receptions.

PITTSBURGH			1960			5-6-1	Game Highlights
9/24/1960	SAT	@	Dallas	35	28	W	Carpenter 5 catch-116 yards-2 TD catch
10/2/1960		@	Cleveland Browns	20	28	L	Layne 296 pass yards-2 TD pass/Dial TD catch
10/9/1969		vs	NEW YORK GIANTS	17	19	L	Layne 147 pass yards-2 TD pass/Dial TD catch
10/16/1960		vs	ST. LOUIS CARDINALS	27	14	W	Dial 4 catch-94 yards-TD catch/Rechichar FGs
10/23/1960		@	Washington	27	27	T	**Lewis fumble recovery TD**/Bukich 265 pass yds
10/30/1960		vs	GREEN BAY	13	19	L	Layne 209 pass yards-2 TD pass
11/6/1960		@	Philadelphia	7	34	L	Tracy TD pass to Dial/Steelers 212 total yards
11/13/1960		@	New York Giants	24	27	L	Dial 4 catch-121 yards-TD catch
11/20/1960		vs	CLEVELAND BROWNS	14	10	W	Tracy & Johnson rush TDs
11/27/1960		vs	WASHINGTON	22	10	W	Tracy 3 FGs-rush TD/Layne 2 FGs
12/11/1960		vs	PHILADELPHIA	27	21	W	Johnson 2 rush TD-TD pass to Dial
12/18/1960		@	St. Louis Cardinals	7	38	L	Layne 173 pass yards-TD pass to Orr

Schedule courtesy of Steve's Football Bible LLC

1960 NFL Eastern Conference	W	L	T	PCT	CONF	PF	PA
Philadelphia Eagles	10	2	0	.833	8–2	321	246
Cleveland Browns	8	3	1	.727	6–3–1	362	217
New York Giants	6	4	2	.600	5–4–1	271	261
St. Louis Cardinals	6	5	1	.545	4–5–1	288	230
Pittsburgh Steelers	**5**	**6**	**1**	**.455**	**4–5–1**	**240**	**275**
Washington Redskins	1	9	2	.100	0–8–2	178	309

1960 NFL Draft

Round	Choice	Player	Position	School
1	6	Jack Spikes	FB	TCU
5	55	Abner Haynes	HB	North Texas
7	76	Leonard Wilson	Back	Purdue
7	78	Lonnie Dennis	Guard	BYU
8	90	Dan Lanphear	DE	Wisconsin
9	102	Marshall Harris	Guard	TCU
10	114	John Kapele	DE	BYU
10	115	Arvie Martin	Center	TCU
12	138	Earl Butler	Tackle	North Carolina
13	150	Joe Womack	HB	Los Angeles State
14	162	Brady Keys	DB	Colorado State
15	174	Larry Essenmacker	Tackle	Alma
16	186	Dave Ames	HB	Richmond
17	198	Dale Chamberlain	FB	Miami-OH
18	210	Charley Lee	Tackle	Iowa
19	222	Howard Turley	End	Louisville
20	234	George Hershberger	Tackle	Wichita State

1961 Pittsburgh Steelers

The 1961 Pittsburgh Steelers, coached by Buddy Parker, missed the playoffs after finishing the NFL regular season in 5th place in the Eastern Conference with a 6-8 record. Johnny Sample {CB} and Gene "Big Daddy" Lipscomb {DT} were selected to various first team All-Pro teams.

Rudy Bukich led the team in passing with 1,253 yards/ Bukich and Bobby Layne each threw 11 touchdown passes. John Henry Johnson led the team in rushing with 787 yards and 6 rushing touchdowns. Buddy Dial led the team in receiving with 53 receptions for 1,047 yards and 12 TD receptions.

PITTSBURGH		1961			6-8	Game Highlights
9/17/1961	@	Dallas	24	27	L	**Sample INT return TD**/Layne TD pass to Dial
9/24/1961	vs	NEW YORK GIANTS	14	17	L	Johnson rush TD/Layne TD pass to Dial
10/1/1961	@	Los Angeles Rams	14	24	L	Johnson rush TD/Bukich TD pass to Dial
10/8/1961	@	Philadelphia	16	21	L	Bukich rush TD/Bukich TD pass to Dial
10/15/1961	vs	WASHINGTON REDSKINS	20	0	W	Bukich 2 pass TDs/Michaels 2 FGs
10/22/1961	vs	CLEVELAND BROWNS	28	30	L	Bukich 275 pass yards/2 TD pass to Dial/Dial 235 yds
10/29/1961	vs	SAN FRANCISCO	20	10	W	Johnson 103 rush yards-rush TD/Michaels 2 FGs
11/5/1961	@	Cleveland Browns	17	13	W	Bukich rush TD-TD pass to Schnelker/Michaels FG
11/12/1961	vs	DALLAS	37	7	W	**Butler INT return TD**/Dial 148 yards reception-2 TDs
11/19/1961	@	New York Giants	21	42	L	Dial 7 catch-117 yards-2 TD catch
11/26/1961	vs	ST. LOUIS CARDINALS	30	27	W	**Sample punt return TD**/Michaels 3 FGs/Johnson TD
12/3/1961	vs	PHILADELPHIA	24	35	L	Layne 179 pass yards-3 TD pass/Johnson rush TD
12/10/1961	@	Washington Redskins	30	14	W	Layne 226 pass yards-2 TD pass to Mack
12/17/1961	@	St. Louis Cardinals	0	36	L	Steelers commit 6 turnovers/Layne 139 pass yds-2 INT

Schedule courtesy of Steve's Football Bible LLC

1961 NFL Eastern Conference	W	L	T	PCT	CONF	PF	PA
New York Giants	10	3	1	.769	9–2–1	368	220
Philadelphia Eagles	10	4	0	.714	8–4	361	297
Cleveland Browns	8	5	1	.615	8–3–1	319	270
St. Louis Cardinals	7	7	0	.500	7–5	279	267
Pittsburgh Steelers	**6**	**8**	**0**	**.429**	**5–7**	**295**	**287**
Dallas Cowboys	4	9	1	.308	2–9–1	236	380
Washington Redskins	1	12	1	.077	1–10–1	174	392

1961 NFL Draft

Round	Choice	Player	Position	School
2	19	Myron Pottios	LB	Notre Dame
5	59	Fred Mautino	End	Syracuse
7	90	Dick Hoak	Back	Penn State
8	103	George Balthazar	Tackle	Tennessee State
10	131	Bill (Red) Mack	Back	Notre Dame
11	146	Henry Clement	Back	North Carolina
12	159	Frank Jackunas	Tackle	Detroit
14	187	Bob Schmitz	Guard	Montana State
15	202	Ray McCown	Back	West Texas State
16	215	Wilbert Scott	Back	Indiana
17	230	Terry Nofsinger	QB	Utah
18	243	John Simko	End	Augustana (ND)
19	258	Bernard Wyatt	Back	Iowa
20	271	Mike Jones	QB	San Jose State

1962 Pittsburgh Steelers

The 1962 Pittsburgh Steelers, coached by Buddy Parker, missed the playoffs after finishing the NFL regular season in 2nd place in the Eastern Conference with a 9-5 record. They played the Detroit Lions in the NFL Playoff Bowl, where they lost 17-10.

Bobby Lane led the team in passing with 1,686 yards and threw 9 touchdown passes. John Henry Johnson led the team in rushing with 1,141 yards and 7 rushing touchdowns. Buddy Dial led the team in receiving with 50 receptions for 981 yards and 6 TD receptions. **Lou Michaels kicked 26 field goals in 1962, setting a new NFL record.**

PITTSBURGH			1962			9-6	Game Highlights
9/16/1962		@	Detroit	7	45	L	Steelers held to 173 yards/Carpenter TD catch
9/23/1962		@	Dallas	30	28	W	Layne 144 pass yards-2 TD pass/Womack 2 TDs
9/30/1962		vs	NEW YORK GIANTS	27	31	L	Johnson 113 rush yards-rush TD/Michaels 2 FGs
10/6/1962	SAT	vs	PHILADELPHIA	13	7	W	**Schmitz INT return TD**/Michaels 2 FGs
10/14/1962		@	New York Giants	20	17	W	Johnson 123 rush yards-TD catch from Layne
10/21/1962		vs	DALLAS	27	42	L	Layne 266 pass yards-2 TD pass to Dial
10/28/1962		vs	CLEVELAND BROWNS	14	41	L	Johnson 94 rush yards/Hoak rush TD
11/4/1962		vs	MINNESOTA	39	31	W	Johnson 91 rush yards-2 rush TD/Michaels 3 FG
11/11/1962		@	St. Louis Cardinals	26	17	W	Johnson 138 rush yards-rush TD/Michaels 2 FG
11/18/1962		vs	WASHINGTON	23	21	W	Brown 179 pass yards/Michaels 3 FGs
11/25/1962		@	Cleveland Browns	14	35	L	Johnson & Womack rush TDs
12/2/1962		vs	ST. LOUIS CARDINALS	19	7	W	**Daniel INT return TD**/Michaels 4 FGs
12/9/1962		@	Philadelphia	26	17	W	Michaels 4 FGs/Carpenter & Johnson TD each
12/16/1962		@	Washington	27	24	W	Layne 201 pass yards-2 TD pass/Michaels 2 FGs
1/6/1963		vs	**Detroit**	**10**	**17**	L	Hoak 64 rush yards-rush TD/Michaels FG

Schedule courtesy of Steve's Football Bible LLC

1962 NFL Eastern Conference	W	L	T	PCT	CONF	PF	PA
New York Giants	12	2	0	.857	10–2	398	283
Pittsburgh Steelers	**9**	**5**	**0**	**.643**	**8–4**	**312**	**363**
Cleveland Browns	7	6	1	.538	6–5–1	291	257
Washington Redskins	5	7	2	.417	4–6–2	305	376
Dallas Cowboys	5	8	1	.385	4–7–1	398	402
St. Louis Cardinals	4	9	1	.308	4–7–1	287	361
Philadelphia Eagles	3	10	1	.231	3–8–1	282	356

1962 NFL Draft

Round	Choice	Player	Position	School
1	5	Bob Ferguson	Back	Ohio State
7	89	Jack Collins	RB	Texas
8	104	Gary Ballman	Back	Michigan State
9	117	John Powers	End	Notre Dame
10	132	Larry Vignali	Guard	Pittsburgh
11	145	Bob Wills	End	California
12	160	Sam Mudie	Back	Rutgers
13	173	Dave Woodward	Tackle	Auburn
14	188	Jim Whitaker	End	Nevada-Reno
15	201	Vern Hatch	End	North Carolina Central
16	216	Bobby Ply	Back	Baylor
17	229	Nat Tucker	Back	Florida A&M
18	244	Ferrell Yarbrough	Tackle	Northwestern State (LA)
19	257	John Kuprok	End	Pittsburgh
20	272	John Knight	Back	Valparaiso

1963 NFL Playoff Bowl

The Lions won the Playoff Bowl again in January of 1963, using their stifling defense to get past the Steelers for a 17-10 victory. A crowd of almost 35,000 was on hand, which was just enough to convince the NFL to keep the game in Miami. Quarterback Milt Plum and running back Kenny Webb led the Detroit offensive attack.

1963 Pittsburgh Steelers

    The Steelers won seven games, and lost four, with three games ending in a tie. As a result, the Steelers finished in fourth place in the NFL Eastern Conference. It was also their final season of splitting home games between Forbes Field and Pitt Stadium before moving all their home games to the latter for the next six seasons. Because tie games were not included in the NFL standings at the time, the Steelers had a chance to play in their first ever NFL Championship Game if they defeated the New York Giants in the season finale, but they fell 33-17. It was their last winning season until 1972. For the first time in 1963, the Steelers wore their trademark black helmets with their logo on one side of the helmet. They had used the logo previously on yellow helmets, but 1963 was the first season in which their now-signature look was used full-time in the regular season. Myron Pottios {LB} was selected to various first team All-Pro teams.

    Ed Brown led the team in passing with 2,982 yards and threw 21 touchdown passes. John Henry Johnson led the team in rushing with 773 yards. Dick Hoak led with 6 rushing touchdowns. Buddy Dial led the team in receiving with 60 receptions for 1,295 yards and 9 TD receptions.

PITTSBURGH			1963			7-4-3		Game Highlights
9/15/1963		@	Philadelphia	21	21	T		Johnson TD catch-rush TD/Michaels 3 FGs
9/22/1963		vs	NEW YORK GIANTS	31	0	W		Johnson 123 rush yards-rush TD/Hoak 2 TDs
9/29/1963		vs	ST. LOUIS CARDINALS	23	10	W		Hoak 85 rush yards-rush TD/Michaels 3 FG
10/5/1963	SAT	@	Cleveland Browns	23	35	L		Brown 289 pass yds-2 pass TD/Michaels 3 FG
10/13/1963		@	St. Louis Cardinals	23	24	L		Mack 3 catch-124 yds-TD catch/Michaels 3 FG
10/20/1963		vs	WASHINGTON	38	27	W		**Haley INT return TD**/Dial 155 yards-TD catch
10/27/1963		vs	DALLAS	27	21	W		Brown 377 pass yards-3 pass TD to Dial
11/3/1963		@	Green Bay	14	33	L		Brown 147 pass yards-TD pass to Mack
11/10/1963		vs	CLEVELAND BROWNS	9	7	W		Brown 215 pass yards-TD pass to Ballman
11/17/1963		@	Washington	34	28	W		**Ballman kickoff return TD**-161 yds-TD catch
11/24/1963		vs	CHICAGO	17	17	T		Brown 134 pass yards-TD pass to Curry
12/1/1963		vs	PHILADELPHIA	20	20	T		Ballman 7 catch-128 yards-2 TD catch
12/8/1963		@	Dallas	24	19	W		Brown 219 pass yards-2 TD pass/Sapp rush TD
12/15/1963		@	New York Giants	17	33	L		Ballman 6 catch-104 yards-TD catch

Schedule courtesy of Steve's Football Bible LLC

1963 NFL Eastern Conference	W	L	T	PCT	CONF	PF	PA
New York Giants	11	3	0	.786	9–3	448	280
Cleveland Browns	10	4	0	.714	9–3	343	262
St. Louis Cardinals	9	5	0	.643	8–4	341	283
Pittsburgh Steelers	**7**	**4**	**3**	**.636**	**7–3–2**	**321**	**295**
Dallas Cowboys	4	10	0	.286	3–9	305	378
Washington Redskins	3	11	0	.214	2–10	279	398
Philadelphia Eagles	2	10	2	.167	2–8–2	242	381

1963 NFL Draft

Round	Choice	Player	Position	School
8	108	Frank Atkinson	Tackle	Stanford
9	123	Gene Carrington	Tackle	Boston College
10	136	Bill Nelsen	QB	USC
11	151	Hewritt Dixon	Back	Florida A&M
12	164	Ry Curry	Back	Jackson State
13	179	Harold Gray	LB	Cal State-Los Angeles
14	192	Robert Dickerson	End	Bethune-Cookman
15	207	Matt Szykowny	Back	Iowa
16	220	Andy Russell	LB	Missouri
17	235	Tim Stein	Center	Miami (OH)
18	248	Jim Bradshaw	Back	Tennessee-Chattanooga
19	263	Roger Berg	Tackle	St. Thomas (MN)
20	276	Jim Traficant	Back	Pittsburgh

1963 Pittsburgh at New York Giants

The Steelers found themselves in the de facto NFL Final Four and in control of their own destiny. Their final regular-season game was against the Giants with the winner going on to play the Bears in the NFL title game. Pittsburgh was 7-3-3 and New York was 10-3, but a win by the Steelers would give them a higher percentage in the Eastern Division. Early in the game the Steelers Gary Ballman was going into the end zone when he decided to switch hands with the ball on the one-yard line avoiding a tackle. The ball squirted loose and was recovered by the Giants and returned to the 34-yard line. While the Giants were scoring 16 points in the first half, Pittsburgh continued to be frustrated in the Giants' red zone. Twice they fell one yard short at the New York 14-yard line. John Henry Johnson was en route to a 100-yard rushing game, but the football gods just wouldn't let them score. Steelers quarterback, Ed Brown, was terrible. He completed 13 passes and threw 20 incompletions for a shameful 39 percent. The Giants advanced to the NFL title game against the Bears where they lost 13-10.

1964 Pittsburgh Steelers

The team played all of their home games at Pitt Stadium, and won five games, while losing nine, resulting in a fifth-place finish in the NFL Eastern Conference. Following the season, the Steelers dismissed head coach Buddy Parker and replaced him with Mike Nixon.

Ed Brown led the team in passing with 1,990 yards and threw 12 touchdown passes. John Henry Johnson led the team in rushing with 1,048 yards and 7 rushing touchdowns. Gary Ballman led the team in receiving with 47 receptions for 935 yards and 7 TD receptions. **Brady Keys set a team record with a 90-yard punt return against the New York Giants on September 20th.**

PITTSBURGH			1964			5-9	Game Highlights
9/13/1964		vs	LOS ANGELES RAMS	14	26	L	Steelers commit 8 turnovers/Ballman TD catch
9/20/1964		vs	NEW YORK GIANTS	27	24	W	**Hinton INT return TD**/Brown 2 rush TD
9/27/1964		vs	DALLAS	23	17	W	Brown 176 pass yards-3 pass TD/Clark FG
10/4/1964		@	Philadelphia	7	21	L	**Bradshaw fumble return TD**/Brown 234 pass yds
10/10/1964	SAT	@	Cleveland Browns	23	7	W	Johnson 200 rush yards-3 rush TD
10/18/1964		@	Minnesota	10	30	L	Brown 162 pass yards-TD pass to Hoak
10/25/1964		vs	PHILADELPHIA	10	34	L	Peaks 101 rush yards-rush TD
11/1/1964		vs	CLEVELAND BROWNS	17	30	L	Johnson 100 rush yards-rush TD/Peaks rush TD
11/8/1964		@	St. Louis Cardinals	30	34	L	Ballman 6 catch-125 yards-2 TD receptions
11/15/1964		vs	WASHINGTON	0	30	L	Steelers commit 5 turnovers/Brown 131 pass yds
11/22/1964		@	New York Giants	44	17	W	Johnson 106 rush yards-2 rush TD/Brown 2 TD
11/29/1964		vs	ST. LOUIS CARDINALS	20	21	L	**Bradshaw fumble return TD**/Clark 2 FGs
12/6/1964		@	Washington	14	7	W	Johnson 93 rush yds-rush TD/Ballman TD catch
12/13/1964		@	Dallas	14	17	L	Hoak TD catch/Ballman TD catch

Schedule courtesy of Steve's Football Bible LLC

1964 NFL Eastern Conference	W	L	T	PCT	CONF	PF	PA
Cleveland Browns	10	3	1	.769	9–2–1	415	293
St. Louis Cardinals	9	3	2	.750	8–2–2	357	331
Philadelphia Eagles	6	8	0	.429	6–6	312	313
Washington Redskins	6	8	0	.429	5–7	307	305
Dallas Cowboys	5	8	1	.385	4–7–1	250	289
Pittsburgh Steelers	**5**	**9**	**0**	**.357**	**5–7**	**253**	**315**
New York Giants	2	10	2	.167	2–8–2	241	399

1964 NFL Draft

Round	Choice	Player	Position	School
1	10	Paul Martha	WR	Pittsburgh
2	28	Jim Kelly	WR	Notre Dame
3	38	Ralph Baker	LB	Penn State
4	51	Ben McGee	Tackle	Jackson State
5	66	T.W. Alley	Tackle	William & Mary
6	79	Tom Gibson	Guard	South Carolina
7	94	Bobby Smith	HB	North Texas State
8	107	Bobby Currington	HB	North Carolina Central
9	122	Bob Nichols	Tackle	Stanford
11	150	Bob Soleau	Guard	William & Mary
12	163	Bob Sherman	HB	Iowa
13	178	Glenn Baker	Tackle	Washington State
14	191	Tom Jenkins	Guard	Ohio State
15	206	Barry Brown	End	Florida
16	219	Ed Kesler	RB	North Carolina
17	234	Dennis Shaw	Center	Detroit
18	247	Oliver Dobbins	HB	Morgan State
19	262	Don Marshall	Tackle	Lehigh
20	275	Bryan Generalovich	End	Pittsburgh

1965 Pittsburgh Steelers

The 1965 Pittsburgh Steelers, coached by Mike Nixon, missed the playoffs after finishing the NFL regular season in 7th place in the Eastern Conference with a 2-12 record. It was the lowest win total for the Steelers since the 1945 season. It was the second of 8 straight losing seasons that wouldn't end until 1972.

Bill Nelsen led the team in passing with 1,917 yards and threw 8 touchdown passes. Dick Hoak led the team in rushing with 426 yards and 5 rushing touchdowns. Gary Ballman led the team in receiving with 40 receptions for 859 yards 5 TD receptions.

PITTSBURGH			1965		2-12		Game Highlights
9/19/1965		vs	GREEN BAY	9	41	L	Nelsen 122 pass yards-3 INT/Clark 3 FGs
9/26/1965		@	San Francisco	17	27	L	**Campbell fumble return TD**/Nelsen 174 pass yd
10/3/1965		vs	NEW YORK GIANTS	13	23	L	Nelsen 263 pass yards-2 INT/Clark 2 FGs
10/9/1965	SAT	@	Cleveland Browns	19	24	L	Hoak 107 rush yds-2 rush TD/Nelsen rush TD
10/17/1965		vs	ST. LOUIS CARDINALS	7	20	L	Ballman rush TD/Steelers commit 4 turnovers
10/24/1965		@	Philadelphia	20	14	W	**Daniel fumble return TD**/Bradshaw INT TD
10/31/1965		vs	DALLAS	22	13	W	Ballman 3 catch-120 yards-2 TD reception
11/7/1965		@	St. Louis Cardinals	17	21	L	Nelsen 216 pass yards-TD pass to Jefferson
11/14/1965		@	Dallas	17	24	L	**Folkins fumble return TD**/Jefferson 108 rec yds
11/21/1965		vs	WASHINGTON REDSKINS	3	31	L	Steelers held to 115 yards/commit 7 turnovers
11/28/1965		vs	CLEVELAND BROWNS	21	42	L	Nelsen 285 pass yards/3 TD pass
12/5/1965		@	New York Giants	10	35	L	Nelsen 164 pass yards/Steelers commit 6 TO's
12/12/1965		vs	PHILADELPHIA	13	47	L	**Woodson INT return TD**/Ballman TD catch
12/19/1965		@	Washington Redskins	14	35	L	Wade 148 pass yards-TD pass to Ballman

Schedule courtesy of Steve's Football Bible LLC

1965 NFL Eastern Conference	W	L	T	PCT	CONF	PF	PA
Cleveland Browns	11	3	0	.786	11–1	363	325
Dallas Cowboys	7	7	0	.500	6–6	325	280
New York Giants	7	7	0	.500	7–5	270	338
Washington Redskins	6	8	0	.429	6–6	257	301
Philadelphia Eagles	5	9	0	.357	5–7	363	359
St. Louis Cardinals	5	9	0	.357	5–7	296	309
Pittsburgh Steelers	**2**	**12**	**0**	**.143**	**2–10**	**202**	**397**

1965 NFL Draft

Round	Choice	Player	Position	School
2	18	Roy Jefferson	WR	Utah
7	87	Charley Browning	Back	Washington
8	102	Bill Howley	End	Pittsburgh
9	115	Tom Neville	Tackle	Mississippi State
10	130	Dave Tobey	Center	Oregon
11	143	Frank Molden	Tackle	Jackson State
12	158	Craig Lofquist	Back	Minnesota
13	171	J.R. Wilburn	Back	South Carolina
14	186	Jim (Cannonball) Butler	Back	Edward Waters
15	199	John Carrell	Tackle	Texas Tech
16	214	Doug Dusenbury	K	Kansas State
17	227	Whit Canale	RB	Tennessee
18	242	Bob Howard	Back	Stanford
19	255	Lonnie Price	Back	Southwestern Louisiana
20	270	Craig Fertig	QB	USC

1966 Pittsburgh Steelers

The 1966 Pittsburgh Steelers, coached by Bill Austin, missed the playoffs after finishing the NFL regular season in 6th place in the Eastern Conference with a 5-8-1 record. The Steelers played at Pitt Stadium and averaged over 35,000 fans per game.

Ron Smith led the team in passing with 1,249 yards and threw 8 touchdown passes. Willie Asbury led the team in rushing with 544 yards and 7 rushing touchdowns. John Hilton led the team in receptions with 46. Gary Ballman led the team with 663 yards receiving and 5 TD receptions.

PITTSBURGH			1966			5-8-1	Game Highlights
9/11/1966		vs	NEW YORK GIANTS	34	34	T	Nelsen 265 pass yards-3 TD pass/Clark 2 FGs
9/18/1966		vs	DETROIT	17	3	W	Smith 188 pass yards-2 pass TD
9/25/1966		vs	WASHINGTON	27	33	L	**Bradshaw INT return TD**/Ballman 2 TD catch
10/2/1966		@	Washington	10	24	L	Hoak rush TD/Clark FG/commit 4 turnovers
10/8/1966	SAT	@	Cleveland Browns	10	41	L	Izo 177 pass yards-TD pass to Jefferson
10/16/1966		vs	PHILADELPHIA	14	31	L	Asbury 96 total yards-rush TD-TD catch
10/30/1966		@	Dallas	21	52	L	**Woodson INT return TD/Butler kickoff TD**
11/6/1966		vs	CLEVELAND BROWNS	16	6	W	Ballman 7 catch-88 yards-TD catch/Clark 3 FG
11/13/1966		vs	ST. LOUIS CARDINALS	30	9	W	**Russell blocked punt return TD**/Clark 3 FGs
11/20/1966		vs	DALLAS	7	20	L	Smith 152 pass yards-TD pass to Asbury
11/27/1966		@	St. Louis Cardinals	3	6	L	Steelers held to 78 yards/Clark FG
12/4/1966		@	Philadelphia	23	27	L	Asbury 70 rush yards-2 rush TD/Clark 3 FGs
12/11/1966		@	New York Giants	47	28	W	Nelsen 322 pass yards-2 pass TDs/Clark FG
12/18/1966		@	Atlanta	57	33	W	**Thomas fumble return TD**/Nelsen 334 pass yds

Schedule courtesy of Steve's Football Bible LLC

1966 NFL Eastern Conference	W	L	T	PCT	CONF	PF	PA
Dallas Cowboys	10	3	1	.769	9–3–1	445	239
Philadelphia Eagles	9	5	0	.643	8–5	326	340
Cleveland Browns	9	5	0	.643	9–4	403	259
St. Louis Cardinals	8	5	1	.615	7–5–1	264	265
Washington Redskins	7	7	0	.500	7–6	351	355
Pittsburgh Steelers	**5**	**8**	**1**	**.385**	**4–8–1**	**316**	**347**
Atlanta Falcons	3	11	0	.214	2–5	204	437
New York Giants	1	12	1	.077	1–11–1	263	501

1966 NFL Draft

Round	Choice	Player	Position	School
1	3	Dick Leftridge	RB	West Virginia
2	19	Larry Gagner	Guard	Florida
3	35	Pat Killorin	Center	Syracuse
7	98	Emerson Boozer	RB	Maryland-Eastern Shore
9	128	Dale Stewart	DE	Pittsburgh
10	143	Jerry Marion	DB	Wyoming
11	158	Charley Washington	RB	Grambling
13	188	Benjy Dial	QB	Eastern New Mexico
14	203	Joe Novogratz	LB	Pittsburgh
15	218	Joe Dobson	Tackle	Idaho
16	233	Jim Long	WR	Purdue
17	248	Mike Brundage	QB	Oregon
18	263	Ken Lucas	QB	Pittsburgh
19	278	Dave Neilson	QB	Albion
20	293	Ron Springer	Tackle	Albion

1967 Pittsburgh Steelers

The 1967 Pittsburgh Steelers, coached by Bill Austin, missed the playoffs after finishing the NFL regular season in 4th place in the Eastern Conference Century Division with a 4-9-1 record. The Steelers played their home games at Pitt Stadium and averaged over 38,500 fans per game. The 1967 season saw the NFL switch to four divisions and the Steelers were placed in the Century Division of the Eastern Conference.

Kent Nix led the team in passing with 1,587 yards. Bill Nelsen led the team with 10 Touchdown passes. Don Shy led the team in rushing with 341 yards and 4 rushing touchdowns. J.R. Wilburn led the team in receiving with 51 receptions for 76 yards and 5 TD receptions.

PITTSBURGH			1967			4-9-1	Game Highlights
9/17/1967		vs	CHICAGO	41	13	W	Asbury 107 rush yards-2 rush TDs
9/24/1967		vs	ST. LOUIS CARDINALS	14	28	L	**Cards Bakken kicks NFL record 7 FGs**
10/1/1967		@	Philadelphia	24	34	L	Hoak & Asbury rush TDs/Wilburn TD catch
10/7/1967	SAT	@	Cleveland Browns	10	21	L	Nix 218 pass yards-TD pass to Hoak
10/15/1967		vs	NEW YORK GIANTS	24	27	L	Nix 220 pass yards-2 TD pass-rush TD
10/22/1967		vs	DALLAS	21	24	L	Nix 313 pass yards-2 TD pass-rush TD
10/29/1967		@	New Orleans	14	10	W	Wilburn TD catch/Shy rush TD-108 rush yds
11/5/1967		vs	CLEVELAND BROWNS	14	34	L	Nelsen 214 pass yards-2 TD pass
11/12/1967		@	St. Louis Cardinals	14	14	T	Nelsen 233 pass yards-TD pass to Jefferson
11/19/1967		@	New York Giants	20	28	L	Nelsen 240 pass yards-2 TD pass/Clark 2 FG
11/26/1967		vs	MINNESOTA	27	41	L	**Kortas fumble return TD**/Steelers 5 turnovers
12/3/1967		@	Detroit	24	14	W	Nix 205 pass yards-TD pass/Shy 2 rush TD
12/10/1967		vs	WASHINGTON REDSKINS	10	15	L	Nix 226 pass yards-TD pass to Jefferson
12/17/1967		@	Green Bay	24	17	W	**McGee INT return TD/Hinton fumble TD**

Schedule courtesy of Steve's Football Bible LLC

1967 NFL Century Division	W	L	T	PCT	DIV	CONF	PF	PA
Cleveland Browns	9	5	0	.643	5–1	7–3	334	297
New York Giants	7	7	0	.500	5–1	7–3	369	379
St. Louis Cardinals	6	7	1	.462	1–4–1	4–5–1	333	356
Pittsburgh Steelers	**4**	**9**	**1**	**.308**	**0–5–1**	**1–8–1**	**281**	**320**

1967 NFL Draft

Round	Choice	Player	Position	School
2	35	Don Shy	RB	San Diego State
3	73	Rockne Freitas	Center	Oregon State
4	89	Ray May	LB	USC
6	140	Mike Haggerty	Tackle	Miami (FL)
8	192	John Foruria	QB	Idaho
8	194	Mike Barnes	Tackle	Purdue
9	220	Paul Otis	DT	Houston
10	246	Bill Wilsey	LB	Fresno State
11	272	Jim Whitcomb	WR	Emporia State
13	324	Jim Homan	Guard	USC
14	350	Chet Anderson	TE	Minnesota
15	376	Mike Love	RB	Abilene Christian
16	402	Bill Smith	Center	Oregon
17	428	Mike Davenport	RB	Wyoming

1968 Pittsburgh Steelers

     1968 continued the team's descent in the NFL's basement, finishing with a third league-worst 2–11–1 record (Eagles and Falcons both 2-12) and the dismissal of head coach Bill Austin at the end of the season, leading to the eventual hiring of Chuck Noll. To this date, Austin is the last head coach to be fired by the Steelers. The season is notable in that the Steelers had their last tied game before the NFL adopted the overtime rule in regular-season games in 1974 in Week 9 against the St. Louis Cardinals in a 28–28 stalemate; that game was the deciding game in the NFL Century Division that season, as the Cardinals had swept the Cleveland Browns but finished the season 9–4–1, 1/2 game behind the 10–4 Browns. Since that game, the Steelers have only had two tied games, both happening after the overtime rule took effect. In addition, the Steelers lost to the Baltimore Colts at home, 41–7, in Week 3, as the Colts went on to play in Super Bowl III, in which they were upset by the AFL's New York Jets. After that loss, the Steelers would go another 40 years before losing to the Colts at home again, winning 12 straight (including three postseason meetings, among them the now-famous 1995 AFC Championship game as well as the 1975 Divisional Playoff Game that saw the introduction of the Terrible Towel) before losing to the now-Indianapolis Colts, 24–20, on November 10, 2008.

     Dick Shiner led the team in passing with 1,856 yards and threw 18 touchdown passes. Dick Hoak led the team in rushing with 858 yards and 3 rushing touchdowns. Roy Jefferson led the team in receiving with 58 receptions for 1,074 yards and 11 TD receptions.

PITTSBURGH			1968			2-11-1	Game Highlights
9/15/1968		vs	NEW YORK GIANTS	20	34	L	Nix 2 pass TD/Hoak rush TD
9/22/1968		@	Los Angeles Rams	10	45	L	Wilburn 5 catch-93 yards/Gros rush TD
9/29/1968		vs	BALTIMORE COLTS	7	41	L	Steelers fall behind 41-0/commit 4 turnovers
10/5/1968	SAT	@	Cleveland Browns	24	31	L	**Martha fumble return TD**/Jefferson 2 TD catch
10/13/1968		@	Washington Redskins	13	16	L	Shiner 131 pass yards/TD pass to Jefferson
10/20/1968		vs	NEW ORLEANS	12	16	L	Hoak 166 rush yards-rush TD/Gros rush TD
10/27/1968		vs	PHILADELPHIA	6	3	W	Hoak 79 rush yards/Lusteg 23 FGs
11/3/1968		@	Atlanta	41	21	W	Jefferson 11 catch-199 yards-4 TD catch
11/10/1968		@	St. Louis Cardinals	28	28	T	**Jefferson punt return TD**/Shiner 3 pass TDs
11/17/1968		vs	CLEVELAND BROWNS	24	45	L	**May punt return TD**/Wilburn 2 TD catch
11/24/1968		@	San Francisco	28	45	L	Jefferson & Kotite 2 TD receptions each
12/1/1968		vs	ST. LOUIS CARDINALS	10	20	L	Steelers held to 167 yards/Hoak rush TD
12/8/1968		@	Dallas	7	28	L	Shiner 152 pass yards-TD pass to Hilton
12/15/1968		@	New Orleans	14	24	L	Jefferson 6 catch-139 yards-TD reception

Schedule courtesy of Steve's Football Bible LLC

1968 NFL Century Division	W	L	T	PCT	DIV	CONF	PF	PA
Cleveland Browns	10	4	0	.714	4–2	7–3	394	273
St. Louis Cardinals	9	4	1	.692	5–0–1	8–1–1	325	289
New Orleans Saints	4	9	1	.308	2–4	3–7	246	327
Pittsburgh Steelers	**2**	**11**	**1**	**.154**	**0–5–1**	**1–8–1**	**244**	**397**

1968 NFL Draft

Round	Choice	Player	Position	School
1	10	Mike Taylor	Tackle	USC
2	36	Ernie Ruple	Tackle	Arkansas
3	61	John Henderson	DB	Colorado State
3	79	Ken Hebert	WR	Houston
7	174	Doug Dalton	RB	New Mexico State
7	189	Bill Glennon	DT	Washington
8	201	Danny Holman	QB	San Jose State
9	228	John Knight	DE	Weber State
11	282	Kim King	QB	Georgia Tech
12	309	Sam Wheeler	LB	Wisconsin
13	335	Joe Roundy	Guard	Puget Sound
14	363	Lou Harris	DE	Kent State
15	390	Bob Lanning	DE	Northern Montana
16	417	Rocky Bleier	RB	Notre Dame
17	444	Bob Cole	LB	South Carolina

1969 Pittsburgh Steelers

It would mark a turning point of the Steelers franchise. 1969 was the first season for Hall of Fame head coach Chuck Noll, the first season for defensive lineman "Mean Joe" Greene and L. C. Greenwood, the first season for longtime Steelers public relations director Joe Gordon, and the team's last season in Pitt Stadium before moving into then-state-of-the-art Three Rivers Stadium the following season. Although considered a turning point in the team's history, the results were not immediate; after winning the season opener against the Detroit Lions, the Steelers lost every game afterwards to finish 1–13. The Steelers became the first team in NFL history since the 1936 Philadelphia Eagles to win its season opener and lose every remaining game. This feat would later be matched by the 2001 Carolina Panthers and the 2020 Jacksonville Jaguars, both teams won their season openers but went on to lose their remaining games. The Steelers finished 1969 4th in the NFL Century Division and tied with the Chicago Bears for last in the NFL. With the Steelers finishing 1–6 at Pitt Stadium, it marked the last time the Steelers finished the season with a losing record at home until 1999. As a result of their 1–13 records, Art Rooney of the Steelers won a coin toss with George Halas of the Bears to determine who would select Louisiana Tech quarterback Terry Bradshaw (the consensus number 1 selection among league teams) with the number one pick in the 1970 draft. By modern NFL tiebreaking rules, the Steelers would have automatically been given the first pick anyway, as the Bears' one win came against the Steelers in Week 8. Roy Jefferson was selected to various first team All-Pro teams.

Dick Shiner led the team in passing with 1,422 yards and threw 7 touchdown passes. Dick Hoak led the team in rushing with 531 yards. Earl Gros led the team with 5 rushing touchdowns. Roy Jefferson led the team in receiving with 67 receptions for 1,079 yards and 9 TD receptions.

PITTSBURGH			1969			1-13	Game Highlights
9/21/1969		vs	DETROIT	16	13	W	Bankston rush TD/Mingo 3 FGs
9/28/1969		@	Philadelphia	27	41	L	Shiner 275 pass yards-2 TD pass/Mingo 2 FGs
10/5/1969		vs	ST. LOUIS CARDINALS	14	27	L	Jefferson 9 catch-115 yards-2 TD receptions
10/12/1969		@	New York Giants	7	10	L	Shiner 132 pass yards-rush TD
10/18/1969	SAT	@	Cleveland Browns	31	42	L	Jefferson 7 catch-110 yards-2 TD catch
10/26/1969		vs	WASHINGTON REDSKINS	7	14	L	Hanratty 156 pass yards-TD pass to Gros
11/2/1969		vs	GREEN BAY	34	38	L	Hanratty 3 TD pass/Jefferson 2 TD catch
11/9/1969		@	Chicago	7	38	L	Steelers held to 86 total yards/Gros rush TD
11/16/1969		vs	CLEVELAND BROWNS	3	24	L	Bankston 96 rush yards/Pitt commits 4 turnovers
11/23/1969		@	Minnesota	14	52	L	**McCall team record 101 yd kickoff return TD**
11/30/1969		@	St. Louis Cardinals	10	47	L	Steelers held to 187 yards/commit 4 turnovers
12/7/1969		vs	DALLAS	7	10	L	Shiner 145 pass yards-TD pass to Henderson
12/14/1969		vs	NEW YORK GIANTS	17	21	L	Jefferson 5 catch-112 yards-2 TD receptions
12/21/1969		@	New Orleans	24	27	L	Shiner 152 pass yards/Gros 3 rush TDs

Schedule courtesy of Steve's Football Bible LLC

1969 NFL Century Division	W	L	T	PCT	DIV	CONF	PF	PA
Cleveland Browns	10	3	1	.769	4–1–1	8–1–1	351	300
New York Giants	6	8	0	.429	4–2	4–6	264	298
St. Louis Cardinals	4	9	1	.308	3–2–1	3–6–1	314	389
Pittsburgh Steelers	**1**	**13**	**0**	**.071**	**0–6**	**0–10**	**218**	**404**

1969 NFL Draft

Round	Pick	Player	Position	College
1	3	Joe Greene	DT	North Texas
2	30	Terry Hanratty	QB	Notre Dame
2	42	Warren Bankston	RB	Tulane
3	56	Jon Kolb	C	Oklahoma State
4	82	Bob Campbell	RB	Penn State
7	160	Chuck Beatty	DB	North Texas
8	186	Joe Cooper	WR	Tennessee State
9	212	John Sodaski	DB	Villanova
10	238	L. C. Greenwood	DE	Arkansas AM&N
11	264	Clarence Washington	DT	Arkansas AM&N
12	290	Doug Fisher	LB	San Diego State
13	315	John Lynch	LB	Drake
14	342	Bob Hourman	RB	Ohio
15	368	Ken Liberto	WR	Louisiana Tech
16	394	Dock Mosley	WR	Alcorn A&M
17	420	Bill Eppright	PK	Kent State

1970 Pittsburgh Steelers

They improved from a league-worst 1–13 record the previous year, finishing with a 5–9 record and third place in the newly formed AFC Central. The Steelers began the decade in a new conference and a new stadium with a new quarterback. After nearly 40 years in the NFL, they shifted to the AFC, to complete the merger between the NFL and AFL. It was the NFL's weakest division that season, as the Steelers finished three games behind the division-winning Cincinnati Bengals—a team that was only in its third year of existence that season.

In the 1970 NFL Draft, only two Hall of Famers were selected in all 17 Rounds and 442 Picks. One being 1st Round, 1st Pick selection Terry Bradshaw, and the second being 3rd Round, 53rd Pick Mel Blount. Bradshaw and Blount, both part of the '70s Steeler Dynasty, were both inducted into the Hall of Fame in 1989.

Terry Bradshaw led the team in passing with 1,410 yards and threw 6 touchdown passes. Bradshaw also threw 24 interceptions. John Fuqua led the team in rushing with 691 yards and 7 rushing touchdowns. Dave Smith and Ron Shanklin led the team with 30 receptions. Shanklin led with 691 yards receiving and 4 TD receptions.

PITTSBURGH			1970			5-9	Game Highlights
9/20/1970		**vs**	HOUSTON OILERS	7	19	L	Steelers 214 total yds/Hanratty TD pass to Shanklin
9/27/1970		@	Denver	13	16	L	Shanklin 6 catch-123 yards/Mingo 2 FGs
10/3/1970	SAT	@	Cleveland Browns	7	15	L	Bradshaw 207 pass yards-3 INTs-rush TD
10/11/1970		**vs**	BUFFALO	23	10	W	Steelers 50 pass yards/Smith TD catch/Mingo 2 FG
10/18/1970		@	Houston Oilers	7	3	W	Bradshaw 208 pass yards-TD pass to Shanklin
10/25/1970		@	Oakland Raiders	14	31	L	Bradshaw 138 pass yds-4 INT-TD pass to Hughes
11/2/1970	MNF	**vs**	CINCINNATI	21	10	W	Hughes 2 catch-99 yards-2 TD catch
11/8/1970		**vs**	NEW YORK JETS	21	17	W	Fuqua 63 yards-rush TD-TD pass from Hanratty
11/15/1970		**vs**	KANSAS CITY	14	31	L	Bradshaw 3 INT-TD pass to Staggers
11/22/1970		@	Cincinnati	7	34	L	Fuqua 119 rush yards-rush TD/Bradshaw 3 INTs
11/29/1970		**vs**	CLEVELAND BROWNS	28	9	W	**Beatty INT return TD**/Shanklin 121 yards-2 TDs
12/6/1970		**vs**	GREEN BAY	12	20	L	Bradshaw3-20-110 yads-4 INT-TD pass to Smith
12/13/1970		@	Atlanta	16	27	L	Fuqua 63 rush yds-2 rush TD/Hanratty 3 INT
12/20/1970		@	Philadelphia	20	30	L	Fuqua 218 rush yards-2 rush TD/Watson 2 FGs

Schedule courtesy of Steve's Football Bible LLC

1970 AFC Central	W	L	T	PCT	DIV	CONF	PF	PA
Cincinnati Bengals	8	6	0	.571	3–3	7–4	312	255
Cleveland Browns	7	7	0	.500	4–2	7–4	286	265
Pittsburgh Steelers	**5**	**9**	**0**	**.357**	**3–3**	**5–6**	**210**	**272**
Houston Oilers	3	10	1	.231	2–4	3–7–1	217	352

1970 NFL Draft

Round	Pick	Player	Position	College
1	1	Terry Bradshaw	QB	Louisiana Tech
2	28	Ron Shanklin	WR	North Texas
3	53	Mel Blount	CB	Southern
4	80	Ed George	T	Wake Forest
5	105	Jon Staggers	DB	Missouri
6	132	Manuel Barrera	LB	Kansas State
6	155	Clarence Kegler	T	South Carolina State
7	157	Terry Brennan	T	Notre Dame
8	184	Dave Smith	WR	Indiana (Pa.)
9	209	Carl Crennel	LB	West Virginia
10	236	Isaiah Brown	DB	Stanford
11	261	Calvin Hunt	C	Baylor
12	288	Rick Sharp	DT	Washington (St. Louis)
13	313	Billy Main	RB	Oregon State
14	340	Bert Askson	LB	Texas Southern
15	365	Glen Keppy	DT	Wisconsin–Platteville
16	392	Frank Yanossy	DT	Tennessee
17	417	Harry Key	TE	Mississippi Valley State

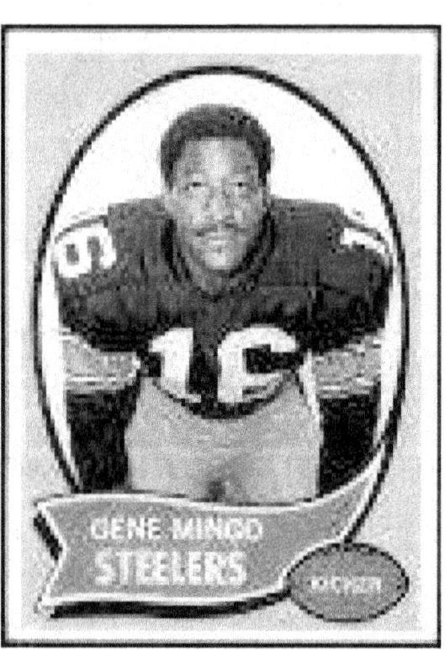

1971 Pittsburgh Steelers

The Steelers showed improvement, finishing in second Place with a 6-8 record. But Terry Bradshaw struggled with turnovers in his second season throwing 22 interceptions to 13 touchdown passes. The Steelers that year drafted wide receiver Frank Lewis, Hall of Fame linebacker Jack Ham, guard Gerry Mullins, defensive end Dwight White, tight end/tackle Larry Brown, defensive tackle Ernie Holmes, and safety Mike Wagner, all key contributors during the Steelers Super Bowl teams of the 1970s.

Bradshaw led the team in passing with 2,259 yards and threw 13 touchdown passes and 22 interceptions. John Fuqua led the team in rushing with 625 yards and 4 rushing touchdowns. Fuqua and Ron Shanklin both had 49 receptions. Shanklin had 6 TD receptions. Dave Smith led with 663 receiving yards.

PITTSBURGH			1971			6-8	Game Highlights
9/19/1971		@	Chicago	15	17	L	**Parson fumble recovery TD**/Gerela 3 FGs
9/26/1971		vs	CINCINNATI	21	10	W	**Staggers punt return TD**/Bradshaw 2 pass TD
10/3/1971		vs	SAN DIEGO CHARGERS	21	17	W	Fuqua 60 rush yds-2 rush TD/Bradshaw rush TD
10/10/1971		@	Cleveland Browns	17	27	L	Bradshaw 126 pass yards-2 TD pass/Gerela FG
10/18/1971	MNF	@	Kansas City	16	38	L	Bradshaw 269 pass yards/Gerela 3 FGS
10/24/1971		vs	HOUSTON OILERS	23	16	W	Fuqua 113 rush yards-rush TD/Gerela 3 FGs
10/31/1971		@	Baltimore Colts	21	34	L	Bradshaw 187 pass yards-2 rush TD-TD pass
11/7/1971		vs	CLEVELAND BROWNS	26	9	W	Fuqua 131 rush yards/Gerela 4 FGs/Smith TD
11/14/1971		@	Miami	21	24	L	Bradshaw 243 pass yards-3 TD pass/Smith 2 TDs
11/21/1971		vs	NEW YORK GIANTS	17	13	W	**Rowser INT return TD**/Shanklin TD catch
11/28/1971		vs	DENVER	10	22	L	Pearson 93 rush yards-TD catch from Hanratty
12/5/1971		@	Houston Oilers	3	29	L	Steelers held to 132 yards-3 turnovers/Gerela FG
12/12/1971		@	Cincinnati	21	13	W	Bradshaw 2 TD pass in 4th quarter
12/19/1971		vs	LOS ANGELES RAMS	14	23	L	Bradshaw 163 pass yards-2 TD pass-4 INTs

Schedule courtesy of Steve's Football Bible LLC

1971 AFC Central	W	L	T	PCT	DIV	CONF	PF	PA
Cleveland Browns	9	5	0	.643	5–1	7–4	285	273
Pittsburgh Steelers	**6**	**8**	**0**	**.429**	**4–2**	**5–6**	**246**	**292**
Houston Oilers	4	9	1	.308	2–4	4–7	251	330
Cincinnati Bengals	4	10	0	.286	1–5	3–8	284	265

1971 NFL Draft

Round	Pick	Player	Position	College
1	8	Frank Lewis	WR	Grambling
2	34	Jack Ham	LB	Penn State
3	60	Steven Davis	RB	Delaware State
4	86	Gerry Mullins	TE	USC
4	104	Dwight White	DE	East Texas State
5	106	Larry Brown	TE	Kansas
5	112	Melvin Holmes	OT	North Carolina A&T
5	126	Ralph Anderson	DB	West Texas State
5	128	Fred Brister	LB	Mississippi
6	138	Craig Hanneman	OT	Oregon State
7	164	Worthy McClure	OT	Mississippi
8	184	Larry Crowe	RB	Texas Southern
8	190	Paul Rogers	PK	Nebraska
8	203	Ernie Holmes	DT	Texas Southern
9	216	Mike Anderson	LB	LSU
10	242	Jim O'Shea	TE	Boston College
11	268	Mike Wagner	DB	Western Illinois
13	320	Alfred Young	WR	South Carolina State
14	346	McKinney Evans	DB	New Mexico Highlands
15	372	Ray Makin	OG	Kentucky
16	398	Walter Huntley	DB	Trinity
17	424	Danny Ehle	RB	Howard Payne

1972 Pittsburgh Steelers

It was the team's third-ever postseason appearance, its first postseason appearance in ten seasons (the Playoff Bowl for third place in the league), and only its second playoff game since 1947. This season is famous for the Immaculate Reception, where the Steelers beat the Oakland Raiders in the playoffs 13-7 on a last second touchdown by Franco Harris. The rebuilding of the franchise that began in 1969 with the hiring of Chuck Noll finally came to fruition in his fourth year. After winning only one game in his first year in 1969 the team that showed steady improvement broke through in 1972 and made the playoffs for the first time since 1947. Their 3 losses were by a combined 11 points. The division title was the first in team history, as was their appearance in the AFC Championship game which they lost to the undefeated Miami Dolphins 21-17. It was the first of 8 straight playoff appearances for the Steelers that led to 4 Super Bowl Championships. Joe Greene {DT} was selected to various first team All-Pro teams.

Terry Bradshaw led the team in passing with 1,887 yards and threw 12 touchdown passes. Franco Harris led the team in rushing with 1,055 yards and 10 rushing touchdowns. Ron Shanklin led the team in receptions with 38 for 669 yards. Frank Lewis led with 5 TD receptions.

PITTSBURGH			1972			12-4	Game Highlights
9/17/1972		vs	OAKLAND RAIDERS	34	28	W	Bradshaw 124 pass yards-TD pass-2 rush TD
9/24/1972		@	Cincinnati	10	15	L	Bradshaw 170 pass yards-rush TD/Gerela FG
10/1/1972		@	St. Louis Cardinals	25	19	W	Bradshaw 229 pass yards-TD pass to Lewis-rush TD
10/8/1972		@	Dallas	13	17	L	**Blount fumble return TD**/Gerela 2 FGs
10/15/1972		vs	HOUSTON OILERS	24	7	W	Harris 115 rush yards-rush TD/Bradshaw rush TD
10/22/1972		vs	NEW ENGLAND	33	3	W	Ham INT return TD/Gerela 4 FGs/Davis rush TD
10/29/1972		@	Buffalo	38	21	W	Harris 138 rush yards-2 rush TD-TD catch
11/5/1972		vs	CINCINNATI	40	17	W	Bradshaw 190 pass yards-3 TD pass/Gerela 2 FGs
11/12/1972		vs	KANSAS CITY	16	7	W	Harris 134 rush yards-rush TD/Gerela 3 FGs
11/19/1972		@	Cleveland Browns	24	26	L	Harris 136 rush yards-rush TD/Fuqua rush TD
11/26/1972		vs	MINNESOTA	23	10	W	Harris 128 rush yards-rush TD/Bradshaw rush TD
12/3/1972		vs	CLEVELAND BROWNS	30	0	W	McMakin 3 catch-113 yds-2 TD catch/Gerela 3 FG
12/10/1972		@	Houston Oilers	9	3	W	Steelers 193 total yards/Gerela 3 FGs
12/17/1972		@	San Diego Chargers	24	2	W	Bradshaw 152 pass yards-TD pass to Shanklin
12/23/1972	SAT	vs	**OAKLAND RAIDERS**	13	7	W	Harris TD catch with 5 seconds left/Gerela 2 FGs
12/31/1972		vs	**MIAMI**	17	21	L	**Mullins fumble recovery TD**/Bradshaw TD pass

Schedule courtesy of Steve's Football Bible LLC

1972 AFC Central	W	L	T	PCT	DIV	CONF	PF	PA
Pittsburgh Steelers	11	3	0	.786	4-2	9-2	343	175
Cleveland Browns	10	4	0	.714	5-1	9-2	268	249
Cincinnati Bengals	8	6	0	.571	3-3	6-5	299	229
Houston Oilers	1	13	0	.071	0-6	1-10	164	380

1972 NFL Draft

Round	Pick	Player	Position	College
1	13	Franco Harris	RB	Penn State
2	38	Gordon Gravelle	OT	BYU
3	63	John McMakin	TE	Clemson
4	80	Lorenzo Brinkley	DB	Missouri
4	88	Ed Bradley	LB	Wake Forest
5	113	Steve Furness	DE	Rhode Island
6	143	Dennis Meyer	DB	Arkansas State
7	159	Joe Colquitt	DE	Kansas State
7	168	Robert Kelly	DB	Jackson State
8	193	Stahle Vincent	RB	Rice
9	217	Don Kelley	DB	Clemson
10	243	Bob Brown	DT	Tampa
11	273	Joe Gilliam	QB	Tennessee State
12	298	Ron Curl	OT	Michigan State
13	323	Ernie Messmer	OT	Villanova
14	348	Tommy Durrance	RB	Florida
15	368	John Hulecki	OG	UMass
15	373	Charles Harrington	OG	Wichita State
16	403	Nate Hawkins	WR	UNLV
17	428	Ron Linehan	LB	Idaho

1972 AFC Divisional Playoffs {"The Immaculate Reception"}

Steelers fullback Franco Harris scored the winning touchdown on what became known as the Immaculate Reception. In a game that was mostly dominated by defense, the contest remained scoreless throughout the entire first half. On the opening drive of the second half, Pittsburgh drove 67 yards to take a 3–0 lead on Roy Gerela's 18-yard field goal. Following two Raiders drives that were shut down by Jack Ham's interception and a fumble recovery by Glen Edwards, Steelers defensive back Mike Wagner fell on a fumble by quarterback Ken Stabler (who had replaced injured starter Daryle Lamonica earlier in the game) at the Oakland 35. Five plays later, Gerela kicked a 29-yard field goal that gave Pittsburgh a 6–0 lead in the fourth quarter. Stabler responded by leading his team 80 yards to score on a 30-yard touchdown run with 1:13 left in the game.

Facing fourth and ten on their own 40-yard line with 22 seconds left, Steelers quarterback Terry Bradshaw threw the ball toward running back John "Frenchy" Fuqua. But the pass bounced off Raiders safety Jack Tatum and was caught by Harris, who then ran the rest of the way downfield to score a 60-yard touchdown that gave the Steelers a 12–7 lead with five seconds left in the game. The play was controversial, as Tatum insisted the ball had bounced off Fuqua, not himself, which would have made the reception illegal under the rules of the time. Replays showing the play are inconclusive as to which player touched the ball (or if both did)

Harris was the sole offensive star of the game, rushing for 64 yards and catching 4 passes for 96 yards and a touchdown. The Raiders managed just 216 yards and started 8 of their 12 drives inside their own 22-yard line, mainly due to excellent punting from Pittsburgh's Bobby Walden, who averaged over 48 yards per punt on his 6 kicks and set AFC playoff records with punts of 62 and 59 yards.

12/23/1972	Line	1	2	3	4	Final
Oakland Raiders		0	0	0	7	7
Pittsburgh Steelers	(-2.0)	0	0	3	10	13

Scoring

Team	
Steelers	Roy Gerela 18 yard field goal
Steelers	Roy Gerela 29 yard field goal
Raiders	Ken Stabler 30 yard rush (George Blanda kick)
Steelers	Franco Harris 60 yard pass from Terry Bradshaw (Roy Gerela kick)

1972 AFC Championship Game

The Dolphins continued their unbeaten streak as quarterback Bob Griese, who had not started a game since week 5, took over the starting spot and led the team to two touchdowns in the second half.

Things started well for Pittsburgh as safety Glen Edwards intercepted a pass from Earl Morrall on the opening drive and returned it 28 yards to the Dolphins 48. Steelers running back Franco Harris subsequently gained 35 yards on 7 carries as the team drove to a third and 2 on the Miami 3-yard line. On the next play, Pittsburgh quarterback Terry Bradshaw fumbled the ball as he tried to run into the end zone, but offensive lineman Gerry Mullins recovered it for a touchdown, giving the Steelers an early 7–0 lead. Unfortunately for the Steelers, Bradshaw was injured on the play and did not return until the fourth 
quarter. The Dolphins tied the game after punter Larry Seiple's 37-yard run on a fake punt set up Morrall's 9-yard touchdown pass to fullback Larry Csonka. The score would remain tied 7–7 at the end of the first half.

On the opening drive of the third quarter, Steelers quarterback Terry Hanratty completed passes to John McMakin and Ron Shanklin for gains of 22 and 24 yards, while John Fuqua added 24 yards on a draw play as the team drove to a 14-yard field goal by Roy Gerela, putting them up 10–7. At this point, Bob Griese, who had been sidelined with a broken leg for 10 weeks, replaced Morrall and threw a 52-yard completion to Paul Warfield on his first pass attempt. Miami also caught a break on the drive when an offsides penalty against Pittsburgh wiped out an interception by linebacker Jack Ham. Eventually, Jim Kiick finished the 11-play, 80-yard drive with a 2-yard touchdown run, giving the Dolphins their first lead at 14–10. Near the end of the third quarter, Seiple's 33-yard punt gave Pittsburgh a first down on the Miami 48. Harris ran for 7 yards on the first play, but this was followed by two incompletions and Gerela's 48-yard field goal attempt was blocked.

Taking over on the Steelers' 49 after the blocked field goal, the Dolphins drove 49 yards on an 11-play drive that only had one pass play. Kiick finished it off with a 3-yard touchdown run, giving Miami a 21-10 fourth quarter lead. However, Bradshaw returned to the game for the Steelers' next drive and quickly led them to a score. He started the drive with a 9-yard pass to tight end Larry Brown and followed it up with consecutive 25-yard completions to Al Young and Shanklin. On the fourth play of the possession, he threw a 12-yard touchdown pass to Young, cutting the score to 21–17. But on Pittsburgh's last two drives, he threw interceptions to Miami linebackers Nick Buoniconti and Mike Kolen, enabling the Dolphins to run out the rest of the clock.

12/31/1972		1	2	3	4	Final
Miami Dolphins	(-3.0)	0	7	7	7	21
Pittsburgh Steelers		7	0	3	7	17

Scoring

Team	
Steelers	Gerry Mullins offensive fumble recovery in end zone (Roy Gerela kick)
Dolphins	Larry Csonka 9 yard pass from Earl Morrall (Garo Yepremian kick)
Steelers	Roy Gerela 14 yard field goal
Dolphins	Jim Kiick 2 yard rush (Garo Yepremian kick)
Dolphins	Jim Kiick 3 yard rush (Garo Yepremian kick)
Steelers	Al Young 12 yard pass from Terry Bradshaw (Roy Gerela kick)

1973 Pittsburgh Steelers

The team finished second in the AFC Central division but qualified for the postseason for the second consecutive season. The Steelers got off to a terrific start winning eight of their first nine games. However, a costly three game losing streak would put their playoff hopes in jeopardy. The Steelers would recover to win their last two games but had to settle for a Wild Card berth with a 10–4 record. The Steelers would lose in the playoffs to the Oakland Raiders 33–14 in Oakland. Joe Greene {DT} and Mike Wagner {S} were selected to various first team All-Pro teams.

Terry Bradshaw led the team in passing with 1,183 yards and threw 10 touchdown passes. Franco Harris led the team in rushing with 698 yards and 3 rushing touchdowns. Ron Shanklin led the team with 30 receptions for 711 yards and 10 TD receptions. Wagner led the team with 8 interceptions.

PITTSBURGH			1973			10-5	Game Highlights
9/16/1973		vs	DETROIT	24	10	W	Bradshaw 154 pass yards-2 TD pass-rush TD
9/23/1973		vs	CLEVELAND	33	6	W	Lewis 3 catch-93 yards-2 TD catch/Gerela 4 FGs
9/30/1973		@	Houston Oilers	36	7	W	**Edwards & Russell INT return TDs**/Gerela 3 FG
10/7/1973		vs	SAN DIEGO CHARGERS	38	21	W	**Wagner fumble recovery TD**/Shanklin 2 TD catch
10/14/1973		@	Cincinnati	7	19	L	Steelers held to 138 total yards/Pearson rush TD
10/21/1973		vs	NEW YORK JETS	26	14	W	Harris 102 rush yards-rush TD/Gerela 4 FGs
10/28/1973		vs	CINCINNATI	20	13	W	Shanklin 3 catch-104 yds-TD catch/Gerela 2 FG
11/5/1973	MNF	vs	WASHINGTON	21	16	W	P. Pearson-B. Pearson-Shanklin TD catch each
11/11/1973		@	Oakland Raiders	17	9	W	Harris 77 rush yards-rush TD/Shanklin TD catch
11/18/1973		vs	DENVER	13	23	L	Hanratty 217 pass yards-TD pass to Shanklin
11/25/1973		@	Cleveland Browns	16	21	L	Gilliam 197 pass yards-TD pass to Shanklin
12/3/1973	MNF	@	Miami	26	30	L	Steelers QBs throw 6 INTs/Fall behind 27-0
12/9/1973		vs	HOUSTON OILERS	33	7	W	**Ham fumble recovery TD**/Gerela 4 FGs
12/15/1973	SAT	@	San Francisco	37	14	W	**Rowser INT return TD**/Gerela 3 FGs
12/22/1973	**SAT**	**@**	**Oakland Raiders**	**14**	**33**	**L**	Bradshaw 167 pass yards-2 TD pass-3 INTs

Schedule courtesy of Steve's Football Bible LLC

1973 AFC Central	W	L	T	PCT	DIV	CONF	PF	PA
Cincinnati Bengals	10	4	0	.714	4–2	8–3	286	231
Pittsburgh Steelers	**10**	**4**	**0**	**.714**	**4–2**	**7–4**	**347**	**210**
Cleveland Browns	7	5	2	.571	4–2	6–3–2	234	255
Houston Oilers	1	13	0	.071	0–6	1–10	199	447

1973 NFL Draft

Rd	Pick	Name	Pos	College
1	24	J.T. Thomas	DB	Florida State
2	50	Ken Phares	DB	Mississippi State
3	76	Roger Bernhardt	G	Kansas
4	102	Gail Clark	LB	Michigan State
5	106	Dave Reavis	T	Arkansas
5	128	Larry Clark	LB	Northern Illinois
6	140	Ron Bell	RB	Illinois State
6	154	Glenn Scolnik	WR	Indiana
7	180	Nate Dorsey	WR	Miss Valley State
8	192	Loren Toews	LB	California
8	206	Bill Janssen	T	Nebraska
9	232	Bracey Bonham	G	North Carolina Central
10	258	Don Wunderly	DT	Arkansas
11	284	Bob White	DB	Arizona
12	310	Willie Lee	RB	Indiana State
13	336	Rick Fergerson	WR	Kansas State
14	362	Roger Cowan	DE	Stanford
15	388	Charles Cross	DB	Iowa
16	414	Glen Nardi	DT	Navy
17	440	Mike Shannon	DT	Oregon State

1973 AFC Divisional Playoffs

The Raiders outgained Pittsburgh in total yards 361 to 223, forced three turnovers without losing any on their side, and scored 16 unanswered points in the second half to defeat the Steelers.

After forcing the Steelers to punt on the game's opening drive, Oakland drove 82 yards in 16 plays, including a 20-yard burst by running back Marv Hubbard, to go up 7-0 on Hubbard's 1-yard touchdown run. In the second quarter, Pittsburgh drove into Raiders territory, only to lose the ball when Terry Bradshaw's pass was deflected by Otis Sistrunk into the arms of linebacker Phil Villapiano for an interception. A 21-yard completion from Ken Stabler to receiver Mike Siani on the ensuing drive set up a 25-yard field goal by George Blanda, increasing the Raiders lead to 10-0 with 8 minutes left in the half. The Steelers were forced to punt on their next drive, but their defense subsequently forced the Raiders to go three-and-out. Then safety Glen Edwards returned Ray Guy's 40-yard punt 20 yards to the Oakland 45-yard line. On the next play, Bradshaw completed a 24-yard pass to running back Preston Pearson. Bradshaw eventually threw an incomplete pass on third down, but a 15-yard roughing the passer penalty gave the Steelers a first down on the Oakland 7. Following a 3-yard running play, Bradshaw finished the drive with a 4-yard touchdown toss to Pearson, cutting the score to 10-7 going into halftime.

Oakland dominated the second half with 16 consecutive points. After Clarence Davis returned the second half kickoff 30 yards to the Raiders 32, a 15-yard roughing the passer penalty against Pittsburgh and a 17-yard completion from Stabler to Hubbard led to Blanda's 31-yard field goal. The Steelers had to punt on their next drive, and George Atkinson returned the ball 13 yards to the Oakland 43, sparking a drive that ended with another Blanda field goal that gave the Raiders a 16-7 lead. Pittsburgh seemed primed to respond when Frank Lewis caught a 17-yard reception that put them in Raiders territory, but on the next play, Willie Brown intercepted a pass from Bradshaw and returned it 54 yards for a touchdown. With the Steelers now facing a 23-7 deficit, the situation continued to unravel as Bradshaw was intercepted again on the next drive, this time by Atkinson, who returned it 8 yards to the Raiders 37. Oakland running back Charlie Smith then took off on a 40-yard run to the Steelers 22, setting up Blanda's third field goal that gave them a 26-7 lead.

With 9:12 left in the fourth quarter, Pittsburgh got one last chance to get back in the game as Bradshaw's 26-yard touchdown pass to Lewis cut the score to 26-14. But after a punt from each team, Oakland put the game away, mainly due to Hubbard, who rushed for gains of 16, 15, 9, and 2 yards before finishing the drive with a 1-yard touchdown run, giving the Raiders a 33-14 lead with 14 seconds left on the clock. Stabler completed 14/17 passes for 142 yards. Hubbard rushed for 91 yards and two touchdowns, while also catching a 17-yard pass. Smith added 73 yards rushing and 10 yards receiving. Bradshaw was held to just 12/25 completions for 167 yards, with 2 touchdowns and 3 interceptions. Future Hall of Fame running back Franco Harris was held to 29 yards on 10 carries.

12/22/1973	Line	1	2	3	4	Final
Pittsburgh Steelers		0	7	0	7	14
Oakland Raiders	(-3.5)	7	3	13	10	33

Scoring

Team	
Raiders	Marv Hubbard 1 yard rush (George Blanda kick)
Raiders	George Blanda 25 yard field goal
Steelers	Barry Pearson 4 yard pass from Terry Bradshaw (Roy Gerela kick)
Raiders	George Blanda 31 yard field goal
Raiders	George Blanda 22 yard field goal
Raiders	Willie Brown 54 yard interception return (George Blanda kick)
Raiders	George Blanda 10 yard field goal
Steelers	Frank Lewis 26 yard pass from Terry Bradshaw (Roy Gerela kick)
Raiders	Marv Hubbard 1 yard rush (George Blanda kick)

1974 Pittsburgh Steelers {Super Bowl IX Champions}

The 1974 Pittsburgh Steelers season was the franchise's 42nd in the National Football League. They improved to a 10–3–1 regular-season record, won the AFC Central division title, sending them to the playoffs for the third consecutive season, and won a Super Bowl championship, the first league title in Steelers' history. This was the first of six consecutive AFC Central division titles for the Steelers, and the first of four Super Bowl championships in the same time. During the offseason, the Steelers held their training camp in St. Vincent College in Latrobe, Pennsylvania. During the 1974 NFL Draft, the Pittsburgh Steelers would draft WR Lynn Swann in Round 1, LB Jack Lambert in Round 2, WR John Stallworth in Round 4, and C Mike Webster in Round 5, and they also signed S Donnie Shell as an undrafted free agent. All five would later be inducted into the Pro Football Hall of Fame. As of 2014, the 1974 Steelers are the only team in NFL history to select four Hall of Fame players in one single draft. Joe Greene {DT}, Jack Ham {LB} and L.C. Greenwood {DE} were selected to various first team All-Pro teams.

After the first two regular-season games, the Steelers had scored a total of 65 points and were 1–0–1, but then lost to the Oakland Raiders at home. The play of the Steelers' starting quarterback at the time, Joe Gilliam, continually deteriorated. By Week 7, the Steelers were 4–1–1 and Gilliam was benched for Terry Bradshaw during a win against the Atlanta Falcons. Bradshaw won the next two games, but after a loss in Cincinnati, Noll benched Bradshaw again, this time in favor of Terry Hanratty. However, Hanratty played horribly in Cleveland. The offense was struggling, but the Steelers had won those tough games behind the still-maturing Steel Curtain defense. When Bradshaw was brought back into the starting lineup, the Steelers beat the Cleveland Browns and the New Orleans Saints. After a loss to Houston, the Steelers played the most important game of their regular season in New England. A win over the Patriots would clinch the AFC Central division title for the Steelers and put them in the playoffs for the third straight year. The Steelers defeated the Patriots, then beat the Cincinnati Bengals, and awaited the playoffs.

Joe Gilliam led the team in passing with 1,274 yards. Terry Bradshaw led the team with 7 touchdown passes. Franco Harris led the team in rushing with 1,006 yards and 5 rushing touchdowns. Frank Lewis led the team in receiving with 30 receptions for 365 yards and 4 TD receptions.

1974 AFC Central	W	L	T	PCT	DIV	CONF	PF	PA
Pittsburgh Steelers	10	3	1	.750	4–2	7–3–1	305	189
Houston Oilers	7	7	0	.500	4–2	7–4	236	282
Cincinnati Bengals	7	7	0	.500	3–3	5–6	283	259
Cleveland Browns	4	10	0	.286	1–5	3–8	251	344

PITTSBURGH			1974			13-3-1	Game Highlights
9/15/1974		vs	BALTIMORE COLTS	30	0	W	Gilliam 257 pass yards-2 TD pass/Gerela FG
9/22/1974		@	Denver (OT)	35	35	T	Gilliam 348 pass yards-TD pass to Davis
9/29/1974		vs	OAKLAND RAIDERS	0	17	L	Steelers held to 203 yards/commit 4 turnovers
10/6/1974		@	Houston Oilers	13	7	W	Pearson 117 rush yards-rush TD/Gerela 2 FGs
10/13/1974		@	Kansas City	34	24	W	**Edwards INT return TD**/Gilliam 214 pass yds
10/20/1974		vs	CLEVELAND BROWNS	20	16	W	Harris & Pearson rush TD each/Gerela 2 FGs
10/28/1974	MNF	vs	ATLANTA	24	17	W	Harris 141 rush yards-rush TD/Bleier rush TD
11/3/1974		vs	PHILADELPHIA	27	0	W	**Blount INT return TD**/Lewis TD catch
11/10/1974		@	Cincinnati	10	17	L	Pearson rush TD/Gerela FG
11/17/1974		@	Cleveland Browns	26	16	W	**Thomas fumble recovery TD**/Gerela 4 FGs
11/25/1974	MNF	@	New Orleans	28	7	W	**Swann punt return TD**/Bradshaw 2 TD pass
12/1/1974		vs	HOUSTON OILERS	10	13	L	Bradshaw TD pass to Harris/Gerela FG
12/8/1974		@	New England Patriots	21	17	W	Harris 136 rush yards-rush TD/Swann TD catch
12/14/1974	SAT	vs	CINCINNATI	27	3	W	Stallworth 6 catch-105 yards-TD catch
12/22/1974		vs	**BUFFALO**	**32**	**14**	**W**	Harris 74 rush yards-2 rush TD/Gerela 2 FGs
12/29/1974		@	**Oakland Raiders**	**24**	**13**	**W**	Harris 111 rush yards-2 rush TD/Bleier 98 yards
1/12/1975		vs	**Minnesota**	**16**	**6**	**W**	Harris 158 rush yards-rush TD/Brown TD catch

Schedule courtesy of Steve's Football Bible LLC

1974 NFL Draft

Round	Pick	Player	Position	College
1	21	Lynn Swann	WR	USC
2	46	Jack Lambert	LB	Kent State
4	82	John Stallworth	WR	Alabama A&M
4	100	Jimmy Allen	S	UCLA
5	125	Mike Webster	C	Wisconsin
6	149	Jim Wolf	DE	Prairie View A&M
6	150	Rick Druschel	Guard	North Carolina State
7	165	Allen Sitterle	T	North Carolina State
7	179	Scott Garske	TE	Eastern Washington
8	204	Mark Gefert	LB	Purdue
9	223	Tommy Reamon	RB	Missouri
9	229	Charlie Davis	DT	TCU
10	243	Jim Kregel	G	Ohio State
10	254	Dave Atkinson	DB	BYU
11	283	Dick Morton	RB	Arkansas
12	308	Hugh Lickiss	LB	Simpson
13	333	Frank Kolch	QB	Eastern Michigan
14	333	Bruce Henley	DB	Rice
15	387	Larry Hunt	DT	Iowa State
16	412	Octavus Morgan	LB	Illinois
17	437	Larry Moore	DE	Angelo State

1974 AFC Divisional Playoffs

Running back Franco Harris led the Steelers to the victory by scoring 3 touchdowns in the second quarter. Pittsburgh outgained the Bills in total yards, 438–264, and first downs, 29–14.

Pittsburgh scored on their first possession with Roy Gerela's 21-yard field goal, but later on, a poor punt from Bobby Walden gave the Bills a first down on their own 44, where they proceeded to drive 56 yards to a 7–3 lead on Joe Ferguson's 27-yard touchdown pass to tight end Paul Seymour.

The Steelers took over the game in the second quarter, scoring 26 unanswered points with an NFL playoff single quarter record 4 touchdowns. Early in the period, Pittsburgh quarterback Terry Bradshaw rushed for 8 yards on 3rd and 7 and later picked another 12 yards on a scramble before finishing the drive with a 27-yard scoring pass to running back Rocky Bleier, giving the team a 9–7 lead after Gerela's extra point was blocked. Following a Bills punt, the team increased their lead to 16–7 with a 66-yard drive that concluded with a 1-yard touchdown run by Harris. Then Buffalo running back Jim Braxton lost a fumble on a combined tackle by Mel Blount and Mike Wagner, which linebacker Jack Ham recovered for Pittsburgh on their 42.

Bradshaw subsequently completed a 19-yard pass to Bleier and 35-yard pass to Lynn Swann as the team drove to a 22–7 lead (due to another blocked extra point) on Harris' 4-yard score. With 16 seconds left before halftime, Harris scored his 3rd rushing touchdown to cap a 56-yard drive, upping his team's lead to 29–7.

Buffalo cut the score to 29–14 in the third quarter with Ferguson's 3-yard touchdown pass to running back O. J. Simpson, but Gerela's 22-yard field goal in the final period would be the only other score of the game. In the only playoff game of his 11-season Hall of Fame career, Simpson was held to 49 rushing yards, 3 receptions for 37 yards, and a touchdown. Ferguson threw for 164 yards, 2 touchdowns, and no interceptions, but completed just 11 of 26 passes. Bradshaw completed 12 of 19 passes for 201 yards and a touchdown, while also rushing for 48 yards on five carries.

12/22/1974	Line	1	2	3	4	Final
Buffalo Bills		7	0	7	0	14
Pittsburgh Steelers	(-6.5)	3	26	0	3	32

Scoring

Team	
Steelers	Roy Gerela 21 yard field goal
Bills	Paul Seymour 22 yard pass from Joe Ferguson (John Leypoldt kick)
Steelers	Rocky Bleier 27 yard pass from Terry Bradshaw
Steelers	Franco Harris 1 yard rush (Roy Gerela kick)
Steelers	Franco Harris 4 yard rush
Steelers	Franco Harris 1 yard rush (Roy Gerela kick)
Bills	O.J. Simpson 3 yard pass from Joe Ferguson (John Leypoldt kick)
Steelers	Roy Gerela 22 yard field goal

1974 AFC Championship Game

After trailing 10–3 at the end of the third quarter, the Steelers scored three touchdowns in the final period to earn their first championship appearance in team history.

The first half was controlled by both defenses. Oakland got a big opportunity in the first quarter when they recovered a muffed punt by Lynn Swann on the Steelers 41-yard line, but Mel Blount's deflection of a 3rd down pass by Ken Stabler forced them to settle for a 40-yard field goal from George Blanda. Meanwhile, the Steelers got close to the Oakland end zone twice, but each time they had to settle for Roy Gerela field goal attempts. He missed his first one from 20 yards in the first quarter but kicked a 23-yard field goal in the second to tie the game at 3 going into halftime.

Steelers linebacker Jack Lambert blocked a Blanda field goal in the second quarter, however in the second half, the Raiders eventually took a 10–3 lead with Ken Stabler's 38-yard touchdown pass to Cliff Branch. But Pittsburgh tied the game again six seconds into the fourth quarter with Franco Harris' 8-yard touchdown run at the end of a 61-yard drive. Then linebacker Jack Ham intercepted a pass from Stabler (his second interception of the day) and returned it to the Raiders' 9-yard line, setting up Bradshaw's 6-yard touchdown pass to Swann. Oakland responded with a drive to the Steelers 7-yard line, featuring a 45-yard reception by Fred Biletnikoff, but on 3rd down, a blitz by defensive back Mike Wagner forced Stabler to throw the ball away, and the team to setting for a 24-yard Blanda field goal, and the Steelers still led, 17–13.

Oakland got the ball back for a chance to drive for a go-ahead touchdown, but J. T. Thomas made a clutch interception and returned the ball 37 yards to the Raiders 24. Harris then scored on a 21-yard rushing touchdown to put the game away. Harris rushed for 111 yards and 2 scores, while Rocky Bleier added 98 rushing yards and 2 receptions for 25. Branch finished the game with 9 receptions for 186 yards and a touchdown.

12/29/1974	Line	1	2	3	4	Final
Pittsburgh Steelers		0	3	0	21	24
Oakland Raiders	(-5.5)	3	0	7	3	13

Scoring

Team	
Raiders	George Blanda 40 yard field goal
Steelers	Roy Gerela 23 yard field goal
Raiders	Cliff Branch 38 yard pass from Ken Stabler (George Blanda kick)
Steelers	Franco Harris 8 yard rush (Roy Gerela kick)
Steelers	Lynn Swann 6 yard pass from Terry Bradshaw (Roy Gerela kick)
Raiders	George Blanda 24 yard field goal
Steelers	Franco Harris 21 yard rush (Roy Gerela kick)

Super Bowl IX

Super Bowl IX was played between the American Football Conference (AFC) champion Pittsburgh Steelers and the National Football Conference (NFC) champion Minnesota Vikings. The game was played on January 12, 1975, at Tulane Stadium in New Orleans, Louisiana. Led by quarterback Terry Bradshaw and the Steel Curtain defense, the Steelers advanced to their first Super Bowl after posting a 10–3–1 regular season record and playoff victories over the Buffalo Bills and the Oakland Raiders. The Vikings were led by quarterback Fran Tarkenton and the Purple People Eaters defense; they advanced to their second consecutive Super Bowl and third overall after finishing the regular season with a 10−4 record and defeating the St. Louis Cardinals and the Los Angeles Rams in the playoffs.

In total, the Steelers limited the Vikings to Super Bowl record lows of nine first downs, 119 total offensive yards, 17 rushing yards, and no offensive scores (Minnesota's only score came on a blocked punt, and they did not even score on the extra point attempt). The Steelers accomplished this despite losing starting linebackers Andy Russell and Jack Lambert, who were injured and replaced by Ed Bradley and Loren Toews for most of the second half. On the other hand, Pittsburgh had 333 yards of total offense. Harris, who ran for a Super Bowl record 158 yards (more than the entire Minnesota offense) and a touchdown, was named the Super Bowl's Most Valuable Player.

Game Summary

The first quarter of Super Bowl IX was completely dominated by both teams' defenses. Pittsburgh managed to get close enough for their kicker Roy Gerela to attempt two field goals, but Gerela missed both attempts. In the second quarter, the Vikings got an opportunity to score when defensive back Randy Poltl recovered a fumble from halfback Rocky Bleier at the Steelers' 24-yard line, but they could only move the ball two yards in their next three plays, and kicker Fred Cox missed a 39-yard field goal attempt. The Steelers then converted a third down with the longest gain so far in the game, a 22-yard pass from Terry Bradshaw to John Stallworth. Pittsburgh was forced to punt, but Bobby Walden booted a 39-yarder, and rookie Sam McCullum did not allow the ball to reach the end zone, then failed to make a return and was downed at the Viking 7-yard line. The first score of the game occurred two plays later, when halfback Dave Osborn fumbled a pitch from Tarkenton at the 10, and the ball rolled backward and across the goal line. Tarkenton quickly dove on the ball in the end zone to prevent a Steeler touchdown, but he was downed by Dwight White for a safety, giving Pittsburgh a 2−0 lead. It was the first safety scored in Super Bowl history.

The Vikings forced a three-and-out, then threatened to score when Tarkenton led them on a 55-yard drive to the Steelers' 20-yard line. With 1:17 left in the half, Tarkenton threw a pass to receiver John Gilliam at the 5-yard line, but Steelers safety Glen Edwards hit him just as he caught the ball. The ball popped out of his hands and right into the arms of Mel Blount for an interception. The half ended with the Steelers leading 2−0, the lowest halftime score in Super Bowl history and lowest possible, barring a scoreless tie.

On the opening kickoff of the second half, Minnesota's Bill Brown lost a fumble on an unintentional squib kick after Gerela slipped on the wet field and only extended his leg halfway for the kick. Marv Kellum recovered the ball for Pittsburgh at the Vikings' 30-yard line. Franco Harris then moved the ball to the 6-yard line with a 24-yard run. After being tackled for a three-yard loss, Harris carried the ball for nine yards and a touchdown, giving the Steelers a 9−0 lead. After an exchange of punts, Minnesota got the ball back on their own 20-yard line. On the second play of drive, Tarkenton's pass was deflected behind the line of scrimmage by Pittsburgh defensive lineman L. C. Greenwood, and bounced back right into the arms of Tarkenton, who then threw a 41-yard completion to Gilliam. Officials ruled Tarkenton's first pass attempt was a completion to himself, and thus his second attempt was an illegal forward pass. After the penalty, facing third and 11, Minnesota got the first down with running back Chuck Foreman's 12-yard run. Three plays later, Tarkenton completed a 28-yard pass to tight end Stu Voigt at the Steelers' 45-yard line. But White deflected Tarkenton's next pass attempt, and Joe Greene intercepted the ball, ending the Vikings' best offensive scoring opportunity.

Early in the fourth quarter, the Vikings got another scoring opportunity when Minnesota safety Paul Krause recovered a fumble from Harris on the Steelers' 47-yard line. On the next play, a deep pass attempt from Tarkenton to Gilliam drew a 42-yard pass interference penalty on Pittsburgh defensive back Mike Wagner that moved the ball up to the 5-yard line. Once again, the Steelers stopped them from scoring when Greene forced and recovered a fumble from Foreman. Pittsburgh failed to get a first down on their next possession and was forced to punt from deep in their own territory. Minnesota linebacker Matt Blair burst through the line to block the punt, and Terry Brown recovered the ball in the end zone for a touchdown. Cox missed the extra point, but the Vikings had cut their deficit to 9–6 and were just a field goal away from a tie.

However, on the ensuing drive, the Steelers put the game out of reach with a 66-yard, 11-play scoring drive that took 6:47 off the clock and featured three successful third down conversions. The first was a key 30-yard pass completion from Bradshaw to tight end Larry Brown. Brown fumbled the ball as he was being tackled, and two officials initially ruled the ball recovered for the Vikings by Jeff Siemon, but head linesman Ed Marion overruled their call, stating that Brown was downed at the contact before the ball came out of his hands. Faced with 2nd and 15 after a penalty, Pittsburgh then fooled the Vikings defense with a misdirection play. Harris ran left past Bradshaw after the snap, drawing in the defense with him, while Bleier took a handoff and ran right through a gaping hole in the line for a 17-yard gain to the Vikings 16-yard line. A few plays later, Bradshaw converted a 3rd and 5 situation with 6-yard pass to Bleier that put the ball on the Vikings' 5-yard line. The Steelers gained just one yard with their next two plays, setting up third and goal from the four. Bradshaw's 4-yard touchdown pass to Brown on third down gave the Steelers a 16–6 lead with only 3:31 remaining. Vikings running back Brent McClanahan returned the ensuing kickoff 22 yards to the 39-yard line, but on the first play of the drive, Tarkenton's pass was intercepted by Wagner.

Harris finished the game with 34 carries for a Super Bowl record 158 yards and a touchdown. Bleier had 65 rushing yards, and two receptions for 11 yards. Pittsburgh finished with a total of 57 rushing attempts. Bradshaw completed nine out of 14 passes for 96 yards and a touchdown. Tarkenton completed 11 of 26 passes for just 102 yards with 3 interceptions, for a passer rating of only 14.1. Foreman was the Vikings' top offensive contributor, finishing the game as the team's leading rusher and receiver with 18 rushing yards and 50 receiving yards. The loss was the Vikings' record-setting third in Super Bowl play.

1/12/1975	Line	1	2	3	4	Final
Pittsburgh Steelers	{-3.0}	0	2	7	7	16
Minnesota Vikings	{33.0}	0	0	0	6	6

Scoring

Team	
Steelers	Tarkenton tackled in End Zone by Dwight White for safety
Steelers	Franco Harris 9 yard run (Roy Gerela kick)
Vikings	Terry Brown recovered blocked punt in end zone (Kick no good)
Steelers	Larry Brown 4 yard pass from Terry Bradshaw (Roy Gerela kick)

1975 Pittsburgh Steelers {Super Bowl X Champions}

The Steelers were defending champions for the first time in their forty-year history and repeated as league champions. The team was led by a dominating defense and a quick offense, and won Super Bowl X over the Dallas Cowboys, 21–17. The 1975 Steelers had one of the greatest defensive teams of all time. The team posted their best defensive numbers since 1946, and scored more points than any other Steelers team, later surpassed by two points in 2010. The 1975 Steelers' +211-point differential stands as the best in franchise history. They won by at least 21 points six times, with their season superlative 37–0 shutout at San Diego in the opener on September 21. Mel Blount {CB}, Jack Ham {LB}, L.C. Greenwood {DE}, Jack Lambert {MLB}, Andy Russell {LB} and Lynn Swann {WR} were selected to various first team All-Pro teams.

Terry Bradshaw led the team in passing with 2,005 yards and threw 18 touchdown passes. Franco Harris led the team in rushing with 1,246 yards and 10 rushing touchdowns. Lynn Swann led the team in receiving with 49 receptions for 781 yards and 11 TD receptions. **Mel Blount set a team record with 11 interceptions.**

PITTSBURGH			1975			15-2	Game Highlights
9/21/1975		@	San Diego Chargers	37	0	W	**Mullins fumble recovery TD**/Gerela 3 FGs
9/28/1975		vs	BUFFALO	21	30	L	Steelers fall behind 23-0/Harris 2 rush TDs
10/5/1975		@	Cleveland Browns	42	6	W	QBs pass for 367 yards-3 TD pass
10/12/1975		vs	DENVER	20	9	W	Bradshaw 191 pass yards-2 TD pass to Swann
10/19/1975		vs	CHICAGO	34	3	W	4 different Steelers score TDs/Gerela 2 FGs
10/26/1975		@	Green Bay	16	13	W	**Collier kickoff return TD**/Gerela 3 FGs
11/2/1975		@	Cincinnati	30	24	W	Swann 6 catch-116 yards-2 TD catch
11/9/1975		vs	HOUSTON OILERS	24	17	W	Bradshaw 219 pass yards-3 TD pass/Gerela FG
11/16/1975		vs	KANSAS CITY	28	3	W	Harris 119 rush yards/Bradshaw 2 TD pass
11/24/1975	MNF	@	Houston Oilers	32	9	W	Harris 149 rush yards-2 rush TD/Swann TD catch
11/30/1975		@	New York Jets	20	7	W	Bradshaw 120 pass yards-2 TD pass/Gerela 2 FGs
12/7/1975		vs	CLEVELAND BROWNS	31	17	W	Harris 103 rush yds-2 rush TD/Swann 2 TD catch
12/14/1975		vs	CINCINNATI	35	14	W	**Thomas fumble return TD**/Harris 118 yds-2 TDs
12/21/1975		@	Los Angeles Rams	3	10	L	Steelers commit 4 turnovers/Gerela FG
12/27/1975	SAT	vs	**BALTIMORE COLTS**	28	10	W	**Russell fumble recovery TD**/Harris 153 yds-TD
1/4/1976		vs	**OAKLAND RAIDERS**	16	10	W	Bradshaw 215 pass yards-TD pass to Stallworth
1/18/1976		vs	**Dallas**	21	17	W	Swann 4 catch-161 yards-TD catch/Gerela 2 FGs

Schedule courtesy of Steve's Football Bible LLC

1975 AFC Central	W	L	T	PCT	DIV	CONF	PF	PA
Pittsburgh Steelers	12	2	0	.857	6–0	10–1	373	162
Cincinnati Bengals	11	3	0	.786	3–3	8–3	340	246
Houston Oilers	10	4	0	.714	2–4	7–4	293	226
Cleveland Browns	3	11	0	.214	1–5	2–8	218	372

1975 NFL Draft

Round	Pick	Player	Position	College
1	26	Dave Brown *	CB	Michigan
2	51	Bob Barber	DE	Grambling
3	78	Walter White	TE	Maryland
4	104	Harold Evans	LB	Houston
5	130	Brent Sexton	DB	Elon
6	156	Marvin Crenshaw	T	Nebraska
7	180	Wayne Mattingly	T	Colorado
8	208	Al Humphrey	DE	Tulsa
9	234	Bruce Reimer	RB	North Dakota State
10	260	Archie Grey	WR	Wyoming
11	286	Randy Little	TE	West Liberty
12	312	Greg Murphy	DE	Penn State
13	337	Bob Gaddis	WR	Mississippi Valley State
14	364	Mike Collier	RB	Morgan State
15	390	Marty Smith	DT	Louisville
16	415	Miller Bassler	TE	Houston
17	442	Stan Hegener	G	Nebraska

1975 AFC Divisional Playoffs

Despite losing 5 turnovers, the Steelers forced 3 turnovers and held the Colts to 154 total yards of offense, while Pittsburgh's Franco Harris shredded Baltimore's defense with 153 rushing yards and a touchdown. The game is also notable in that it was the debut game for the Terrible Towel.

The Steelers scored first after linebacker Jack Ham's interception set up a 61-yard touchdown drive. Terry Bradshaw's 34-yard completion to receiver Frank Lewis paved the way for Harris' 8-yard scoring run. Baltimore responded in the second quarter when Lloyd Mumphord returned an interception 58 yards to set up Glenn Doughty's 5-yard touchdown catch from Marty Domres. Then Harris lost a fumble that was recovered by Colts defensive back Nelson Munsey on the Steelers 19, leading to Toni Linhart's 27-yard field goal that gave Baltimore a 10–7 lead going into halftime.

On the second half kickoff, Munsey recovered a fumble from Steelers returner Dave Brown. But a few plays later, Pittsburgh cornerback Mel Blount intercepted a pass and returned it 20 yards to the Baltimore 7-yard line. From there, Rocky Bleier scored on a 7-yard rushing touchdown giving the Steelers a 14–10 lead. In the fourth quarter, a short punt from David Lee gave the Steelers favorable field position, and they scored on Bradshaw's 2-yard run, increasing their lead to 21–10. Now with the game slipping away, Colts coach Ted Marchibroda benched Domres (who had completed only 2 of 11 passes) and replaced him with Bert Jones (who had earlier left the game due to injury), who promptly gave the team a golden opportunity to rally back with a 58-yard completion to Doughty on the Steelers 3-yard line. But on the next play, Ham knocked the ball out of Jones' hand as he was winding up for a pass. Linebacker Andy Russell recovered the fumble returned it for an NFL playoff record 93 yards to the end zone. Russell's play is claimed by some as the longest single football play in time duration. Sports Illustrated called the play the "longest, slowest touchdown ever witnessed."

12/27/1975	Line	1	2	3	4	Final
Baltimore Colts		0	7	3	0	10
Pittsburgh Steelers	(-10.5)	7	0	7	14	28

Scoring

Team	
Steelers	Franco Harris 8 yard rush (Roy Gerela kick)
Colts	Glenn Doughty 5 yard pass from Marty Domres (Toni Linhart kick)
Colts	Toni Linhart 21 yard field goal
Steelers	Rocky Bleier 7 yard rush (Roy Gerela kick)
Steelers	Terry Bradshaw 2 yard rush (Roy Gerela kick)
Steelers	Andy Russell 93 yard defensive fumble return (Roy Gerela kick)

1975 AFC Championship Game

A defensive struggle in which both teams combined for 12 turnovers (7 for Pittsburgh, 5 for Oakland) turned into an offensive battle as the Steelers managed to stop the Raiders' final drive for the winning score as time ran out. As the two dominant teams of the era in the AFC, Oakland and Pittsburgh would eventually face in five consecutive playoff games from 1972–1976. The Raiders and Steelers also played in three consecutive AFC Championship games from 1974–1976. Already bitter rivals dating back to the 1972 AFC Divisional Playoff game (see: the Immaculate Reception), Raiders' officials, including team owner Al Davis and head coach John Madden, accused the Steelers and Three Rivers Stadium groundskeepers of intentionally allowing the artificial playing surface to ice over, in an effort to slow Oakland's propensity for using a wide-open aerial attack as part of its offensive game plan.

The game started out ugly, as Pittsburgh quarterback Terry Bradshaw was picked off twice in the first quarter. However, Oakland fared no better, as George Blanda's missed 38-yard field goal attempt after Bradshaw's second interception was the closest they would get to scoring in the first half. In the second quarter, Steelers safety Mike Wagner intercepted a pass from Ken Stabler to set up Roy Gerela's 36-yard field goal. This would be the only score of the first three quarters. In the third quarter, the Raiders blew two big scoring chances. After recovering a fumbled punt by the Steelers, the Raiders got a first down on the Pittsburgh 16-yard line. Then quarterback Ken Stabler threw a short pass to Pete Banaszak, only to watch him fumble the ball as he turned upfield, and linebacker Jack Lambert recovered it. Then after Raiders defensive back Jack Tatum recovered a fumble from Lynn Swann at midfield, Oakland gave the ball back again when Lambert recovered a fumble from running back Clarence Davis on the Steelers 30-yard line. The turnover led to a 5-play, 70-yard drive that ended on running back Franco Harris' 25-yard touchdown run to give the Steelers a 10–0 lead. Oakland stormed back, scoring in less than two minutes on a drive that lasted just six plays, three of them receptions by tight end Dave Casper. Stabler finished the drive with a 14-yard touchdown pass to Mike Siani that cut the score to 10–7.

Midway through the fourth quarter, Lambert recorded his third fumble recovery, this one from running back Marv Hubbard on the Oakland 25, setting up Bradshaw's 20-yard touchdown pass to receiver John Stallworth. Bobby Walden fumbled the snap on the PAT, which kicker Roy Gerela recovered but failed to convert on a drop kick, keeping the score at 16–7. Later on, Bradshaw was knocked out of the game when he took a knee-hit to the head by linebacker Monte Johnson. A few plays later, Oakland recovered their fourth fumble of the day with 1:31 left in the game. The Raiders then drove to the Pittsburgh 24-yard line, where they faced third down and 2 yards to go with 18 seconds left on the clock. They opted to have George Blanda kick a 41-yard field goal (his longest of the season and last of his NFL career) to pull the deficit to 6 points. Then Hubbard recovered the ensuing onside kick with 9 seconds remaining to give Oakland one last attempt to win the game. Cliff Branch then caught a 37-yard reception, but he was stopped at the Pittsburgh 15-yard line by Mel Blount before he could get out of bounds and the clock ran out. Aside from his touchdown run, Harris ran for 54 yards on 26 carries, while also catching 5 passes for 58 yards.

Raiders defender George Atkinson knocked Swann into a severe concussion that would have him hospitalized for 2 days. Swann, however, would go on to win the Super Bowl MVP award with yardage records. Lambert set an AFC Championship Game record with three fumble recoveries in the game. This was Oakland's 6th AFC championship loss in the last 8 years.

1/4/1976	Line	1	2	3	4	Final
Oakland Raiders		0	0	0	10	10
Pittsburgh Steelers	(-6.5)	0	3	0	13	16

Scoring

Team	
Steelers	Roy Gerela 36 yard field goal
Steelers	Franco Harris 25 yard rush (Roy Gerela kick)
Raiders	Mike Siani 14 yard pass from Ken Stabler (George Blanda kick)
Steelers	John Stallworth 20 yard pass from Terry Bradshaw
Raiders	George Blanda 41 yard field goal

Super Bowl X

The game was played at the Orange Bowl in Miami, Florida, on January 18, 1976, one of the first major national events of the United States Bicentennial year. Both the pre-game and halftime show celebrated the Bicentennial, while players on both teams wore special patches on their jerseys with the Bicentennial logo. Super Bowl X featured a contrast of playing styles between the Steelers and the Cowboys, which were, at the time, the two most popular teams in the league. The Steelers, dominating teams with their "Steel Curtain" defense and running game, finished the regular season with a league best 12–2 record and defeated the Baltimore Colts and the Oakland Raiders in the playoffs. The Cowboys, with their offense and "flex" defense, became the first NFC wild-card team to advance to the Super Bowl after posting a 10–4 regular season record and postseason victories over the Minnesota Vikings and the Los Angeles Rams.

On the opening kickoff, the Cowboys ran a reverse where rookie linebacker Thomas "Hollywood" Henderson took a handoff from Preston Pearson and returned the ball a Super Bowl-record 48 yards before kicker Roy Gerela forced him out of bounds at the Steelers' 44-yard line. Gerela suffered badly bruised ribs that appeared to affect his kicking performance all afternoon. On the first play of the game, Steelers defensive lineman L. C. Greenwood sacked Cowboys quarterback Roger Staubach, forcing him to fumble. Although Dallas recovered the fumble, they eventually were forced to punt. The sack was a foreshadow of things to come for Staubach, who was sacked seven times on the day. The Steelers managed to get one first down and advanced to their own 40-yard line, but then they too were forced to punt. Steelers punter Bobby Walden fumbled the snap. Walden managed to recover his own fumble, but Dallas took over on the Steelers' 29-yard line. On the very next play, Staubach threw a 29-yard touchdown pass to wide receiver Drew Pearson, taking a 7–0 lead. The score was the first touchdown permitted in the first quarter by the Steelers' defense in 1975. Instead of trying to immediately tie the game on a long passing play, the Steelers ran the ball on the first four plays of their ensuing possession, and then quarterback Terry Bradshaw completed a 32-yard pass to wide receiver Lynn Swann to reach the Cowboys' 16-yard line. Swann soared over the outstretched reach of defensive back Mark Washington before tight roping the sideline to make the reception. Two running plays further advanced the ball to the 7-yard line. Then on third down and one, the Steelers managed to fool the Cowboys. Pittsburgh brought in two tight ends, which usually signals a running play. After the snap, tight end Randy Grossman faked a block to the inside as if it were a running play, but then ran a pass route into the end zone, and Bradshaw threw the ball to him for a touchdown, tying the game, 7–7. This marked the first Super Bowl that both teams scored in the first quarter.

Dallas responded on their next drive, advancing the ball 51 yards, all rushing, (30 of them on five carries from fullback Robert Newhouse) before incurring a third down false start penalty, and scoring on kicker Toni Fritsch's 36-yard field goal to take a 10–7 lead early in the second quarter. The 51 rushing yards the Cowboys amassed on the drive tripled what the Minnesota Vikings gained against Pittsburgh for all of Super Bowl IX. The Steelers subsequently advanced to the Cowboys' 36-yard line on their next possession, but on fourth down and two, Bradshaw's pass was broken up by Dallas safety Cliff Harris. Later in the period, Dallas drove to the Steelers' 20-yard line. But in three plays, the Cowboys lost 25 yards. On first down, Newhouse was tackled for a 3-yard loss by linebacker Andy Russell. Then Greenwood sacked Staubach for a 12-yard loss. And on third down, Staubach was sacked again, this time for a 10-yard loss, by defensive end Dwight White. The sacks pushed Dallas out of field goal range, and they were forced to punt. The Steelers' offense got the ball back their own 6-yard line with 3:47 left in the half. On the drive, Bradshaw completed a 53-yard pass to Swann to advance the ball to the Cowboys' 37-yard line; Swann's catch has become one of the most memorable acrobatic catches in Super Bowl history. On the very next play, Bradshaw just missed connections with Swann at the Dallas 6. Pittsburgh drove to the 19-yard line after the two-minute warning, but the drive stalled there and ended with no points after Gerela missed a 36-yard field goal attempt with 22 seconds remaining in the period.

Early in the third quarter, Pittsburgh got a great scoring opportunity when defensive back J. T. Thomas intercepted a pass from Staubach and returned it 35 yards to the Cowboys' 25-yard line. However, once again the Steelers failed to score as the Dallas defense kept Pittsburgh out of the end zone and Gerela missed his second field goal, a 33-yard attempt. After the miss, Harris mockingly patted Gerela on his helmet and thanked him for "helping Dallas out," but was immediately thrown to the ground by Steeler linebacker Jack Lambert. Lambert could have been ejected from the game for defending his teammate, but the officials decided to allow him to remain.

The third quarter was completely scoreless, and the Cowboys maintained their 10–7 lead going into the final period. However, early in the fourth quarter, Dallas punter Mitch Hoopes was forced to punt from inside his own goal line. As Hoopes stepped up to make the kick, Steelers running back Reggie Harrison broke through the line and blocked the punt. The ball went through the end zone for a safety, cutting the Dallas lead to 10–9. It was the second safety recorded in Super Bowl history, the first occurring a year earlier when White downed Minnesota's Fran Tarkenton on a fumble recovery in the end zone.

Then Steelers running back Mike Collier returned the free kick 25 yards to the Cowboys' 45-yard line. Dallas halted the ensuing drive at the 20-yard line, but this time Gerela successfully kicked a 36-yard field goal to give Pittsburgh their first lead of the game, 12–10. Then on the first play of the Cowboys' next drive, Steelers defensive back Mike Wagner intercepted a pass from Staubach and returned it 19 yards to the Dallas 7-yard line. Wagner's interception came off the same play Dallas used to score their opening touchdown. Instead of surveying the middle of the field, Wagner watched Pearson and recognized the pattern. Staubach later said: "It was our bread and butter play all season long. It was the first time it didn't work." The Cowboys defense again managed to prevent a touchdown, but Gerela kicked an 18-yard field goal to increase the Steelers lead to 15–10. The Steelers forced a punt and regained possession of the ball on their own 30-yard line with 4:25 left in the final period, giving them a chance to either increase their lead or run out the clock to win the game. But after two plays, the Steelers found themselves facing 3rd-and-4 on their own 36-yard line. Assuming that the Cowboys would be expecting a short pass or a run, Bradshaw decided to try a long pass and told Swann in the huddle to run a deep post pattern. As Bradshaw dropped back to pass, Harris and linebacker D.D. Lewis both blitzed in an attempt to sack him. But Bradshaw managed to dodge Lewis and throw the ball just before being leveled by Harris and lineman Larry Cole, who landed a helmet-to-helmet hit on Bradshaw. Swann then caught the ball at the 5-yard line and ran into the end zone for a 64-yard touchdown completion. Bradshaw never saw Swann's catch or the touchdown since Cole's hit to Bradshaw's helmet knocked him out of the game with a head injury. It was only after he was assisted to the locker room that he was told what happened.

After play resumed, Gerela missed the extra point attempt, but the Steelers now had a 21–10 lead with 3:02 left in the game, and the Cowboys needed two touchdowns to come back. Staubach then led his team 80 yards in 5 plays on the ensuing drive, scoring on a 34-yard touchdown pass to wide receiver Percy Howard and cutting their deficit to 21–17 (Howard's touchdown reception was the only catch of his NFL career; he was not mentioned by name by John Facenda in the highlight package produced by NFL Films). After Gerry Mullins recovered Dallas' onside kick attempt, the Steelers then tried to run out the clock on the next drive with four straight running plays, but the Cowboys defense stopped them on fourth down at their 39-yard line, giving Dallas one more chance to win. Some questioned why Noll would elect to go for it on fourth down but as later explained by NFL Films, his entire kicking game had been suspect all game long with Gerela missing an extra point and two field goals while Walden fumbled a snap on a punt, and nearly had two punts blocked. (Gerela's problems may have begun on the opening kickoff when he was forced to make a touchdown saving tackle on Hollywood Henderson.)

With 1:22 left in the game, Staubach started out the drive with an 11-yard scramble to midfield, and then followed it up with a 12-yard completion to Preston Pearson at the Steelers' 38-yard line. Pearson inexplicably ran towards the middle rather than running out of bounds to stop the clock. On the next play, Staubach couldn't handle a low snap but managed to recover the ball and throw it downfield for an incompletion. On second down with 12 seconds left, he threw a pass intended for Howard in the end zone, but the ball bounced off Howard's helmet and a Hail Mary replay was not to be. Had Howard positioned himself inches back from his position in the end zone as the ball came down, he would have had a better opportunity to catch the ball and write himself into Cowboy folklore. Then on third down, Staubach once again tried to complete a pass to Howard in the end zone, but the ball was tipped by Wagner into the arms of safety Glen Edwards for an interception as time expired, sealing Pittsburgh's victory. Bradshaw finished the game with 9 out of 19 pass completions for 209 yards and two touchdowns, with no interceptions. He also added another 16 yards rushing the ball. Staubach completed 15 out of 24 passes for 204 yards and two touchdowns with three interceptions. He also rushed for 22 yards on five carries but was sacked seven times. Steelers running back Franco Harris was the leading rusher of the game with 82 rushing yards and caught a pass for 26 yards. Newhouse was the Cowboys top rusher with 56 yards and caught two passes for 12 yards. Greenwood recorded a Super Bowl record of four sacks, but it has gone unrecognized since the NFL didn't officially record sacks until 1982.

1/4/1976	Line	1	2	3	4	Final
Dallas Cowboys	(36.0}	7	3	0	7	17
Pittsburgh Steelers	(-7.0)	7	0	0	14	21

Scoring

Team	
Cowboys	Drew Pearson 29 yard pass from Roger Staubach (Toni Fritsch kick)
Steelers	Randy Grossman 7 yard pass from Terry Bradshaw (Roy Gerela kick)
Cowboys	Toni Fritsch 36 yard field goal
Steelers	Safety, Harrison blocked Hoopes kick through end zone
Steelers	Roy Gerela 36 yard field goal
Steelers	Roy Gerela 18 yard field goal
Steelers	Lynn Swann 64 yard pass from Terry Bradshaw
Cowboys	Percy Howard 34 yard pass from Roger Staubach (Toni Fritsch kick)

1976 Pittsburgh Steelers

The Steelers started the season looking to become the first team in the Super Bowl era to win three-straight league championships (and first since the 1929–1931 and 1965–1967 Green Bay Packers). However, many thought that would be in doubt after the team started 1–4 and saw quarterback Terry Bradshaw injured in the week 5 loss to the Cleveland Browns after a vicious sack by Joe "Turkey" Jones that has since become immortalized in NFL Films as part of the Browns-Steelers rivalry. The 1976 Steelers' 9.9 points allowed per game in the regular season is the best in franchise history. Despite the setbacks, the Steelers would turn it around behind the strength of the Steel Curtain and its dual threat at running back in Franco Harris and Rocky Bleier, who each rushed for over 1,000 yards with the latter having the best season of his career, Pittsburgh finished 10–4 and posted five shutouts, the most in a single season in the Super Bowl era. Rookie quarterback Mike Kruczek wound up going 6–0 starting in place of Bradshaw, largely due to the strength of the ground game. Injuries to both Bleier and Harris in the AFC Divisional Playoff game against the Baltimore Colts sidelined them both for the following week's AFC Championship game against the Oakland Raiders. Without both of their 1,000-yard rushers, the Steelers lost to the Raiders by a score of 24-7. Jack Ham {LB}, Jack Lambert {MLB} and Me3l Blount {CB} were selected to various first team All-Pro teams.

Terry Bradshaw led the team in passing with 1,177 yards and threw 10 touchdown passes. Franco Harris led the team in rushing with 1,128 yards and **his 14 rushing touchdowns set a franchise record.** Lynn Swann led the team in receiving with 28 receptions for 516 yards and 3 TD receptions. Mel Blount and Glenn Edwards led the team with 6 interceptions.

PITTSBURGH			1976			11-5	Game Highlights
9/12/1976		@	Oakland Raiders	28	31	L	Steelers blow 14-point 4th quarter lead
9/19/1976		vs	CLEVELAND BROWNS	31	14	W	Harris 118 rush yards-rush TD/Stallworth 2 TDs
9/26/1976		vs	NEW ENGLAND	27	30	L	Bradshaw 291 pass yards-TD pass to Grossman
10/4/1976	MNF	@	Minnesota	6	17	L	Steelers commit 6 turnovers/Cunningham TD
10/10/1976		@	Cleveland Browns	16	18	L	Harris & Kruczek rush TDs/Gerela FG
10/17/1976		vs	CINCINNATI	23	6	W	Harris 143 rush yards-2 rush TD/Gerela 3 FGs
10/24/1976		@	New York Giants	27	0	W	Harris 106 rush yards-2 rush TD/Gerela 2 FGs
10/31/1976		vs	SAN DIEGO CHARGERS	23	0	W	Harrison 108 rush yards/Bradshaw & Fuqua TDs
11/7/1976		@	Kansas City	45	0	W	Harris 117 rush yards-2 rush TD/Bleier 102 yds
11/14/1976		vs	MIAMI	14	3	W	Harris & Bleier 110 rush yards each/Harris TD
11/21/1976		vs	HOUSTON OILERS	32	16	W	Harrison 2 rush TD/Gerela 3 FGs
11/28/1976		@	Cincinnati	7	3	W	Bleier 97 rush yds/Harris 87 rush yds-rush TD
12/5/1976		vs	TAMPA BAY	42	0	W	Bleier 118 rush yards-3 rush TDs/Swann 2 TDs
12/11/1976	SAT	@	Houston Oilers	21	0	W	Bleier 107 rush yds/Harris 104 rush yds-rush TD
12/19/1976		@	**Baltimore Colts**	**40**	**14**	**W**	Bradshaw 264 pass yds-3 Td pass/Harrison 2 TD
12/26/1976		@	**Oakland Raiders**	**7**	**24**	**L**	Steelers held to 72 rush yards/Harrison rush TD

Schedule courtesy of Steve's Football Bible LLC

1976 AFC Central	W	L	T	PCT	DIV	CONF	PF	PA	STK
Pittsburgh Steelers	**10**	**4**	**0**	**.714**	**5–1**	**9–3**	**342**	**138**	**W9**
Cincinnati Bengals	10	4	0	.714	4–2	8–4	335	210	W1
Cleveland Browns	9	5	0	.643	3–3	7–5	267	287	L1
Houston Oilers	5	9	0	.357	0–6	3–9	222	273	L2

1976 NFL Draft

Round	Choice	Player	Position	School
1	28	Bennie Cummingham	TE	Clemson
2	37	Ray Pinney	G	Washington
2	47	Mike Kruczek	QB	Boston College
2	56	James Files	C	McNeese State
3	70	Ron Coder	DT	Penn State
3	88	Ernest Pough	WR	Texas Southern
4	112	Wonder Monds	DB	Nebraska
4	120	Theo Bell	WR	Arizona
5	152	Rodney Norton	LB	Rice
6	159	Gary Dunn	DT	Miami (FL)
6	182	Jack Deloplaine	RB	Salem
7	209	Barry Burton	TE	Vanderbilt
8	237	Ed McAleney	DT	Massachusetts
9	265	Wentford Gaines	DB	Cincinnati
10	291	Gary Campbell	LB	Colorado
11	319	Rolland Fuchs	RB	Arkansas
12	347	Bill Carroll	WR	East Texas State
13	375	Larry Kain	TE	Ohio State
14	403	Wayne Field	DB	Florida
15	431	Mel Davis	DE	North Texas State
16	459	Randy Butts	RB	Kearney State
17	487	Kelvin Kirk	WR	Dayton

1976 AFC Divisional Playoffs

The Steelers, who lost four of their first five games during the season, dominated the Colts with 526 yards of total offense, while limiting Baltimore to only 170. Quarterback Terry Bradshaw completed 14 of 18 passes for 267 yards and three touchdowns, including a 76-yard one to Frank Lewis on the third play of the game, giving him the first perfect 158.3 passer rating in NFL playoff history. Steelers running back Franco Harris racked up 132 rushing yards on 18 carries, and caught 3 passes for 24 yards, despite leaving the game with an injury early in the third quarter.

Lewis' touchdown catch and a 45-yard Roy Gerela field goal gave the Steelers are early 9-0 lead. The Colts made it 9-7 late in the first period with Bert Jones' 17-yard touchdown pass to Roger Carr, but Theo Bell's 60-yard kickoff return set up a 32-yard drive to get the Steelers up 16-7 on Reggie Harrison's 1-yard touchdown run. Following a punt, they blew a scoring chance when Harrison lost a fumble at the Colts 2-yard line. But they soon made up for it with two scores in the final minute of the half. After getting the ball back, Bradshaw put the Steelers ahead 23-7 with a 29-yard touchdown pass to Lynn Swann. Then Glen Edwards intercepted a pass from Jones and returned it 26 yards to set up a 25-yard Gerela field goal that gave Pittsburgh a 26-7 halftime lead.

In the third quarter, The Colts had an odd drive in which they gained only 36 net yards in 13 plays. They faced an early 3rd and 6, but a sack on Jones was eliminated by a holding penalty that gave them a first down. Then Lydell Mitchell appeared to lose a fumble, but officials ruled him down by contact before he lost the ball. David Lee soon came on to punt, but a roughing the kicker penalty on Larry Brown allowed them to keep the ball again. The drive finally ended with a turnover on downs at the Steelers 32, and Pittsburgh went on to drive 68 yards in 11 plays, scoring on Bradshaw's 11-yard touchdown pass to Swann. Now with a 33-7 fourth quarter lead, all that remained would be a touchdown from each team, a 1-yard run by Roosevelt Leaks and a 9-yard score by Harrison.

Less than ten minutes after the conclusion of the game, a small charter plane crashed into the upper deck at Memorial Stadium. There were no deaths or injuries in the accident.

12/19/1976	Line	1	2	3	4	Final
Pittsburgh Steelers	{-3.5}	9	17	0	14	40
Baltimore Colts		7	0	0	7	14

Scoring

Team	
Steelers	Frank Lewis 76 yard pass from Terry Bradshaw
Steelers	Roy Gerela 45 yard field goal
Colts	Roger Carr 17 yard pass from Bert Jones (Toni Linhart kick)
Steelers	Reggie Harrison 1 yard rush (Roy Gerela kick)
Steelers	Lynn Swann 29 yard pass from Terry Bradshaw (Roy Gerela kick)
Steelers	Roy Gerela 25 yard field goal
Steelers	Lynn Swann 11 yard pass from Terry Bradshaw (Roy Gerela kick)
Colts	Roosevelt Leaks 1 yard rush (Toni Linhart kick)
Steelers	Reggie Harrison 10 yard rush (Ray Mansfield kick)

1976 AFC Championship Game

Pittsburgh had defeated the Raiders in the AFC championship game in each of the last two seasons. But with Steelers running backs Franco Harris and Rocky Bleier out of the game with injuries, this time the Raiders easily shut down Pittsburgh's offense. The Raiders would not host another AFC Title game in Oakland again until 2000 (although they hosted the title game in 1983 when they were the Los Angeles Raiders). Late in the first quarter, Bobby Walden's rushed punt went just 19 yards and gave Oakland the ball at the Steelers 38, setting up Errol Mann's 39-yard field goal. Then in the second quarter, Raiders linebacker Willie Hall intercepted a pass from Terry Bradshaw and returned it 25 yards to the

Steelers 1-yard line. Three plays later, Clarence Davis' 1-yard touchdown run gave them a 10-0 lead. Although the game would end up as a defensive struggle with both teams combining for 14 punts (7 each) and only 457 yards (237 for Pittsburgh, 220 for Oakland), Hall's interception would be the only turnover of the day for either team.

The Steelers responded with Bradshaw's completions to Lynn Swann for gains of 18 and 30 yards leading to Reggie Harrison's 3-yard rushing touchdown. Oakland responded with a methodical 14-play, 69-yard scoring drive. With 19 seconds left in the first half, the Raiders faced first down at the Pittsburgh 4-yard line following a 16-yard burst by Clarence Davis. Oakland lined up three tight ends as if they were to run the ball, but quarterback Ken Stabler threw a play action pass to Warren Bankston for a touchdown to give the Raiders a 17–7 lead at halftime. Oakland controlled the entire second half, including a 12-play, 63-yard drive that featured a 28-yard completion from Stabler to receiver Cliff Branch. Stabler finished the drive with a 5-yard touchdown pass to Pete Banaszak that put the game out of reach at 24-7.

12/26/1976	Line	1	2	3	4	Final
Pittsburgh Steelers	{-4.0}	0	7	0	0	7
Oakland Raiders		3	14	7	0	24

Scoring

Raiders	Errol Mann 39 yard field goal
Raiders	Clarence Davis 1 yard rush (Errol Mann kick)
Steelers	Reggie Harrison 3 yard rush (Ray Mansfield kick)
Raiders	Warren Bankston 4 yard pass from Ken Stabler (Errol Mann kick)
Raiders	Pete Banaszak 5 yard pass from Ken Stabler (Errol Mann kick)

1977 Pittsburgh Steelers

The 1977 Pittsburgh Steelers season was the franchise's 45th in the National Football League. After what was considered the franchise's greatest season ever in 1976, the 1977 Pittsburgh Steelers failed to improve on their 10-4 record from 1976 and finished with a 9-5 record, however they appeared in the playoffs for their 6th straight season and won the AFC Central again. They had a hard time for most of the season as their record hovered around .500. Even the Steel curtain seemed to have a little wear and tear allowing 243 points on the season, more than 100 more than the previous season. The sloppy plays would catch up with them in the Divisional Playoffs when they were knocked off by the Broncos 34–21 in Denver. The 1977 season is remembered as one of the most turbulent in franchise history, as numerous players were involved with off-the-field issues. Defensive tackle Ernie Holmes was arrested for cocaine possession, and despite being found not guilty, lawsuits followed. Head coach Chuck Noll was also subject to a defamation lawsuit, as Oakland Raiders safety George Atkinson sued Noll and the Steelers for a disparaging comment in which Noll called Atkinson part of the "criminal element" in football. Though Atkinson lost the lawsuit, Noll was forced to bring Steelers cornerback Mel Blount into the suit, which upset Blount as he was one of many Steelers players engaged in a contract holdout, with others including linebacker Jack Lambert and safety Glen Edwards. Disputes between these players and Steelers owner Art Rooney were often publicized, and the overall drama played a significant part in the regression of the Steel Curtain defense. Jack Ham {LB}, Franco Harris {RB}, Lynn Swann {WR}, Joe Greene {DT} and Mel Blount {CB} were selected to various first team All-Pro teams.

Terry Bradshaw led the team in passing with 2,523 yards and threw 23 touchdown passes. Franco Harris led the team in rushing with 1,162 yards and 11 rushing touchdowns. Lynn Swann led the team with 50 receptions for 789 yards. Swann and John Stallworth both had 7 TD receptions.

PITTSBURGH			1977			9-6	Game Highlights
9/19/1977	MNF	vs	SAN FRANCISCO	27	0	W	Harris 100 rush yards-2 rush TD/Gerela 2 FGs
9/25/1977		vs	OAKLAND RAIDERS	7	16	L	Steelers commit 5 turnovers/Cunningham TD catch
10/2/1977		@	Cleveland Browns	28	14	W	Swann 7 catch-71 yards-2 TD catch/Lewis TD catch
10/9/1977		@	Houston Oilers	10	27	L	Steelers commit 9 turnovers/Bleier rush TD
10/17/1977	MNF	vs	CINCINNATI	20	14	W	Bleier 2 rush TD/Thornton rush TD
10/23/1977		vs	HOUSTON OILERS	27	10	W	Bradshaw 227 pass yards-2 TD pass/Harris 2 TDs
10/30/1977		@	Baltimore Colts	14	31	L	Steelers fall behind 24-0/Harris 2 rush TD
11/6/1977		@	Denver	7	21	L	Steelers held to 216 yards/Stallworth TD catch
11/13/1977		vs	CLEVELAND BROWNS	35	31	W	Stallworth 6 catch-129 yards-2 TD catch/Swann TD
11/20/1977		vs	DALLAS	28	13	W	Harris 179 rush yds-2 rush TD/Bradshaw 2 TD pass
11/27/1977		@	New York Jets	23	20	W	Bradshaw 143 pass yards-2 TD pass/Harris rush TD
12/4/1977		vs	SEATTLE	30	20	W	Bradshaw 2 rush TD-TD pass to Swann-Gerela 3 FG
12/10/1977	SAT	@	Cincinnati	10	17	L	Steelers commit 5 turnovers/Harris rush TD
12/18/1977		@	San Diego Chargers	10	9	W	Bradshaw 139 pass yards/Thornton rush TD
12/24/1977	**SAT**	**@**	**Denver**	**21**	**34**	**L**	Bradshaw 177 pass yards-TD pass-3 INTs

Schedule courtesy of Steve's Football Bible LLC

1977 AFC Central	W	L	T	PCT	DIV	CONF	PF	PA
Pittsburgh Steelers	**9**	**5**	**0**	**.643**	**4–2**	**7–5**	**276**	**243**
Houston Oilers	8	6	0	.571	3–3	6–6	299	230
Cincinnati Bengals	8	6	0	.571	3–3	6–5	238	235
Cleveland Browns	6	8	0	.429	2–4	5–7	269	267

1977 NFL Draft

Round	Choice	Player	Position	School
1	21	Robin Cole	LB	New Mexico
2	48	Sidney Thornton	RB	Northwest Louisiana
3	60	Tom Beasley	DT	Virginia Tech
3	75	Jim Smith	WR	Michigan
4	93	Ted Petersen	Center	Eastern Illinois
4	99	Laverne Smith	RB	Kansas
4	106	Dan Audick	Guard	Hawaii
5	121	Cliff Stoudt	QB	Youngstown State
5	125	Steve Courson	Guard	South Carolina
5	132	Dennis Winston	LB	Arkansas
6	159	Paul Harris	LB	Alabama
7	186	Randy Frisch	DT	Missouri
8	217	Phil August	WR	Miami (FL)
9	244	Roosevelt Kelly	TE	Eastern Kentucky
10	253	Alvin Cowans	DB	Florida
10	271	Dave LaCrosse	LB	Wake Forest
11	298	Lou West	DB	Cincinnati
12	310	Jimmy Stephens	TE	Florida

1977 AFC Divisional Playoffs

In Denver's first postseason football contest, linebacker Tom Jackson's 2 interceptions and a fumble recovery set up 17 points, 10 of them in the 4th quarter, as the Broncos defeated the Steelers for the first playoff win in their 18-year history.

Denver scored first after Broncos receiver John Schultz blocked a punt from Rick Engles and recovered the ball on the Steelers 17-yard line to set up running back Rob Lytle's 7-yard rushing touchdown. Pittsburgh responded with a 56-yard drive, including a 19-yard reception by tight end Bennie Cunningham on 4th down and 1, to tie the score on quarterback Terry Bradshaw's 1-yard rushing touchdown.

In the second quarter, Broncos defensive tackle Lyle Alzado forced a fumble from Franco Harris, which linebacker Randy Gradishar recovered and returned 5 yards before fumbling himself. The second fumble was recovered by Tom Jackson, who returned it 25 yards to the Pittsburgh 10-yard line. On the next play, running back Otis Armstrong ran the ball into the end zone to give the Broncos a 14–7 lead. However, Pittsburgh quickly struck back starting with Jim Smith's 28-yard kickoff return to the Steelers 34-yard line. Bradshaw then hit John Stallworth for a 21-yard completion and Harris ripped off a 20-yard burst before he finished the drive with a 1-yard touchdown run to tie the game at 14 with 1:41 left in the half.

In the third quarter, the Broncos drove 52 yards to the Pittsburgh 1-yard line, only to lose the ball when Jim Jensen was stuffed for no gain by Jack Lambert and Jim Allen on 4th down. But after a punt, they drove 43 yards to go up 21-14 on Craig Morton's 30-yard touchdown pass to tight end Riley Odoms.

Early in the 4th quarter, Pittsburgh managed to tie the game with a 48-yard catch by Stallworth setting up Bradshaw's 1-yard touchdown pass to tight end Larry Brown. But this would be their last score as Denver soon took over the game. First, Jim Turner put the Broncos up 24-21 by kicking 44-yard field goal with 7:17 left on the clock. Then Jackson intercepted a pass from Bradshaw and returned it 32 yards to the Steelers 9-yard line, setting up Turner's 24-yard field goal to make the score 27-21. On Pittsburgh's ensuring drive, Jackson struck again, intercepting another pass and returning this one 17 yards to the Steelers 33. Rather than sitting on their one-score lead and trying to run out the clock with running plays, Denver took to the air, scoring the game clinching touchdown on Morton's 34-yard pass to Jack Dolbin with 1:44 left in the game.

Harris finished the game with 92 rushing yards, 4 receptions for 20 yards, and a touchdown. Morton only completed 11 of 23 passes, but he threw for 167 yards and two touchdowns with no interceptions.

12/24/1977	Line	1	2	3	4	Final
Pittsburgh Steelers		0	14	0	7	21
Denver Broncos	{-2.0}	7	7	7	13	34

Scoring

Team	
Broncos	Rob Lytle 7 yard rush (Jim Turner kick)
Steelers	Terry Bradshaw 1 yard rush (Roy Gerela kick)
Broncos	Otis Armstrong 10 yard rush (Jim Turner kick)
Steelers	Franco Harris 1 yard rush (Roy Gerela kick)
Broncos	Riley Odoms 30 yard pass from Craig Morton (Jim Turner kick)
Steelers	Larry Brown 1 yard pass from Terry Bradshaw (Roy Gerela kick)
Broncos	Jim Turner 44 yard field goal
Broncos	Jim Turner 25 yard field goal
Broncos	Jack Dolbin 34 yard pass from Craig Morton (Jim Turner kick)

1978 Pittsburgh Steelers {Super Bowl XIII Champions}

The season concluded with the team winning Super Bowl XIII to become the first franchise in the NFL to win three Super Bowl titles. The championship run was led by quarterback Terry Bradshaw and the team's vaunted Steel Curtain defense. This team is regarded as one of the greatest defensive teams of all time and one of the greatest teams in NFL history. **Bradshaw put together the best year of his career to that point, becoming only the second Steeler to win the NFL MVP award.** Ten Steelers players were named to the Pro Bowl team, and four were judged as first-team All-Pros by the AP. Head coach Chuck Noll returned for his tenth season—moving him ahead of Walt Kiesling as the longest tenured head coach in the team's history to that point. The Steelers entered the season as defending champions of the AFC Central Division, coming off a 9–5 record in 1977. Their two losses were by a combined 10 points. Despite winning their division, the previous season was a difficult one for the team (both on and off the field) which culminated in a division round playoff loss to the Denver Broncos on Christmas Eve. The team began the 1978 season with seven straight victories, a franchise-best start to a season that stood for 42 years, before losing to the Houston Oilers in prime time on Monday Night Football. They finished the season with a league-best 14–2 record, including a 5-game winning streak to close the season. This record assured them they would play at home throughout the 1978 playoffs. It was also the best record compiled in the team's history (since surpassed only by a 15–1 mark in 2004).

The NFL instituted several major changes for the 1978 season. Chief among these were the extension of the regular season and playoff expansion. The regular season was extended from 14 to 16 games, with an offsetting decrease in the number of preseason games from six to four. Two playoff slots were added expanding the field from eight teams to ten, with each conference adding a second wild card entrant. Additionally, several rules were changed to help open the offense, particularly the passing game. One rule which prohibited defenders from contacting receivers more than five yards from the line of scrimmage, came to be known as the "Mel Blount rule" after the Steelers notably physical cornerback. Another rule allowed offensive linemen to use their hands in blocking. Jack Ham {LB}, Lynn Swann {WR}, Mike Webster {C} and Terry Bradshaw {QB} were selected to various first team All-Pro teams.

Bradshaw led the team in passing with 2,915 yards and threw 28 touchdown passes. Franco Harris led the team in rushing with 1,082 yards and 8 rushing touchdowns. Lynn Swann led the team in receiving with 61 receptions for 880 yards and 11 TD receptions. Tony Dungy led with 6 interceptions.

1978 AFC Central	W	L	T	PCT	DIV	CONF	PF	PA
Pittsburgh Steelers	**14**	**2**	**0**	**.875**	**5–1**	**11–1**	**356**	**195**
Houston Oilers	10	6	0	.625	4–2	8–4	283	298
Cleveland Browns	8	8	0	.500	1–5	4–8	334	356
Cincinnati Bengals	4	12	0	.250	2–4	2–10	252	284

Pittsburgh at Buffalo

The Steel Curtain defense was dominant early, holding the Bills to just 59 total yards and only six first downs in first three quarters of play. New defensive coordinator George Perles employed the blitz to a much greater degree than the team had in the past. Bills quarterback Joe Ferguson, who was coming off a knee injury suffered in the pre-season, struggled with just three completions and 20 yards on ten passing attempts before being pulled from the game. Meanwhile, the Steelers scored two second-quarter touchdowns, the first coming on a throw from Terry

Bradshaw to John Stallworth. Stallworth caught three passes of twenty yards or longer in the Steelers first two possessions. The Steelers second score came on a one-yard plunge by Franco Harris. When the Steelers scored again on a Sidney Thornton rush at the start of the fourth quarter to go up 21–0, the game appeared to be all but over. However, Bill Munson came into the game in relief of Ferguson and sparked the Bills to two quick scores that brought the Bills to within 11 points. The Steelers put the game away with a 73-yard drive capped by Bradshaw's second touchdown of the game.

PITTSBURGH			1978			17-2	Game Highlights
9/3/1978		@	Buffalo	28	17	W	Bradshaw 217 pass yards-2 TD pass
9/10/1978		vs	SEATTLE	21	10	W	Bradshaw 213 pass yards-2 TD pass/Harris TD
9/17/1978		@	Cincinnati	28	3	W	Bradshaw 242 pass yards-2 TD pass/Swann TD
9/24/1978		vs	CLEVELAND (OT)	15	9	W	Gerela 3 FG/Bradshaw TD pass to Cunningham
10/1/1978		@	New York Jets	28	17	W	Swann 7 catch-100 yards-2 TD catch
10/8/1978		vs	ATLANTA	31	7	W	Harris 104 rush yards/Belier 2 rush TDs
10/15/1978		@	Cleveland Browns	34	14	W	**Anderson kickoff return TD**/Gerela 2 FGs
10/23/1978	MNF	vs	HOUSTON OILERS	17	24	L	Grossman 9 catch-116 yards/Swann 2 TD catch
10/29/1978		vs	KANSAS CITY	27	24	W	**Shell fumble return TD**/Harris 2 rush TD
11/5/1978		vs	NEW ORLEANS	20	14	W	Bradshaw 200 pass yds-2 TD pass/Gerela 2 FG
11/12/1978	SNF	@	Los Angeles Rams	7	10	L	Steelers held to 174 yards/Swann TD catch
11/19/1978		vs	CINCINNATI	7	6	W	Steelers held to 154 yards/Bleier rush TD
11/27/1978	MNF	@	San Francisco	24	7	W	Swann 8 catch-134 yards-2 TD catch
12/3/1978		@	Houston Oilers	13	3	W	Bradshaw TD pass to Stallworth/Gerela 2 FGs
12/10/1978		vs	BALTIMORE COLTS	35	13	W	Bradshaw 240 pass yds-3 TD pass/Harris 2 TD
12/17/1978		vs	DENVER	21	17	W	Bradshaw 131 pass yards-2 TD pass/Harris TD
12/30/1978	**SAT**	**vs**	**DENVER**	**33**	**10**	**W**	Stallworth 10 catch-156 yards-TD catch
1/7/1979		**vs**	**HOUSTON OILERS**	**34**	**5**	**W**	Bradshaw 200 pass yards-2 TD pass
1/21/1979		**vs**	**Dallas**	**35**	**31**	**W**	Bradshaw 318 pass yards-4 TD pass

Schedule courtesy of Steve's Football Bible LLC

1978 NFL Draft

Round	Pick #	Player	Position	College
1	22	Ron Johnson	Defensive back	Eastern Michigan
2	49	Willie Fry	Defensive end	Notre Dame
3	76	Craig Colquitt	Punter	Tennessee
4	101	Larry Anderson	Defensive back	Louisiana Tech
6	160	Randy Reutershan	Wide receiver	Pitt
7	187	Mark Dufresne	Tight end	Nebraska
8	208	Rick Moser	Running back	Rhode Island
8	214	Andre Keys	Wide receiver	Cal Poly
9	241	Lance Reynolds	Offensive tackle	BYU
10	268	Doug Becker	Linebacker	Notre Dame
10	276	Tom Jurich	Placekicker	Northern Arizona
11	279	Nat Terry	Defensive back	Florida State
11	300	Tom Brzoza	Center	Pitt
12	327	Brad Carr	Linebacker	Maryland

1978 AFC Divisional Playoffs

The Steelers dominated the Broncos by gaining 425 yards of total offense and dominated Denver starting quarterback Craig Morton so effectively that his team gained just 49 yards on their first five possessions before he was replaced by Norris Weese in the second quarter, who ended up getting sacked 5 times.

After Denver scored first on a field goal, Pittsburgh responded by driving 66 yards in 8 plays to score on running back Franco Harris' 1-yard touchdown run, giving the team a 6-3 lead after Roy Gerela missed the extra point. Then on the Steelers' next drive, Harris ran 18 yards to the end zone for his second touchdown. In the second quarter, the Steelers increased their lead to 16-3 with Gerela's 24-yard field goal. However, linebacker Tom Jackson later recovered a fumble from Pittsburgh quarterback Terry Bradshaw on the Steelers 49-yard line, where the Broncos went on to score on Dave Preston's 3-yard touchdown run that made the score 16-10. The Steelers responded with Gerela's second field goal of the day to take a 19-10 lead going into halftime.

In the third quarter, Denver mounted their most promising drive of the day, advancing the ball 73 yards. But it ended with no points when Joe Greene blocked Jim Turner's 29-yard field goal attempt. In the fourth quarter, Bradshaw threw two touchdowns, the first a 45-yarder to wide receiver John Stallworth. Then Dennis Winston recovered a fumble from Denver's Rick Upchurch on the ensuing kickoff, setting up Bradshaw's 38-yard touchdown pass. to wide receiver Lynn Swann.

Bradshaw completed 16 of 29 passes for 272 yards and 2 touchdowns, Stallworth had 10 receptions for 156 yards and a touchdown, and Harris rushed for 105 yards and 2 touchdowns.

12/30/1978	Line	1	2	3	4	Final
Denver Broncos		3	7	0	0	10
Pittsburgh Steelers	{-7.0}	6	13	0	14	33

Scoring

Team	
Broncos	Jim Turner 37 yard field goal
Steelers	Franco Harris 1 yard rush
Steelers	Franco Harris 18 yard rush (Roy Gerela kick)
Steelers	Roy Gerela 24 yard field goal
Broncos	Dave Preston 3 yard rush (Jim Turner kick)
Steelers	Roy Gerela 27 yard field goal
Steelers	John Stallworth 45 yard pass from Terry Bradshaw (Roy Gerela kick)
Steelers	Lynn Swann 38 yard pass from Terry Bradshaw (Roy Gerela kick)

1978 AFC Championship Game

On a wet, slick, and slippery field, the Steelers dominated the Oilers by forcing 9 turnovers and only allowing 5 points. Pittsburgh took the early lead by driving 57 yards to score on running back Franco Harris' 7-yard touchdown run. Then, linebacker Jack Ham recovered a fumble at the Houston 17-yard line, which led to running back Rocky Bleier's 15-yard rushing touchdown.

In the second quarter, a 19-yard field goal by Oilers kicker Toni Fritsch cut the score 14–3, but then the Steelers scored 17 points during the last 48 seconds of the second quarter. First, Houston running back Ronnie Coleman lost a fumble, and moments later Pittsburgh wide receiver Lynn Swann caught a 29-yard touchdown reception. Then Johnnie Dirden fumbled the ensuing kickoff, which led to Steelers wide receiver John Stallworth's 17-yard reception. After the Oilers got the ball back, Coleman fumbled again, and Roy Gerela kicked a field goal to increase Pittsburgh's lead, 31–3. Houston never posed a threat for the rest of the game as they turned over the ball four times in their six second-half possessions.

1/7/1979	Line	1	2	3	4	Final
Houston Oilers		0	3	2	0	5
Pittsburgh Steelers	{-7.0}	14	17	3	0	34

Scoring

Team	Detail
Steelers	Franco Harris 7 yard rush (Roy Gerela kick)
Steelers	Rocky Bleier 15 yard rush (Roy Gerela kick)
Oilers	Toni Fritsch 19 yard field goal
Steelers	Lynn Swann 29 yard pass from Terry Bradshaw (Roy Gerela kick)
Steelers	John Stallworth 17 yard pass from Terry Bradshaw (Roy Gerela kick)
Steelers	Roy Gerela 37 yard field goal
Steelers	Roy Gerela 22 yard field goal
Oilers	Safety, Washington tackled Bleier in end zone

Super Bowl XIII {"Battle of Champions"}

The game was played on January 21, 1979, at the Orange Bowl in Miami, the fifth and last time that the Super Bowl was played in that stadium. This was the first Super Bowl that featured a rematch of a previous one (the Steelers had previously beaten the Cowboys, 21–17, in Super Bowl X), and both teams were attempting to be the first club to win a third Super Bowl. Dallas was also the defending Super Bowl XII champion and finished the 1978 regular season with a 12–4 record and posted playoff victories over the Atlanta Falcons and the Los Angeles Rams. Pittsburgh entered the game after posting a 14–2 regular season record, and playoff wins over the Denver Broncos and the Houston Oilers. Super Bowl XIII is also the only Super Bowl to date that featured two teams (and quarterbacks) that had previously won two Super Bowls in the same decade. The Dallas Cowboys (quarterbacked by Roger Staubach) won Super Bowl VI during the 1971-72 season and Super Bowl XII during the 1977-78 season. The Pittsburgh Steelers (quarterbacked by Terry Bradshaw) won Super Bowl IX during the 1974-75 season, and Super Bowl X during the 1975-76 season. Steelers quarterback Terry Bradshaw, who was named Super Bowl MVP, completed 17 out of 30 passes for Super Bowl records of 318 passing yards and 4 touchdown passes.

Super Bowl XIII can arguably be called the greatest collection of NFL talent for a game. In addition to coaches Noll and Landry, 16 players would end up being voted into the Pro Football Hall of Fame. Of the 16 Hall of Fame players to play in this game, ten were Pittsburgh players (Bradshaw, Harris, Shell, Swann, Stallworth, Webster, Greene, Lambert, Ham, and Blount), and six were Dallas players (Staubach, Dorsett, Harris, White, Wright, and Jackie Smith).

On their opening drive, the Cowboys advanced to the Pittsburgh 38-yard line, with running back Tony Dorsett gaining 38 yards off 3 running plays. But they lost the ball on a fumbled handoff while attempting to fool the Steelers defense with a reverse-pass play. Receiver Drew Pearson later explained, "We practiced that play for three weeks. It is designed for me to hit Billy Joe 15 to 17 yards downfield. We practiced the play so much it was unbelievable we could fumble it. I expected the handoff a bit lower, but I should have had it. Billy Joe was in the process of breaking into the clear when the fumble occurred." The play was similar to the near turnover by Butch Johnson in the previous Super Bowl. After defensive lineman John Banaszak recovered the loose ball on the Pittsburgh 47-yard line, the Steelers attempted 2 running plays with running back Franco Harris carrying the ball, but only gained 1 yard. Then on third down, wide receiver John Stallworth caught a 12-yard pass to the Cowboys' 40-yard line. Then after throwing an incomplete pass, Terry Bradshaw completed 2 consecutive passes, the second one a 28-yard touchdown completion to Stallworth to take a 7–0 lead. On their next drive, the Cowboys responded by advancing to the Steelers 39-yard line but were pushed back to their own 39-yard line after quarterback Roger Staubach was sacked twice, and they were forced to punt. On the Steelers' ensuing drive, Bradshaw threw a 22-yard pass to Harris and followed it up with a 13-yard pass to receiver Lynn Swann to move the ball to the Dallas 30-yard line. But on the next play, Dallas linebacker D. D. Lewis ended the drive by intercepting a pass intended for Stallworth. It was the first interception thrown by Bradshaw in Super Bowl play. With a little more than a minute to go in the period, Bradshaw fumbled the ball while being sacked by Cowboys lineman Harvey Martin, and defensive end Ed "Too Tall" Jones recovered it. Staubach then capitalized on Bradshaw's mistake three plays later with a 39-yard scoring strike to receiver Tony Hill, tying the game at 7 as the first quarter expired. Pittsburgh sent eight men on an all-out blitz, but Staubach got the pass away just before he was hit by Steelers' safety Mike Wagner. Hill beat Donnie Shell in single-coverage and scored the only first-quarter touchdown surrendered by Pittsburgh all season (In Super Bowl X, the Cowboys also scored a first-quarter touchdown against a Steeler team that hadn't permitted one all year). Drew Pearson ensured the play's success by distracting Steelers cornerback Mel Blount, who was oblivious of Hill as he raced past Blount and Pearson en route to the end zone.

The Steelers took possession at the start of the second quarter and advanced to their own 48-yard line. On the next play, Dallas linebackers Mike Hegman and Thomas "Hollywood" Henderson went after Bradshaw on a blitz. After taking the snap, Bradshaw collided with Franco Harris and the ball popped loose. Bradshaw scooped it up and rolled to his right, looking to pass, but Henderson wrapped him up before he could throw, while Hegman ripped the ball out of his hands and returned the fumble 37 yards for a touchdown, giving the Cowboys a 14–7 lead. The Steelers had now turned the ball over on three consecutive possessions, but the Cowboys' lead didn't last long. On the third play of Pittsburgh's ensuing possession, Stallworth caught a pass from Bradshaw at the Steelers 35-yard line. He then broke a tackle from defensive back Aaron Kyle, waited for Swann and blockers to cross in front of him, turned toward the inside and outraced every other defender to the end zone, making a simple 10-yard pass into a 75-yard touchdown completion to tie the score, 14–14.

Pittsburgh's "Steel Curtain" defense then dominated the Dallas offense on their ensuing drive. First, Banaszak tackled fullback Robert Newhouse for 4-yard loss. Next, linebacker Jack Ham tackled Dorsett for a 3-yard loss on an attempted sweep. On third down, defensive tackle Joe Greene sacked Staubach, forcing a fumble that bounced through the hands of Steelers' defensive lineman Steve Furness. Cowboys lineman Tom Rafferty eventually recovered at the Dallas 13-yard line. Theo

Bell then returned Danny White's ensuing 38-yard punt 3 yards to the Dallas 48-yard line. The Steelers began their ensuing drive with Bradshaw's 26-yard completion to Swann. Jones tackled Harris for an 8-yard loss on the next play, but a subsequent holding penalty on Henderson gave Pittsburgh a first down at the Dallas 25-yard line. However, after an incomplete pass and a 2-yard run by Harris, Hegman sacked Bradshaw for an 11-yard loss on third down, pushing the ball back to the 34-yard line. The Steelers then came up empty after kicker Roy Gerela's 51-yard field goal attempt hit the crossbar. With less than two minutes remaining in the half, Dallas advanced to the Pittsburgh 32-yard line, after starting from their own 34-yard line. But Blount exacted revenge from the first quarter by intercepting a pass from Staubach and returning it 13 yards to the 29, with a personal foul on Dallas tight end Billy Joe DuPree adding another 15 yards and giving the Steelers the ball at their own 44-yard line (note: the interception happened on exactly the same play that Drew Pearson scored on in the first quarter of Super Bowl X; Mike Wagner intercepted Staubach on exactly the same play call in the 4th quarter of the same game). Following a penalty, Bradshaw completed 2 passes to Swann for gains of 29 and 21 yards, moving the ball to the 16-yard line with 40 seconds left in the half. Next, after dropping a pass intended for him, Harris ran the ball to the 7-yard line. Then with just 26 seconds left, Bradshaw completed a 7-yard touchdown pass to fullback Rocky Bleier, giving the Steelers a 21–14 lead at halftime.

The torrid scoring pace slowed during much of the third quarter, as both teams began to assert themselves on the defensive side of the ball. But late in the quarter, a 12-yard punt return by Cowboys receiver Butch Johnson gave Dallas good field position on their 42-yard line. The Cowboys subsequently drove down to the Steelers 10-yard line, mostly with Dorsett's rushing. Then on third down with less than three minutes remaining in the period, Staubach spotted 38-year-old reserve tight end Jackie Smith wide open in the end zone and threw him the ball. Head coach Tom Landry said Staubach tried to throw the ball soft when he saw how wide-open Smith was and that it came in low, and that when Smith tried to stop, his feet seemed to come out from under him. Jackie Smith states that it was still a catchable ball and that he should have made the play. Instead, Smith dropped the pass and the Cowboys had to settle for a field goal from kicker Rafael Septién, cutting their deficit to 21–17. Though Smith played 16 years in the league and is now enshrined in the Pro Football Hall of Fame, he is perhaps best known for this dropped touchdown, particularly in a championship game that was ultimately decided by four points.

Two controversial penalties early in the fourth quarter paved the way for the Steelers to score 14 unanswered points. The Steelers advanced to their own 44-yard line after a crucial 3rd down pass from Bradshaw to tight end Randy Grossman, a 13-yard pass to Swann, and a 5-yard run by Harris. Bradshaw then attempted a pass to Swann, but the receiver collided with Cowboys defensive back Benny Barnes and fell to the ground as the ball rolled incomplete. However, official Fred Swearingen (the referee of the Immaculate Reception game of 1972) called Barnes for pass interference. Replays showed that it could have been incidental contact, as Swann seemed to run into Barnes. The penalty gave Pittsburgh a first down at Dallas' 23-yard line. Two plays later, the Steelers faced 3rd down and 4 from the Dallas 17. Henderson sacked Bradshaw for a 12-yard loss, but the play was nullified by a delay of game penalty on Pittsburgh, bringing up 3rd down and 9 instead of a fourth down. Replays clearly showed the whistle blew before the play's onset, plus most of the players pulled up and stopped playing after a whistle sounded. Franco Harris confronted Henderson for taunting Bradshaw after the whistle, and on the next play, Bradshaw handed the ball off to Harris, who raced untouched, with help from the Umpire Art Demmas impeding Cowboys safety Charlie Waters' attempt to tackle him, up the middle for a 22-yard touchdown run. The next day Waters was quoted as saying, "I don't know what I could do – maybe knock him [Umpire Demmas] flat and maybe he'd knock Franco flat? Our safeties play a vital role in the run. That official gets in the way a lot. He screened me off." This score increased Pittsburgh's lead to 28–17. The run would be the Steelers' longest touchdown run in Super Bowl competition until Willie Parker scampered 75 yards for a score against the Seattle Seahawks in Super Bowl XL. On the ensuing kickoff, video shows that Gerela slipped when trying to plant his foot, causing him to squib the ball, which bounced to Cowboys lineman Randy White at the 24-yard line. White, who was playing the game with a cast on his broken left hand, fumbled the ball before being hit by Tony Dungy, and Pittsburgh linebacker Dennis Winston recovered the ball at the Dallas 18-yard line. Remarkably, Winston wasn't even in the middle of the scrum when the fumble first occurred; he was standing by several teammates and decided to join the battle for the ball before referees intervened. On the next play, Bradshaw threw an 18-yard touchdown pass to Swann, increasing the Steelers' lead to 35–17 with less than 7 minutes left in the game. The touchdown was Bradshaw's last pass of the game. Some of the Steelers were already celebrating victory on the sidelines, but the Cowboys refused to give up. On their next drive, Dallas drove 89 yards in 8 plays, including an 18-yard scramble by Staubach on 3rd and 11 and a 29-yard run by Dorsett, to score on Staubach's 7-yard touchdown pass to DuPree. Then after Dallas' Dennis Thurman recovered an onside kick at 2:19, Drew Pearson caught 2 passes for gains of 22 and 25 yards (the second catch on 4th down and 18) as the Cowboys drove 52 yards in 9 plays to score on Staubach's 4-yard touchdown pass to Butch Johnson. With the ensuing extra point, the Steelers' lead was cut to 35–31 with just 0:22 left in the game. But the Cowboys' second onside kick attempt was unsuccessful. Bleier recovered the ball, and the Steelers were able to run out the clock to win the game.

Swann was the leading receiver in the game with 7 receptions for 124 yards and a touchdown. Stallworth recorded 115 yards and two touchdowns off just 3 receptions. Stallworth and Swann became the first pair of teammates to each have 100 yards receiving in a Super Bowl and first time two receivers did it in the same game. Dorsett was the top rusher of the game with 96 rushing yards and caught 5 passes for 44 yards. Harris was Pittsburgh's leading rusher with 68 yards, and he caught a pass for 22 yards. Staubach finished the game with exactly as many passing attempts (30) and completions (17) as Bradshaw, good for 228 passing yards, 3 touchdowns, and 1 interception. Butch Johnson caught 2 passes for 30 yards and a touchdown, returned 3 kickoffs for 63 yards, and gained 33 yards on 2 punt returns, giving him 126 total yards. Drew Pearson hauled in 4 passes for 73 yards, all in the fourth quarter.

1/21/1979	Line	1	2	3	4	Final
Pittsburgh Steelers	{-3.5}	7	14	0	14	35
Dallas Cowboys	{37.0}	7	7	3	14	31

Scoring

Team	
Steelers	John Stallworth 28 yard pass from Terry Bradshaw (Roy Gerela kick)
Cowboys	Tony Hill 39 yard pass from Roger Staubach (Rafael Septien kick)
Cowboys	Mike Hegman 37 yard defensive fumble return (Rafael Septien kick)
Steelers	John Stallworth 75 yard pass from Terry Bradshaw (Roy Gerela kick)
Steelers	Rocky Bleier 7 yard pass from Terry Bradshaw (Roy Gerela kick)
Cowboys	Rafael Septien 27 yard field goal
Steelers	Franco Harris 22 yard rush (Roy Gerela kick)
Steelers	Lynn Swann 18 yard pass from Terry Bradshaw (Roy Gerela kick)
Cowboys	Billy Joe DuPree 7 yard pass from Roger Staubach (Rafael Septien kick)
Cowboys	Butch Johnson 4 yard pass from Roger Staubach (Rafael Septien kick)

1979 Pittsburgh Steelers {Super Bowl XIV Champions}

The Steelers successfully defended their Super Bowl Championship from the previous year, despite not improving on their 14-2 record from last year with a 12–4 record. They went on to defeat the Los Angeles Rams in Super Bowl XIV. The Steelers started out to a 4-0 record. Adding to the previous season, the Steelers had won 12 in a row. They finished the regular season at 12-4. In six of those games the opponents were held to a touchdown or less. In the playoffs Pittsburgh defeated Miami, 34-14 and then for the second consecutive season beat Houston 27-13, in the AFC championship game. The Steelers ended the decade by defeating the Los Angeles Rams 31-19 in Super Bowl XIV. Despite them and the San Diego Chargers having 12-4 records, the Chargers were awarded the top seed in the AFC because of their victory over the Steelers. Jack Ham {LB}, John Stallworth {WR}, Mike Webster {C}, Jack Lambert {MLB}, Joe Greene {DT}, Donnie Shell {S} and Jon Kolb {T} were selected to various first team All-Pro teams.

Terry Bradshaw led the team in passing with 3,724 yards and threw 26 touchdown passes. Franco Harris led the team in rushing with 1,186 yards and 11 rushing touchdowns. John Stallworth led the team in receiving with 70 receptions for 1,183 yards and 8 TD receptions. Jack Lambert led the team with 6 interceptions.

PITTSBURGH			1979			14-5	Game Highlights
9/3/1979	MNF	@	New England (OT)	16	13	W	Thornton 2 TDs/Bahr GW FG in overtime
9/9/1979		vs	HOUSTON OILERS	38	7	W	**Winston INT return TD**/Thornton 2 TDs
9/16/1979		@	St. Louis Cardinals	24	21	W	Bradshaw 206 pass yards-2 TD pass/Bahr GW FG
9/23/1979		vs	BALTIMORE COLTS	17	13	W	Bradshaw 249 pass yards-2 pass TD/Thornton 129 yds
9/30/1979		@	Philadelphia	14	17	L	Bradshaw 176 pass yards-TD pass to Stallworth
10/7/1979		@	Cleveland	51	35	W	Harris 153 rush yards-2 rush TD/Thornton 98 yards
10/14/1979		@	Cincinnati	10	34	L	Steelers commit 9 turnovers/Stallworth TD catch
10/22/1979	MNF	vs	DENVER	42	7	W	Bradshaw 267 pass yards-2 TD pass/Harris 2 TDs
10/28/1979		vs	DALLAS	14	34	L	Harris 102 rush yards-2 rush TD/Thornton 68 yards
11/4/1979		vs	WASHINGTON	38	7	W	Stallworth 6 catch-126 yards-2 TD catch/Moser TD
11/11/1979		@	Kansas City	30	3	W	Bradshaw 232 pass yards-3 TD pass/Bahr 3 FGs
11/18/1979		@	San Diego Chargers	7	35	L	Steelers commit 8 turnovers/Belier rush TD
11/25/1979		vs	CLEVELAND (OT)	33	10	W	Harris 151 rush yards-2 rush TD-TD catch/Bahr 4 FG
12/2/1979		vs	CINCINNATI	37	17	W	Swann 5 catch-192 yards-2 TD catch/Bahr 3 FGs
12/10/1979	MNF	@	Houston Oilers	17	20	L	Bradshaw 237 pass yards-TD pass to Stallworth
12/16/1979		vs	BUFFALO	28	0	W	Harris 100 rush yards-2 rush TD/Swann TD catch
12/30/1979		vs	**MIAMI**	**34**	**14**	**W**	Bradshaw 230 pass yards-2 TD pass
1/7/1980		vs	**HOUSTON OILERS**	**27**	**13**	**W**	Bradshaw 2019 pass yards-2 TD pass/Bahr 2 FGs
1/21/1980		vs	**Los Angeles Rams**	**31**	**19**	**W**	Stallworth 3 catch-121 yards-Td catch/Harris 2 TDs

Schedule courtesy of Steve's Football Bible LLC

1979 AFC Central	W	L	T	PCT	DIV	CONF	PF	PA
Pittsburgh Steelers	**12**	**4**	**0**	**.750**	**4–2**	**9–3**	**416**	**262**
Houston Oilers	11	5	0	.688	4–2	9–3	362	331
Cleveland Browns	9	7	0	.563	2–4	6–6	359	352
Cincinnati Bengals	4	12	0	.250	2–4	2–10	337	421

1979 NFL Draft

Round	Choice	Player	Position	School
1	28	Greg Hawthorne	RB	Baylor
2	56	Zack Valentine	LB	East Carolina
4	86	Russell Davis	RB	Michigan
4	110	Calvin Sweeney	WR	USC
5	137	Dwaine Board	DE	North Carolina A&T
6	157	Bill Murrell	TE	Winston-Salem State
6	161	Dwayne Woodruff	DB	Louisville
6	165	Matt Bahr	K	Penn State
7	192	Bruce Kimball	Guard	Massachusetts
8	220	Tom Graves	LB	Michigan State
9	248	Rick Kirk	DE	Denison
10	275	Tod Thompson	TE	Brigham Young
11	303	Charlie Moore	Center	Wichita State
12	322	Ed Smith	LB	Vanderbilt
12	330	Mike Almond	WR	Northwest Louisiana

1979 AFC Divisional Playoffs

The Steelers scored 20 points in the first quarter and held the Dolphins to 25 rushing yards. Miami future hall of fame running back Larry Csonka was held to just 20 rushing yards on 10 carries in the final game of his career, while Steelers quarterback Terry Bradshaw threw for 230 yards and 2 touchdowns.

On the opening drive of the game, Pittsburgh marched 62 yards in 13 plays to score on running back Sidney Thornton's 1-yard touchdown run. On their second possession, the Steelers advanced another 62 yards in 9 plays, 36 of them on carries by Thornton, to score on wide receiver John Stallworth's 17-yard touchdown reception (although the extra point was blocked). And on their third drive, they moved the ball 56 yards to score on wide receiver Lynn Swann's 20-yard touchdown reception.

In the second quarter, the Dolphins moved the ball 63 yards to the Pittsburgh 6-yard line, but then lost it when a safety blitz by J. T. Thomas forced quarterback Bob Griese to throw a rushed pass that was intercepted by linebacker Dennis Winston. Miami soon got another chance to score when Larry Gordon recovered Thornton's fumble on the Steelers 5, but all this resulted in was a turnover on downs. Faced with 4th and 2, Griese tried to connect with tight end Bruce Hardy in the end zone, but Hardy collided with receiver Nat Moore and the pass fell 
incomplete. The Steelers had a chance to increase their lead even more right before halftime when they

tackled Dolphins punter George Roberts on the Miami 21 before he could make a kick. But Matt Bahr's 30-yard field goal was eliminated by a Pittsburgh holding penalty, which ran off the final seconds of the half.

In the second half, Pittsburgh primarily relied on their rushing game to protect their lead. Despite Miami having the second highest ranked run defense during the season, and an injury that sidelined Thornton in the second half, the Steelers ended up running the ball 40 times during the game, with Franco Harris gaining 83 yards on 21 carries. Miami finally scored in the third quarter after defensive back Don Bessillieu recovered a punt that bounced into the leg of Pittsburgh blocker Dwayne Woodruff on the Steelers 11-yard line, leading to Griese's 7-yard touchdown pass to Duriel Harris. However, the Steelers responded by advancing 69 yards to score on running back Rocky Bleier's 1-yard touchdown. Harris' 5-yard touchdown in the fourth quarter put the game out of reach.

This was the final NFL game for Csonka, as well as the final playoff game for Griese, who completed just 14 of 26 passes for 118 yards and was sacked 8 times before being replaced by Don Strock with 8:55 left in the fourth quarter. Strock ended up with more passing yards, going 8/14 for 125 yards and leading the team 76 yards to their final score on a 1-yard Csonka run.

12/30/1979	Line	1	2	3	4	Final
Miami Dolphins		0	0	7	7	14
Pittsburgh Steelers	{-9.5}	20	0	7	7	34

Scoring

Team	
Steelers	Sidney Thornton 1 yard rush (Matt Bahr kick)
Steelers	John Stallworth 17 yard pass from Terry Bradshaw
Steelers	Lynn Swann 20 yard pass from Terry Bradshaw (Matt Bahr kick)
Dolphins	Duriel Harris 7 yard pass from Bob Griese (Uwe von Schamann kick)
Steelers	Rocky Bleier 1 yard rush (Matt Bahr kick)
Steelers	Franco Harris 5 yard rush (Matt Bahr kick)
Dolphins	Larry Csonka 1 yard rush (Uwe von Schamann kick)

1979 AFC Championship Game

The Steelers held the Oilers to only 24 rushing yards but were also aided by a controversial non-touchdown call to come away with a 27–13 win. Houston jumped to a 7–0 lead with just 2:30 into the game when Vernon Perry returned an interception 75 yards for a touchdown. Then after the teams exchanged field goals, Pittsburgh quarterback Terry Bradshaw completed two touchdown passes, a 16-yarder to tight end Bennie Cunningham and a 20-yard one to wide receiver John Stallworth.

With the Steelers leading 17–10, the controversial play occurred during the last seconds of the third quarter after the Oilers advanced to the Pittsburgh 6-yard line. With a chance to tie the game, Quarterback Dan Pastorini threw a pass to Mike Renfro at the back of the end zone, and Renfro appeared to have caught it for a touchdown with both feet in bounds before he fell out of the end zone. TV replays suggested a catch for a touchdown. Despite this, the officials ruled the pass incomplete, saying that Renfro did not have complete control of the ball before going out of bounds. The Oilers then had to settle for a 23-yard field goal. The Steelers would then score 10 unanswered points in the fourth quarter to clinch the victory. A 78-yard drive ended with a field goal and running back Rocky Bleier scored on a 4-yard rushing touchdown. Steelers running back Franco Harris rushed for 85 yards and caught 6 passes for 50 yards. Houston running back Earl Campbell, the NFL's leading rusher during the season, finished the game with just 15 yards on 17 carries.

1/6/1980	Line	1	2	3	4	Final
Houston Oilers		7	3	0	3	13
Pittsburgh Steelers	{-9.5}	3	14	0	10	27

Scoring

Team	
Oilers	Vernon Perry 75 yard interception return (Toni Fritsch kick)
Steelers	Matt Bahr 21 yard field goal
Oilers	Toni Fritsch 21 yard field goal
Steelers	Bennie Cunningham 16 yard pass from Terry Bradshaw (Matt Bahr kick)
Steelers	John Stallworth 20 yard pass from Terry Bradshaw (Matt Bahr kick)
Oilers	Toni Fritsch 23 yard field goal
Steelers	Matt Bahr 39 yard field goal
Steelers	Rocky Bleier 4 yard rush (Matt Bahr kick)

Super Bowl XIV

The game was played on January 20, 1980, at the Rose Bowl in Pasadena, California, and was attended by a Super Bowl record 103,985 spectators. The Rams became the first team to reach the Super Bowl after posting nine wins or fewer during the regular season since the NFL season expanded to 16 games in 1978. Their 9–7 regular season record was followed by postseason wins over the Dallas Cowboys and the Tampa Bay Buccaneers. The Steelers were the defending Super Bowl XIII champions and finished the 1979 regular season with a 12–4 record and posted playoff victories over the Miami Dolphins and the Houston Oilers.

Despite being the underdogs, the Rams managed to hang onto a 13–10 lead at halftime, and a 19–17 lead at the beginning of the fourth quarter. But the Steelers held the Rams scoreless in the fourth quarter and scored two touchdowns for the win. Despite the game's uneven matchup and the final score, this game is regarded by some as one of the most competitive games in Super Bowl history. Overall, the lead changed seven times between both teams, a Super Bowl record (Pittsburgh took the lead 4 times, while Los Angeles took it 3 times).

The Rams took the opening kickoff but the Steel Curtain, however, managed to force a three-and-out. Then on the Steelers' 7th play of their first possession, quarterback Terry Bradshaw completed a 32-yard pass to running back Franco Harris to reach the Los Angeles 26-yard line. But a third down pass fell incomplete, forcing Pittsburgh to settle for a 41-yard field goal from rookie kicker Matt Bahr. Bahr's ensuing kickoff was very short, giving the Rams great field position at their 41-yard line. On the first play of the drive, Los Angeles running back Wendell Tyler caught a 6-yard pass from Vince Ferragamo. Then on the next play, Tyler took a handoff, ran left, broke some tackles, and ran 39 yards to the Steelers 14-yard line before he was finally dragged down by Pittsburgh defensive back Donnie Shell, the longest run against the Steelers all season. Shell saved the touchdown by making the tackle after previously being knocked to the turf five yards past the line of scrimmage. 6 plays later, fullback Cullen Bryant scored on a 1-yard touchdown run to give the Rams a 7–3 lead. The score was the Steelers' first rushing touchdown allowed in Super Bowl competition in franchise history. But the lead did not last long. Pittsburgh defensive back Larry Anderson returned the ensuing kickoff 45 yards to his own 47-yard line, and then the Steelers marched 53 yards in 9 plays using every offensive weapon in their arsenal. First, Harris ran for 12 yards, fullback Rocky Bleier ran for 1, then tight end Bennie Cunningham caught a pass for 8. Bleier ran again for 2, followed by Bradshaw's 12-yard completion to receiver Lynn Swann on the last play of the first quarter.

The second period opened with Bradshaw's 13-yard completion to Cunningham to reach the Los Angeles 5-yard line, and then Harris ran through the middle to the 4. Wide receiver John Stallworth was then stopped at the 1-yard line, but then Harris ran to the right untouched and scored a touchdown on the next play, giving the Steelers a 10–7 lead. However, like the Rams' previous lead, the Steelers' lead also turned out to be short-lived. Aided by a 20-yard pass interference penalty against Shell, Los Angeles advanced 67 yards in 10 plays to score on 31-yard field goal from kicker Frank Corral to tie the game. Anderson gave the Steelers great field position after returning the ensuing kickoff 38 yards to the Pittsburgh 46-yard line, but the Steelers could not move the ball and had to punt. The Rams were also forced to punt on their next possession after only gaining 6 yards. But on the first play of the Steelers' next drive, Los Angeles defensive back Dave Elmendorf intercepted a pass from Bradshaw and returned it 10 yards to Pittsburgh's 39-yard line. On the first two plays after the turnover, Ferragamo was sacked for a 10-yard loss and threw an incomplete pass. But he managed to overcome the situation with a 12-yard completion to Bryant on third down and a 10-yard completion to receiver Billy Waddy on 4th down and 8. Ferragamo's next pass was complete to tight end Terry Nelson for a first down at the 13-yard line, but after throwing two incompletions, Pittsburgh lineman John Banaszak sacked Ferragamo on third down. However, Corral kicked a 45-yard field goal to give the Rams a 13–10 halftime lead. The heavily favored Steelers trailed at the end of the half. Anderson once again gave the Steelers great starting field position, returning the opening kickoff of the second half 37 yards to the Pittsburgh 39-yard line. The Steelers lulled the Rams defense by running the ball on three consecutive plays of the drive, and then Bradshaw burned them with a 47-yard touchdown completion to Swann, who made a leaping catch at the Los Angeles 2-yard line and tumbled into the end zone to give Pittsburgh a 17–13 lead.

But they didn't hold it. After two plays of the ensuing drive, Ferragamo completed a 50-yard pass to Waddy. Then on the next play, Ferragamo handed the ball off to running back Lawrence McCutcheon, who started to run to the right. The Steelers' defense came up to tackle him behind the line of scrimmage, only to watch him throw a 24-yard touchdown pass to Ron Smith. Corral missed the extra point attempt, but  the Rams had retaken the lead, 19–17. The Steelers had some success advancing into Rams territory on their next two possessions, only to see the Rams intercept the ball both times. First, Rams free safety Eddie Brown stopped the ensuing Steelers drive with an interception, lateraling to Pat Thomas to gain an additional two yards. Then after a punt, Pittsburgh drove all the way to the Rams 16-yard line, but Los Angeles defensive back Rod Perry intercepted a pass intended for Stallworth. Thus, the third quarter ended with the Rams still in the lead, 19–17, seemingly in control of the game. Worse yet, Pittsburgh lost Swann to injury, when he was knocked out of the game by Pat Thomas. With 12:59 left in the game, Rams punter Ken Clark's 59-yard punt planted Pittsburgh back on their own 25-yard line. Then faced with 3rd down and 8, Bradshaw took the snap, dropped back, and then threw a pass to Stallworth, who was running a streak pattern down the middle of the field. Stallworth caught the ball barely beyond the outstretched hand of Perry and took it all the way to the end zone for a 73-yard go-ahead touchdown to make the score 24–19 for the Steelers. The NFL Films highlight film notes that safety Eddie Brown was supposed to help Perry in covering Stallworth, but for some reason, Brown ignored the Steeler receiver.

On the ensuing kickoff, the Rams tried a reverse, which resulted in poor field position. After an exchange of punts, the Rams mounted one final, spirited drive to regain the lead. Ferragamo smartly moved the Rams down the field, completing 3 out of 4 passes around runs by Tyler. His 15-yard completion to Waddy on 3rd and 13 moved the Rams to the Pittsburgh 32-yard line with just under 6 minutes remaining. However, on the following play, Ferragamo made his first and only mistake of the game. Even though Waddy had broken free down the right side of the field, Ferragamo had zeroed in on Ron Smith down the middle of the field, but he didn't notice Pittsburgh linebacker Jack Lambert playing behind Smith. As Ferragamo released the ball, Lambert jumped in front of Smith and intercepted the pass with 5:24 remaining.

When faced with a 3rd down and 7 on their ensuing drive, Bradshaw once again made a crucial long pass completion to Stallworth, this time a 45-yard reception to the Rams 22-yard line, barely beyond the outstretched hand of Perry. Two plays later, a pass interference penalty on Los Angeles cornerback Pat Thomas in the end zone gave the Steelers a first down at the 1-yard line. The Rams managed to keep Bleier and Harris out of the end zone for two plays, but Harris then scored on a third-down, 1-yard touchdown run to give the Steelers a 31–19 lead and put the game away. The Rams responded by driving to Pittsburgh's 37-yard line but ended up turning over the ball on downs with 39 seconds left in the game, and the Steelers ran out the clock for the win.

1/20/1980	Line	1	2	3	4	Final
Los Angeles Rams	{36.0}	7	6	6	0	19
Pittsburgh Steelers	{-10.5}	3	7	7	14	31

Scoring

Team	
Steelers	Matt Bahr 41 yard field goal
Rams	Cullen Bryant 1 yard rush (Frank Corral kick)
Steelers	Franco Harris 1 yard rush (Matt Bahr kick)
Rams	Frank Corral 31 yard field goal
Rams	Frank Corral 45 yard field goal
Steelers	Lynn Swann 47 yard pass from Terry Bradshaw (Matt Bahr kick)
Rams	Ron Smith 24 yard pass from Lawrence McCutcheon
Steelers	John Stallworth 73 yard pass from Terry Bradshaw (Matt Bahr kick)
Steelers	Franco Harris 1 yard rush (Matt Bahr kick)

1980 Pittsburgh Steelers

The 1980 Pittsburgh Steelers season was the franchise's 48th season in the National Football League. The Steelers struggled for the first time in many years. The aging defense was not as effective as it had been in the 1978 and '79 seasons, falling from 2nd to 15th in yards allowed. The Steelers also surrendered 313 points, ranked 15th in the league, compared to 262 points (5th in the league) the previous season. The Pittsburgh defense only garnered 18 quarterback sacks. The offense was still plagued with 42 total turnovers, 42 total, but ranking 6th in total offense, and scoring 352 points. Despite the team's troubles, the Steelers could have again obtained home-field advantage throughout the playoffs had they not lost several close games, including games against Cincinnati and Cleveland in which they lost despite having large leads in the fourth quarter. Pittsburgh remained in the playoff hunt until a 28–13 loss to Buffalo in week 12 and then a 6–0 loss to Houston effectively eliminated Pittsburgh from the postseason. To many, these two losses marked the end of the Steeler Dynasty. Several key players retired after the 1980 season and the team was never the same again. The 1980 season was the first in which the Steelers did not qualify for the playoffs since 1971. Donnie Shell {S}, Jack Lambert {MLB} and Mike Webster {C} were selected to various first team All-Pro teams.

Terry Bradshaw led the team in passing with 3,339 yards and threw 24 touchdown passes. Franco Harris led the team in rushing with 789 yards and 4 rushing touchdowns. Lynn Swann led the team in receiving with 44 receptions. Theo Bell led with 748 receiving yards. Jim Smith led with 9 TD receptions. Donnie Shell led with 7 interceptions.

PITTSBURGH			1980			9-7	Game Highlights
9/7/1980		vs	HOUSTON OILERS	31	17	W	Bradshaw 254 pass yards-2 TD pass-rush TD
9/14/1980		@	Baltimore Colts	20	17	W	Bradshaw 282 pass yards-2 TD pass/Bahr 2 FGs
9/21/1980		@	Cincinnati	28	30	L	Bradshaw 265 pass yards-3 TD pass/Swann 2 TDs
9/28/1980		vs	CHICAGO	38	3	W	Smith 6 catch-131 yards-3 TD catch/Bahr FG
10/5/1980		@	Minnesota	23	17	W	Bradshaw 236 pas yards-TD pass-rush TD
10/12/1980		vs	CINCINNATI	16	17	L	Bradshaw 231 pass yds-TD pass to Smith/Bahr FG
10/20/1980	MNF	vs	OAKLAND RAIDERS	34	45	L	Bradshaw 299 pass yards-2 TD pass/Smith 2 TDs
10/26/1980		@	Cleveland Browns	26	27	L	Stoudt 310 pass yards/Hawthorne 2 rush TD
11/2/1980		vs	GREEN BAY	22	20	W	Bradshaw 135 pass yards-2 TD pass/Bahr 2 FGs
11/9/1980		@	Tampa Bay	24	21	W	**Winston fumble recovery TD**/Swann TD catch
11/16/1980		vs	CLEVELAND BROWNS	16	13	W	Swann 9 catch-138 yards-TD catch/Smith TD catch
11/23/1980		@	Buffalo	13	28	L	Bradshaw 155 pass yds/Harris rush TD/Bahr 2 FG
11/30/1980		vs	MIAMI	23	10	W	Bradshaw 289 yards-TD pass to Swann/Bahr 3 FG
12/4/1980	TH	@	Houston Oilers	0	6	L	Steelers commit 5 turnovers/Bradshaw 3 INTs
12/14/1980		vs	KANSAS CITY	21	16	W	Bradshaw 197 pass yards-2 TD pass/Bleier rush TD
12/22/1980	MNF	@	San Diego Chargers	17	26	L	Bradshaw 272 pass yards-TD pass to Cunningham

Schedule courtesy of Steve's Football Bible LLC

1980 AFC Central	W	L	T	PCT	DIV	CONF	PF	PA
Cleveland Browns	11	5	0	.688	4–2	8–4	357	310
Houston Oilers	11	5	0	.688	4–2	7–5	295	251
Pittsburgh Steelers	**9**	**7**	**0**	**.563**	**2–4**	**5–7**	**352**	**313**
Cincinnati Bengals	6	10	0	.375	2–4	4–8	244	312

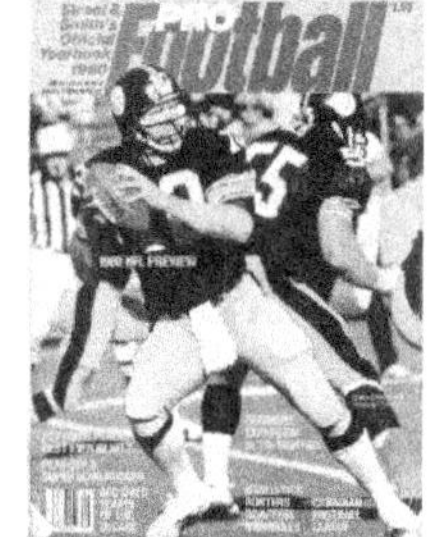

1980 NFL Draft

Round	Pick	Player	Position	College
1	28	Mark Malone	Quarterback	Arizona State
2	35	Bob Kohrs	Linebacker	Arizona State
2	56	John Goodman	Defensive end	Oklahoma
3	83	Ray Sydnor	Tight end	Wisconsin
4	110	Bill Hurley	Defensive back	Syracus
5	138	Craig Wolfley	Guard	Syracuse
6	165	Tunch Ilkin *	Tackle	Indiana State
7	193	Nate Johnson	Wide receiver	Hillsdale
8	221	Ted Walton	Defensive back	UConn
9	249	Ron McCall	Wide receiver	Arkansas–Pine Bluff
10	250	Woodrow Wilson	Defensive back	NC State
10	277	Ken Fritz	Guard	Ohio State
11	305	Frank Pollard	Running back	Baylor
12	306	Charles Vaclavik	Defensive back	Texas
12	333	Tyrone McGriff	Guard	Florida A&M

Oakland Raiders at Pittsburgh {Monday Night Football}

Without the availability of future Hall of Famers Harris, Swann and Stallworth, Terry Bradshaw marched the Pittsburgh offense down the field on their opening drive. He connected on a 19-yard scoring pass to Jim Smith to complete a six-play, 67-yard drive to give Pittsburgh the early lead. They quickly added to the advantage as a fumble by Kenny King on the first offensive play by the Raiders led to a Matt Bahr field goal and a 10-0 Pittsburgh lead. Undaunted, King recovered from his miscue to score the first touchdown of the game for the Raiders on a 27-yard run that completed a six-play, 85-yard Oakland drive. The Steelers increased their advantage to 17-7 as a one-yard touchdown run by Greg Hawthorne completed a 10-play, 84-yard drive. Later in the quarter, the Raiders answered with a one-yard touchdown run of their own by Mark van Eeghen following an interception by future Hall of Famer Ted Hendricks. Oakland took the lead for the first time at 21-17 as a sack of Bradshaw by Cedric Hardman resulted in a fumble and a 34-yard return for a touchdown by Rod Martin. led by Cliff Stoudt, the Steelers suffered their third straight turnover as Hendricks intercepted a Stoudt pass for his second pick of the quarter. Oakland increased their lead to 28-17 as Jim Plunkett hit Morris Bradshaw on a 45-yard touchdown pass with 1:22 remaining in the half. Stoudt led the Steelers down the field and cut the halftime lead to 28-24 with a 13-yard touchdown pass to Smith. On their first possession of the second half, Plunkett hit Cliff Branch with a 56-yard touchdown pass to give the Raiders an 11-point lead at 35-24. Terry Bradshaw returned for the Steelers in the second half and led the Steelers to a touchdown in their first possession of the half. He connected with Theo Bell on a 36-yard touchdown pass to make the score 35-31. the Steelers were unable to turn an Oakland fumble into a touchdown. Instead, they settled for a 32-yard field goal by Matt Bahr to make the score 35-34. Oakland answered in the fourth quarter as Plunkett hit Cliff Branch for a 36-yard touchdown to again make it a two-possession game. Oakland put the game away with a time-consuming drive in the final minutes that culminated in a 36-yard field goal by Chris Bahr to make the final score 45-34.

1981 Pittsburgh Steelers

After enduring an injury plagued 9–7 season the previous year and missing the playoffs for the first time since 1971, the Steelers had hoped that the 1980 season was just a small hiatus from contending for championships. However, while the Steelers had flashes of their former glory years after starting the season with 2 unimpressive losses, the 1981 season would end in an 8–8 record and eventually prove the end of the Steelers great dynasty of the 1970s. Mike Webster {C}, Jack Lambert {MLB}, Donnie Shell {S} and Mel Blount {CB} were selected to various first team All-Pro teams.

Terry Bradshaw led the team in passing with 2,887 yards and threw 22 touchdown passes. Franco Harris led the team in rushing with 987 yards and 8 rushing touchdowns. John Stallworth led the team with 68 receptions for 1,098 yards. Jim Smith led with 7 TD receptions. Jack Lambert and Mel Blount led the team with 6 interceptions each.

PITTSBURGH			1981			8-8	Game Highlights
9/6/1981		vs	KANSAS CITY	33	37	L	Bradshaw 319 pass yds-2 TD pass/Harris 2 rush TD
9/14/1981	TH	@	Miami	10	30	L	Bradshaw 222 pass yards-TD pass to Smith
9/20/1981		vs	NEW YORK JETS	38	10	W	Davis 100 rush yards-rush TD/Pollard 2 rush TD
9/27/1981		vs	NEW ENGLAND	27	21	W	Bradshaw 247 pass yards-2 TD pass/Swann GW TD
10/4/1981		@	New Orleans	20	6	W	Bradshaw 276 pass yards-2 TD pass/Trout 2 FGs
10/11/1981		vs	CLEVELAND BROWNS	13	7	W	Bradshaw 199 pass yards-TD pass to Stallworth
10/18/1981		@	Cincinnati	7	34	L	Steelers 205 total yards/ Bradshaw TD pass to Smith
10/26/1981	MNF	vs	HOUSTON OILERS	26	13	W	Smith 5 castch-100 yards-TD catch/Trout 2 FGs
11/1/1981		vs	SAN FRANCISCO	14	17	L	**Blount INT return TD**/Smith TD catch
11/8/1981		@	Seattle	21	24	L	Bradshaw 212 pass yards-TD pass to Malone
11/15/1981		@	Atlanta	34	20	W	Bradshaw 253 pass yds-5 TD pass/Stallworth 2 TDs
11/22/1981		@	Cleveland Browns	32	10	W	Bradshaw 223 pass yards-2 TD pass
11/29/1981		vs	LOS ANGELES RAMS	24	0	W	Harris 114 rush yards-rush TD/ Bradshaw rush TD
12/7/1981	MNF	@	Oakland Raiders	27	30	L	Malone 244 pass yards-2 TD pass/Smith 2 TD catch
12/13/1981		vs	CINCINNATI	10	17	L	Steelers held to 207 yards/Harris TD catch
12/20/1981		@	Houston Oilers	20	21	L	Stallworth 6 catch-90 yards/Malone rush TD

Schedule courtesy of Steve's Football Bible LLC

1981 AFC Central	W	L	T	PCT	DIV	CONF	PF	PA
Cincinnati Bengals	12	4	0	.750	4–2	10–2	421	304
Pittsburgh Steelers	**8**	**8**	**0**	**.500**	**3–3**	**5–7**	**356**	**297**
Houston Oilers	7	9	0	.438	4–2	6–6	281	355
Cleveland Browns	5	11	0	.313	1–5	2–10	276	375

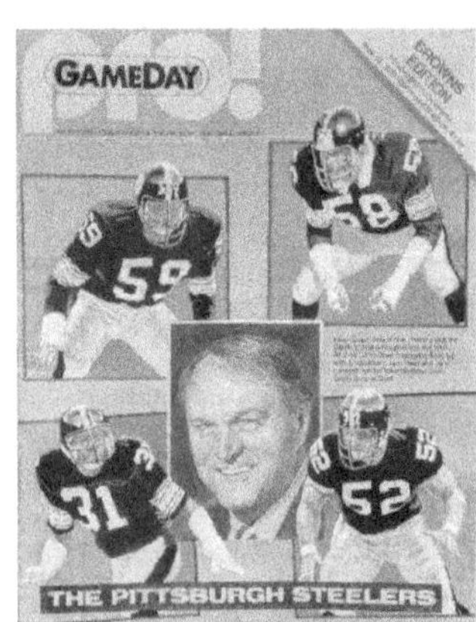

1981 NFL Draft

Round	Choice	Player	Position	School
1	17	Keith Gary	DE	Oklahoma
2	44	Anthony Washington	DB	Fresno State
3	73	Rick Donnalley	Center	North Carolina
4	100	Robbie Martin	WR	Cal Poly-San Luis Obispo
5	127	Ricky Martin	WR	New Mexico
6	156	Bryan Hinkle	LB	Oregon
7	183	David Little	LB	Florida
8	209	Frank Wilson	RB	Rice
9	239	James Hunter	Tackle	USC
10	265	Mike Mayock	DB	Boston College
11	292	Rick Trocano	QB	Pittsburgh

Houston at Pittsburgh {Monday Night Football}

The Steelers scored on the first series of the game, but they had to settle for a 19-yard Dave Trout field goal after getting a 1st-and-goal at the Houston 2. A pass by Terry Bradshaw to Benny Cunningham was incomplete on first down, running back Frank Pollard gained 1 yard on second down and then lost that yard on third down, forcing Pittsburgh to settle for three points. the Steelers made up for their early inconsistency in their second series, marching 89 yards in 10 plays to take a 10-0 lead on Bradshaw's 46-yard scoring pass to Jim Smith 26 seconds before the end of the first quarter. Houston and Pittsburgh exchanged turnovers midway through the second period, and the Oilers used Vernon Perry's 12-yard return of an interception of a Bradshaw pass to set up a 34-yard field goal by Tony Fritsch to bring Houston within 10-3. The Oilers closed to within 13-10 two minutes into the fourth quarter on a 52-yard pass from Stabler to Dave Casper. The Oilers would tie the game on Fritsch 44-yard field goal, but the Steelers would put the game away on a Terry Bradshaw 6-yard TD pass to John Stallworth and a Franco Harris 1 yard TD run.

1982 Pittsburgh Steelers

The Steelers returned to the playoffs after missing the playoffs for two years. This was also the Steelers 50th Anniversary season. Although the season was shortened because of the 1982 strike, the Steelers finished with a strong 6–3 record, good enough for fourth in the AFC. Although division standings were thrown out because of the strike, the Steelers unofficially finished second in the AFC Central, one game behind defending AFC Champion Cincinnati. The 1982 season is best remembered as the final seasons for Hall of Famers Lynn Swann and Jack Ham and the "unofficial" final season of fellow Hall of Famer Terry Bradshaw, who would miss much of the 1983 season due to injuries before retiring. On the flip side, it would also be the first year of placekicker Gary Anderson and the first year of the team using a 3-4 defense, a style still used by the team as of 2019. The Steelers would lose in the first round of the playoffs to the San Diego Chargers, in what would be the last home playoff game for the Steelers for the next ten years. Jack Lambert {MLB}, Mike Webster {C} and Donnie Shell {S} were selected to various first team All-Pro teams.

Terry Bradshaw led the team in passing with 1,768 yards and threw 17 touchdown passes. Franco Harris led the team in rushing with 604 yards. Harris led the team in receptions with 31. John Stallworth led the team with 441 receiving yards and 7 TD receptions. Donnie Shell and Dwayne Woodruff led the team with 5 interceptions.

PITTSBURGH			1982			6-4	Game Highlights
9/13/1982	MNF	@	Dallas	36	28	W	Bradshaw 246 pass yards-3 TD pass/Anderson 3 FGs
9/19/1982		vs	CINCINNATI	26	20	W	Bradshaw 298 pass yards-3 TD pass/Anderson 2 FGs
11/21/1982		@	Houston Oilers	24	10	W	Bradshaw 228 pass yards-3 TD pass/Smith TD catch
11/28/1982		@	Seattle	0	16	L	Steelers commit 5 turnovers-held to 218 total yards
12/5/1982		vs	KANSAS CITY	35	14	W	Stallworth 6 catch-107 yards-2 TD catch/Harris rush TD
12/12/1982		@	Baltimore Colts	0	13	L	Steelers commit 4 turnover-held to 94 total yards
12/19/1982		@	Cleveland	9	10	L	Bradshaw 4 INTs-TD pass to Stallworth
12/26/1982		vs	NEW ENGLAND	37	14	W	Bradshaw 282 pass yards-2 TD pass/Anderson 3 FGs
1/2/1983		vs	CLEVELAND	37	21	W	**Rodgers blocked punt return TD**/ Bradshaw 269 pass yards
1/9/1983		vs	**SAN DIEGO**	28	31	L	**Ruff fumble recovery TD**/Stallworth 8 catch-116 yards-TD

Schedule courtesy of Steve's Football Bible LLC

1982 AFC Central	W	L	T	PCT	DIV	CONF	PF	PA
Cincinnati Bengals	7	2	0	.778	3–1	6–2	232	177
Pittsburgh Steelers	**6**	**3**	**0**	**.667**	**3–1**	**5–3**	**204**	**146**
Cleveland Browns	4	5	0	.444	2–2	4–3	140	182
Houston Oilers	1	8	0	.111	0–4	1–5	136	245

Pittsburgh at Dallas {Monday Night Football}

Terry Bradshaw drilling passes to his wide receivers, John Stallworth and Jim Smith, threw three touchdown passes as the Pittsburgh Steelers defeated the Dallas Cowboys, 36-28, tonight in the National Football League's first Monday game of the season. Pittsburgh exploded for 17 points in the third quarter to overcome a 14-13 deficit as the Steelers capitalized on a blocked punt and two interceptions. Gary Anderson, a rookie obtained from Buffalo last week, kicked a 40-yard field goal with 1:02 left to lock up the victory. The Steelers had to overcome four touchdown passes by White, including two in the final quarter. Interceptions by Rick Woods and Jack Ham put the Steelers in position for Bradshaw's second touchdown pass to Smith, a 15-yarder, and Anderson's 26-yard field goal. Stallworth, who caught an 8-yard scoring pass in the first half, grabbed a 21-yard pass to set up the field goal. Anderson also kicked a 43-yard field goal in the fourth quarter before Dallas rallied as White threw touchdown passes of 45 yards to Tony Hill and 5 yards to the tight end Billie Joe DuPree. Bradshaw's other touchdown pass came in the second period, a 7-yard strike to Smith that gave Pittsburgh a 13-7 lead.

1982 NFL Draft

Round	Choice	Player	Position	School
1	12	Walter Abercrombie	RB	Baylor
2	43	John Meyer	Tackle	Arizona State
3	70	Mike Merriweather	LB	Pacific
4	97	Rick Woods	DB	Boise State
5	124	Ken Dallafior	Tackle	Minnesota
6	155	Mike Perko	DT	Utah State
6	167	Craig Bingham	LB	Syracuse
7	172	Edmund Nelson	DT	Auburn
7	182	Emil Boures	Center	Pittsburgh
8	209	John Goodson	Punter	Texas
9	236	Mike Hirn	TE	Central Michigan
10	267	Sal Sunseri	LB	Pittsburgh
11	293	Mikal Abdul-Saboor	Guard	Morgan State
12	320	Al Hughes	DE	Western Michigan

1982 AFC Wild Card

The game began disastrously for the Chargers when James Brooks fumbled the opening kickoff, which was recovered for a touchdown by Guy Ruff of the Steelers. But San Diego battled back, winning by overcoming an 11-point deficit in the fourth quarter. Quarterback Dan Fouts threw for 333 yards and three touchdowns with no interceptions to lead his team to victory. Quarterback Terry Bradshaw threw for 325 yards and two touchdowns and scored a rushing touchdown in his final postseason game but was intercepted twice. Chargers running back Chuck Muncie rushed for 126 yards and caught a pass for 12, while tight end Kellen Winslow caught seven passes for 102 yards and two touchdowns. Steelers receiver John Stallworth caught eight passes for 116 yards and a touchdown.

Amazingly, Brooks fumbled the next kickoff after Ruff's touchdown, but he managed to recover it on the 2-yard line. San Diego then drove inside the Steelers red zone where Rolf Benirschke made a 25-yard field goal to cut the score to 7–3. Pittsburgh responded with a 40-yard reception by receiver Jim Smith that set up a 1-yard touchdown run by Bradshaw near the end of the first quarter. In the second quarter, Brooks' 15-yard touchdown cut the score to 14–10. Later, Fouts' 33-yard completion to Wes Chandler set up his 10-yard touchdown pass to Eric Sievers to give the Chargers a 17–14 lead. The Steelers had a chance to tie or retake the lead with a drive into San Diego territory just before halftime, but Chargers safety Bruce Laird made a clutch interception to prevent them from scoring.

Bradshaw threw a 2-yard touchdown pass to tight end Bennie Cunningham in the third quarter, and later a 9-yard touchdown pass to Stallworth that gave the Steelers a 28–17 lead three plays into the fourth quarter. But this would be the end of his success as he completed only three of his next 11 passes in the final quarter. The next time Pittsburgh had the ball, cornerback Jeff Allen intercepted Bradshaw's pass and returned it eight yards to the Steelers 29-yard line. Pittsburgh defensive back Mel Blount intercepted a pass in the end zone on the second play of the ensuing drive, but it was eliminated by a holding penalty on linebacker Jack Ham. Five plays later, Fouts cut the score to 28–24 with an 8-yard touchdown pass to Winslow. Following six consecutive handoffs by Bradshaw, San Diego got the ball back on their own 36-yard line due to a 20-yard punt by John Goodson with four minutes left in the game. Four runs by Muncie moved the ball 33 yards to a third and 7 situation on the Steelers 12-yard line. On the next play, Fouts connected with Winslow on a screen pass, and the tight end took it all the way to the end zone for the game winning score with less than a minute left on the clock.

This marked Bradshaw's final appearance at Three Rivers Stadium. He sat out nearly all of the 1983 season with an elbow injury, appearing in just one half of a late-season game against the Jets in what turned out to be their final game at Shea Stadium. The game was also the final one of the career of Hall of Fame linebacker Jack Ham.

1/9/1983	Line/Total	1	2	3	4	Final
San Diego Chargers	{53.0}	3	14	0	14	31
Pittsburgh Steelers	{-1.5}	14	0	7	7	28

Scoring

Team	
Steelers	Guy Ruff special teams fumble recovery in end zone (Gary Anderson kick)
Chargers	Rolf Benirschke 25 yard field goal
Steelers	Terry Bradshaw 1 yard rush (Gary Anderson kick)
Chargers	James Brooks 18 yard rush (Rolf Benirschke kick)
Chargers	Eric Sievers 10 yard pass from Dan Fouts (Rolf Benirschke kick)
Steelers	Bennie Cunningham 2 yard pass from Terry Bradshaw (Gary Anderson kick)
Steelers	John Stallworth 14 yard pass from Terry Bradshaw (Gary Anderson kick)
Chargers	Kellen Winslow 8 yard pass from Dan Fouts (Rolf Benirschke kick)
Chargers	Kellen Winslow 12 yard pass from Dan Fouts (Rolf Benirschke kick)

1983 Pittsburgh Steelers

The 1983 Pittsburgh Steelers, coached by Chuck Noll, lost the Division Championship after finishing the NFL regular season in 1st place in the AFC Central with a 10-6 record. Jack Lambert {MLB} and Mike Webster {C} were selected to various first team All-Pro teams.

Cliff Stoudt led the team in passing with 2,553 yards and threw 12 touchdown passes. Franco Harris led the team in rushing with 1,007 yards and 5 rushing touchdowns. Calvin Sweeney led the team in receiving with 39 receptions for 577 yards and 5 TD receptions.

PITTSBURGH			1983		10-7		Game Highlights
9/4/1983		vs	DENVER	10	14	L	Stoudt 217 pass yards-3 INT/Harris rush TD
9/11/1983		@	Green Bay	25	21	W	Harris 118 rush yards-rush TD/Stoudt rush TD
9/18/1983		@	Houston Oilers	40	28	W	**Hinkle INT return TD**/Harris 115 rush yds-TD
9/25/1983		vs	NEW ENGLAND	23	28	L	Stoudt 265 pass yards-2 TD pass/Anderson 3 FG
10/2/1983		vs	HOUSTON OILERS	17	10	W	Pollard rush TD/Abercrombie TD catch
10/10/1983	MNF	@	Cincinnati	24	14	W	**Johnson & Clayton INT return TDs**/Woods TD
10/16/1983		vs	CLEVELAND BROWNS	44	17	W	**Merriweather INT return TD/Best fumble TD**
10/23/1983		@	Seattle	27	21	W	Harris 132 rush yards-rush TD/Anderson 2 FGs
10/30/1983		vs	TAMPA BAY	17	12	W	Stoudt 233 pass yards-TD pass to Capers
11/6/1983		vs	SAN DIEGO CHARGERS	26	3	W	**Blount fumble return TD**/Anderson 4 FGs
11/13/1983		@	Baltimore Colts	24	13	W	Sweeny 6 catch-104 yards-TD catch
11/20/1983		vs	MINNESOTA	14	17	L	Stoudt 168 pass yards-TD pass to Cunningham
11/24/1983	TH	@	Detroit	3	45	L	Steelers commit 5 turnovers/held to 218 yards
12/4/1983		vs	CINCINNATI	10	23	L	Steelers commit 5 turnovers/held to 154 yards
12/11/1983		@	New York Jets	34	7	W	Stoudt 2 TD pass to Sweeny/Bradshaw 2 TD pass
12/18/1983		@	Cleveland Browns	17	38	L	Malone 108 pass yards-TD pass to Harris
12/25/1983		@	**Los Angeles Raiders**	10	38	L	Stoudt 187 pass yards-TD pass to Stallworth

Schedule courtesy of Steve's Football Bible LLC

1983 AFC Central	W	L	T	PCT	DIV	CONF	PF	PA
Pittsburgh Steelers	**10**	**6**	**0**	**.625**	**4–2**	**8–4**	**355**	**303**
Cleveland Browns	9	7	0	.563	3–3	7–5	356	342
Cincinnati Bengals	7	9	0	.438	4–2	4–8	346	302
Houston Oilers	2	14	0	.125	1–5	1–11	288	460

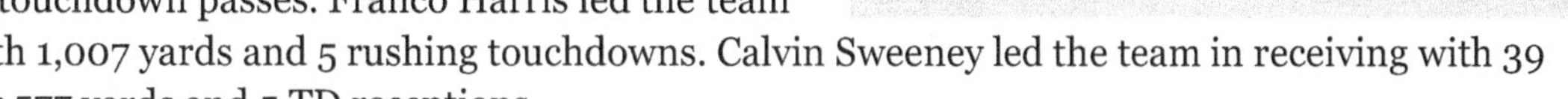

Pittsburgh at Cincinnati {Monday Night Football}

Ron Johnson and Harvey Clayton returned interceptions for fourth-quarter touchdowns tonight to help the Pittsburgh Steelers score a 24-14 victory over the Cincinnati Bengals. Johnson returned a pass by the Bengals' backup quarterback, Turk Schonert, 34 yards to put Pittsburgh ahead by 17-14 with 11 minutes 4 seconds left. Clayton ran 70 yards with another Schonert pass with 1:20 left. The Steelers, who had 20 sacks in their first 5 games, dropped Cincinnati quarterbacks a club-record 9 times for 77 yards in losses. Pittsburgh safety Rick Woods ran 38 yards for a touchdown with a first-quarter fumble recovery, and Gary Anderson kicked a 35-yard field goal for a 10-0 lead in the second quarter. The Bengals got a pair of touchdowns before the half on Pete

Johnson's 1-yard plunge and the rookie James Griffin's 41-yard interception return. The Bengals had a chance to tie after Ron Johnson's interception return for his first professional touchdown, but Jim Breech's 47-yard field- goal attempt hit the left upright with 3:40 to play.

Pittsburgh at New York Jets {Bradshaw's last game}

The Steelers, who clinched a playoff berth with the victory, did it with two names that evoked memories of Super Bowls past: Terry Bradshaw, the 35-year-old quarterback, and Franco Harris, the 33-year-old fullback. In his first appearance in 11 months following elbow surgery, Bradshaw threw for two touchdowns before reinjuring his right arm, and Harris produced the 47th 100-yard game of his career. The loss, which dropped the Jets to a 7-8 mark with one game remaining, ended with hundreds of young fans rushing the field and tearing up the sod for souvenirs. Bradshaw led the Steelers to a 14-0 edge before reinjuring his right elbow after tossing his second touchdown early in the second quarter. Cliff Stoudt replaced him. Stoudt helped the Steelers take a 20- 0 halftime edge by leading the team close enough for Gary Anderson to kick a pair of field goals, from 29 and 40 yards.

1983 NFL Draft

Round	Choice	Player	Position	School
1	21	Gabriel Rivera	DT	Texas Tech
2	52	Wayne Capers	WR	Kansas
3	79	Todd Seabaugh	LB	San Diego State
4	106	Bo Scott Metcalf	DB	Baylor
5	133	Paul Skansi	WR	Washington
5	140	Gregg Garrity	WR	Penn State
6	164	Eric Williams	DB	North Carolina State
7	191	Mark Kirchner	G	Baylor
8	199	Henry Odom	RB	South Carolina State
8	218	Craig Dunaway	TE	Michigan
9	244	Blake Wingle	G	UCLA
10	275	Roosevelt Straughter	DB	N.E. Louisiana
11	302	Mark Raugh	TE	West Virginia
12	330	Roger Wiley	RB	Sam Houston State

1983 AFC Divisional Playoffs

The Raiders scored three touchdowns in the third quarter en route to a 38–10 win over the Steelers, who were playing without Hall of Fame quarterback Terry Bradshaw due to injury.

In the first quarter, a 15-yard run by Steelers running back Frank Pollard and Cliff Stoudt's 44-yard completion to Wayne Capers sparked a 78-yard drive, but when faced with fourth down and inches near the goal line, they opted for kicker Gary Anderson's 17-yard field goal. The Steelers defense forced a punt on the next drive, but Ray Guy's 34-yard kick pinned them on their own 14-yard line, and on the next play, Raiders defensive back Lester Hayes returned an interception 18 yards for a touchdown, making the score 7–3.

After forcing a punt, Los Angeles running back Marcus Allen started off a drive with two carries for 13 yards. Then Jim Plunkett got his team rolling, completing a 9-yard pass to tight end Todd Christensen, a 17-yard pass to Allen, and two passes to Cliff Branch for 34 yards, moving the ball to the Steelers 5-yard line. Allen eventually finished the drive with a 4-yard touchdown run, increasing the

Raiders lead to 14–3 in the second quarter. Later on, after Los Angeles received a Steelers punt with 1:02 left in the half, Allen's 21-yard run and Plunkett's 17-yard completion to Branch set up a 45-yard field goal from Chris Bahr, giving the Raiders a 17–3 halftime lead.

The Raiders then scored three touchdowns in the third quarter to put the game out of reach. First, they took the opening kickoff and stormed 72 yards to a 9-yard touchdown run by Kenny King. Then after a punt, Allen scored on a 49-yard touchdown run, increasing his team's lead to 31–3. Pittsburgh managed to respond with Stoudt's 58-yard touchdown pass to receiver John Stallworth. But Los Angeles stormed right back, scoring on Frank Hawkins' 2-yard touchdown run to make the score 38–10. This turned out to be the last score of the game, as both teams' defenses took over during the fourth quarter.

Allen finished the game with 121 rushing yards and two touchdowns on just 13 carries, while also catching five passes for 38 yards. Raiders defensive end Lyle Alzado had 2.5 sacks.

1/1/1984	Line/Total	1	2	3	4	Final
Pittsburgh Steelers	{43.0}	3	0	7	0	10
Los Angeles Raiders	{-7.0}	7	10	21	0	38

Scoring

Team	
Steelers	Gary Anderson 17 yard field goal
Raiders	Lester Hayes 18 yard interception return (Chris Bahr kick)
Raiders	Marcus Allen 4 yard rush (Chris Bahr kick)
Raiders	Chris Bahr 45 yard field goal
Raiders	Kenny King 9 yard rush (Chris Bahr kick)
Raiders	Marcus Allen 49 yard rush (Chris Bahr kick)
Steelers	John Stallworth 58 yard pass from Cliff Stoudt (Gary Anderson kick)
Raiders	Frank Hawkins 2 yard rush (Chris Bahr kick)

1984 Pittsburgh Steelers

Most of the stars from the 1970s had departed, but the Steelers showed signs of their past glory by amassing a 9–7 record to capture the AFC Central Title again. The highlight of the season was an October 14 win over the 49ers in San Francisco. It was the only loss the 49ers suffered all season. Also serving up highlights that season was WR Louis Lipps who won the Offensive Rookie of the Year. In the playoffs the Steelers stunned the Broncos 24–17 in Denver to earn a trip to the AFC Championship. However, the Steelers season would end with a 45–28 thrashing at the hands of the Dolphins in Miami. This season was the last time the Steelers appeared in a playoff game until 1989, marking the end of the long lived and storied Steel Curtain. 1984 would prove to be somewhat of a transition year for the Steelers, as it would mark the final season of several key members of their 1970s dynasty -- most notably Jack Lambert (who missed several games during the season due to a recurring turf toe injury), but also Larry Brown and Craig Colquitt -- as well as the retirement of Mel Blount in mid-March and the unexpected retirement of Terry Bradshaw in late July. Louis Lipps {WR} and Mike Merriweather {LB} were selected to various first team All-Pro teams.

Mark Malone led the team in passing with 2,137 yards and threw 16 touchdown passes. Frank Pollard led the team in rushing with 851 yards and 6 rushing touchdowns. John Stallworth led the team in receiving with 80 receptions for 1,395 yards and 11 TD receptions. Donnie Shell led the team with 7 interceptions.

PITTSBURGH			1984			10-8	Game Highlights
9/2/1984		vs	KANSAS CITY	27	37	L	Lipps 6 catch-183 yards-2 TD catch
9/6/1984	TH	@	New York Jets	23	17	W	Woodley 187 pass yds-2 TD pass/Anderson 3 FG
9/16/1984		vs	LOS ANGELES RAMS	24	14	W	**Washington INT return TD**/Woodley 2 TD pass
9/23/1984		@	Cleveland	10	20	L	**Washington INT return TD**/Anderson FG
10/1/1984	MNF	vs	CINCINNATI	38	17	W	**Woodruff & Shell INT return TDs**/Woodley 252 yds
10/7/1984		vs	MIAMI	7	31	L	Malone 228 pass yards/Pollard rush TD
10/14/1984		@	San Francisco	20	17	W	Stallworth 6 catch-78 yards-TD catch/Erenberg TD
10/21/1984		@	Indianapolis Colts	16	17	L	Stallworth 5 catch-101 yards/Lipps TD catch
10/28/1984		vs	ATLANTA	35	10	W	**Woodruff fumble return TD**/Stallworth 2 TD catch
11/4/1984		vs	HOUSTON OILERS	35	7	W	**Hinkle fumble return TD**/Stallworth 3 TD catch
11/11/1984		@	Cincinnati	20	22	L	Stallworth 7 catch-76 yds/Anderson 2 FG/Lipps TD
11/19/1984	MNF	@	New Orleans	24	27	L	**Lipps punt return TD**-TD catch-4 catch-81 yards
11/25/1984		vs	SAN DIEGO	52	24	W	Stallworth 7 catch-116 yards-3 TD catch/Lipps TD
12/2/1984		@	Houston Oilers	20	23	L	Malone 193 pass yards-2 TD pass/Lipps TD catch
12/9/1984		vs	CLEVELAND	23	20	W	Lipps 3 catch-97 yards-TD catch/Pollard rush TD
12/16/1984		@	Los Angeles Raiders	13	7	W	Abercrombie 111 rush yards/Pollard rush TD
12/30/1984		@	**Denver**	**24**	**17**	**W**	Pollard 99 rush yards-2 rush TD/Lipps TD catch
1/6/1985		@	**Miami**	**28**	**45**	**L**	Stallworth 4 catch-111 yards-2 TD catch

Schedule courtesy of Steve's Football Bible LLC

Pittsburgh at Indianapolis Colts

This game was particularly frustrating to Steeler fans. One week previously, the Steelers beat the 49ers in San Francisco – becoming the solitary team to achieve this as the 49ers finished 15-1 on the way to winning the Super Bowl. Then coming back east to play one of the worst teams of the season, the Indianapolis Colts – who had only two wins at that point and were to win just four games for the season – they lost on a last-minute improbable play after leading throughout the game. The Colts' third-string quarterback, Mike Pagel, came off the bench in the third quarter and was leading a final minute drive from their 20. On the Colts 40 with 34 seconds left, Pagel avoided a near sack, scrambled right and threw down the middle of the field to WR Bernard Henry. The ball however went directly to the hands of Steeler CB Sam Washington who bobbled the ball. Between Washington and a few other Steeler defenders, WR Ray Butler burst through the gap, snatched the ball in the air and ran untouched 54 yards for the touchdown. The extra point sealed the game.

1984 AFC Central	W	L	T	PCT	DIV	CONF	PF	PA
Pittsburgh Steelers	**9**	**7**	**0**	**.563**	**3–3**	**6–6**	**387**	**310**
Cincinnati Bengals	8	8	0	.500	5–1	6–6	339	339
Cleveland Browns	5	11	0	.313	3–3	4–8	250	297
Houston Oilers	3	13	0	.188	1–5	3–9	240	437

1984 NFL Draft

Round	Choice	Player	Position	School
1	23	Louis Lipps	WR	Southern Mississippi
2	52	Chris Kolodziejski	TE	Wyoming
4	108	Weegie Thompson	WR	Florida State
4	111	Terry Long	Guard	East Carolina
5	135	Van Hughes	DT	Southwest Texas State
6	164	Chris Brown	DB	Notre Dame
7	191	Scott Campbell	QB	Purdue
8	220	Randy Rasmussen	Center	Minnesota
9	247	Rich Erenberg	RB	Colgate
10	276	Kirk McJunkin	Tackle	Texas
11	303	Elton Veals	RB	Tulane
12	332	Gernandars Gillespie	RB	William Jewell
13	359	Duane Gunn	WR	Indiana
14	388	Tom Dixon	Center	Michigan
15	415	Phillip Boren	Tackle	Arkansas

1984 AFC Divisional Playoffs

Steelers running back Frank Pollard led the team to victory with 99 rushing yards, 4 receptions for 48 yards, and two touchdowns, the second in the game's closing minutes to the put Pittsburgh ahead for good.

The Broncos got their first chance to score after the opening drive, in which Rulon Jones's sack of Steelers quarterback Mark Malone forced a fumble that was recovered by defensive end Andre Townsend on the Steelers 23-yard line. But Denver only gained 1 yard with their next three plays and Rich Karlis missed a 39-yard field goal attempt. On the next play, Denver's Tom Jackson recovered a fumbled snap from Malone on the Steelers 22 set up quarterback John Elway's 9-yard touchdown pass to Jim Wright. Pittsburgh responded by moving the ball 62 yards to the Broncos 11-yard line, where Gary Anderson's 28-yard field goal made the score 7-3. Denver then drove to a 3rd and goal from the Steelers 6-yard line, only to lose the ball when Elway threw a pass that was intercepted by Pittsburgh lineman Gary Dunn. Late in the second quarter, Pollard rushed 4 times for 45 yards on a 78-yard drive that ended with his 1-yard touchdown run, giving the Steelers a 10-7 lead with 1:14 left in the half.

Denver tied the game in the third period when safety Roger Jackson blocked a punt give them a first and goal on the Pittsburgh 4-yard line, leading to Karlis' 21-yard field goal. The next time Denver got the ball, they drove 54 yards to take a 17-10 lead on Elway's 20-yard touchdown pass to Steve Watson (who finished with 11 receptions for 177 yards). But the Steelers tied the game with quarterback Mark Malone's 10-yard touchdown to Louis Lipps. With 3 and half minutes left in the game, Pittsburgh drove into position for Anderson to attempt a go-ahead field goal, but he missed the kick from 26 yards. A few plays later, Steelers safety Eric Williams intercepted a pass from Elway and returned it 28 yards to the Broncos' 2-yard line to set up Pollard's winning 1-yard touchdown run.

Malone finished the game with 227 passing yards and a touchdown. Elway threw for 184 yards and two scores but was sacked four times and intercepted twice. This was Elway's first playoff game as a starter; because of the Broncos' elimination, he was denied the opportunity to play in the only Super Bowl to be held at his college home field, Stanford Stadium. The Steelers outgained Denver in total yards 381-250 and held them to just 51 yards on the ground. Running back Sammy Winder, who rushed for 1,153 yards during the season, was held to just 37 yards on 15 carries.

12/30/1984	Line/Total	1	2	3	4	Final
Pittsburgh Steelers	{36.0}	0	10	7	7	24
Denver Broncos	{-5.5}	7	0	10	0	17

Scoring

Team	
Broncos	James Wright 9 yard pass from John Elway (Rich Karlis kick)
Steelers	Gary Anderson 28 yard field goal
Steelers	Frank Pollard 1 yard rush (Gary Anderson kick)
Broncos	Rich Karlis 21 yard field goal
Broncos	Steve Watson 20 yard pass from John Elway (Rich Karlis kick)
Steelers	Louis Lipps 10 yard pass from Mark Malone (Gary Anderson kick)
Steelers	Frank Pollard 2 yard rush (Gary Anderson kick)

1984 AFC Championship Game

Pittsburgh racked up 455 yards of offense and converted 54% of their third downs, but it still wasn't enough to keep pace with Miami, who gained 569 yards in 71 plays en route to their fifth Super Bowl in franchise history. Dolphins quarterback Dan Marino led the Dolphins to a victory by throwing for 421 yards and 4 touchdowns (both AFC championship records) with 1 interception. Marino's record setting day was particularly noteworthy considering he threw his last pass with 11:05 left in the game. Steelers quarterback Mark Malone recorded 312 yards and 3 touchdowns but was intercepted 3 times.

Miami scored first on Marino's 40-yard touchdown pass to wide receiver Mark Clayton, but Pittsburgh countered with running back Rich Erenberg's 7-yard rushing touchdown. Then after Dolphins kicker Uwe von Schamann made a 26-yard field goal, the Steelers took the lead, 14–10, with wide receiver John Stallworth's 65-yard touchdown reception. Marino struck back with a 41-yard touchdown to wide receiver Mark Duper. Then Dolphins safety Lyle Blackwood picked off a pass from Malone and returned it 4 yards to the Steelers 35. After an 11-yard run by Tony Nathan, the Dolphins suffered a setback when a touchdown pass was wiped out by a penalty. But Marino easily shook this off, completing a 28-yard pass to tight end Joe Rose at the 1-yard line on the next play. Nathan finished off the drive with a 2-yard touchdown run to give Miami a 24-14 halftime lead.

On the opening drive of the second half, Marino completed a 36-yard touchdown pass to Duper. Then after Stallworth caught a 19-yard touchdown, the Dolphins scored two more touchdowns, including Marino's fourth score, to clinch the victory. Malone threw a 29-yard touchdown pass to Wayne Capers in the final period to close out the scoring. Duper finished the game with 5 receptions for 148 yards and 2 touchdowns. Clayton caught 4 passes for 95 yards and a score. Nathan rushed for 61 yards and a touchdown, while also catching 8 passes for 114 yards. Stallworth caught 4 passes for 111 yards and 2 touchdowns in the final postseason game of his Hall of Fame career.

1/6/1985	Line/Total	1	2	3	4	Final
Pittsburgh Steelers	{43.5}	7	7	7	7	28
Miami Dolphins	{-9.5}	7	17	14	7	45

Scoring

Team	
Dolphins	Mark Clayton 40 yard pass from Dan Marino (Uwe von Schamann kick)
Steelers	Rich Erenberg 7 yard rush (Gary Anderson kick)
Dolphins	Uwe von Schamann 26 yard field goal
Steelers	John Stallworth 65 yard pass from Mark Malone (Gary Anderson kick)
Dolphins	Mark Duper 41 yard pass from Dan Marino (Uwe von Schamann kick)
Dolphins	Tony Nathan 2 yard rush (Uwe von Schamann kick)
Dolphins	Mark Duper 36 yard pass from Dan Marino (Uwe von Schamann kick)
Steelers	John Stallworth 19 yard pass from Mark Malone (Gary Anderson kick)
Dolphins	Woody Bennett 1 yard rush (Uwe von Schamann kick)
Dolphins	Nat Moore 6 yard pass from Dan Marino (Uwe von Schamann kick)
Steelers	Wayne Capers 29 yard pass from Mark Malone (Gary Anderson kick)

1985 Pittsburgh Steelers

The Steelers challenged for the AFC Central most of the season, sitting at 6–5 after their first eleven games. However, losing 4 out of their final 5 games dropped the Steelers to a 7–9 overall record, their first season with a losing record in fourteen years. Louis Lipps {WR} and Gary Anderson {K} were selected to various first team All-Pro teams. **Louis Lipps set a franchise record with 2 punt returns for touchdowns.**

Mark Malone led the team in passing with 1,428 yards and threw 13 touchdown passes. Frank Pollard led the team in rushing with 991 yards. Walter Abercrombie led with 7 rushing touchdowns. John Stallworth led the team with 75 receptions. Louis Lipps led the team with 1,134 receiving yards and 12 TD receptions. Dwayne Woodruff led the team with 5 interceptions.

PITTSBURGH			1985			7-9	Game Highlights
9/8/1985		vs	INDIANAPOLIS COLTS	45	3	W	Lipps 9 catch-154 yards-3 TD catch/Malone 5 TDs
9/16/1985	MNF	@	Cleveland	7	17	L	Steelers held to 54 rush yards/Malone TD pass
9/22/1985		vs	HOUSTON OILERS	20	0	W	Malone 2 TD pass to Lipps/Anderson 2 FGs
9/30/1985	MNF	vs	CINCINNATI	24	37	L	Malone 374 pass yds-3 TD pass/Stallworth 151 yds
10/6/1985		@	Miami	20	24	L	Abercrombie 91 rush yds-rush TD/Anderson 2 FG
10/13/1985		@	Dallas	13	27	L	Abercrombie rush TD/Anderson 2 FGs
10/20/1985		vs	ST. LOUIS CARDINALS	23	10	W	Malone 184 pass yds/Lipps TD/Anderson 3 FG
10/27/1985		@	Cincinnati	21	26	L	**Lipps punt return TD**-TD catch from Woodley
11/3/1985		vs	CLEVELAND	10	9	W	Defense hold Browns to 153 yds/Abercrombie TD
11/10/1985		@	Kansas City	36	28	W	**Lipps punt return TD**/Anderson 5 FGs
11/17/1985		@	Houston Oilers	30	7	W	Pollard 123 rush yards-rush TD/Anderson 3 FGs
11/24/1985		vs	WASHINGTON	23	30	L	Lipps 5 catch-121 yards-TD catch/Anderson 3 FGs
12/1/1985		vs	DENVER	23	31	L	**Merriweather INT return TD**/Anderson 3 FGs
12/8/1985	SNF	@	San Diego Chargers	44	54	L	Woodley 287 pass yards-3 TD pass/Anderson 4 FG
12/15/1985		vs	BUFFALO	30	24	W	Lipps 4 catch-116 yards-TD catch/Anderson 3 FG
12/22/1985		@	New York Giants	10	28	L	Campbell TD pass to Stallworth/Anderson FG

Schedule courtesy of Steve's Football Bible LLC

1985 AFC Central	W	L	T	PCT	DIV	CONF	PF	PA
Cleveland Browns	8	8	0	.500	4–2	7–5	287	294
Cincinnati Bengals	7	9	0	.438	4–2	5–7	441	437
Pittsburgh Steelers	**7**	**9**	**0**	**.438**	**3–3**	**6–6**	**379**	**355**
Houston Oilers	5	11	0	.313	1–5	4–8	284	412

Buffalo at Pittsburgh

Buffalo entered the game with a 2-13 record to Pittsburgh's 7-8 record and were ten-point underdogs according to sportsbook odds. Buffalo was able to get on the scoreboard first thanks to a 77-yard rush the Steelers couldn't shut down that went the distance by Greg Bell. Jerry Butler scored on a 33-yard pass from Bruce Mathison and Don Wilson was able to grab a ball the Steelers' offense fumbled and carried it for 61 yards into the end zone to put Buffalo up 21-0. Scott Campbell found veteran receiver Louis Lipps open for a 13-yard pass and touchdown that gave the Steelers their first points in the game. The Steelers would then get a four-yard burst on the ground into the end zone from Frank Pollard to close the score to 21-14 after Gary Anderson converted both PAT's. Anderson was able to successfully kick two field goals (26-yard and 31-yard) in the third quarter, closing the gap to 1 point. Scott Norwood got just one final opportunity to give Buffalo points in the game when he kicked a 24-yard field goal. The Steelers answered with a 45-yarder. Walter Abercrombie would seal the win for the Steelers by plunging into the end zone on a 2-yard rush to set up Anderson for the PAT. Donnie Shell and Dwayne Woodruff both had picks in the game.

1985 NFL Draft

Round	Choice	Player	Position	School
1	20	Darryl Sims	DE	Wisconsin
2	47	Mark Behning	T	Nebraska
3	74	Liffort Hobley	DB	Louisiana State
4	101	Dan Turk	C	Wisconsin
5	136	Cam Jacobs	LB	Kentucky
6	160	Gregg Carr	LB	Auburn
7	187	Alan Andrews	TE	Rutgers
8	214	Harry Newsome	P	Wake Forest
9	241	Fred Small	LB	Washington
9	242	Andre Harris	DB	Minnesota
10	268	Oliver White	TE	Kentucky
11	300	Terry Matichak	DB	Missouri
12	327	Jeff Sanchez	DB	Georgia

50 • DAVID LITTLE
Linebacker   Ht: 6-1   Wt: 238

16 • MARK MALONE
Quarterback   Ht: 6-4   Wt: 225

56 • ROBIN COLE
Linebacker   Ht: 6-2   Wt: 225

1986 Pittsburgh Steelers

The 1986 Pittsburgh Steelers season was the franchise's 54th season as a member of the National Football League. The Steelers failed to improve upon their 7–9 record from 1985: they instead finished 6–10 and failed to reach the playoffs for a second consecutive season.

Mark Malone led the team in passing with 2,444 yards and threw 15 touchdown passes. Earnest Jackson led the team in rushing with 910 yards. Walter Abercrombie led with 6 rushing touchdowns. Abercrombie led the team with 47 receptions. Louis Lipps led with 590 receiving yards. Weegie Thompson led with 5 TD receptions.

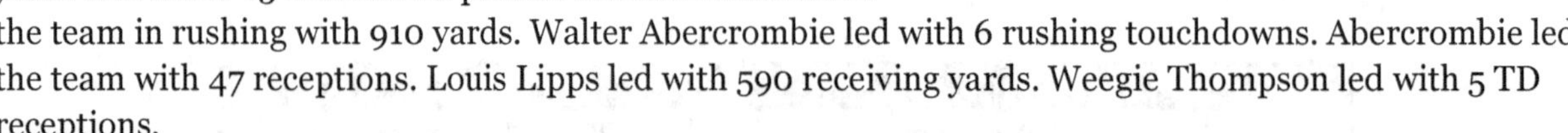

PITTSBURGH			1986		5-11		Game Highlights
9/7/1986		@	Seattle	0	30	L	Steelers held to 146 yards/commit 5 turnovers
9/15/1986	MNF	vs	DENVER	10	21	L	Steelers held to 30 rush yards/Erenberg rush TD
9/21/1986		@	Minnesota	7	31	L	Steelers held to 81 rush yds/Abercrombie TD catch
9/28/1986		@	Houston Oilers	22	16	W	Sweeney 4 catch-88 yards-TD catch/Anderson 3 FG
10/5/1986		vs	CLEVELAND	24	27	L	Malone 143 pass yards-TD pass-rush TD
10/13/1986	MNF	@	Cincinnati	22	24	L	Brister 191 pass yards-rush TD/Anderson 2 FGs
10/19/1986		vs	NEW ENGLAND	0	34	L	Steelers held to 168 yards/commit 4 turnovers
10/26/1986		vs	CINCINNATI	30	9	W	Jackson 132 rush yards-rush TD/Anderson 3 FGs
11/2/1986		vs	GREEN BAY	27	31	L	Malone 195 pass yards-3 TD pass to Thompson
11/9/1986		@	Buffalo	12	16	L	Jackson rush TD/Thompson TD catch
11/16/1986		vs	HOUSTON OILERS	21	10	W	Abercrombie & Jackson rush TD-Erenberg TD catch
11/23/1986		@	Cleveland Browns	31	37	L	Abercrombie & Malone 2 rush TD each
11/30/1986		@	Chicago	10	13	L	Newsome TD pass to Gothard/Anderson TD
12/7/1986		vs	DETROIT	27	17	W	Lipps 8 catch-150 yards-2 TD catch/Anderson 2 FG
12/14/1986		@	New York Jets	45	24	W	**Sanchez INT return TD**/Abercrombie 3 TDs
12/21/1986		vs	KANSAS CITY	19	24	L	Malone 351 pass yards-rush TD/Anderson 4 FGs

Schedule courtesy of Steve's Football Bible LLC

1986 AFC Central	W	L	T	PCT	DIV	CONF	PF	PA
Cleveland Browns	12	4	0	.750	5–1	10–2	391	310
Cincinnati Bengals	10	6	0	.625	3–3	7–5	409	394
Pittsburgh Steelers	**6**	**10**	**0**	**.375**	**3–3**	**4–8**	**307**	**336**
Houston Oilers	5	11	0	.313	1–5	3–9	274	329

Kansas City Chiefs at Pittsburgh

The Kansas City Chiefs, overcoming an offense that generated only three points, scored three first-half touchdowns on special teams plays and beat the Pittsburgh Steelers, 24-19. Deron Cherry fell on a blocked punt in the end zone to account for a first-quarter touchdown and Boyce Green and Lloyd Burruss scored in the second quarter on a 97-yard kickoff return and a 78-yard return of a blocked field goal. The Chiefs' offense, which produced only a 47-yard Nick Lowery field goal, was outgained 515 yards to 171 and generated only eight first downs to the Steelers' 28. But the Chiefs, who led 24-6 at halftime, held on to win despite failing to score in the second half. The Steelers lost even though quarterback Mark Malone completed 22 of 43 passes for 351 yards and ran 9 yards for a third-quarter touchdown. The Steelers had a chance to win when they marched to a first down at the Chiefs' 33 with 2:30 to play in the game. But Malone's off-balance pass was intercepted by cornerback Albert Lewis.

1986 NFL Draft

Round	Choice	Player	Position	School
1	9	John Rienstra	G	Temple
2	36	Gerald Williams	DE	Auburn
3	67	Bubby Brister	QB	N.E. Louisiana
4	94	Bill Callahan	DB	Pittsburgh
5	122	Erroll Tucker	DB	Utah
5	135	Brent Jones	TE	Santa Clara
6	148	Domingo Bryant	DB	Texas A&M
7	175	Rodney Carter	RB	Purdue
8	207	Cap Boso	TE	Illinois
9	234	Anthony Henton	LB	Troy State
10	260	Warren Seitz	WR	Missouri
11	287	Larry Station	LB	Iowa
12	314	Mike Williams	LB	Tulsa

34 • WALTER ABERCROMBIE
Running Back   Ht: 6-0   Wt: 210

31 • DONNIE SHELL
Safety   Ht: 5-11   Wt: 190

67 • GARY DUNN
Nose Tackle   Ht: 6-5   Wt: 265

1987 Pittsburgh Steelers

The team improved from a 6-10 record from 1986 and finishing 8-7 record and fail to reach the playoffs for a third straight season. Noll was renowned as a stoic character, but in complete contrast was his reaction to Jerry Glanville, the head coach of the Oilers. After the Steelers second meeting, Noll in the postgame handshake grabbed Glanville and told him he'd better watch out or he'd get jumped on. This was in reaction to Glanville's earlier comments on how the Oilers field was the 'house of pain' and his prediction that his players would intentionally hurt the Steelers. Mike Webster {C} was selected to various first team All-Pro teams.

Mark Malone led the team in passing with 1,896 yards and threw 6 touchdown passes. Earnest Jackson led the team in rushing with 696 yards. John Stallworth led the team with 41 receptions for 521 yards. Swayne Woodruff led the team with 5 interceptions.

PITTSBURGH			1987			8-7	Game Highlights
9/14/1987		vs	SAN FRANCISCO	30	17	W	**Hall fumble return TD**/Anderson 3 FGs
9/21/1987		@	Cleveland Browns	10	34	L	**Shell fumble return TD**/Anderson FG/Malone 5 Int
10/4/1987		@	Atlanta	28	12	W	STRIKE GAMES
10/11/1987		@	Los Angeles Rams	21	31	L	STRIKE GAMES
10/18/1987		vs	INDIANAPOLIS COLTS	21	7	W	STRIKE GAMES
10/25/1987		vs	CINCINNATI	23	20	W	**Hall INT return TD**/Stallworth 7 catch-100 yds/TD
11/1/1987		@	Miami	24	35	L	**Shell INT return TD**/Malone TD pass to Lockett
11/8/1987		@	Kansas City	17	16	W	Malone 157 pass ayrds-2 TD pass to Carter
11/15/1987		vs	HOUSTON OILERS	3	23	L	Steelers held to 170 yards-commit 3 turnovers
11/22/1987		@	Cincinnati	30	16	W	**Woodson INT return TD**/Anderson 3 FGs
11/29/1987		vs	NEW ORLEANS	16	20	L	**Woodruff INT return TD**/Abercrombie rush TD
12/6/1987		vs	SEATTLE	13	9	W	Pollard 106 rush yards-rush TD/Anderson 2 FGs
12/13/1987		@	San Diego Chargers	20	16	W	Pollard & Malone rush TDs-Anderson 2 FGs
12/20/1987		@	Houston Oilers	16	24	L	Malone 181 pass yards-rush TD/Anderson 3 FGs
12/26/1987	SAT	vs	CLEVELAND BROWNS	13	19	L	**Gowdy INT return TD**/Anderson 2 FGs

Schedule courtesy of Steve's Football Bible LLC

1987 AFC Central	W	L	T	PCT	DIV	CONF	PF	PA
Cleveland Browns	10	5	0	.667	5–1	8–3	390	239
Houston Oilers	9	6	0	.600	5–1	7–4	345	349
Pittsburgh Steelers	**8**	**7**	**0**	**.533**	**2–4**	**6–5**	**285**	**299**
Cincinnati Bengals	4	11	0	.267	0–6	3–9	285	370

82 • JOHN STALLWORTH
Wide Receiver Ht: 6-2 Wt: 202

Pittsburgh at San Diego Chargers

The Steelers improved to 8-5 with a 20-16 triumph, remaining tied with Cleveland atop the AFC Central. Pittsburgh trailed 9-0 in the first quarter, but quarterback Mark Malone and Frank Pollard ran for touchdowns and Gary Anderson kicked two field goals in the comeback victory. The Chargers outgained Pittsburgh 435 yards to 254, but San Diego committed five turnovers and Vince Abbott missed all three of his field-goal tries. The Steelers capitalized on a San Diego turnover with an 8-yard run by Pollard that cut the lead to 9-7 with 5:23 left in the half. Pittsburgh took over on the San Diego 38 when James muffed a punt, and Dwight Stones recovered for the Steelers. Pollard scored his fifth TD of the year four plays later. Pittsburgh took the lead for the first time, 14-9, when Malone was flushed from the pocket, but raced 7 yards to end zone at 6:36 of the third quarter. Anderson kicked a 43-yard field goal with 37 seconds remaining in the third quarter to extend Pittsburgh's lead to 17-9. The Steelers went ahead 20-9 with 9:04 to play when Anderson converted a 33-yard field goal. The Chargers lost three turnovers in Pittsburgh territory. Their only offensive points came on a pass of 15 yards from Fouts to Lionel James, making it 20-16 with 2:56 left. Fouts drove San Diego to the Steelers 24 with 20 seconds to play, but Wes Chandler, who had seven catches for 117 yards, dropped two passes and another was knocked away at the goal line by safety Thomas Everett.

1987 NFL Draft

Round	Choice	Player	Position	School
1	10	Rod Woodson	DB	Purdue
2	38	Delton Hall	DB	Clemson
3	66	Charles Lockett	WR	Long Beach State
4	94	Thomas Everett	DB	Baylor
5	122	Hardy Nickerson	LB	California
6	141	Tim Johnson	DT	Penn State
6	150	Greg Lloyd	LB	Fort Valley State
7	178	Chris Kelly	TE	Akron
8	205	Charles Buchanan	DE	Tennessee State
9	233	Joey Clinkscales	WR	Tennessee
10	261	Merril Hoge	RB	Idaho State
11	289	Paul Oswald	C	Kansas
12	317	Theo Young	TE	Arkansas

1988 Pittsburgh Steelers

Hall of Fame team founder and owner Art Rooney died at age 87 less than two weeks before the start of the season on August 25. The team wore AJR patches on the left shoulder the entire season in memory of "The Chief". The team finished the season at 5–11 failing to improve on their 8-7 record from 1987 and had their worst record since finishing an NFL-worst 1–13 in 1969. As of 2020, the 5–11 mark remains the team's worst record since 1969, and they have only finished with ten losses twice since, in 1999 and 2003. The Steelers got off to a disappointing start.] After winning their home opener against the Dallas Cowboys, the team lost six straight, their first six-game losing streak since 1969. The team never recovered after the skid, and at one point had a 2–10 record after a 27–7 loss to the Cleveland Browns. It was the Steelers worst start to a season since the merger. The Steelers did, however, finish the season on a positive note, winning 3 of their last 4 games to finish the season 5-11. To date, this represents the only time since the AFL-NFL merger the Steelers have finished the season in last place in their division. The Steelers saw two of its last three remaining players who won all four Super Bowls retire in wide receiver John Stallworth and strong safety Donnie Shell, who were both from the team's famous Class of 1974 that saw four players go on to the Pro Football Hall of Fame.

Bubby Brister led the team in passing with 2,634 yards and threw 11 touchdown passes. Merril Hoge led the team in rushing with 705 yards. Brister led the team with 6 rushing touchdowns. Hoge and Louis Lipps tied for the team lead in receptions with 50. Lipps led with 973 receiving yards and 5 TD receptions.

PITTSBURGH			1988			5-11	Game Highlights
9/4/1988		vs	DALLAS	24	21	W	Jackson 2 rush TD/Brister rush TD/Anderson FG
9/11/1988		@	Washington Redskins	29	30	L	Brister 280 pass yards-2 TD pass-rush TD
9/18/1988		vs	CINCINNATI	12	17	L	Steelers commit 6 turnovers/Brister TD pass to Lipps
9/25/1988		@	Buffalo	28	36	L	Brister 330 pass yards-2 TD pass-2 rush TD
10/2/1988		vs	CLEVELAND	9	23	L	Steelers held to 183 yards-5 turnovers/Anderson 3 FGs
10/9/1988		@	Phoenix Cardinals	14	31	L	**Woodson kickoff return TD**/Hoge TD catch
10/16/1988		vs	HOUSTON OILERS	14	34	L	Blackledge 251 pass yards-TD pass to Lockett
10/23/1988		vs	DENVER	39	21	W	Carter 105 rush yds- rush TD-TD catch/Anderson 6 FGs
10/30/1988		@	New York Jets	20	24	L	Brister 238 pass yards-TD pass to Carter/Anderson 2 FG
11/6/1988		@	Cincinnati	7	42	L	Steelers held to 198 total yards/Brister rush TD
11/13/1988		vs	PHILADELPHIA	26	27	L	Lipps 6 catch-171 yards-TD catch/Anderson 4 FGs
11/20/1988		@	Cleveland	7	27	L	Steelers commit 4 turnover/Carter rush TD
11/27/1988		vs	KANSAS CITY	16	10	W	Hoge rush TD/Anderson 3 FGs
12/4/1988	SNF	@	Houston Oilers	37	34	W	**Stone kickoff return TD**/Hoge 2 rush TD/Lipps 2 TD
12/11/1988		@	San Diego Chargers	14	20	L	Brister 206 pass yards-TD pass to Gothard-rush TD
12/18/1988		vs	MIAMI	40	24	W	**Woodruff & Jordan INT return TD**/Anderson 4 FGs

Schedule courtesy of Steve's Football Bible LLC

1988 AFC Central	W	L	T	PCT	DIV	CONF	PF	PA
Cincinnati Bengals	12	4	0	.750	4–2	8–4	448	329
Cleveland Browns	10	6	0	.625	4–2	6–6	304	288
Houston Oilers	10	6	0	.625	3–3	7–5	424	365
Pittsburgh Steelers	**5**	**11**	**0**	**.313**	**1–5**	**4–8**	**336**	**421**

1988 NFL Draft

Round	Choice	Player	Position	School
1	18	Aaron Jones	DE	Eastern Kentucky
2	44	Dermontti Dawson	C	Kentucky
3	70	Chuck Lanza	C	Notre Dame
5	121	Darin Jordan	LB	Northeastern
5	128	Jerry Reese	DT	Kentucky
6	155	Warren Williams	RB	Miami (FL)
7	182	Marc Zeno	WR	Tulane
8	209	Mark Nichols	DT	Michigan State
8	211	Mike Hinnant	TE	Temple
9	236	Gordie Lockbaum	RB	Holy Cross
10	252	John Jackson	T	Eastern Kentucky
11	295	Bobby Dawson	DB	Illinois
12	322	James Earle	LB	Clemson

Pittsburgh at Houston Oilers {Sunday Night Football}

After a Tony Zendejas field goal tied the score at three in the 2nd quarter, Dwight Stone returned the ensuing kickoff 92 yards to give the Steelers a 10-3 lead. The Oilers answered right back with 10 points of their own to take a 13-10 lead. Right before halftime, Bubby Brister hooked up with Louis Lipps for an 80-yard bomb and the Steelers had a 17-13 lead at the break. Early in the 3rd quarter when Brister once again connected with Lipps, this time on a 65-yard touchdown pass, and the Steelers were now ahead, 24-13. Lorenzo White answered with a 90-yard kickoff return and the Oilers were immediately back in the game, 24-20. Houston took the lead later in the quarter on a Warren Moon 2-yard touchdown run. Pittsburgh answered in the 4th and took a 31-27 lead on Merril Hoge's 2-yard touchdown run. The Oilers regained the lead late on another Warren Moon rushing touchdown. With time running out, Brister marched the Steelers down the field and hit Hoge with a 16-yard touchdown pass with less than 30 seconds left. Gary Anderson missed the extra point to give the Steelers a 37-34 lead and they would thwart the Oilers chance at a comeback and hold on for the victory.

53 · BRYAN HINKLE
Linebacker   Ht: 6-2   Wt: 220

6 · BUBBY BRISTER
Quarterback   Ht: 6-3   Wt: 210

62 · TUNCH ILKIN
Offensive Tackle   Ht: 6-3   Wt: 265

1989 Pittsburgh Steelers

They were considered a rebuilding team filled with many young players, especially after the release of longtime center Mike Webster in the offseason. The young team showed its inexperience in the first game of the season, when they lost at home to the archrival Cleveland Browns 51–0. The loss marked the Steelers worst defeat in franchise history. The following week wasn't much better, losing 41–10 to another division rival, the defending AFC Champion Cincinnati Bengals. However, the Steelers clinched the final playoff spot in the last week in the season with a 9–7 record. Chuck Noll, in his 21st season as the team's head coach, was named the NFL's Coach of the Year for the only time in his coaching career. In the first round of the playoffs, the Steelers would have a memorable come-from-behind overtime victory over the division-rival Houston Oilers 26–23, which saw Gary Anderson kick a game-winning, 50-yard field goal in the extra period. The following week, the Steelers nearly pulled off a major upset against the Denver Broncos at Mile High Stadium before losing 24–23 on a Melvin Bratton one-yard touchdown run with 2:22 remaining in the game. Though the Steelers would not make the playoffs again under Chuck Noll (missing in 1990 with an identical 9–7 record and again in 1991 at 7–9 despite a second place finish that year), the season did set the tone for the team's return to prominence in the 1990s under his successor, Bill Cowher. Rod Woodson {CB} was selected to various first team All-Pro teams.

Bubby Brister led the team in passing with 2,365 yards and threw 9 touchdown passes. Tim Worley led the team in rushing with 770 yards. Merril Hoge led with 8 rushing touchdowns. Louis Lipps led the team in receiving with 50 receptions for 944 yards and 5 TD receptions. Dwayne Woodruff led the team with 4 interceptions.

PITTSBURGH		1989			10-8	Game Highlights
9/10/1989	vs	CLEVELAND BROWNS	0	51	L	Steelers held to 53 total yards-commit 8 turnovers
9/17/1989	@	Cincinnati	10	41	L	Brister 244 pass yards-TD pass to Hill
9/24/1989	vs	MINNESOTA	27	14	W	Hoge & Worley rush TD/Anderson 2 FGs
10/1/1989	@	Detroit	23	3	W	Lipps 7 catch-126 yards-TD catch
10/8/1989	vs	CINCINNATI	16	26	L	Brister TD pass to Carter/Anderson 3 FGs
10/15/1989	@	Cleveland Browns	17	7	W	Blackledge 143 pass yards-TD pass to Carter
10/22/1989	@	Houston Oilers	0	27	L	Steelers held to 132 total yards-commit 4 turnovers
10/29/1989	vs	KANSAS CITY	23	17	W	Lipps 7 catch-130 yards-2 TD catch/Anderson 3 FGs
11/5/1989	@	Denver	7	34	L	Steelers 170 total yards/Brister TD pass to Carter
11/12/1989	vs	CHICAGO	0	20	L	Steelers commit 6 turnovers/Lipps 4 catch-112 yards
11/19/1989	vs	SAN DIEGO CHARGERS	20	17	W	**Woodson kickoff return TD**/Anderson 2 FGs
11/26/1989	@	Miami	34	14	W	**Woodruff fumble return TD**/Hoge 3 rush TD
12/3/1989	vs	HOUSTON OILERS	16	23	L	Hoge rush TD/Anderson 3 FGs
12/10/1989	@	New York Jets	13	0	W	Worley rush TD/Anderson 2 FGs
12/17/1989	vs	NEW ENGLAND PATRIOTS	28	10	W	Worley 104 rush yards-rush TD/Hoge 2 rush TD
12/24/1989	@	Tampa Bay	31	22	W	Lipps 4 catch-137 yds-2 TD catch/Worley 2 rush TD
12/31/1989	**@**	**Houston Oilers**	**26**	**23**	**W**	Hoge 100 rush yards-rush TD/Anderson 4 FGs
1/7/1990	**@**	**Denver**	**23**	**24**	**L**	Brister 229 pass yds-TD pass to Lipps-Anderson 3 FG

Schedule courtesy of Steve's Football Bible LLC

1989 AFC Central	W	L	T	PCT	DIV	CONF	PF	PA
Cleveland Browns	9	6	1	.594	3–3	6–5–1	334	254
Houston Oilers	9	7	0	.563	3–3	6–6	365	412
Pittsburgh Steelers	**9**	**7**	**0**	**.563**	**1–5**	**6–6**	**265**	**326**
Cincinnati Bengals	8	8	0	.500	5–1	6–6	404	285

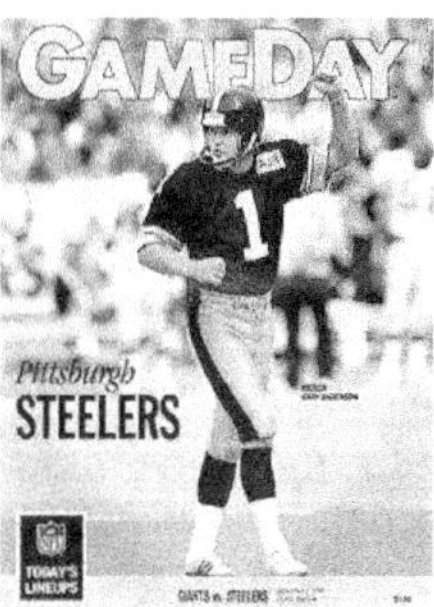

1989 NFL Draft

Round	Choice	Player	Position	School
1	7	Tim Worley	RB	Georgia
1	24	Tom Ricketts	T	Pittsburgh
2	34	Carnell Lake	DB	UCLA
3	61	Derek Hill	WR	Arizona
4	91	Jerrol Williams	LB	Purdue
5	118	David Arnold	DB	Michigan
6	144	Mark Stock	WR	Virginia Military Inst
7	174	David Johnson	DB	Kentucky
8	201	Chris Asbeck	DT	Cincinnati
9	228	A.J. Jenkins	DE	Fullerton State
10	258	Jerry Olsavsky	LB	Pittsburgh
11	285	Brian Slater	WR	Washington
12	312	Carlton Haselrig	G	Pittsburgh-Johnstown

1989 AFC Wild Card

Steelers defensive back Rod Woodson recovered a fumble to set up Gary Anderson's winning 50-yard field goal in overtime to give Pittsburgh the win. Houston took the opening kickoff and drove to the Steelers 40-yard line but were stopped there and Tony Zendejas missed a 55-yard field goal. Later in the quarter, Steelers rookie Jerry Olsavsky blocked a punt from Greg Montgomery and Pittsburgh recovered on the Oilers 23. Eventually facing fourth and 1 on the Houston 9-yard line, Steelers coach Chuck Noll decided to go for the first down. This paid off as running back Tim Worley took a pitch and ran all the way to the end zone, evading linebacker Robert Lyles and plowing right through safety Bubba McDowell on the way to a 7–0 Steelers lead with 2:36 left in the first quarter.

Houston responded on their next drive, moving the ball 96 yards to the Steelers 3-yard line, but could go no further and settled for a 26-yard Zendejas field goal. Then McDowell recovered a fumble from Worley on the Pittsburgh 41. From there the Oilers advanced to the 17-yard line, but when faced with fourth and 1 they decided to settle for another Zendejas field goal, cutting the score to 7–6. Pittsburgh struck back with a drive to the Oilers 9, featured a 49-yard run by Merril Hoge. However, they also ended up facing fourth and 1, and would settle for an Anderson field goal to put them up 10–6 going into halftime.

The field goal battle continued in the third quarter, with Zendejas kicking one more and Anderson adding another two, making the score 16–9 at the start of the fourth quarter. But quarterback Warren Moon finally got his team to the end zone with a 10-play, 80-yard drive to score on his 18-yard touchdown pass to Ernest Givins that tied the game. Following a Pittsburgh three-and-out, Harry Newsome's punt went just 25 yards to the Steelers 38-yard line. From there it took just five plays for Houston to take their first lead of the game, scoring on Moon's 9-yard pass touchdown pass to Givins that put them up 23–16 with 5:16 left in regulation. Starting from their own 18 after the kickoff, Pittsburgh drove 82 yards, featuring a 22-yard run by receiver Dwight Stone (the only time he touched the ball all game) on a reverse play, to score on Hoge's 2-yard touchdown run with 46 seconds left, tying the game and sending it into overtime.

Pittsburgh won the coin toss and received the ball first, but were quickly forced to punt, and another short kick from Newsome gave Houston the ball with great field position on the Steelers 45-yard line. On the Oilers first play, Moon handed the ball off to Lorenzo White, who was quickly leveled by Woodson and defensive end Tim Johnson, causing a fumble that Woodson recovered and returned four yards to the Oilers 46. From there, Pittsburgh could gain just 13 yards with a few Hoge carries before facing a fourth down. But it was enough for Anderson to kick a 50-yard field goal, his longest attempt of the season, which he sent perfectly through the uprights to give the Steelers the win. Hoge finished the game with 100 rushing yards on just 17 carries, along with three receptions for 26 yards. Moon threw for 315 yards and two touchdowns. Givins caught 11 passes for 136 yards. Pittsburgh won despite being outgained in total yards 380–289. Oilers coach Jerry Glanville was fired a few days after this game. This was a particularly satisfying win for the Steelers, who had started the season with a 51–0 loss to Cleveland and a 41–10 loss to Cincinnati. They had been shutout three times, outgained by their opponents in ten consecutive games, and had to recover from a 4–6 record to get into the playoffs by winning five of their last six games.

12/31/1989	Line/Total	1	2	3	4	OT	Final
Pittsburgh Steelers	{43.0}	7	3	3	10	3	26
Houston Oilers	{-6.5}	0	6	3	14	0	23

Scoring

Steelers	Tim Worley 9 yard rush (Gary Anderson kick)
Oilers	Tony Zendejas 26 yard field goal
Oilers	Tony Zendejas 35 yard field goal
Steelers	Gary Anderson 25 yard field goal
Oilers	Tony Zendejas 26 yard field goal
Steelers	Gary Anderson 30 yard field goal
Steelers	Gary Anderson 48 yard field goal
Oilers	Ernest Givins 18 yard pass from Warren Moon (Tony Zendejas kick)
Oilers	Ernest Givins 9 yard pass from Warren Moon (Tony Zendejas kick)
Steelers	Merril Hoge 2 yard rush (Gary Anderson kick)
Steelers	Gary Anderson 50 yard field goal

1989 AFC Divisional Playoffs

The Broncos recovered from two early 10-point deficits to eventually win on a 71-yard drive that was capped by Mel Bratton's 1-yard touchdown run with 2:27 left in the game. For the second game in a row, Steelers running back Merril Hoge had a superb performance, rushing for 120 yards on 16 carries and catching eight passes for 60 yards. But this time it wasn't enough to lift his team to victory. Broncos receiver Mark Jackson caught five passes for 111 yards.

The Steelers jumped to an early 3–0 lead with a 32-yard field goal by Gary Anderson. On the first play of the second quarter, Hoge ripped off a 45-yard run, the longest of his career. He ended up rushing for 60 yards on the Steelers drive, including a 7-yard touchdown carry to increase the Steelers lead to 10–0. Denver responded with a 12-play, 75-yard drive to score on Bratton's

1-yard touchdown run, cutting the lead to 10–7. But the Steelers stormed right back, with Bubby Brister completing a 25-yard pass to tight end Mike Mularkey and rookie running back Tim Worley contributing a 19-yard carry on the way to a 9-yard scoring reception by Louis Lipps. Shortly before the end of the half, Broncos kicker David Treadwell made a 43-yard field goal, putting the score at 17-10 going into halftime.

In the third quarter, Broncos defenders Karl Mecklenburg and Greg Kragen forced a fumble from Worley that defensive back Tyrone Braxton recovered on the Steelers 37-yard line, setting up quarterback John Elway's 37-yard touchdown pass to wide receiver Vance Johnson to tie the game at 17. Brister struck back, completing a 19-yard screen to Hoge and a 30-yard pass to rookie receiver Mark Stock on the way to a 35-yard Anderson field goal. Then in the fourth quarter, Pittsburgh defensive back Thomas Everett intercepted an Elway pass and returned it 26 yards to midfield, setting up Anderson's 32-yard field goal to make the score 23–17. The Steelers appeared to have a big chance to put the game away following a Denver punt. But after a productive start to their drive, Braxton tackled Hodge 1-yard short of a first down at the Denver 41 to bring up fourth down and force a punt.

Now with seven minutes left in the game, Elway led the Broncos 71 yards in nine plays, including a 36-yard completion to Jackson and a 15-yarder to Ricky Nattiel. Bratton finished the drive with his second 1-yard touchdown of the game, this one with 2:27 left. This time, the Steelers had no ability to respond. On first down of their ensuring possession, Brister fired a pass to a wide-open Stock, but he tried to turn upfield before securing the catch and it fell to the turf incomplete. Then after another incompletion, Brister fumbled a low snap from backup center Chuck Lanza (filling in for injured All-Pro center Dermontti Dawson) in shotgun formation, and Broncos safety Randy Robbins recovered the ball to secure the win. Brister completed 19/29 passes for 224 yards and a touchdown. Elway threw for 239 yards and a touchdown, with one interception, and rushed for 44 yards.

1/7/1990	Line/Total	1	2	3	4	Final
Pittsburgh Steelers	{38.0}	3	14	3	3	23
Denver Broncos	{-10.0}	0	10	7	7	24

Scoring

Team	
Steelers	Gary Anderson 32 yard field goal
Steelers	Merril Hoge 7 yard rush (Gary Anderson kick)
Broncos	Mel Bratton 1 yard rush (David Treadwell kick)
Steelers	Louis Lipps 9 yard pass from Bubby Brister (Gary Anderson kick)
Broncos	David Treadwell 43 yard field goal
Broncos	Vance Johnson 37 yard pass from John Elway (David Treadwell kick)
Steelers	Gary Anderson 35 yard field goal
Steelers	Gary Anderson 32 yard field goal
Broncos	Mel Bratton 1 yard rush (David Treadwell kick)

1990 Pittsburgh Steelers

The Steelers did not score an offensive touchdown until the 5th game of the season but did rebound to a 9–7 record (the same they posted the previous season). Unlike the previous season, 9–7 was not enough to gain a playoff berth. The Steelers continued to show improvement overcoming a 1-3 start to find themselves in a showdown with the Oilers in Houston for the AFC's final playoff spot in the final game of the season. However, the Steelers were never in the game as the Oilers beat the Steelers 34-14 ending their season without the playoffs. Rod Woodson {CB} was selected to various first team All-Pro teams.

Bubby Brister led the team in passing with 2,725 yards and threw 20 touchdown passes. Merril Hoge led the team in rushing with 772 yards and 7 rushing touchdowns. Louis Lipps led the team in receiving with 50 receptions for 682 yards. Eric Green led with 7 TD receptions. Woodson led the team with 5 interceptions.

PITTSBURGH			1990			9-7	Game Highlights
9/9/1990		@	Cleveland Browns	3	13	L	Steelers held to 49 rush yards-commit 3 turnovers
9/16/1990	SNF	vs	HOUSTON OILERS	20	9	W	**Johnson INT return TD/Woodson punt return Td**
9/23/1990		@	Los Angeles Raiders	3	20	L	Steelers held to 90 rush yards-commit 3 turnovers
9/30/1990		vs	MIAMI	6	28	L	Steelers held to 41 rush yards-commit 3 turnovers
10/7/1990		vs	SAN DIEGO	36	14	W	Brister 2 TD pass to Green/Anderson 2 FGs
10/14/1990		@	Denver	34	17	W	Brister 353 pass yards-3 TD pass to Green
10/21/1990		@	San Francisco	7	27	L	Steelers held to 200 total yards/Brister TD pass
10/29/1990	MNF	vs	LOS ANGELES RAMS	41	10	W	Hoge rush TD-2 TD catch/Brister 4 TD pass
11/4/1990		vs	ATLANTA	21	9	W	Williams 89 rush yards-rush TD/Brister 2 TD pass
11/18/1990	SNF	@	Cincinnati	3	27	L	Brister 112 pass yards/Anderson FG
11/25/1990		@	New York Jets	27	7	W	Brister 187 pass yards-2 TD pass/Hoge rush TD
12/2/1990		vs	CINCINNATI	12	16	L	Steelers held to 79 rush yards/Anderson 4 FGs
12/9/1990		vs	NEW ENGLAND	24	3	W	Hoge 117 rush yards-2 rush TD/Green TD catch
12/16/1990		@	New Orleans	9	6	W	Steelers win FG contest/Anderson 3 FGs
12/23/1990		vs	CLEVELAND BROWNS	35	0	W	Brister 139 pass yards-4 TD pass/Mularkey 2 TD
12/30/1990	SNF	@	Houston Oilers	14	34	L	Hoge 2 rush TD/Brister 240 pass yards

Schedule courtesy of Steve's Football Bible LLC

1990 AFC Central	W	L	T	PCT	DIV	CONF	PF	PA
Cincinnati Bengals	9	7	0	.563	5–1	8–4	360	352
Houston Oilers	9	7	0	.563	4–2	8–4	405	307
Pittsburgh Steelers	**9**	**7**	**0**	**.563**	**2–4**	**6–6**	**292**	**240**
Cleveland Browns	3	13	0	.188	1–5	2–10	228	462

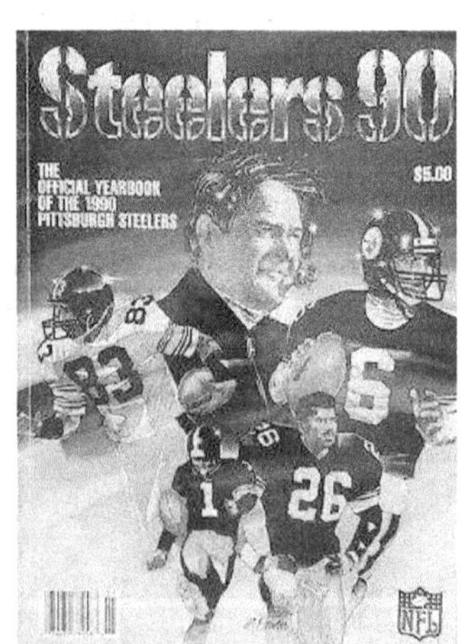

1990 NFL Draft

Round	Choice	Player	Position	School
1	21	Eric Green	TE	Liberty
2	43	Kenny Davidson	DE	Louisiana State
3	70	Neil O'Donnell	QB	Maryland
3	81	Craig Veasey	DT	Houston
4	97	Chris Calloway	WR	Michigan
5	128	Barry Foster	RB	Arkansas
6	155	Ron Heard	WR	Bowling Green
7	182	Dan Grayson	LB	Washington State
8	209	Karl Dunbar	DT	Louisiana State
9	239	Gary Jones	DB	Texas A&M
10	266	Eddie Miles	LB	Minnesota-Duluth
11	293	Justin Strzelczyk	T	Maine
12	319	Richard Bell	RB	Nebraska

95 • GREG LLOYD
Linebacker   Ht: 6-2   Wt: 224

43 • EARNEST JACKSON
Running Back   Ht: 5-9   Wt: 225

37 • CARNELL LAKE
Strong Safety   Ht: 6-1   Wt: 205

1991 Pittsburgh Steelers

The Steelers struggled early as Neil O'Donnell took over from Bubby Brister at quarterback. The Steelers ended the season winning their last two games, 17–10, over the Cincinnati Bengals and Cleveland Browns at Three Rivers Stadium to finish with a 7–9 record. Following the season Chuck Noll announced his retirement, ending his 23-year career in which, he won four Super Bowls while posting an overall record of 209–156–1.

Neil O'Donnell led the team in passing with 1,963 yards and threw 11 touchdown passes. Merril Hoge led the team in rushing with 610 yards. Warren Williams led with 4 rushing touchdowns. Louis Lipps led the team in receiving with 55 receptions for 671 yards. Eric Green led with 6 TD receptions. Thomas Everett led the team with 4 interceptions.

PITTSBURGH			1991			7-9	Game Highlights
9/1/1991		vs	SAN DIEGO CHARGERS	26	20	W	Stone 4 catch-124 yards-TD catch/Anderson 4 FG
9/8/1991		@	Buffalo	34	52	L	**Hinkle INT return TD**/Foster 121 rush yards
9/15/1991		vs	NEW ENGLAND	20	6	W	Brister 262 pass yards-TD pass to Green
9/22/1991		@	Philadelphia	14	23	L	Green 8 catch-158 yards-TD catch
10/6/1991	SNF	@	Indianapolis Colts	21	3	W	Brister 181 pass yds-2 TD pass/Hoge rush TD
10/14/1991	MNF	vs	NEW YORK GIANTS	20	23	L	Steelers rally from down 20/O'Donnell 2 TD pass
10/20/1991		vs	SEATTLE	7	27	L	O'Donnell 184 pass yards-TD pass to Stone
10/27/1991		@	Cleveland Browns	14	17	L	Steelers held to 75 rush yards-commit 2 turnovers
11/3/1991	SNF	@	Denver	13	20	L	O'Donnell 204 pass yards-TD pass to Green
11/10/1991		@	Cincinnati (OT)	33	27	W	**Williams fumble return TD**/O'Donnell 3 TD pass
11/17/1991		vs	WASHINGTON	14	41	L	O'Donnell 289 pass yards-2 TD pass
11/24/1991		vs	HOUSTON OILERS	26	14	W	Stone TD catch-Williams rush TD/Anderson 4 FG
11/28/1991	TH	@	Dallas	10	20	L	Williams rush TD/Anderson FG
12/8/1991		@	Houston Oilers	6	31	L	Steelers 85 rush yards/Anderson 2 FGs
12/15/1991		vs	CINCINNATI	17	10	W	Brister 184 pass yards-2 rush TD/Anderson FG
12/22/1991		vs	CLEVELAND BROWNS	17	10	W	**Shelton INT return TD**/Stone TD catch

Schedule courtesy of Steve's Football Bible LLC

1991 AFC Central	W	L	T	PCT	DIV	CONF	PF	PA
Houston Oilers	11	5	0	.688	5–1	10–2	386	251
Pittsburgh Steelers	**7**	**9**	**0**	**.438**	**4–2**	**7–5**	**292**	**344**
Cleveland Browns	6	10	0	.375	2–4	6–6	293	298
Cincinnati Bengals	3	13	0	.188	1–5	2–10	263	435

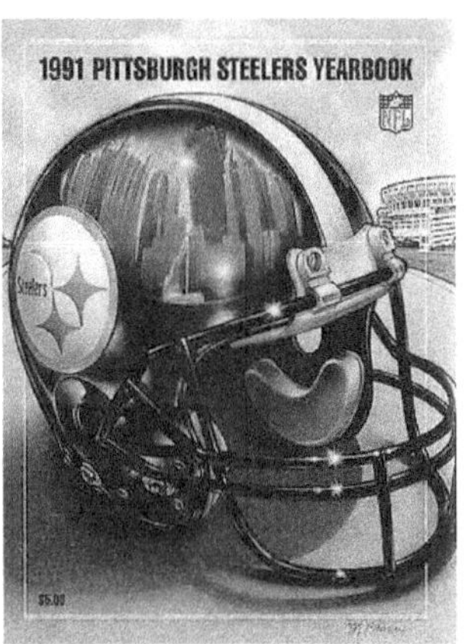

Pittsburgh at Cincinnati

Neil O'Donnell connected with tight end Eric Green on a 26-yard touchdown pass at 6:32 of overtime to give the Steelers the victory. Boomer Esiason passed for 361 yards and 1 TD, and Eddie Brown had 10 catches for Cincinnati.

1991 NFL Draft

Round	Pick	Player	Position	College
1	17	Huey Richardson	Defensive end	Florida
2	46	Jeff Graham	Wide receiver	Ohio State
3	73	Ernie Mills	Wide receiver	Florida
4	88	Sammy Walker	Cornerback	Texas Tech
4	103	Adrian Cooper	Tight end	Oklahoma
6	158	Leroy Thompson	Running back	Penn State
7	185	Andre Jones	Linebacker	Notre Dame
8	212	Dean Dingman	Guard	Michigan
9	238	Bruce McGonnigal	Tight end	Virginia
10	269	Ariel Solomon	Tackle	Colorado
11	296	Efrum Thomas	Defensive back	Alabama
12	323	Jeff Brady	Linebacker	Kentucky

Houston Oilers at Pittsburgh

The Pittsburgh Steelers came up with five interceptions and got four field goals from Gary Anderson to down the Oilers, 26-14. Anderson's field goals came from 20, 28, 33 and 24 yards. Anderson kicked two first-quarter field goals of 20 and 28 yards to give the Steelers a 6-0 lead, but Moon capped an eight-play, 72-yard drive with a 9-yard scoring strike to Ernest Givens early in the second quarter. Following a punt, the Oilers were forced to start a drive from their own 1-yard line. Moon, struggling in the Pittsburgh cold, threw an interception to cornerback Shawn Vincent, who returned the ball to the 17. Anderson then kicked a 33-yard field goal to put Pittsburgh on top 9-7. In the closing moments of the first half, O'Donnell combined with Dwight Stone on a 43-yard touchdown strike to give the Steelers a 16-7 advantage. Pittsburgh added to its lead on a 1-yard touchdown run by Warren Williams following a Bryan Hinkle interception at the Houston 36-yard line. Haywood Jefferies caught a 15-yard touchdown pass from Moon three minutes into the fourth quarter, but Anderson's 24-yard field goal in the fourth quarter clinched the win.

1992 Pittsburgh Steelers

The Pittsburgh Steelers celebrated their 60th Anniversary season in 1992. This was also Bill Cowher's first season as head coach following the retirement of Chuck Noll after 23 seasons. The team was coming off a 7–9 season in 1991. Cowher led the Steelers to an 11–5 record in his first season and the top seed in the AFC playoffs. However, in what later became commonplace in Cowher's reign as coach of the Steelers, the team failed to capitalize on the seeding and lost to the eventual AFC champion Buffalo Bills in the divisional playoffs. Rod Woodson {CB} and Barry Foster {RB} were selected to various first team All-Pro teams.

Neil O'Donnell led the team in passing with 2,283 yards and threw 13 touchdown passes. **Barry Foster set a new franchise record rushing for 1,690 yards on 390 attempts** and rushed for 11 touchdowns. Jeff Graham led the team in receiving with 49 receptions for 711 yards. Darren Perry led the team with 6 interceptions.

PITTSBURGH			1992			11-6	Game Highlights
9/6/1992		@	Houston Oilers	29	24	W	O'Donnell 223 pass yds-2 TD pass/Anderson 3 FG
9/13/1992		vs	NEW YORK JETS	27	10	W	**Griffin INT return TD**/Foster 190 rush yds-2 TD
9/20/1992		@	San Diego Chargers	23	6	W	O'Donnell 215 pass yards-2 TD pass-rush TD
9/27/1992		@	Green Bay	3	17	L	Foster 117 rush yards/Anderson FG
10/11/1992		@	Cleveland Browns	9	17	L	O'Donnell 241 pass yards/Anderson 3 FGs
10/19/1992	MNF	vs	CINCINNATI	20	0	W	O'Donnell 287 pass yards-2 TD pass to Stone
10/25/1992	SNF	@	Kansas City	27	3	W	**Woodson punt return TD**/Foster 105 rush yards
11/1/1992		vs	HOUSTON OILERS	21	20	W	Foster 118 rush yds-rush TD/O'Donnell 2 pass TD
11/8/1992		@	Buffalo	20	28	L	O'Donnell 158 pass yds-2 TD pass/Anderson 2 FG
11/15/1992		vs	DETROIT	17	14	W	Foster 106 rush yards/Mills & Jorden TD catch
11/22/1992		vs	INDIANAPOLIS COLTS	30	14	W	Foster 168 rush yards-2 rush TD/Anderson 3 FGs
11/29/1992		@	Cincinnati	21	9	W	**Davenport fumble return TD**/Foster 2 rush TD
12/6/1992		vs	SEATTLE	20	14	W	Foster 125 rush yards-rush TD/Anderson 2 FGs
12/13/1992		@	Chicago	6	30	L	Steelers held to 140 total yards-commit 4 turnovers
12/20/1992		vs	MINNESOTA	3	6	L	Foster 118 rush yards/Anderson FG
12/27/1992		vs	CLEVELAND BROWNS	23	13	W	Foster 103 rush yards-rush TD/Anderson 3 FGs
1/9/1993	SAT	vs	**BUFFALO**	3	24	L	Steelers commit 3 turnovers/Anderson FG

Schedule courtesy of Steve's Football Bible LLC

1992 AFC Central	W	L	T	PCT	DIV	CONF	PF	PA
Pittsburgh Steelers	**11**	**5**	**0**	**.688**	**5–1**	**10–2**	**299**	**225**
Houston Oilers	10	6	0	.625	3–3	7–5	352	258
Cleveland Browns	7	9	0	.438	3–3	5–7	272	275
Cincinnati Bengals	5	11	0	.313	1–5	4–8	274	364

Pittsburgh at Houston Oilers

Warren Moon threw five interceptions to the Pittsburgh Steelers. And in a major upset, the Houston Oilers lost the game, 29-24, as Bill Cowher won his first start as Pittsburgh's second coach in three decades. Houston, which broke on top, 14-0, and held on through a 24-16 first half, but failed to score in the second half. The decisive plays were Cowher's gambles, which included a run on fourth and four, a fake punt, and other unexpected calls. The fake punt was a pass. It set up the touchdown that changed Houston's first-quarter advantage from 14-0 to 14-7. Neil O'Donnell drove the Steelers to the winning touchdown, sustaining the drive for 43 yards through the suddenly dispirited Houston defense, and throwing the game-deciding pass nine yards to tight end Adrian Cooper.

1992 NFL Draft

Round	Pick	Player	Position	College
1	11	Leon Searcy	Tackle	Miami (FL)
2	38	Levon Kirkland	Linebacker	Clemson
3	67	Joel Steed	Nose tackle	Colorado
4	94	Charles Davenport	Wide receiver	North Carolina State
5	123	Alan Haller	Cornerback	Michigan State
7	179	Russ Campbell	Tight end	Kansas State
7	188	Scottie Graham	Running back	Ohio State
8	203	Darren Perry	Free safety	Penn State
8	206	Hesham Ismail	Guard	Florida
8	215	Nate Williams	Defensive tackle	Mississippi State
9	235	Elnardo Webster	Linebacker	Rutgers
10	262	Mike Saunders	Running back	Iowa
11	262	Kendall Gammon	Long snapper	Pittsburg State
12	318	Cornelius Benton	Quarterback	Connecticut

1992 AFC Divisional Playoffs

The Bills forced four fumbles, three turnovers, and seven sacks as they held the Steelers to just a field goal. Buffalo quarterback Frank Reich threw for 160 yards, two touchdowns, and no interceptions, while running back Kenneth Davis rushed for 104 yards. Steelers running back Barry Foster rushed for 104 yards and caught a pass for seven yards. Pittsburgh had led the NFL with 43 takeaways during the season, but they were not able to force any in this game. On the opening drive of the game, the Bills drove to the Pittsburgh 46-yard line. But on fourth and 1, fullback Carwell Gardner was stuffed by linebackers David Little and Hardy Nickerson for no gain. The turnover on downs led to Gary Anderson's 38-yard field goal to give Pittsburgh a 3-0 lead. However, Steelers quarterback Neil O'Donnell, who had missed the last three games of the season with a leg injury, ended up turning the ball over three times on the team's next four drives. First, he threw a pass that was deflected by Phil Hansen into the arms of Nate Odomes for an interception. Following a punt from each team, Bruce Smith forced a fumble from O'Donnell, which Hansen recovered on the Bills 41-yard line. Buffalo then advanced 59 yards, including a 19-yard catch by receiver Don Beebe on the Steelers 1-yard line. On the next play, the team scored on Reich's 1-yard touchdown pass to Mitch Frerotte, an eligible offensive lineman playing out of the fullback position. Although there would be no more scoring in the first half, Pittsburgh's struggles would continue. On their next drive, O'Donnell was intercepted by defensive back James Williams.

On the opening drive of the second half, the Bills moved the ball 80 yards and scored with Reich's 17-yard touchdown pass to James Lofton, increasing their lead to 14-3. On the play before the touchdown, Reich had thrown the ball right into the hands of defensive back Richard Shelton while trying to connect with Beebe, but Shelton dropped the pass, costing his team what would have been an easy touchdown return. "I was just running before I caught the ball, and that really hurt", Shelton said after the game. "I could have had six." In the final quarter, a botched Steelers field goal attempt set up a 44-yard drive that ended with Bills kicker Steve Christie's 43-yard field goal. The next time Buffalo got the ball, they drove 86 yards and scored on a 1-yard run from Gardner.

1/9/1993	Line/Total	1	2	3	4	Final
Buffalo Bills	{36.0}	0	7	7	10	24
Pittsburgh Steelers	{-1.0}	3	0	0	0	3

Scoring

Steelers	Gary Anderson 38 yard field goal
Bills	Mitch Frerotte 1 yard pass from Frank Reich (Steve Christie kick)
Bills	James Lofton 17 yard pass from Frank Reich (Steve Christie kick)
Bills	Steve Christie 43 yard field goal
Bills	Carwell Gardner 1 yard rush (Steve Christie kick)

86 · ERIC GREEN
Tight End   Ht: 6-5   Wt: 280

14 · NEIL O'DONNELL
Quarterback   Ht: 6-3   Wt: 226

BILL COWHER
Head Coach

1993 Pittsburgh Steelers

The Steelers looked to continue the progress made under second year head coach Bill Cowher. However, the team would take a slight step backwards, finishing 9–7 (three games behind the eventual AFC Central champion Houston Oilers). Despite that, the Steelers clinched the final wild card spot, making the playoffs for the second consecutive year. The team would lose to the Kansas City Chiefs 27–24 in overtime in the AFC Wild Card Round of the playoffs, in what is considered one of the best playoff games in NFL history even though the Steelers were on the losing end. Notable about the season came in the second week, when the Steelers suffered a rare shutout loss to the Los Angeles Rams 27–0 in one of the team's last visit to the Los Angeles area in the foreseeable future. The day was highlighted by the emergence of Rams rookie Jerome Bettis running over the Steelers defense. Though no one knew it at the time, it would foreshadow what was to come with Bettis' career—as a member of the Steelers, who would acquire Bettis in a draft day trade with the Rams three years later. 1993 was also the season in which the Steelers began their policy of "blacking out" regular season contract negotiations. Early in the season the Steelers had reached contract extensions with Rod Woodson and Barry Foster and continued negotiations with other players. However, this led to discord in the locker room, and management felt that contract talk was taking the team's focus from winning. At mid-season the Steelers broke off all contract negotiations and have refused to negotiate contracts during the regular season since. Rod Woodson {CB}, Dermontti Dawson {C} and Greg Lloyd {LB} were selected to various first team All-Pro teams.

Neil O'Donnell led the team in passing with 3,208 yards and threw 14 touchdown passes. Leroy Thompson led the team in rushing with 763 yards. Barry Foster led with 8 rushing touchdowns. Eric Green led the team in receiving with 63 receptions for 942 yards and 5 TD receptions. Woodson led the team with 8 interceptions.

PITTSBURGH			1993			9-8	Game Highlights
9/5/1993		vs	SAN FRANCISCO	13	24	L	Steelers 211 total yards/Foster TD/Anderson 2 FG
9/12/1993		@	Los Angeles Rams	0	27	L	Steelers 175 total yards-commit 3 turnovers
9/19/1993		vs	CINCINNATI	34	7	W	O'Donnell 189 pass yards-3 TD pass/Stone 2 TDs
9/27/1993	MNF	@	Atlanta	45	17	W	**Davidson fumble return TD**/Foster 3 rush TD
10/10/1993		vs	SAN DIEGO CHARGERS	16	3	W	**Kirkland fumble return TD**/Anderson 3 FGs
10/17/1993		vs	NEW ORLEANS	37	14	W	**Woodson INT return TD**/Anderson 3 FGs
10/24/1993		@	Cleveland Browns	23	28	L	O'Donnell 355 pass yards/Foster 2 rush TD
11/7/1993		@	Cincinnati	24	16	W	O'Donnell 244 pass yds-2 TD pass/Foster rush TD
11/15/1993	MNF	vs	BUFFALO	23	0	W	Thompson 108 rush yards-rush TD/Anderson 3 FG
11/21/1993		@	Denver	13	37	L	Tomczak TD pass to Thigpen/Anderson 2 FGs
11/28/1993	SNF	@	Houston Oilers	3	23	L	Steelers 65 rush yards-commit 4 turnovers
12/5/1993		vs	NEW ENGLAND	17	14	W	Hoge 2 TD catch from O'Donnell/Anderson FG
12/13/1993	MNF	@	Miami	21	20	W	Thompson 81 rush yds-2 rush TD/Hoge TD catch
12/19/1993		vs	HOUSTON OILERS	17	26	L	Steelers 400 pass yards/Green TD catch/Hoge TD
12/26/1993		@	Seattle	6	16	L	O'Donnell 285 pass yards/Anderson 2 FGs
1/2/1994		vs	CLEVELAND BROWNS	16	9	W	O'Donnell 226 pass yards-TD pass to Green
1/8/1994	**SAT**	**@**	**Kansas City (OT)**	**24**	**27**	**L**	O'Donnell 286 pass yards-3 TD pass

Schedule courtesy of Steve's Football Bible LLC

1993 AFC Central	W	L	T	PCT	PF	PA	STK
Houston Oilers	12	4	0	.750	368	238	W11
Pittsburgh Steelers	**9**	**7**	**0**	**.563**	**308**	**281**	**W1**
Cleveland Browns	7	9	0	.438	304	307	L1
Cincinnati Bengals	3	13	0	.188	187	319	L1

1993 NFL Draft

Round	Pick	Player	Position	College
1	23	Deon Figures	Cornerback	Colorado
2	44	Chad Brown *	Linebacker	Colorado
3	76	Andre Hastings	Wide Receiver	Georgia
4	108	Kevin Henry	Defensive end	Mississippi State
5	135	Lonnie Palelei	Guard	UNLV
5	140	Marc Woodard	Linebacker	Mississippi State
6	162	Willie Williams	Cornerback	Western Carolina
7	185	Jeff Zgonina	Defensive tackle	Purdue
7	189	Craig Keith	Tight end	Lenoir–Rhyne
8	216	Alex Van Pelt	Quarterback	Pittsburgh

1993 AFC Wild Card

Chiefs kicker Nick Lowery made the winning 32-yard field goal after 11:03 of overtime, to earn themselves a win over the Steelers in a game in which both teams combined for 770 yards, no fumbles lost, and no interceptions. The Steelers scored first by driving 66 yards, featuring a 32-yard reception by running back Merril Hoge, and scoring on Neil O'Donnell's 10-yard touchdown pass to tight end Adrian Cooper. Later in the first quarter, Kansas City drove 75 yards in seven plays and tied the game after backup quarterback Dave Krieg, who temporarily replaced injured starter Joe Montana, threw a 23-yard touchdown to wide receiver J. J. Birden.

The Steelers responded with a long 15-play drive to retake the lead on Gary Anderson's 30-yard field goal, making the score 10–7. After a punt, Pittsburgh drove back to the Chiefs 35-yard line, only to turn the ball over on downs. Kansas City then took over and drove to the Steelers 42, but on fourth down and 1, defensive end Gerald Williams sacked Montana for a 7-yard loss, giving his team the ball on their own 49 with under a minute left. The Steelers made the most of their opportunity, scoring on O'Donnell's 26-yard touchdown completion to Ernie Mills that increased their lead to 17–7 at the end of the half.

Most of the third quarter was a defensive struggle until the Chiefs put together a 49-yard drive to score on Lowery's 23-yard field goal. Then in the fourth quarter, Montana connected with Willie Davis for 22 yards and Birden for 19 on the way to Marcus Allen's 2-yard touchdown run that tied the game at 17. O'Donnell led the Steelers right back though, completing a 26-yard pass to Dwight Stone before hooking up with Eric Green for a 22-yard touchdown throw to retake the lead, 24–17.

In the final minutes of regulation, tight end Keith Cash blocked a Pittsburgh punt and Fred Jones returned it 31 yards to the Steelers 9-yard line. On fourth down, Montana threw a 7-yard touchdown pass to wide receiver Tim Barnett, tying the game at 24 with 1:43 left in the game. Then after forcing Pittsburgh to punt, Kansas City drove 47 yards to set up Lowery's 43-yard field-goal attempt in the closing seconds, but the kick was wide right and thus the game went into overtime.

Kansas City won the coin toss to receive the overtime kickoff but went three and out. Pittsburgh then drove to midfield before they also had to punt. At this point, Montana completed several passes, including an 18-yarder to Cash to move the Chiefs into position for Lowery's game winning score.

Montana finished the game 23/42 for 276 passing yards and a touchdown, with no interceptions. O'Donnell completed 23/42 passes for 286 yards and three scores.

1/8/1994	Line/Total	1	2	3	4	OT	Final
Pittsburgh Steelers	{35.5}	7	10	0	7	0	24
Kansas City Chiefs	{-8.0}	7	0	3	14	3	27

Scoring

Team	
Steelers	Adrian Cooper 10 yard pass from Neil O'Donnell (Gary Anderson kick)
Chiefs	J.J. Birden 23 yard pass from Dave Krieg (Nick Lowery kick)
Steelers	Gary Anderson 30 yard field goal
Steelers	Ernie Mills 26 yard pass from Neil O'Donnell (Gary Anderson kick)
Chiefs	Nick Lowery 23 yard field goal
Chiefs	Marcus Allen 2 yard rush (Nick Lowery kick)
Steelers	Eric Green 22 yard pass from Neil O'Donnell (Gary Anderson kick)
Chiefs	Tim Barnett 7 yard pass from Joe Montana (Nick Lowery kick)
Chiefs	Nick Lowery 32 yard field goal

33 · MERRIL HOGE
Fullback   Ht: 6-2   Wt: 230

72 · LEON SEARCY
Offensive Tackle   Ht: 6-3   Wt: 304

26 · ROD WOODSON
Cornerback   Ht: 6-0   Wt: 200

1994 Pittsburgh Steelers

This season marked their third consecutive trip to the playoffs under head coach Bill Cowher. For the second time in Cowher's three seasons as head coach of the Steelers the team was the top seed in the AFC playoffs. Pittsburgh won its first playoff game since 1989 with a win in the divisional playoffs over their division rival Cleveland Browns but failed to advance to the Super Bowl after losing to the San Diego Chargers in the AFC Championship Game. Dermontti Dawson {C}, Greg Lloyd {LB}, Rod Woodson {CB} and Kevin Greene {LB} were selected to various first team All-Pro teams.

Neil O'Donnell led the team in passing with 2,443 yards and threw 13 touchdown passes. Barry Foster led the team in rushing with 851 yards. Bam Morris led with 7 rushing touchdowns. John Williams led the team with 51 receptions. Eric Green led the team with 618 yards and 4 TD receptions. Darren Perry led the team with 7 interceptions. **Mark Royals set a franchise record with 97 punts during the season.**

PITTSBURGH			1994			13-5	Game Highlights
9/4/1994		vs	DALLAS	9	26	L	Steelers held to 126 total yards/O'Donnell TD
9/11/1994		@	Cleveland Browns	17	10	W	O'Donnell 199 pass yards-TD pass to Thigpen
9/18/1994		vs	INDIANAPOLIS	31	21	W	O'Donnell 254 pass yards-2 TD pass/Anderson FG
9/25/1994		@	Seattle	13	30	L	O'Donnell 282 pass yards-TD pass-4 INTs
10/3/1994	MNF	vs	HOUSTON OILERS	30	14	W	Foster 115 rush yards-rush TD/Anderson 3 FGs
10/16/1994		vs	CINCINNATI	14	10	W	O'Donnell 190 pass yards-2 TD pass
10/23/1994		@	New York Giants	10	6	W	Morris 146 rush yards-rush TD/Anderson FG
10/30/1994	SNF	@	Arizona (OT)	17	20	L	O'Donnell 260 pass yards-TD pass to Thigpen
11/6/1994		@	Houston Oilers (OT)	12	9	W	O'Donnell 154 pass yards/Anderson 4 FGs
11/14/1994	MNF	vs	BUFFALO	23	10	W	**Woodson INT return TD/Williams fumble return TD**
11/20/1994		vs	MIAMI (OT)	16	13	W	Tomczak 343 pass yards/Foster TD/Anderson 3 FGs
11/27/1994		@	Los Angeles Raiders	21	3	W	Tomczak 2 TD pass/Morris rush TD
12/4/1994		@	Cincinnati	38	15	W	**Woodson INT return TD**/Morris 108 rush yds-2 TD
12/11/1994		vs	PHILADELPHIA	14	3	W	Defense holds Eagles to 105 yards/Williams rush TD
12/18/1994		vs	CLEVELAND	17	7	W	Foster 106 rush yards-rush TD/Thigpen TD catch
12/24/1994	SAT	@	San Diego	34	37	L	Tomczak 248 pass yds-2 TD pass/Johnson 2 TD catch
1/7/1995	SAT	vs	**CLEVELAND**	29	9	W	Foster 133 rush yards/O'Donnell 2 TD pass
1/15/1995		vs	**SAN DIEGO**	13	17	L	O'Donnell 349 pass yards-TD pass to Williams

Schedule courtesy of Steve's Football Bible LLC

1994 AFC Central	W	L	T	PCT	PF	PA
Pittsburgh Steelers	12	4	0	.750	316	234
Cleveland Browns	11	5	0	.688	340	204
Cincinnati Bengals	3	13	0	.188	276	406
Houston Oilers	2	14	0	.125	226	352

1994 NFL Draft

Round	Pick	Player	Position	College
1	17	Charles Johnson	Wide Receiver	Colorado
2	50	Brentson Buckner	Defensive end	Clemson
3	88	Jason Gildon	Linebacker	Oklahoma State
3	91	Bam Morris	Running back	Texas Tech
4	122	Ta'ase Faumui	Defensive end	Hawaii
5	140	Myron Bell	Safety	Michigan State
5	148	Gary Brown	Tackle	Georgia Tech
6	178	Jim Miller	Quarterback	Michigan State
6	180	Eric Ravotti	Linebacker	Penn State
7	209	Brice Abrams	Running back	Michigan State

1994 AFC Divisional Playoffs

Pittsburgh had defeated Cleveland twice during the season and proved to be more than capable of doing so again. Aided by running back Barry Foster's 133 rushing yards, the Steelers controlled the game by scoring on their first three possessions and holding the ball for 42:27. The Steelers finished the game with 424 yards of offense, including 238 yards on the ground, while holding the Browns to a mere 186 total yards.

On Pittsburgh's opening drive, they moved the ball 65 yards in 13 plays to score on Gary Anderson's 39-yard field goal. Cleveland had to punt on their next drive, and Tom Tupa's kick went just 26 yards to the Steelers 47-yard line. Pittsburgh then went 53 yards in eight plays, including a 21-yard completion from Neil O'Donnell to Ernie Mills, to go up 10–0 on O'Donnell's 2-yard touchdown pass to tight end Eric Green. On the Steelers next possession, Foster rushed three times for 40 yards as the team drove 74 yards to score on John L. Williams' 26-yard touchdown burst with 9:03 left in the second quarter.

After being completely dominated up to this point, Cleveland finally caught a break when Mark Carrier returned Mark Royals' 43-yard punt 20 yards to the Steelers 30-yard line, leading to Matt Stover's 22-yard field goal to cut the lead to 17–3, but in the closing seconds of the quarter, Steelers defensive back Tim McKyer intercepted a pass from Cleveland quarterback Vinny Testaverde and returned it 21 yards to the Browns 6-yard line. O'Donnell then completed a 9-yard touchdown to wide receiver Yancey Thigpen with 16 seconds left in the first half.

In the third quarter, the Steelers drove 72 yards to go up 27–3 on a 40-yard Anderson field goal. In the final quarter, the Browns took advantage of a 35-yard pass interference penalty on Steelers defensive back Deon Figures, converting it into a score with Testaverde's 20-yard touchdown pass to wide receiver Keenan McCardell. But on their next drive, the Cleveland quarterback was sacked in the end zone by Pittsburgh defensive back Carnell Lake for a safety with 2:45 left in the game.

O'Donnell finished the game 18/23 for 186 yards and two touchdowns. His top receiver was Mills, who caught five passes for 117 yards. This was the first playoff win for Steelers coach Bill Cowher, who had watched his team get eliminated from the playoffs in the first round in each of the past three seasons.

1/7/1995	Line/Total	1	2	3	4	Final
Cleveland Browns	{32.0}	0	3	0	6	9
Pittsburgh Steelers	{-3.5}	3	21	3	2	29

Scoring

Team	
Steelers	Gary Anderson 39 yard field goal
Steelers	Eric Green 2 yard pass from Neil O'Donnell (Gary Anderson kick)
Steelers	John Williams 26 yard rush (Gary Anderson kick)
Browns	Matt Stover 22 yard field goal
Steelers	Yancey Thigpen 9 yard pass from Neil O'Donnell (Gary Anderson kick)
Steelers	Gary Anderson 40 yard field goal
Browns	Keenan McCardell 20 yard pass from Vinny Testaverde (pass failed)
Steelers	Safety, Lake sacked Testaverde in end zone

1994 AFC Championship Game

The Chargers scored 14 unanswered points in the second half to upset the heavily favored Steelers. In one of the greatest games in his career, Junior Seau recorded 16 tackles while playing with a pinched nerve in his neck. Although Pittsburgh held advantages in total plays (80–47), total offensive yards (415–226), and time of possession (37:13–22:47), it was San Diego who made the big plays.

The Steelers took the opening kickoff and drove 67 yards to a score on Neil O'Donnell's 16-yard touchdown pass to fullback John L. Williams. O'Donnell also made two big completions to Andre Hastings on the drive, the first for 18 yards, and the second for 11 yards on fourth down and 2. Later in the quarter, the Chargers got a big opportunity when safety Darren Carrington recovered a fumble from Steelers running back Barry Foster on the San Diego 41, but Pittsburgh's defense stepped up and forced a punt. Pittsburgh then advanced the ball to the Chargers 27-yard line, but a holding penalty pushed them out of field goal range, and they ended up punting it back. In the second quarter, San Diego's offense finally managed to get a drive going, with running back Natrone Means rushing for 17 yards and catching a pass for 15. On the next play, a long pass interference penalty gave them a first down on the Steelers 3-yard line, but they could not get into the end zone and settled for John Carney's field goal, cutting the score to 7–3. Pittsburgh struck back with a 12-play, 51-yard drive, including three first down completions from O'Donnell to receiver Ernie Mills, and scored on Gary Anderson's 39-yard field goal with 13 seconds left in the half. Although their halftime lead was only 10–3, Pittsburgh seemed in control of the game. They had outgained San Diego in total yards 229–46, and first downs 13–4.

The situation kept getting better for Pittsburgh in the second half. Humphries was intercepted by cornerback Rod Woodson on the third play of the quarter, and O'Donnell's 33-yard aerial strike to tight end Eric Green set up Anderson's 23-yard field goal, increasing their lead to 13–3. But on the fifth play of the Chargers ensuing drive, quarterback Stan Humphries faked a handoff, fooling the Steelers defensive backs long enough to find tight end Alfred Pupunu wide open to complete a 43-yard touchdown. The score was cut to 13–10 and would remain so going into the fourth quarter. Early in the final quarter, Humphries completed consecutive passes to Pupunu for 31 yards, moving the ball across midfield. Then with 5:13 left in the game, Humphries threw a 43-yard touchdown pass to wide receiver Tony Martin, who out-jumped defensive back Tim McKyer to make the catch and give the Chargers a 17–13 lead. O'Donnell then completed seven consecutive passes, the longest a 21-yard gain to Green that gave them a first and goal at the Chargers 9-yard line and put them in position for a potential winning touchdown. However, Foster was dropped for a one-yard loss on the next play, followed by an incompletion and a 7-yard catch by Williams. On fourth down, Chargers linebacker Dennis Gibson sealed the victory by tipping away O'Donnell's pass intended for Foster. The Steelers lost for the first time during the season in which they held a lead at halftime. (In 1994, they were 9–0 when leading at halftime prior to this game.) O'Donnell completed 32 of 54 passes for 349 yards and a touchdown. His top receiver was Mills, who caught eight passes for 106 yards. Humphries completed 11 of 22 passes for 165 yards, two touchdowns, and an interception.

1/15/1995	Line/Total	1	2	3	4	Final
San Diego Chargers	{36.0}	0	3	7	7	17
Pittsburgh Steelers	{-9.0}	7	3	3	0	13

Scoring

Team	
Steelers	John Williams 16 yard pass from Neil O'Donnell (Gary Anderson kick)
Chargers	John Carney 20 yard field goal
Steelers	Gary Anderson 39 yard field goal
Steelers	Gary Anderson 23 yard field goal
Chargers	Alfred Pupunu 43 yard pass from Stan Humphries (John Carney kick)
Chargers	Tony Martin 43 yard pass from Stan Humphries (John Carney kick)

1995 Pittsburgh Steelers

This season saw the Steelers return to the Super Bowl for the first time in sixteen years (Super Bowl XIV). The team's 11–5 finish was good enough for the AFC Central championship and the second seed in the conference. For the second consecutive season, Pittsburgh hosted the AFC Championship Game, by virtue of the Indianapolis Colts' upset of the top-seeded Kansas City Chiefs at Arrowhead Stadium. The Steelers won the conference championship game but lost to the Dallas Cowboys in the Super Bowl in a matchup of teams that were looking to join the San Francisco 49ers as the only other team (at the time) to win five Super Bowls. It was the first time in three Super Bowl meetings that the Steelers had lost to the Cowboys, and their first Super Bowl loss overall. Pittsburgh coach Bill Cowher became (at the time) the youngest head coach to lead his team to the Super Bowl. After the Super Bowl loss, quarterback Neil O'Donnell signed as a free agent with the New York Jets. The Steelers would not return to the Super Bowl until ten years later. Dermontti Dawson {C} and Greg Lloyd {LB} were selected to various first team All-Pro teams.

Neil O'Donnell led the team in passing with 2,970 yards and threw 17 touchdown passes. Erric Pegram led the team in rushing with 813 yards. Bam Morris led the team with 9 rushing touchdowns. Yancey Thigpen led the team in receiving with 85 receptions for 1,307 yards. Ernie Mills led with 8 TD receptions. Willie Williams led the team with 7 interceptions.

PITTSBURGH			1995			13-6	Game Highlights
9/3/1995		vs	DETROIT	23	20	W	Bam Morris 2 rush TDs/Johnson 3 FGs
9/10/1995		@	Houston Oilers	34	17	W	**Hastings punt return TD/Lake INT return TD**
9/18/1995	MNF	@	Miami	10	23	L	Miller 202 pass yards-TD pass to Mills/Johnson FG
9/24/1995		vs	MINNESOTA	24	44	L	Pegram 2 rush TD/Thigpen 10 catch-141 yards-TD
10/1/1995		vs	SAN DIEGO	31	16	W	**Williams & Mays INT return TDs**/Morris 2 rush TD
10/8/1995		@	Jacksonville	16	20	L	O'Donnell 282 pass yards-TD pass to Avery
10/19/1995	TH	vs	CINCINNATI	9	27	L	O'Donnell 359 pass yards/Johnson 3 FGs
10/29/1995		vs	JACKSONVILLE	24	7	W	O'Donnell 178 pass yards-2 TD pass/Pegram rush TD
11/5/1995		@	Chicago (OT)	37	34	W	O'Donnell 341 pass yds-2 TD pass/Pegram 2 rush TD
11/13/1995	MNF	vs	CLEVELAND	20	3	W	Pegram 112 rush yards/O'Donnell 167 pass yards-TD
11/19/1995		@	Cincinnati	49	31	W	O'Donnell 377 pass yards-3 TD pass/Morris 3 rush TD
11/26/1995		@	Cleveland	20	17	W	Thigpen 5 catch-106 yards/Johnson 2 FGs
12/3/1995		vs	HOUSTON OILERS	21	7	W	Morris 102 rush yards-rush TD/O'Donnell 2 TD pass
12/10/1995		@	Oakland Raiders	29	10	W	O'Donnell 230 pass yards-2 TD pass to Mills
12/16/1995	SAT	vs	NEW ENGLAND	41	27	W	**Buckner & Oldham fumble return TDs**/Johnson 2 FG
12/24/1995		@	Green Bay	19	24	L	O'Donnell 318 pass yards-TD pass to Mills
1/6/1996	SAT	vs	**BUFFALO**	**40**	**21**	**W**	Morris 106 rush yards-2 rush TD/Johnson 4 FGs
1/14/1996		vs	**INDIANAPOLIS**	**20**	**16**	**W**	O'Donnell TD pass to Stewart/Johnson 2 FGs
1/28/1996		vs	**Dallas**	**17**	**27**	**L**	O'Donnell 239 pass yards-TD pass to Mills/Morris TD

Schedule courtesy of Steve's Football Bible LLC

1995 AFC Central	W	L	T	PCT	PF	PA
Pittsburgh Steelers	**11**	**5**	**0**	**.688**	**407**	**327**
Cincinnati Bengals	7	9	0	.438	349	374
Houston Oilers	7	9	0	.438	348	324
Cleveland Browns	5	11	0	.313	289	356
Jacksonville Jaguars	4	12	0	.250	275	404

1995 NFL Draft

Round	Pick	Player	Position	College
1	27	Mark Bruener	Tight end	Washington
2	60	Kordell Stewart	Quarterback	Colorado
3	91	Brenden Stai	Guard	Nebraska
4	120	Oliver Gibson	Defensive tackle	Notre Dame
4	125	Donta Jones	Linebacker	Nebraska
5	151	Lethon Flowers	Safety	Georgia Tech
5	161	Lance Brown	Safety	Indiana
6	199	Barron Miles	Cornerback	Nebraska
7	235	Henry Bailey	Wide receiver	UNLV
7	247	Cole Ford	Placekicker	USC

1995 AFC Divisional Playoffs

Running back Bam Morris scored two touchdowns in the fourth quarter as the Steelers stopped the Bills, minus Hall of Fame defensive end Bruce Smith who fell ill the day before the game, from coming back from a 20–0 deficit. By the end of the game, the Steelers outgained them in total yards 409–250 and forced four turnovers.

Pittsburgh started off the scoring with a 76-yard drive in which receiver Yancy Thigpen caught a 43-yard pass and fullback John L. Williams finished it off with a 1-yard touchdown run. The Bills responded with a drive to the Steelers 21-yard line, but then Darick Holmes was tackled for a 13-yard loss by defensive back Carnell Lake and Steve Christie missed a 52-yard field goal attempt. Morris then rushed for 44 yards on a 58-yard possession that ended on Neil O'Donnell's 13-yard touchdown completion to Ernie Mills.

Early in the second quarter, Steelers receiver Andre Hastings returned a punt 12 yards to the Bills 43-yard line, setting up Norm Johnson's 45-yard field goal. Now facing a 17–0 deficit, the Bills offense self-destructed on their next drive. Facing 3rd and 8, Jim Kelly was sacked by linebacker Kevin Greene and fumbled the ball. Center Kent Hull recovered the fumble for Buffalo, but it didn't help much. On the next play, Lee Flowers stormed into the backfield and tackled punter Chris Mohr on the Bills 12-yard line, leading to another Johnson field goal that gave Pittsburgh a 20–0 lead. Buffalo responded with a drive to the Steelers 30-yard line, only to lose the ball when Lake forced a fumble from Thurman Thomas that was recovered by defensive back Chris Oldham. However, the Bills soon got the ball back with excellent field position after Rohn Stark punted the ball 33 yards to the Steelers 49. Kelly then got the team to the 1-yard line with three completions, hitting Tony Cline for 17 yards, Andre Reed for 5, and Steve Tasker for 26. Thomas then ran the ball into the end zone, cutting the score to 20–7. Only 45 seconds remained in the half, but O'Donnell proved up to the challenge of earning his team some more points, completing 4 consecutive passes for 53 yards to get the team to the Bills 16-yard line. Johnson finished the drive with his third field goal, giving the Steelers a 23–7 halftime lead.

In the third quarter, Lake intercepted a pass from Kelly and returned it 3 yards to the Buffalo 25-yard line, leading to Johnson's fourth field goal that put the team up 26–7. Both teams had to punt on their following drives, and Tasker returned Stark's 30-yard punt 4 yards to the Steelers 42-yard line. A few plays later, he took a handoff on a reverse and ran 40 yards to the 3. Alex Van Pelt (who replaced an injured Jim Kelly) finished the drive with 2-yard touchdown pass to Cline, making the score 26–14.

Early in the fourth quarter, Buffalo took advantage of yet another poor punt from Stark, this one a 31-yard kick that gave them the ball on the Pittsburgh 36. Van Pelt then guided the team to the 11-yard line, where Kelly returned to the field and eventually hit Thomas for a 9-yard scoring completion, cutting the score to 26–21 with 11:23 left in the game. But Pittsburgh then marched 76 yards, including O'Donnell's 3rd down conversion passes to Thigpen and Andre Hastings for gains of 21 and 17 yards, to score on Morris'  13-yard touchdown run, increasing their lead to 33–21. The following three drives would result in interceptions, with Kelly throwing a pick to Jerry Olsavsky and Matt Darby nabbing a pass from O'Donnell. On the next play, Linebacker Levon Kirkland intercepted a pass from Kelly and returned it 4 yards to the Bills 23-yard line to set up Morris' 2-yard score with 1:58 remaining to clinch the victory.

With the Steelers win, they snapped the Bills' 10 game postseason winning streak against the AFC dating back to 1990. Morris rushed for 106 yards and caught 2 passes for 7. Lake had an interception and a fumble recovery.

1/6/1996	Line/Total	1	2	3	4	Final
Buffalo Bills	{42.5}	0	7	7	7	21
Pittsburgh Steelers	{-6.5}	7	16	3	14	40

Scoring

Team	
Steelers	John Williams 1 yard rush (Norm Johnson kick)
Steelers	Ernie Mills 10 yard pass from Neil O'Donnell (Norm Johnson kick)
Steelers	Norm Johnson 45 yard field goal
Steelers	Norm Johnson 38 yard field goal
Bills	Thurman Thomas 1 yard rush (Steve Christie kick)
Steelers	Norm Johnson 34 yard field goal
Steelers	Norm Johnson 39 yard field goal
Bills	Tony Cline 2 yard pass from Alex Van Pelt (Steve Christie kick)
Bills	Thurman Thomas 9 yard pass from Jim Kelly (Steve Christie kick)
Steelers	Bam Morris 13 yard rush (Norm Johnson kick)
Steelers	Bam Morris 2 yard rush (Norm Johnson kick)

1995 AFC Championship Game {"60 Minutes"}

On the Steelers opening drive, Neil O'Donnell's first pass of the game was tipped by defensive tackle Tony Siragusa and intercepted by Jeff Herrod, who returned it to the Pittsburgh 24-yard line. But the Colts drive was halted when Ray Seals tackled running back Lamont Warren for a loss on third down and one. On the next play, Cary Blanchard hit the right upright on his 34-yard field goal, but it still bounced in, and the Colts took a 3–0 lead. After each team punted, Pittsburgh's Norm Johnson kicked a field goal to even the game with under two minutes left in the first quarter. The field goal occurred after Kordell Stewart dropped a pass in the end zone. Replays showed Colts safety Jason Belser contacted Stewart just before the ball arrived, but no penalty flag was thrown.

In the second quarter, a 30-yard reception by Colts receiver Sean Dawkins set up Blanchard's second field goal. But later, Pittsburgh drove 80 yards in 17 plays, featuring three third down conversion runs by Kordell Stewart, and scored on O'Donnell's 5-yard third and goal touchdown pass to Stewart with 13 seconds left in the half to make it 10–6. Replays showed Stewart had put half a foot out of bounds before making the catch, which would have made him an ineligible receiver, but the penalty was not called.

On Indianapolis' first drive of the second half, they drove 61 yards in nine plays, featuring a 29-yard completion from Jim Harbaugh to tight end Ken Dilger. Blanchard finished the drive with his third field goal to cut their deficit to 10–9. Then after forcing a three and out, Indy drove 35 yards in nine plays to set up another field goal try, which would have put the Colts up 12–10. But this time Blanchard's 47-yard attempt sailed wide right. Taking over on their own 37, Pittsburgh mounted a drive in Colts territory where Johnson's 37-yard field goal put them back up by four points, at 13–9.

Early in the fourth quarter, a long punt return by Steelers receiver Andre Hastings gave them the ball at midfield. But all they got out of their great field position was a missed field goal. After that, Harbaugh threw a 47-yard touchdown pass to wide receiver Floyd Turner to take the lead, 16–13. After a Steelers punt, their defense got a big chance when Warren fumbled deep in Colts territory, but guard Joe Staysniak recovered the ball in mid-air to keep the drive going. Later on, defensive back Willie Williams tackled Warren behind the line on third down and one to force a punt, giving Pittsburgh the ball back with 3:03 left in the game.

Pittsburgh then marched 67 yards to score the winning touchdown. Running back Byron Bam Morris scored the game-winning 1-yard touchdown run with 1:34 remaining in the game to pull Pittsburgh ahead for good. The drive was aided by O'Donnell's 9-yard completion to Hastings on fourth down and 3 from the 47-yard line, as well as an earlier dropped potential interception that went in and out of the arms of linebacker Quentin Coryatt. On the next play after Hastings' fourth down conversion catch, O'Donnell completed a 37-yard pass to Ernie Mills on the Indianapolis 1-yard line, setting up Morris' 1-yard scoring run. The Colts got the ball back and advanced to the Steelers' 29 with 5 seconds left, narrowly avoiding a turnover when defensive back Chris Oldham dropped a wide-open interception. On the game's final play, Harbaugh attempted a hail mary pass which he lofted high and came down into a crowd of players in the end zone; the ball momentarily was against the Colts' WR Aaron Bailey's chest but it hit the turf before he could haul it in.

The Colts were the first No. 5 seed to advance to a conference championship game since the 1990 playoff expansion. Harbaugh completed 21 of 33 passes for 267 yards and a touchdown.

1/14/1996	Line/Total	1	2	3	4	Final
Indianapolis Colts	{41.0}	3	3	3	7	16
Pittsburgh Steelers	{-11.5}	3	7	3	7	20

Scoring

Team	
Colts	Cary Blanchard 34 yard field goal
Steelers	Norm Johnson 31 yard field goal
Colts	Cary Blanchard 36 yard field goal
Steelers	Kordell Stewart 5 yard pass from Neil O'Donnell (Norm Johnson kick)
Colts	Cary Blanchard 37 yard field goal
Steelers	Norm Johnson 36 yard field goal
Colts	Floyd Turner 47 yard pass from Jim Harbaugh (Cary Blanchard kick)
Steelers	Bam Morris 1 yard rush (Norm Johnson kick)

Super Bowl XXX

The game was played on January 28, 1996, at Sun Devil Stadium in Tempe, Arizona, the first time the Super Bowl was played in the Phoenix metropolitan area. Both teams entered the game trying to tie the San Francisco 49ers for the record for most Super Bowl wins by a franchise (5). The Cowboys, who posted a 12–4 regular season record, were making their eighth Super Bowl appearance, while the Steelers, who recorded an 11–5 regular season record, were making their fifth appearance. This game was also the fifth rematch between Super Bowl teams. Moreover, it was the third meeting between the two longtime rivals in a Super Bowl (after Super Bowl X and Super Bowl XIII), the most between any two NFL teams. Dallas became the first team to win three Super Bowls in four years, while Pittsburgh's defeat was their first Super Bowl loss in team history. The NBC television broadcast broke the then-record for most watched sporting event ever on American television, and the second-most watched program of all time, trailing only the final episode of M*A*S*H.

Super Bowl XXX began with Dallas wide receiver Kevin Williams returning the opening kickoff 18 yards to the 29-yard line. On the Cowboys' first possession, quarterback Troy Aikman completed a 20-yard pass on second down to wide receiver Michael Irvin, which was followed by a 23-yard rush by running back Emmitt Smith to advance to the Pittsburgh 28-yard line. The run would be Smith's longest of the day and the longest for either team. On 3rd-and-8 from the 26-yard line, Williams could only gain 2 yards on a reverse play, forcing Dallas to settle for a 42-yard Chris Boniol field goal.

On the Steelers' first possession, the Dallas defense forced a three-and-out and subsequent punt, which Cowboys cornerback Deion Sanders returned 11 yards to the 25-yard line. After two Smith runs, Aikman completed two quick passes, the first to Irvin for an 11-yard gain and the second to Sanders (who was brought in on offense as an extra receiver) for 47 yards. Sanders became the only player in Super Bowl history to record a Super Bowl interception on defense and a reception on offense (he recorded an interception as a member of the 49ers a year earlier in Super Bowl XXIX). Four plays later, Aikman completed a 3-yard  touchdown pass to tight end Jay Novacek (playing in what would be his last game, as Novacek missed the following season due to back injuries before retiring), increasing Dallas' lead to 10–0. It was the second Super Bowl in which Novacek scored Dallas's first touchdown (he also scored their first touchdown in Super Bowl XXVII). After the Steelers managed to advance to the Dallas 36-yard line on their ensuing drive, the possession fell apart due to a miscue by center Dermontti Dawson. Pittsburgh had lined up in the shotgun formation, and Dawson's snap sailed over quarterback Neil O'Donnell's head. O'Donnell managed to recover the fumble, but the Steelers were unable to recover from the 13-yard loss, and they had to punt two plays later.

After the punt, Dallas drove to the Steelers' 24-yard line. However, a pass interference penalty on Irvin nullified a 24-yard touchdown reception and moved the ball back to the 34-yard line. On the next play, Aikman completed a 19-yard pass to Novacek, bringing up second down and 1 from the 15-yard line. However, the Steelers' defense stopped Smith for no gain on the next play, and then tackled him for a 3-yard loss on third down. Boniol then kicked a 35-yard field goal, increasing Dallas' lead to 13–0. After an exchange of punts, Steelers wide receiver Andre Hastings returned John Jett's punt 11 yards to the Pittsburgh 46-yard line. After O'Donnell's first-down pass fell incomplete, Dallas linebacker Charles Haley then sacked the Steelers quarterback for a 10-yard loss, forcing third down and 20. O'Donnell's next pass was a 19-yard completion to Hastings, and then a 3-yard run on fourth down by wide receiver/backup quarterback Kordell Stewart netted a first down. Nine plays later, O'Donnell threw a 6-yard touchdown pass to wide receiver Yancey Thigpen with just 13 seconds left in the half, cutting Pittsburgh's deficit to 13–7.

After the third quarter began with another exchange of punts, the Steelers advanced the ball to their own 48-yard line. However, on third down, Cowboys cornerback Larry Brown intercepted O'Donnell's pass at the Dallas 38-yard line and returned it 44 yards to the Pittsburgh 18-yard line. Aikman then completed a 17-yard pass to Irvin to reach the 1-yard line, setting up a 1-yard touchdown run by Smith to increase Dallas' lead to 20–7. On their next drive, the Steelers faced second down and 2 on their own 47-yard line but turned the ball over on downs after running back Bam Morris was tackled for no gain on three consecutive running plays: a draw play to the left, a run to the left, and one to the middle. The Steelers defense held, however, forcing Dallas into a three-and-out; after a 6-yard run by Smith and an incompletion, Aikman's third-down pass was broken up by defensive back Rod Woodson (who had missed most of the season due to a knee injury), forcing the Cowboys to punt.

On their next drive, the Steelers advanced from their own 20-yard line to the Dallas 19. However, Dallas defensive end Tony Tolbert sacked O'Donnell on third down for a 9-yard loss, one of four Dallas sacks in the game, forcing Pittsburgh to settle for kicker Norm Johnson's 46-yard field goal with 11:20 left in the game, cutting the deficit to 20–10. On the ensuing kickoff, Pittsburgh surprised the Cowboys by executing a successful onside kick, with defensive back Deon Figures recovering the ball for Pittsburgh at their own 47-yard line. O'Donnell hit Hastings on two consecutive passes for 23 total yards. His next pass went to wide receiver Ernie Mills for 7 yards, and then Morris ran for 5 yards and caught a pass for a 6-yard gain to the Dallas 11-yard line. Three plays later, Morris scored on a 1-yard touchdown run, cutting Pittsburgh's deficit to 20–17. With the aid of linebacker Levon Kirkland's 8-yard sack of Aikman, the Cowboys were forced to punt on their next drive, and Pittsburgh regained possession of the ball at their own 32-yard line with 4:15 remaining. However, on second down, Brown intercepted another O'Donnell pass and returned it 33 yards to the Steelers' 6-yard line. The play was a mirror image of O'Donnell's first interception to Brown; a throw in the right flat thrown under a heavy Cowboys blitz into the arms of Brown with no Steelers receiver in sight. After the game, O'Donnell said that he was throwing in the spot he expected receiver Corey Holliday to be on the second interception, stating that he expected Holliday to make an out-cut instead of an in-cut. Mills responded by questioning why O'Donnell would throw to a spot and not a man in a Super Bowl. Brown said he was all alone on both picks because he expected O'Donnell to throw to the outside to seemingly get rid of the ball amidst the Cowboys' blitz.

Two plays following the interception, Smith scored once again with 3:43 left in the game, increasing the Cowboys' lead to 27–17. Despite being held to 49 yards on the ground and only 9 in the second half, Smith scored the game-clinching touchdown by making a devastating cutback on Kirkland, the best player on Pittsburgh's defense that day. The Steelers responded by driving to the Dallas 40-yard line, but after O'Donnell threw four consecutive incompletions, Pittsburgh turned the ball over on downs with 1:42 left in the game. After that, Dallas ran out most of the clock with  three quarterback kneels and an intentional delay of the game penalty before punting the ball back to the Steelers. Pittsburgh regained possession of the ball with three seconds remaining, but O'Donnell's Hail Mary pass was intercepted by Dallas safety Brock Marion on the final play of the game. The Steelers had outgained the Cowboys in total yards, 310–254 (201–61 in the second half), had 25 first downs compared to the Cowboys' 15, and limited Dallas' powerful running attack to just 56 yards. However, they were unable to overcome O'Donnell's interceptions, which led to two Cowboys touchdowns. The irony of the game was that O'Donnell entered Super Bowl XXX as the NFL's all-time leader in fewest interceptions per pass attempt.

Troy Aikman finished the game with 15 out of 23 completions for 209 yards and a touchdown (Aikman became just the third quarterback to win three Super Bowl games; Terry Bradshaw and Joe Montana each won four). Smith was the Cowboys' leading rusher with 49 yards and 2 rushing touchdowns

(Smith became just the fifth player to score a touchdown in three Super Bowl games, joining Lynn Swann, Franco Harris, Thurman Thomas, and Jerry Rice; he also became the first player to rush for two touchdowns in two Super Bowls). Irvin was Dallas' top receiver with 5 catches for 76 yards. Novacek caught 5 passes for 50 yards and a touchdown. Defensive end Chad Hennings recorded 2 of the 4 Dallas sacks in the game. The Dallas defense did not allow a play from scrimmage longer than 20 yards. Although his 3 interceptions were costly, O'Donnell recorded 28 of 49 completions for 239 yards and a touchdown. Morris was the top rusher of the game with 73 yards and a touchdown and caught 3 passes for 18 yards. Hastings was the top receiver of the game with 10 receptions for 98 yards and returned 2 punts for 18 yards. Mills caught 8 passes for 78 yards and gained 79 yards on 4 kickoff returns, giving him 157 total yards. A knee injury he sustained in the fourth quarter would keep him out for most of the 1996 season.

1/28/1996	Line/Total	1	2	3	4	Final
Dallas Cowboys	{-13.5}	10	3	7	7	27
Pittsburgh Steelers	{52.0}	0	7	0	10	17

Scoring

Team	Detail
Cowboys	Chris Boniol 42 yard field goal
Cowboys	Jay Novacek 3 yard pass from Troy Aikman (Chris Boniol kick)
Cowboys	Chris Boniol 35 yard field goal
Steelers	Yancey Thigpen 6 yard pass from Neil O'Donnell (Norm Johnson kick)
Cowboys	Emmitt Smith 1 yard rush (Chris Boniol kick)
Steelers	Norm Johnson 46 yard field goal
Steelers	Bam Morris 1 yard rush (Norm Johnson kick)
Cowboys	Emmitt Smith 4 yard rush (Chris Boniol kick)

1996 Pittsburgh Steelers

This was Bill Cowher's fifth season as head coach of the Steelers, which resulted in yet another trip to the playoffs for the team, as Pittsburgh won the AFC Central championship for the fourth time under Cowher. The team's 10–6 record was not enough to earn the Steelers a first-round bye. In their first playoff game, a rematch of the previous year's AFC Championship Game, the Steelers defeated the Colts, However, their season would come to a halt a week later as the Steelers lost to the New England Patriots, 28–3. Chad Brown {LB}, Dermontti Dawson {C} and Jerome Bettis {FB} were selected to various first team All-Pro teams.

Mike Tomczak led the team in passing with 2,767 yards and threw 15 touchdown passes. Jerome Bettis led the team in rushing with 1,431 yards and 11 rushing touchdowns. Andre Hasting led the team with 72 receptions and 6 TD receptions. Charles Johnson led with 1,008 receiving yards. Darren Perry led the team with 5 interceptions.

PITTSBURGH			1996			11-7	Game Highlights
9/1/1996		@	Jacksonville	9	24	L	Steelers 187 total yards/Johnson 3 FGs
9/8/1996		vs	BALTIMORE RAVENS	31	17	W	**Woodson INT return TD**/Bettis 116 rush yds-TD
9/16/1996	MNF	vs	BUFFALO	24	6	W	**Lake INT return TD**/Bettis 133 rush yds-2 TD
9/29/1996		vs	HOUSTON OILERS	30	16	W	**Perry INT return TD**/Bettis 115 rush yards
10/7/1996	MNF	@	Kansas City	17	7	W	Bettis 103 rush yards-rush TD/Johnson 3 FGs
10/13/1996		vs	CINCINNATI	20	10	W	**Woodson fumble return TD**/Bettis 109 rush yards
10/20/1996		@	Houston Oilers	13	23	L	Tomczak TD pass to C. Johnson/Johnson 2 FGs
10/27/1996		@	Atlanta	20	17	W	Bettis 126 rush yards-rush TD/Johnson 2 FGs
11/3/1996		vs	ST. LOUIS RAMS	42	6	W	**Pegram kickoff return TD**/Bettis 129 yds-2 TD
11/10/1996		@	Cincinnati	24	34	L	Bettis 111 rush yards-2 rush TD/Stewart rush TD
11/17/1996		vs	JACKSONVILLE	28	3	W	**Lake fumble return TD**/Thigpen 2 TD catch
11/25/1996	MNF	@	Miami	24	17	W	Tomczak 252 pass yards-TD pass to Mills
12/1/1996		@	Baltimore Ravens	17	31	L	Tomczak 221 pass yards-2 TD pass to Hastings
12/8/1996		vs	SAN DIEGO CHARGERS	16	3	W	Johnson 3 FGs/Hastings TD catch
12/15/1996		vs	SAN FRANCISCO	15	25	L	Tomczak 253 pass yards/TD pass to Stewart
12/22/1996		@	Carolina	14	18	L	Stewart 102 rush yards-rush TD/Hastings TD
12/29/1996		vs	**INDIANAPOLIS**	**42**	**14**	**W**	Bettis 102 rush yds-2 rush TD/Stewart 2 rush TD
1/5/1997		@	**New England Patriots**	**3**	**28**	**L**	Steelers held to 213 total yards/Johnson FG

Schedule courtesy of Steve's Football Bible LLC

1996 AFC Central	W	L	T	PCT	PF	PA
Pittsburgh Steelers	**10**	**6**	**0**	**.625**	**344**	**257**
Jacksonville Jaguars	9	7	0	.563	325	335
Cincinnati Bengals	8	8	0	.500	372	369
Houston Oilers	8	8	0	.500	345	319
Baltimore Ravens	4	12	0	.250	371	441

1996 NFL Draft

Round	Choice	Player	Position	School
1	29	Jamain Stephens	T	North Carolina A&T
3	72	Steven Conley	LB	Arkansas
3	92	Jon Witman	RB	Penn State
4	126	Earl Holmes	LB	Florida A&M
4	132	Jahine Arnold	WR	Fresno State
5	163	Israel Raybon	DE	North Alabama
6	200	Orpheus Roye	DE	Florida State
6	203	Spence Fischer	QB	Duke
7	242	Carlos Emmons	LB	Arkansas State

1996 AFC Wild Card

The Steelers blew a 13-point lead in the first half but scored 29 unanswered points in the second half. Meanwhile, Pittsburgh held the Colts to 146 total yards of offense, while gaining 407 yards for themselves (236 on the ground).

Pittsburgh drove 51 yards in eight plays, including a 30-yard reception by receiver Charles Johnson, to score on Norm Johnson's 29-yard field goal on their first drive. After the Colts next drive, Steelers receiver Jahine Arnold returned their punt 36 yards to the Colts 31-yard line. One play later, Mike Tomczak completed a 20-yard pass to Charles Johnson at the 8. Backup quarterback Kordell Stewart, who was routinely used by the team in short-yardage situations, eventually finished the drive with a 1-yard touchdown run, giving the Steelers a 10–0 lead with 4:55 left in the first quarter. Following another Colts punt, Pittsburgh increased their lead to 13–0 with Norm Johnson's 50-yard field goal 10 seconds into the second quarter.

Pittsburgh seemed to be taking control of the game, but with 4:35 left in the half, Tomczak threw a short pass intended for Ernie Mills that was too far behind the receiver. Defensive back Eugene Daniel intercepted the ball and returned it 59 yards for a touchdown. On the Steelers next possession, Tomczak threw an interception to safety Ray McElroy on the Colts 40-yard line. On the next play, Jim Harbaugh completed a 48-yard pass to Marvin Harrison at the Steelers 12, and he eventually converted a third and 7 situation with a 9-yard touchdown pass to receiver Aaron Bailey, giving the team a 14–13 lead with 31 seconds left before halftime.

However, the Steelers dominated the rest of the game. They started out the second half with a 16-play, 91-yard possession that ate 9:30 off the clock. Tomczak completed 5/5 passes for 37 yards on the drive, while Jerome Bettis caught one of them and rushed for 42 yards on eight carries, the last a 1-yard touchdown run. Then Stewart completed a 2-point conversion pass to tight end John Farquhar, giving the team a 21–14 lead. Harbaugh was intercepted by Levon Kirkland on the next drive, and after a Steelers punt, running back Marshall Faulk fumbled a pitch from him which safety Carnell Lake recovered on the

Indy 18-yard line. Five plays later, Bettis scored another 1-yard touchdown run to give the Steelers a 28–14 lead less than a minute into the fourth quarter.

Stewart ended up starting for the Steelers for the rest of the game. He finished with just one pass attempt, but his 24-yard run on a quarterback draw set up running back Jon Witman's 31-yard touchdown play. Stewart added a 3-yard touchdown run with 3:10 left in the game, making the final score 42–14. It was the second straight year the Steelers eliminated the Colts from the playoffs.

Bettis rushed for 102 yards and two touchdowns (his 11th 100-yard game of the year), while also catching a pass for four yards. Johnson caught five passes for 109 yards. Neither starting quarterback had a big day. Tomczak completed 13 of 21 passes for 176 yards, with two interceptions and no touchdowns. Harbaugh completed 12 of 32 passes for 134 yards and a touchdown with one pick. He was also sacked four times, three by lineman Chad Brown.

12/29/1996	Line/Total	1	2	3	4	Final
Indianapolis Colts	{37.0}	0	14	0	0	14
Pittsburgh Steelers	{-8.0}	10	3	8	21	42

Scoring

Team	
Steelers	Norm Johnson 29 yard field goal
Steelers	Kordell Stewart 1 yard rush (Norm Johnson kick)
Steelers	Norm Johnson 50 yard field goal
Colts	Eugene Daniel 59 yard interception return (Cary Blanchard kick)
Colts	Aaron Bailey 9 yard pass from Jim Harbaugh (Cary Blanchard kick)
Steelers	Jerome Bettis 1 yard rush (John Farquhar pass from Kordell Stewart)
Steelers	Jerome Bettis 1 yard rush (Norm Johnson kick)
Steelers	Jon Witman 31 yard rush (Norm Johnson kick)
Steelers	Kordell Stewart 3 yard rush (Norm Johnson kick)

1996 AFC Divisional Playoffs

In their first home playoff game in 18 years, the Patriots blew out the Steelers 28–3 with 346 yards of total offense, while limiting the Steelers to 213.

On the first play from scrimmage, the Steelers got a taste of what lay in store as Pats quarterback Drew Bledsoe completed a 53-yard pass to Terry Glenn that set up Curtis Martin's 2-yard touchdown run. Pittsburgh was quickly forced to punt, and New England took just four plays to score again, the last a 34-yard touchdown on a screen pass from Bledsoe to fullback Keith Byars, giving the team a 14–0 lead just over seven minutes into the first quarter. Then on the first play of the second quarter, Martin burst through a hole in the right line, dodged a tackle attempt by Carnell Lake, and raced 78 yards for a touchdown. This would end up not only being the longest run of his Hall of Fame career, but this was the second longest scoring run in NFL postseason history. Near the end of the half, Steelers defensive back Willie Williams intercepted a pass from Bledsoe to give his team a chance to get back in the game. But Pittsburgh turned the ball over on downs on the Pats 24-yard line and the score remained 21-0 going into halftime.

The Steelers lone score of the game occurred with 3:50 left in the third quarter, when linebacker Chad Brown's interception of a Bledsoe pass led to a 29-yard field goal by Norm Johnson. Pittsburgh then got the ball back on their own 36 following a Patriots punt, but any hope of a comeback was dashed when safety Lawyer Milloy intercepted a pass from Mike Tomczak on the New England 39-

yard line. Six plays later, Martin's 23-yard touchdown run increased New England's lead to 28–3. In the fourth quarter, the Steelers managed a drive to the Patriots 15, only to lose the ball again on an interception by linebacker Willie Clay.

Martin finished the day with 166 rushing yards and three touchdowns, while running back Dave Meggett returned seven punts for 72 yards and rushed for 18. Tomczak was held to 110 passing yards and intercepted twice in the final postseason game of his career. He was periodically replaced by versatile quarterback Kordell Stewart, but he fared no better, finishing the game 0/10 on pass attempts. Steelers running back Jerome Bettis, who rushed for 1,431 yards during the season and 102 yards in the previous playoff game, was held to just 43 yards on the ground and was limited by groin and ankle injuries. This was New England's first playoff win since their 1985 Super Bowl season.

1/5/1997	Line/Total	1	2	3	4	Final
Pittsburgh Steelers	{40.0}	0	0	3	0	3
New England Patriots	{-3.0}	14	7	0	7	28

Scoring

Team	
Patriots	Curtis Martin 2 yard rush (Adam Vinatieri kick)
Patriots	Keith Byars 34 yard pass from Drew Bledsoe (Adam Vinatieri kick)
Patriots	Curtis Martin 78 yard rush (Adam Vinatieri kick)
Steelers	Norm Johnson 29 yard field goal
Patriots	Curtis Martin 23 yard rush (Adam Vinatieri kick)

1997 Pittsburgh Steelers

This season was considered a transitional year due to many key free agent losses in the offseason, as well as the first season of Kordell Stewart starting at quarterback. The Steelers finished with an 11–5 record, their fourth consecutive AFC Central top seed, and their sixth straight playoff appearance. In doing so, Steelers head coach Bill Cowher tied Hall of Fame coach Paul Brown with most consecutive playoff appearances to start a head coaching career in the NFL—a record Cowher still co-owns with Brown, as the Steelers missed the playoffs the following year. The Steelers had 572 rushing attempts in 1997, the most in the 1990s.[1] Their 2,479 total rushing yards were the third-most of the decade by any team. The Steelers went into the season introducing a new font style numbers on jerseys matching the ones they wear on the helmets and the Steelers logo patch on uniform. The Steelers would host the AFC Championship Game for the third time in four years; however, they would ultimately lose to the eventual Super Bowl champion Denver Broncos. That game was the last playoff appearance for the Steelers during the 1990s and they did not return to the postseason until 2001. Carnell Lake {CB}, Levon Kirkland {LB} and Dermontti Dawson {C} were selected to various first team All-Pro teams.

Kordell Stewart led the team in passing with 3,020 yards and threw 21 touchdown passes. Jerome Bettis led the team in rushing with 1,665 yards. Stewart led with 11 rushing touchdowns. Yancey Thigpen led the team in receiving with 79 receptions for 1,398 yards and 7 TD receptions. Darren Perry and Donnell Woolford led the team with 4 interceptions each.

PITTSBURGH			1997			12-6	Game Highlights
8/31/1997		vs	DALLAS	7	37	L	Steelers 174 total yards/Stewart TD pass to Breuner
9/7/1997		vs	WASHINGTON	14	13	W	Bettis 134 rush yards-rush TD/Stewart rush TD
9/22/1997	MNF	@	Jacksonville	21	30	L	Stewart 155 pass yards-2 TD pass-rush TD
9/28/1997		vs	TENNESSEE TITANS	37	24	W	**Gildon fumble return TD**/Johnson 3 FGs
10/5/1997		@	Baltimore Ravens	42	34	W	Steelers fall behind 21-0/Stewart 3 TD pass
10/12/1997	SNF	vs	INDIANAPOLIS COLTS	24	22	W	**Lake fumble return TD**/Bettis 164 rush yds-TD
10/19/1997		@	Cincinnati	26	10	W	Bettis 135 rush yards-rush TD/Stewart 2 TD pass
10/26/1997		vs	JACKSONVILLE (OT)	23	17	W	Stewart 317 pass yards-3 TD pass-rush TD
11/3/1997	MNF	@	Kansas City	10	13	L	Steelers blow 10-0 lead/Hawkins TD catch
11/9/1997	SNF	vs	BALTIMORE RAVENS	37	0	W	Bettis 114 rush yards-rush TD/Johnson 3 FGs
11/16/1997		vs	CINCINNATI	20	3	W	Stewart 128 pass yards-2 TD pass/Johnson 2 FG
11/23/1997		@	Philadelphia	20	23	L	Stewart 294 pass yards-2 TD pass/Johnson 2 FG
11/30/1997		@	Arizona Cardinals (OT)	26	20	W	Bettis 142 rush yards-3 rush TD/Johnson 2 FG
12/7/1997		vs	DENVER	35	24	W	Thigpen 6 catch-175 yds-3 TD catch/Stewart 2 TD
12/13/1997	SAT	@	New England (OT)	24	21	W	Stewart 266 pass yards-TD pass to Breuner
12/21/1997		@	Tennessee Titans	6	16	L	Thigpen 6 catch-84 yards/Johnson 2 FGs
1/3/1998	SAT	vs	**NEW ENGLAND**	**7**	**6**	W	Defense force 4 turnovers/Stewart rush TD
1/11/1998		vs	**DENVER**	**21**	**24**	L	Bettis 105 rush yards-rush TD/Stewart rush TD

Schedule courtesy of Steve's Football Bible LLC

1997 AFC Central	W	L	T	PCT	PF	PA
Pittsburgh Steelers	**11**	**5**	**0**	**.688**	**372**	**307**
Jacksonville Jaguars	11	5	0	.688	394	318
Tennessee Oilers	8	8	0	.500	333	310
Cincinnati Bengals	7	9	0	.438	355	405
Baltimore Ravens	6	9	1	.406	326	345

1997 NFL Draft

Round	Pick	Player	Position	College
1	24	Chad Scott	Cornerback	Maryland
2	53	Will Blackwell	Wide receiver	San Diego State
3	82	Paul Wiggins	Tackle	Oregon
3	91	Mike Vrabel *	Linebacker	Ohio State
5	154	George Jones	Running back	San Diego State
6	186	Daryl Porter	Safety	Boston College
6	199	Rod Manuel	Defensive end	Oklahoma
7	223	Mike Adams	Wide Receiver	Texas

1997 AFC Divisional Playoffs

Quarterback Kordell Stewart's 40-yard touchdown run in the first quarter was the difference in a defense-dominated game.

The Patriots were severely depleted by injuries, playing without star running back Curtis Martin. Pro Bowl tight end Ben Coates was limited to just a few plays, while receiver Terry Glenn was out of the game a few minutes into the fourth quarter. On the third play of the game, rookie defensive back Chad Scott intercepted a pass from New England quarterback Drew Bledsoe and returned it 27 yards to the Steelers 38. Stewart then got the team to the Patriots 40-yard line, converting two third downs with 10-yard completions to Charles Johnson before taking the ball the rest of the way to the end zone on a 40-yard score, the longest touchdown run in Steelers playoff history at the time.

In the second quarter, Bledsoe completed two passes to Shawn Jefferson for 29 yards and a 36-yard throw to Glenn on a 65-yard drive that ended with Adam Vinatieri's 31-yard field goal, making the score 7-3. Later, Pittsburgh drove to the New England 33-yard line, but defensive back Steve Israel intercepted a pass from Stewart. The only remaining highlight of the quarter would be Steelers receiver Will Blackwell's 58-yard punt return on the last play of the half.

On the last play of the third quarter, Bledsoe's 39-yard completion to Glenn led to a 46-yard field goal from Vinatieri, cutting their deficit to 7-6. After a punt from each team, the Steelers had a chance to put the game away with a drive to the Patriots 1-yard line. On fourth down, coach Bill Cowher tried to ice the game with a conversion attempt, but Stewart was stuffed for no gain with 3:24 left in regulation. This gave New England one last chance to drive for a winning field goal and they managed to reach their own 42, but rookie linebacker Mike Vrabel stripped the ball from Bledsoe, and fellow linebacker Jason Gildon recovered it. The Patriots managed to get it back with 34 seconds left, but linebacker Levon Kirkland intercepted Bledsoe's Hail Mary pass on the game's final play.

For the third time in four years, Pittsburgh would play and host the AFC Championship Game. Jefferson was the sole offensive star of the game with nine receptions for 106 yards. Jerome Bettis led the Steelers with 74 yards from scrimmage but was held in check by New England's defense. Blackwell had four punt returns for 78 yards and three kickoff returns for 36. Gildon had a sack and two fumble recoveries.

1/3/1998	Line/Total	1	2	3	4	Final
New England Patriots	{41.0}	0	3	0	3	6
Pittsburgh Steelers	{-7.5}	7	0	0	0	7

Scoring

Team	
Steelers	Kordell Stewart 40 yard rush (Norm Johnson kick)
Patriots	Adam Vinatieri 31 yard field goal
Patriots	Adam Vinatieri 46 yard field goal

1997 AFC Championship Game

For the second week in a row, Denver eliminated a team on the road who had beat them in the regular season. In Week 15, Pittsburgh had defeated the Broncos 35–24, with quarterback Kordell Stewart throwing for 303 yards and three touchdowns, while running for two more. But this time, Denver intercepted three of his passes and recovered a fumble, while also sacking him three times.

Most of the scoring came in the first half. Pittsburgh got an early scoring opportunity when Levon Kirkland intercepted a pass from Denver quarterback John Elway on the Broncos 43-yard line. The Steelers then moved the ball to the 20, only to have Norm Johnson miss a 38-yard field goal attempt. On the next play Denver running back Terrell Davis took off for a 43-yard run to the Steelers 29-yard line, and the team went on to score on Davis' 8-yard touchdown run. Will Blackwell returned the ensuing kickoff 18 yards to the 35-yard line, where Pittsburgh went on to move the ball 65 yards to tie the game. On the final two plays, Stewart completed a 20-yard pass to Yancey Thigpen and then ran the ball the final 33 yards to the end zone. Steelers defensive back Darren Perry ended Denver's next drive by forcing and recovering a fumble from Davis on the Pittsburgh 32-yard line. Pittsburgh then drove 68 yards in 11 plays to go up 14-7 on Jerome Bettis' 1-yard touchdown run a few minutes into the second quarter.

The Broncos took the ball back and went on a 10-play, 45-yard drive to score on kicker Jason Elam's 43-yard field goal. Both teams had to punt on their next drives, and Blackwell's 19-yard return gave the Steelers a first down on the Broncos 43-yard line. But two plays later, Stewart forced a throw into double coverage and safety Ray Crockett intercepted his pass in the end zone. After the turnover, Elway led the Broncos 80 yards to score on his 15-yard touchdown pass to fullback Howard Griffith, giving the Broncos the lead, 17-14. The Steelers had to punt on their next drive, and Darrien Gordon returned the ball 19 yards to the Broncos 46, setting up a 54-yard drive that ended on Elway's 1-yard touchdown pass to Ed McCaffrey that gave Denver a 24-14 lead with 13 seconds left in the half. 34 of their 54 yards came from a pass interference penalty on Steelers defensive back Carnell Lake on the first play of the drive.

Both defenses controlled most of the second half. The Steelers took the opening drive of the second half and moved the ball methodically down the field and had a great scoring chance at the Broncos 5-yard line. But linebacker Allen Aldridge ended the possession with an interception in the end zone. The next time the Steelers got the ball, they moved it to the Broncos 32, only to lose it again when Neil Smith forced a fumble while sacking Stewart and Denver's Mike Lodish made the recovery.

Late in the fourth quarter, Stewart completed seven of eight passes for 68 yards and rushed twice for 11 yards on a 79-yard drive that ended with his 14-yard touchdown pass to Charles Johnson, cutting the score to 24-21 with 2:46 left in regulation. At the two-minute warning, facing third down and 5 on their own 15-yard line on their ensuing drive, Elway connected on an 18-yard completion to Shannon Sharpe for a first down. Then on the next play, he completed a 10-yard pass to McCaffrey for another first down, enabling his team to run out the rest of the clock. Sharpe later said that Elway made up the converting play in the huddle, seconds before the snap.

Davis rushed for 139 yards and a touchdown. Bettis rushed for 105 yards and a touchdown. This would be the final playoff game at Three Rivers Stadium.

1/11/1998	Line/Total	1	2	3	4	Final
Denver Broncos	{-2.5}	7	17	0	0	24
Pittsburgh Steelers	{41.5}	7	7	0	7	21

Scoring

Team	
Broncos	Terrell Davis 8 yard rush (Jason Elam kick)
Steelers	Kordell Stewart 33 yard rush (Norm Johnson kick)
Steelers	Jerome Bettis 1 yard rush (Norm Johnson kick)
Broncos	Jason Elam 43 yard field goal
Broncos	Howard Griffith 16 yard pass from John Elway (Jason Elam kick)
Broncos	Ed McCaffrey 1 yard pass from John Elway (Jason Elam kick)
Steelers	Charles Johnson 15 yard pass from Kordell Stewart (Norm Johnson kick)

1998 Pittsburgh Steelers

This season marked the first time since the 1991 season that the Steelers failed to make the playoffs. Pittsburgh finished 7–9 after starting the season 5–2, losing their last five games to lose a spot in the playoffs. It was Bill Cowher's first losing record as coach of the Steelers. The season was marked by a controversial ending to the team's Thanksgiving Day game against the Detroit Lions, where Jerome Bettis claimed he called the coin toss in overtime as "tails" although referee Phil Luckett heard "heads." The Lions won 19–16 and started the Steelers' losing streak to finish the season. The inept plays of Kordell Stewart were cited as another conflict, as the fans slowly began to turn on him. After their 11–5 1997 season, Pittsburgh lost two key offensive components: Chan Gailey, the offensive coordinator who went on to become head coach of the Dallas Cowboys, and their leading receiver, Yancey Thigpen, a Pro Bowler for Pittsburgh in 1997, who joined the Tennessee Oilers. Dermontti Dawson {C} was selected to various first team All-Pro teams. Kordell Stewart led the team in passing with 2,560 yards and threw 11 touchdowns. Jerome Bettis led the team in rushing with 1,185 yards and 3 rushing touchdowns. Courtney Hawkins led the team with 66 receptions. Charles Johnson led the team with 815 yards receiving and 7 TD receptions. DeWayne Washington led the team with 5 interceptions.

PITTSBURGH			1998			7-9	Game Highlights
9/6/1998		@	Baltimore Ravens	20	13	W	Stewart 173 pass yards-TD pass/Johnson 2 FGs
9/13/1998		vs	CHICAGO	17	12	W	Bettis 131 rush yards-rush TD/Stewart TD pass
9/20/1998		@	Miami	0	21	L	Steelers 200 total yards-commit 3 turnovers
9/27/1998		vs	SEATTLE	13	10	W	Bettis 138 rush yards/Johnson 2 FGs
10/11/1998		@	Cincinnati	20	25	L	Huntley & Bettis rush TDs/Johnson 2 FGs
10/18/1998		vs	BALTIMORE RAVENS	16	6	W	Stewart 196 pass yards-TD pass/Johnson 3 FGs
10/26/1998	MNF	@	Kansas City	20	13	W	**McAfee blocked punt return TD**/Johnson 2 FGs
11/1/1998		vs	TENNESSEE TITANS	31	41	L	Hawkins 14 catch-147 yards-TD catch/Johnson 3 TD
11/9/1998	MNF	vs	GREEN BAY	27	20	W	Stewart 231 pass yards-TD pass/Johnson 2 FGs
11/15/1998		@	Tennessee Titans	14	23	L	Stewart 239 pass yards-2 TD pass/Steelers 79 rush yds
11/22/1998		vs	JACKSONVILLE	30	15	W	**Washington two INT return TDs**/Johnson 3 FGs
11/26/1998	TH	@	Detroit (OT)	16	19	L	Stewart 225 pass yards-TD pass to Blackwell
12/6/1998		vs	NEW ENGLAND	9	23	L	Steelers 54 rush yards/Johnson 3 FGs
12/13/1998		@	Tampa Bay	3	16	L	Steelers 166 total yards/Johnson FG
12/20/1998		vs	CINCINNATI	24	25	L	**Lake INT return TD**/Oldham fumble return TD
12/28/1998	MNF	@	Jacksonville	3	21	L	Bettis 139 rush yards/Johnson FG

Schedule courtesy of Steve's Football Bible LLC

1998 AFC Central	W	L	T	PCT	PF	PA
Jacksonville Jaguars	11	5	0	.688	392	338
Tennessee Oilers	8	8	0	.500	330	320
Pittsburgh Steelers	**7**	**9**	**0**	**.438**	**263**	**303**
Baltimore Ravens	6	10	0	.375	269	335
Cincinnati Bengals	3	13	0	.188	268	452

1998 NFL Draft

Round	Pick	Player	Position	College
1	26	Alan Faneca *	Guard	LSU
2	41	Jeremy Staat	Defensive end	Arizona State
3	66	Chris Conrad	Tackle	Fresno State
3	92	Hines Ward *	Wide Receiver	Georgia
4	117	Deshea Townsend	Cornerback	Alabama
4	123	Carlos King	Running back	NC State
5	137	Jason Simmons	Safety	Arizona State
6	178	Chris Fuamatu-Ma'afala	Fullback	Utah
6	186	Ryan Olson	Defensive tackle	Colorado
7	221	Angel Rubio	Defensive tackle	SE Missouri State

Green Bay Packers at Pittsburgh {Monday Night Football}

Pittsburgh's 27-20 win over the visiting Green Bay Packers in front of a raucous Three Rivers Stadium crowd on November 9, 1998, was a true roller coaster ride. Pittsburgh rolled out to a seemingly insurmountable lead only to barely escape Brett Favre's gallant second half comeback bid. After a Kordell Stewart touchdown pass to Charles Johnson put the Steelers on the scoreboard barely three minutes into the game, Slash scored again from a yard out to give the home team a 14-0 lead at the end of the first quarter. With the Steelers defense harassing Brett Favre and stonewalling his rushing attack, Pittsburgh's offense continued to pile onto their lead. Rookie Chris Fuamatu-Ma'afala's first career touchdown followed by a Norm Johnson field goal capped off a perfect first half for the Black and Gold, who led 24-0 at intermission. A 21-yard-field goal by Norm Johnson, which made the score 27-0 with a little more than a quarter and a half left to play, appeared to put this one on ice. Trailing 27-3, the Packers' Keith McKenzie scooped up a Steelers fumble at the Green Bay 12-yard-line and screamed 88 yards into the end zone. The play was the first of three Packers scores in the game's final stanza, as Favre engineered two furious scoring drives in the game's final minutes. A short touchdown run by Raymont Harris, a two-point conversion to Antonio Freeman and another field goal by Ryan Longwell cut Pittsburgh's lead to 27-20 with 2:58 remaining.

1999 Pittsburgh Steelers

For the second consecutive season the Steelers failed to make the playoffs after starting off the season by winning 5 of their first 8 games. Losing seven of the remaining eight dropped Pittsburgh to 6–10 for the year, their worst record under Bill Cowher. The 1999 Steelers are the only NFL team since at least 1940 to concede so many as five safeties in one season.

Mike Tomczak led the team in passing with 1,625 yards and threw 12 touchdown passes. Jerome Bettis led the team in rushing with 1,091 yards and 7 rushing touchdowns. Hines Ward and Troy Edwards led the team in receptions with 61. Edwards led with 714 receiving yards. Hines led with 7 TD receptions. DeWayne Washington and Scott Shields led the team with 4 interceptions each.

PITTSBURGH			1999			6-10	Game Highlights
9/12/1999	SNF	@	Cleveland	43	0	W	Huntley rush TD-2 TD catch/Brown 3 FGs
9/19/1999		@	Baltimore Ravens	23	20	W	Stewart & Huntley rush TDs/Brown 3 FGs
9/26/1999		vs	SEATTLE	10	29	L	Steelers fall behind 26-0/Edwards TD catch
10/3/1999		vs	JACKSONVILLE	3	17	L	Steelers 216 total yards/Brown FG
10/10/1999		@	Buffalo	21	24	L	Stewart 216 rush yards-2 TD pass/Bettis rush TD
10/17/1999		@	Cincinnati	17	3	W	Bettis 111 rush yards-rush TD/Brown FG
10/25/1999	MNF	vs	ATLANTA	13	9	W	Stewart TD pass to Huntley/Brown 2 FGs
11/7/1999		@	San Francisco	27	6	W	Stewart TD pass to Ward/Bettis 2 TD/Brown 2 FG
11/14/1999		vs	CLEVELAND	15	16	L	Huntley rush TD/Brown 3 FGs
11/21/1999		@	Tennessee Titans	10	16	L	Stewart 177 pass yards-TD pass to Edwards
11/28/1999		vs	CINCINNATI	20	27	L	Tomczak 264 pass yards-2 Td pass/Brown 2 FG
12/2/1999	TH	@	Jacksonville	6	20	L	Steelers 63 pass yards/Brown 2 FGs
12/12/1999		vs	BALTIMORE RAVENS	24	31	L	Tomczak 249 pass yards-2 TD pass/Brown FG
12/18/1999	SAT	@	Kansas City	19	35	L	Tomczak 278 pass yards-2 TD pass-4 INTs
12/26/1999		vs	CAROLINA	30	20	W	**Davis 102-yard fumble return TD**/Bettis 137 yards
1/2/2000		vs	TENNESSEE TITANS	36	47	L	**Porter fumble return TD**/Tomczak 309 yds-2 TD

Schedule courtesy of Steve's Football Bible LLC

1999 AFC Central	W	L	T	PCT	PF	PA
Jacksonville Jaguars	14	2	0	.875	396	217
Tennessee Titans	13	3	0	.813	392	324
Baltimore Ravens	8	8	0	.500	324	277
Pittsburgh Steelers	**6**	**10**	**0**	**.375**	**317**	**320**
Cincinnati Bengals	4	12	0	.250	283	460
Cleveland Browns	2	14	0	.125	217	437

1999 NFL Draft

Round	Pick	Player	Position	College
1	13	Troy Edwards	Wide Receiver	Louisiana Tech
2	59	Scott Shields	Safety	Weber State
3	73	Joey Porter *	Linebacker	Colorado State
3	74	Kris Farris	Tackle	UCLA
3	95	Amos Zereoué	Running back	West Virginia
4	109	Aaron Smith *	Defensive end	Northern Colorado
5	136	Jerame Tuman	Tight end	Michigan
5	166	Malcolm Johnson	Wide Receiver	Notre Dame
7	214	Antonio Dingle	Defensive tackle	Virginia
7	219	Chad Kelsay	Linebacker	Nebraska
7	228	Kris Brown	Kicker	Nebraska

Atlanta Falcons at Pittsburgh {Monday Night Football}

The Steelers sacked Chris Chandler seven times, then overcame Chandler's late heroics with two goal-line stands in the final two minutes to preserve a 13-9 victory Monday night. The Falcons trailed 13-0 and never threatened offensively until Chandler hit Terance Mathis on a 5-yard scoring pass with 6:42 to play. Chandler then found Mathis again on a 40-yard completion to the Steelers' 7 following Jerome Bettis' midfield fumble. But after Ken Oxendine ran 6 yards to set up a second-and-goal at the 1, the Steelers' defense stuffed three successive running plays. The Falcons eschewed the short pass to run again on fourth down, but Earl Holmes and Kirkland teamed to stop Oxendine inches short of the goal line on fourth down. The Steelers, unable to get a first down that would run out the clock, then took a safety rather than punt out of the end zone on fourth down to make it 13-9. Chandler wasn't done, finding Tim Dwight for 27 yards to the Steelers' 5 with five seconds left. But, after spiking the ball to save time for one last play, Chandler couldn't find an open Dwight over the middle on the final play.

2000 Pittsburgh Steelers

The season began with the team trying to improve on their 6–10 record from 1999 in which they failed to qualify for the playoffs. While Pittsburgh did improve to 9–7 and had their first winning season since 1997, it was not enough for the team to qualify for the playoffs. This season also marked the Steelers' last at Three Rivers Stadium. Coach Bill Cowher named Kent Graham the team's starting quarterback for the season over former starter Kordell Stewart. After a 0–3 start, Graham was injured, and Stewart reclaimed the starting job. Graham was released at the end of the season.

Kordell Stewart led the team in passing with 1,860 yards and threw 11 touchdown passes. Jerome Bettis led the team in rushing with 1,341 yards and 8 rushing touchdowns. Hines Ward led the team in receiving with 48 receptions for 672 yards and 4 TD receptions. DeWayne Washington and Chad Scott led the team with 5 interceptions.

PITTSBURGH			2000			9-7	Game Highlights
9/3/2000		vs	BALTIMORE RAVENS	0	16	L	Steelers held to 30 rush yards in shutout
9/17/2000		@	Cleveland	20	23	L	Bettis 133 rush yards-rush TD/Brown 2 FGs
9/24/2000		vs	TENNESSEE TITANS	20	23	L	Graham 254 pass yards/Stewart rush TD
10/1/2000		@	Jacksonville	24	13	W	Bettis 97 rush yards-2 rush TDs/Brown FG
10/8/2000		@	New York Jets	20	3	W	Bettis 107 rush yards-rush TD/Brown 2 FGs
10/15/2000		vs	CINCINNATI	15	0	W	Graham 173 pass yards-77 yd TD pass to Ward
10/22/2000		vs	CLEVELAND	22	0	W	Bettis 105 rush yards-rush TD/Brown 5 FGs
10/29/2000		@	Baltimore Ravens	9	6	W	Stewart TD pass to Ward/Brown FG
11/5/2000		@	Tennessee Titans	7	9	L	Steelers held to 167 yards/Breuner TD catch
11/12/2000		vs	PHILADELPHIA (OT)	23	26	L	**Porter fumble return TD**/Brown 3 FGs
11/19/2000	SNF	vs	JACKSONVILLE	24	34	L	Stewart 2 rush TD-TD pass to Ward
11/26/2000		@	Cincinnati	48	28	W	**Gildon fumble return TD**/Stewart 3 TD pass
12/3/2000		vs	OAKLAND RAIDERS	21	20	W	Stewart 136 pass yards-2 TD pass-rush TD
12/10/2000		@	New York Giants	10	30	L	Steelers held to 47 rush yds/Stewart TD pass
12/16/2000	SAT	vs	WASHINGTON REDSKINS	24	3	W	**Poteat punt return TD**/Huntley 2 rush TD
12/24/2000		@	San Diego Chargers	34	21	W	**Blackwell kickoff return TD**/Hawkins TD catch

Schedule courtesy of Steve's Football Bible LLC

2000 AFC Central	W	L	T	PCT	PF	PA
Tennessee Titans	13	3	0	.813	346	191
Baltimore Ravens	12	4	0	.750	333	165
Pittsburgh Steelers	**9**	**7**	**0**	**.563**	**321**	**255**
Jacksonville Jaguars	7	9	0	.438	367	327
Cincinnati Bengals	4	12	0	.250	185	359
Cleveland Browns	3	13	0	.188	161	419

2000 NFL Draft

Round	Pick	Player	Position	College
1	8	Plaxico Burress	Wide receiver	Michigan State
2	38	Marvel Smith *	Offensive tackle	Arizona State
3	72	Kendrick Clancy	Defensive tackle	Mississippi
3	77	Hank Poteat	Cornerback	Pittsburgh
4	103	Danny Farmer	Wide receiver	UCLA
5	137	Clark Haggans	Outside linebacker	Colorado State
5	163	Tee Martin	Quarterback	Tennessee
6	173	Chris Combs	Defensive end	Duke
6	204	Jason Gavadza	Tight end	Kent State

Oakland Raiders at Pittsburgh

In the first quarter, Kordell Stewart threw a 19-yard touchdown pass to Bobby Shaw for a 7-0 lead. However, the Steelers fell behind 17-7 in the second quarter. A calf injury to Stewart forced him to the sidelines, and in his relief appearance, Kent Graham threw a pass that was intercepted by Eric Allen and returned 27 yards for a touchdown. Then with 1:06 to go in the half, Rich Gannon found tight end Randy Jordan on a screen pass for a 21-yard touchdown make the score 17-7 Raiders at the half. In the second half, Kordell Stewart returned to play despite his injury and drove the Steelers down to the Raiders's 6-yard line. This drive featured a play where Stewart fumbled at his own 14-yard line but recovered the ball and escaped the Raiders for 17 yards. On second and goal, Stewart threw a pass in the right flat to tight end Mark Bruener at the 1, when Raiders safety Calvin Branch went into Breuner at full speed and shoved him backwards towards the 5. Unwilling to be stopped short, Breuner fought back and dragged Branch into the end zone with him just before he could be shoved out of bounds, making the score 17-14.

On the first play of the fourth quarter, Stewart ran for a 17-yard touchdown for the Steelers to regain the lead, 21-17. Raiders kicker Sebastian Janikowski kicked a 42 yard field goal to make it 21-20, but with 4 minutes to play, missed another field goal that would have given the Raiders the lead. The Raiders got the ball back with 1:39 left with one last chance to win the game. Rich Gannon completed passes to receivers James Jett and Andre Rison for 11 and 14 yards, then found Tim Brown to convert a fourth down at midfield. The game came down to a controversial call. The Raiders had a fourth and one at the Steelers' 41-yard line, but the sideline crew was slow to switch the down markers from 3 to 4, so Raiders quarterback Rich Gannon called for a pass out in the flat to fullback Jon Ritchie. The Steelers blitzed and forced Gannon to throw incomplete, when the Raiders began to challenge their turnover on downs. Referee Tom White conferred with scorekeeper Charles Heberling to review the down and distance for the previous four plays, and Heberling confirmed that because the previous play was in fact fourth down despite what was labeled, the Steelers would be awarded the ball.

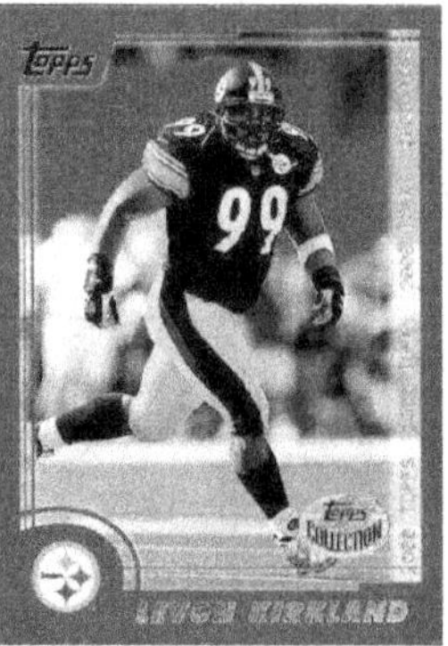

2001 Pittsburgh Steelers

After finishing the previous three seasons a combined 22–26, the Steelers returned to the top seed in the AFC, rolling to a 13–3 record in their first playoff berth since 1997 and playing at Heinz Field. The Steelers went 7–1 in their new home stadium, with the only loss coming to the defending Super Bowl champion Baltimore Ravens (a loss the Steelers avenged in the divisional playoffs). However, for the third time in Bill Cowher's coaching tenure, the Steelers fell in the AFC Championship Game at home. This time, the eventual champion New England Patriots defeated the top-seeded Steelers. Alan Faneca {G} and Jason Gildon {LB} were selected to various first team All-Pro teams.

Kordell Stewart led the team in passing with 3,109 yards and threw 14 touchdown passes. Jerome Bettis led the team in rushing with 1,072 yards. Stewart led the team with 5 rushing touchdowns. Hines Ward led the team with 94 receptions. Plaxico Burress led with 1,008 yards receiving and 6 TD receptions. Chad Scott led the team with 5 interceptions.

PITTSBURGH			2001			14-4	Game Highlights
9/9/2001		@	Jacksonville	3	21	L	Steelers commit 4 turnovers/Brown FG
9/30/2001		@	Buffalo	20	3	W	**Washington fumble return TD**/Brown 2 FGs
10/7/2001		vs	CINCINNATI	16	7	W	Bettis 153 rush yds/Stewart rush TD/Brown 3 FGs
10/14/2001		@	Kansas City	20	17	W	**Scott INT return TD**/Bettis 112 yds/Brown 2 FGs
10/21/2001		@	Tampa Bay	17	10	W	Bettis 143 rush yards-rush TD/Tuman TD catch
10/29/2001	MNF	vs	TENNESSEE TITANS	34	7	W	Bettis 2 rush TD/Stewart TD pass to Ward
11/4/2001		vs	BALTIMORE RAVENS	10	13	L	Stewart 236 pass yards/TD pass to Burress
11/11/2001		@	Cleveland (OT)	15	12	W	Bettis 163 rush yards/Brown 5 FGs
11/18/2001		vs	JACKSONVILLE	20	7	W	Stewart 266 pass yds-TD pass to Ward
11/25/2001		@	Tennessee Titans	34	24	W	**Scott INT return TD**/Burress 8 catch-114 yds-TD
12/2/2001		vs	MINNESOTA	21	16	W	Bettis-Zereoue-Edwards rush TDs
12/9/2001		vs	NEW YORK JETS	18	7	W	Ma'afala rush TD/Brown 4 FGs
12/16/2001	SNF	@	Baltimore Ravens	26	21	W	Stewart 333 pass yards-2 TD pass/Brown 2 FGs
12/23/2001		vs	DETROIT	47	14	W	**Gildon fumble return TD**/Stewart 3 TD pass
12/30/2001		@	Cincinnati (OT)	23	26	L	Burress 6 catch-106 yards-2 TD catch
1/6/2002		vs	CLEVELAND	28	7	W	**Edwards fumble return TD**/Shaw TD catch
1/20/2002		vs	**BALTIMORE**	**27**	**10**	**W**	Zereoue 2 rush TDs/Brown 2 FGs/Burress TD
1/27/2002		vs	**NEW ENGLAND**	**17**	**24**	**L**	Bettis & Zereoue rush TDs/Stewart 3 INTs

Schedule courtesy of Steve's Football Bible LLC

2001 AFC Central	W	L	T	PCT	PF	PA
Pittsburgh Steelers	13	3	0	.813	352	212
Baltimore Ravens	10	6	0	.625	303	265
Cleveland Browns	7	9	0	.438	285	319
Tennessee Titans	7	9	0	.438	336	388
Jacksonville Jaguars	6	10	0	.375	294	286
Cincinnati Bengals	6	10	0	.375	226	309

2001 NFL Draft

Round	Pick	Player	Position	College
1	18	Casey Hampton *	Defensive Tackle	Texas
2	39	Kendrell Bell *	Linebacker	Georgia
4	111	Mathias Nkwenti	Tackle	Temple
5	146	Chukky Okobi	Center	Purdue
6	181	Rodney Bailey	Defensive end	Ohio State
6	182	Roger Knight	Linebacker	Wisconsin
7	218	Chris Taylor	Wide Receiver	Texas A&M

2001 AFC Divisional Playoffs

Steelers running back Jerome Bettis, sidelined for much of the regular season, was scheduled to make his return in the first playoff game at their new home, Heinz Field, but was sidelined at the last minute due to a painkiller mishap. It did not matter as the Pittsburgh offense rushed for 150 yards and held the ball for over 40 minutes. Their defense limited the defending champion Ravens to 150 yards and seven first downs, forced four turnovers, and recorded three sacks. Bettis' replacement, Amos Zereoué, rushed for two touchdowns.

The first half was a disaster for Baltimore. Their first six drives resulted in two interceptions, three punts without gaining a first down, and a fumble. Steelers defensive back Chad Scott started out the dominance by intercepting Baltimore quarterback Elvis Grbac's first pass of the game and returning it 19 yards to the Ravens 43-yard line. Pittsburgh's offense subsequently gained 37 yards on their first three plays. Linebacker Jamie Sharper managed to halt the drive by tackling Chris Fuamatu-Ma'afala for a 1-yard loss on third down and goal, but Kris Brown kicked a field goal to give Pittsburgh a 3–0 lead. The next time Baltimore had the ball, they were forced to punt after linebacker Mike Jones sacked Grbac for a 10-yard loss on third down and 10. Pittsburgh's offense then drove 51 yards in seven plays, featuring two completions from Kordell Stewart to receivers Plaxico Burress and Hines Ward for gains of 17 and 20 yards. Zereoue finished the drive with a 2-yard touchdown run to make it 10–0.

In the second quarter, Baltimore defensive back Chris McAlister gave the offense a great chance to score when he intercepted a pass from Stewart and returned it 18 yards to the Steelers 7-yard line. But on the next play, safety Brent Alexander intercepted Grbac's pass in the end zone for a touchback. The Steelers took over and drove to the Ravens 9-yard line, but on third down, Stewart was sacked for an 8-yard loss by Larry Webster and Brown's ensuing field goal attempt was wide left. Following another three and out for Baltimore, receiver Troy Edwards returned their punt 27-yards to the Ravens 43-yard line, setting up Zereoue's second touchdown run. Then linebacker Jason Gildon recovered a fumble from Terry Allen on Baltimore's next drive and the Steelers capitalized with a 46-yard field goal from Brown, increasing their lead to 20–0 with 4:23 left in the half. After going all this time without a single first down, Baltimore finally managed to respond on their next drive. Tight end Shannon Sharpe caught four passes for 48 yards on an 11-play, 57-yard drive. Matt Stover capped it off with a 26-yard field goal, cutting their deficit to 20–3 at halftime. Late in the third quarter, Baltimore receiver Jermaine Lewis returned a punt 88 yards for a touchdown. But the Steelers responded by driving 83 yards in 12 plays and scoring with Stewart's 32-yard touchdown pass to Burress.

1/20/2002	Line/Total	1	2	3	4	Final
Baltimore Ravens	{32.0}	0	3	7	0	10
Pittsburgh Steelers	{-6.0}	10	10	0	7	27

Scoring

Team	
Steelers	Kris Brown 21 yard field goal
Steelers	Amos Zereoue 1 yard rush (Kris Brown kick)
Steelers	Amos Zereoue 1 yard rush (Kris Brown kick)
Steelers	Kris Brown 46 yard field goal
Ravens	Matt Stover 26 yard field goal
Ravens	Jermaine Lewis 88 yard punt return (Matt Stover kick)
Steelers	Plaxico Burress 32 yard pass from Kordell Stewart (Kris Brown kick)

2001 AFC Championship Game

The Patriots' storybook season continued as Drew Bledsoe came into the game in the second quarter in place of an injured Tom Brady – who replaced Bledsoe himself early in the season when he suffered a sheared blood vessel. Both defenses controlled the game early on, and with just over four minutes left in the first quarter, the Steelers had to punt the ball from their own 13-yard line. Josh Miller appeared to bail his team out with a 64-yard punt, but Steelers receiver Troy Edwards was penalized for going out of bounds before tackling Troy Brown on the return. This turned out to make a big difference, as the punt was redone and on the second attempt, Brown returned it 55 yards for a touchdown. Pittsburgh responded by driving 65 yards in 10 plays, one of them a 34-yard run by quarterback Kordell Stewart and scoring with a 30-yard field goal from Kris Brown, cutting the score to 7–3. Later, with under two minutes left in the half, Brady completed a 28-yard pass to Brown at the Steelers 40-yard line but was knocked out of the game by a hit from safety Lethon Flowers. Bledsoe took over without missing a beat, rushing for four yards and completing three passes to David Patten for 36 yards, the last one an 11-yard touchdown to give the Patriots a 14–3 lead.

On the first drive of the second half, New England linebacker Tedy Bruschi recovered a fumbled snap on the Steelers 35-yard line. But the Patriots gained only two yards on their next four plays and ended up turning the ball over on downs. Pittsburgh subsequently drove 52 yards to the 16-yard line to set up Brown's second field goal attempt, but this time his kick was blocked by defensive tackle Brandon Mitchell and Troy Brown recovered the ball. After returning it 11 yards, Brown threw a lateral pass to Antwan Harris, who took the ball the remaining 45 yards for a touchdown to increase New England's lead to 21–3. The Steelers struck back with Stewart completing a 24-yard pass to Hines Ward and a 19-yard screen pass to Amos Zereoué on an 8-play, 79-yard drive. Jerome Bettis finished it off with a 1-yard touchdown run, cutting the score to 21–10 with 5:11 left in the third quarter. New England was forced to punt after linebacker Jason Gildon sacked Bledsoe on third down, and Edwards returned the punt 28 yards to the Patriots 32-yard line. Five plays later, Zereoue scored with an 11-yard touchdown run, making the score 21–17.

Early in the fourth quarter, Adam Vinatieri's 44-yard field goal at the end of a 45-yard drive increased New England's lead to 24–17. Later in the quarter, the Patriots made two key stops to clinch the victory. First, safety Tebucky Jones intercepted a pass from Stewart and returned it 19 yards to the Steelers 34-yard line. Pittsburgh's defense managed to prevent a first down and Vinatieri missed a 50-yard field goal attempt that would have sealed the game, giving the Steelers the ball back on their own 40-yard line, but a few plays later, Lawyer
Milloy intercepted a pass from Stewart with 2:02 left to seal the game, and the Patriots were able to run out the clock. Brown was the top offensive performer of the day with eight receptions for 121 yards, along

with three punt returns for 80 yards. Brady completed 12 of 18 passes for 115 yards, while Bledsoe completed 10 of 21 passes for 102 yards and a touchdown.

1/27/2002	Line/Total	1	2	3	4	Final
New England Patriots	{37.0}	7	7	7	3	24
Pittsburgh Steelers	{-10.0}	0	3	14	0	17

Scoring

Team	
Patriots	Troy Brown 55 yard punt return (Adam Vinatieri kick)
Steelers	Kris Brown 30 yard field goal
Patriots	David Patten 11 yard pass from Drew Bledsoe (Adam Vinatieri kick)
Patriots	Antwan Harris 49 yard blocked field goal return (Adam Vinatieri kick)
Steelers	Jerome Bettis 1 yard rush (Kris Brown kick)
Steelers	Amos Zereoue 11 yard rush (Kris Brown kick)
Patriots	Adam Vinatieri 44 yard field goal

2002 Pittsburgh Steelers

The Steelers were coming off a 13–3 record in 2001 and making an appearance in the AFC Championship Game. The team failed to improve their 13–3 record, finishing 10–5–1, although this record was good enough for a division championship. With their finish, the Steelers became the first champions of the newly created AFC North. Bill Cowher's team won the

Wild Card Game, defeating the Cleveland Browns at home, but lost to AFC South champion Tennessee Titans in the divisional round. Week 4 saw Kordell Stewart's final game as the Steelers' starting quarterback, as he was replaced by Tommy Maddox during the game and although he did relieve an injured Maddox, never regained his job as he was released following the season. Alan Faneca {G} and Joey Porter {LB} were selected to various first team All-Pro teams.

Tommy Maddox led the team in passing with 2,836 yards and threw 20 touchdown passes. Amos Zereoue led the team in rushing with 762 yards. Jerome Bettis led with 9 rushing touchdowns. Hines Ward led the team in receiving with 112 receptions for 1,329 yards and 12 TD receptions. Joey Porter and Brent Alexander led the team with 4 interceptions.

PITTSBURGH			2002			11-6-1	Game Highlights
9/9/2002	MNF	@	New England Patriots	14	30	L	Stewart 242 pass yards-TD pass to Ward
9/15/2002	SNF	vs	OAKLAND RAIDERS	17	30	L	Ward 7 catch-92 yards-2 TD catch
9/29/2002		vs	CLEVELAND (OT)	16	13	W	Ward 9 catch-104 yards/Peterson 3 FGs
10/6/2002		@	New Orleans	29	32	L	Maddox 268 pass yards-3 TD pass/Bettis 84 yds
10/13/2002		@	Cincinnati	34	7	W	Bettis 109 rush yards-2 rush TD/Peterson 2 FGs
10/21/2002	MNF	vs	INDIANAPOLIS COLTS	28	10	W	Bettis 2 rush TD/Ward 2 TD catch
10/27/2002		@	Baltimore Ravens	31	18	W	Zereoue 2 rush TD/Burress 2 TD catch
11/3/2002		@	Cleveland	23	20	W	Maddox 239 pass yards-TD pass/Peterson 3 FGs
11/10/2002		vs	ATLANTA (OT)	34	34	T	Maddox 473 pass yards-4 TD pass/Burress 2 TD
11/17/2002		@	Tennessee Titans	23	31	L	Ward 10 catch-168 yards-2 TD catch
11/24/2002		vs	CINCINNATI	29	21	W	Bettis 2 rush TD/Ward 5 catch-125 yds-TD catch
12/1/2002		@	Jacksonville	25	23	W	Reed 6 FGs/Stewart rush TD-202 pass yards
12/8/2002		vs	HOUSTON TEXANS	6	24	L	Texans score 3 defensive TDs/47 total yds in win
12/15/2002		vs	CAROLINA	30	14	W	Bettis 2 rush TDs/Reed 3 FGs/Burress TD catch
12/23/2002	MNF	@	Tampa Bay	17	7	W	**Scott INT return TD**/Maddox TD pass to Randle
12/29/2002		vs	BALTIMORE RAVENS	34	31	W	Zereoue 104 rush yards-2 rush TD/Reed 2 FGs
1/5/2003		vs	**CLEVELAND**	**36**	**33**	**W**	**Randle-El punt return TD**/Maddox 3 TD pass
1/11/2003	SAT	@	**Tennessee (OT)**	**31**	**34**	**L**	Ward 7 catch-82 yards-2 TD catch/Reed 3 FGs

Schedule courtesy of Steve's Football Bible LLC

2002 AFC North	W	L	T	PCT	DIV	CONF	PF	PA
Pittsburgh Steelers	**10**	**5**	**1**	**.656**	**6–0**	**8–4**	**390**	**345**
Cleveland Browns	9	7	0	.563	3–3	7–5	344	320
Baltimore Ravens	7	9	0	.438	3–3	7–5	316	354
Cincinnati Bengals	2	14	0	.125	0–6	1–11	279	456

Houston Texans at Pittsburgh

Aaron Glenn scored twice on long interception returns and the Texans scored the first three defensive touchdowns in their history, all off Tommy Maddox turnovers, to stun the Pittsburgh Steelers 24-6. The Texans were outgained 422-47, the fewest yards ever by a winning team in NFL history. the Steelers lost to an expansion team in its first season of existence for the third time since 1995. Maddox couldn't have had a much worse day in his first game since being briefly paralyzed by a hit Nov. 17 in Tennessee, despite throwing for 325 yards. His fumble was returned 40 yards for a touchdown by Kenny Wright on Pittsburgh's first possession, and Glenn's 70-yard interception return for a TD the next time the Steelers had the ball made it 14-0. All of Houston's points came on defense or special teams.

2002 NFL Draft

Round	Pick	Player	Position	College
1	30	Kendall Simmons	Guard	Auburn
2	63	Antwaan Randle El	Wide receiver	Indiana
3	94	Chris Hope *	Safety	Florida State
4	128	Larry Foote	Linebacker	Michigan
5	166	Verron Haynes	Running back	Georgia
6	202	Lee Mays	Wide receiver	Texas El Paso
7	212	Lavar Glover	Defensive back	Cincinnati
7	242	Brett Keisel *	Defensive end	Brigham Young

2002 AFC Wild Card

An amazing performance from Browns quarterback Kelly Holcomb, was overshadowed by journeyman quarterback Tommy Maddox, who led the Steelers to 29 second half points to overcome a 17-point deficit. A 3-yard touchdown run by Chris Fuamatu-Ma'afala with 54 seconds left capped the game-winning 58-yard drive. On the third play of the game, Holcomb completed an 83-yard pass to Kevin Johnson at the Steelers 1-yard line, setting up William Green's 1-yard touchdown run and giving the Browns a 7–0 lead after just 1:16 had elapsed in the game.

Most of the rest of the quarter would be taken up by drives that ended in punts, but the Steelers got a big scoring opportunity when Amos Zereoué's 36-yard run gave them a first down on the Cleveland 23-yard line. This would only amount to nothing though, as Maddox was intercepted by Browns defensive back Daylon McCutcheon on the next play.

One play into the second quarter, Steelers receiver Antwaan Randle El fumbled a Browns punt, and Chris Akins recovered the ball for Cleveland on the Steelers 32-yard line. On the next play, Cleveland took a 14–0 lead with Holcomb's 32-yard touchdown pass to Dennis Northcutt. The Browns seemed to be taking control of the game now, particularly when another Steelers drive into field goal range was again snuffed out by a McCutheon interception (the Steelers' third turnover in less than six minutes). But suddenly Randle El brought the team right back into the game by returning a punt 66 yards for a touchdown, making the score 14–7. Cleveland stormed right back, as Holcomb's 29-yard pass to Johnson and two completions to running back Jamel White for 22 total yards earned the team a Phil Dawson field goal that made the score 17-7 going into halftime.

Early in the third quarter, Northcutt returned Tom Rouen's 37-yard punt 59 yards to the Pittsburgh 14-yard line, setting up Holcomb's 15-yard touchdown pass to Northcutt that increased the Browns lead to 24-7. Then after a punt, Cleveland drove to the Steelers 32-yard line. They were now in position to build a near-insurmountable lead, but defensive back Mike Logan made a clutch interception to keep the team's victory hopes alive. Maddox then completed 7/8 passes for 62 yards, one of them a 24-

yard completion to Randle El and rushed for eight as he led the team 71 yards to score on his 6-yard touchdown pass to Plaxico Burress, cutting the deficit to 24–14 with four minutes left in the third quarter. Cleveland responded by driving 64 yards in eight plays, featuring a 43-yard completion from Holcomb to receiver André Davis, to score on Dawson's 24-yard field goal on the second play of the final quarter, increasing their lead to 27–14. On Pittsburgh's ensuing drive, Maddox completed three passes to Randle-El for gains of 20, 30, and six yards before finding tight end Jerame Tuman with a 3-yard touchdown pass early in the fourth quarter. But the Browns stormed back, with Green's 23-yard run sparking a 61-yard drive that ended on Holcomb's 22-yard touchdown pass to Davis, giving them a 33–21 lead after the 2-point conversion failed. With 3:06 left in the game, Maddox finished off a 77-yard drive with a 5-yard touchdown pass to Hines Ward, cutting the score to 33–28. The Browns tried to run out the clock on their ensuing possession, but Northcutt dropped a potential first down catch on third down and 12, forcing his team to punt. Taking over at their own 42-yard line, Maddox threw to Burress for 24 yards, Ward for 10, Burress again for 17, and Ward again for seven before Fuamatu-Ma'afala finished the drive with a 3-yard touchdown run. Then Tuman scored the two-point conversion to give the Steelers a 36–33 lead. The Browns attempted to drive for the tying field goal, but time expired in the game on Holcomb's 16-yard completion to Andre King at the Steelers 29-yard line. Maddox completed 30 of 48 passes for a franchise postseason record 367 yards and three touchdowns, with two interceptions. Burress caught six passes for 100 yards and a touchdown, while Ward caught 11 passes for 104 yards and a score. Randle El caught five passes for 85 yards and returned a punt 66 yards for a touchdown. In his first career playoff game, Holcomb completed 26 of 43 passes for 429 yards, three touchdowns, and an interception. Johnson caught four passes for 140 yards, while Northcutt caught six passes for 92 yards and two touchdowns and returned two punts for 70 yards.

1/5/2003	Line/Total	1	2	3	4	Final
Cleveland Browns	{41.0}	7	10	7	9	33
Pittsburgh Steelers	{-8.0}	0	7	7	22	36

Scoring

Team	
Browns	William Green 1 yard rush (Phil Dawson kick)
Browns	Dennis Northcutt 32 yard pass from Kelly Holcomb (Phil Dawson kick)
Steelers	Antwaan Randle El 66 yard punt return (Jeff Reed kick)
Browns	Phil Dawson 31 yard field goal
Browns	Dennis Northcutt 15 yard pass from Kelly Holcomb (Phil Dawson kick)
Steelers	Plaxico Burress 6 yard pass from Tommy Maddox (Jeff Reed kick)
Browns	Phil Dawson 24 yard field goal
Steelers	Jerame Tuman 3 yard pass from Tommy Maddox (Jeff Reed kick)
Browns	Andre' Davis 22 yard pass from Kelly Holcomb (pass failed)
Steelers	Hines Ward 5 yard pass from Tommy Maddox (Jeff Reed kick)
Steelers	Chris Fuamatu-Ma'afala 3 yard rush (Jerame Tuman pass from Antwaan Randle El)

2002 AFC Divisional Playoffs

The third time was the charm for Titans kicker Joe Nedney. After missing the potential game-winning field goal at the end of regulation time, and a second failed kick in overtime was negated because of a controversial running-into-the-kicker penalty on Pittsburgh's Dewayne Washington, Nedney won the game from 26 yards out 2:15 into overtime. Steelers coach Bill Cowher was incensed, saying he called a timeout before the winning kick took place.

Titans defensive back Samari Rolle gave his team an early scoring opportunity when he intercepted Tommy Maddox's first pass of the game and returned it 16 yards to the Tennessee 48-yard line. The Titans then drove 52 yards in seven plays to score on quarterback Steve McNair's 8-yard scramble. Following a Steelers punt, Tennessee drove 76 yards in 16 plays to score on Eddie George's 1-yard touchdown run. The key player of the drive was receiver Drew Bennett, who was responsible for two of the drive's four third down conversions. He caught a 19-yard pass on third and 16 from the Titans 36, and later hauled in a 9-yard catch on third and 8 from the Steelers 43. However, Pittsburgh ended up dominating the second quarter. After punting on their next drive, Steelers defensive back Lethon Flowers recovered a fumble from George (his first fumble of the season) on the Titans 8-yard line, leading to Maddox's 8-yard touchdown pass to Hines Ward. Then Tennessee lost another turnover when McNair threw a pass that was intercepted by Chad Scott on the Steelers 41. On the next play, Maddox completed a 40-yard pass to Plaxico Burress, setting up Jeff Reed's 30-yard field goal that made the score 14–10. The next time they had the ball, they took advantage of a 35-yard pass interference penalty against Rolle, along with three key plays by Ward, who caught two passes for 18 yards and rushed for 11. Reed finished the drive with a 39-yard field goal on the last play of the half, making the score 14-13 going into halftime.

On the first play of the second half, Steelers defensive tackle Casey Hampton forced a fumble from George that Aaron Smith recovered for Pittsburgh on the Titans 31-yard line. On the next play, the team took a 20–14 lead with a 31-yard touchdown run by Amos Zereoué. But Tennessee stormed right back, going into a no-huddle offense and scoring twice in a span of five minutes. First, they responded by driving 70 yards in eight plays, including a 39-yard reception by tight end Frank Wycheck, and scored on McNair's 7-yard touchdown toss to Wycheck that retook the lead. The Steelers had to punt on their next drive, and Derrick Mason returned the ball nine yards to the Titans 42-yard line. McNair then completed two passes to Mason for 24 total yards and one to Wycheck for 21 on the way to his 2-yard touchdown pass to tight end Erron Kinney, giving Tennessee a 28–20 lead with 2:53 left in the third quarter.

The momentum seemed to be back in Tennessee's favor, particularly when Reed missed a 44-yard field goal attempt early in the fourth quarter. But after a Titans punt, Pittsburgh drove 65 yards in seven plays to score on Maddox's 21-yard touchdown pass to Ward. Then Burress caught a pass for a 2-point conversion that tied the game at 28. On the first play after the following kickoff, Deshea Townsend intercepted a pass from McNair on the Steelers 43, leading to Reed's 40-yard field goal that gave the team a 31–28 lead. Titans running back John Simon returned the ensuing kickoff 38 yards to the Steelers 42-yard line, where the team proceeded to drive 38 yards, including a 20-yard catch by Bennett, to tie the game with Nedney's 43-yard field goal. After the next three drives ended in punts, the Titans drove for a potential game-winning field goal, only to have Nedney miss a 48-yard kick on the last play of regulation.

In the first overtime period, referee Ron Blum announced that each team had three timeouts. This caused some confusion because, compared with the regular season, overtime in the postseason utilizes slightly different rules. The Titans took the opening kickoff and McNair threw completions to Justin McCareins for gains of 31 and 22 yards before Robert Holcombe's 3-yard run put the ball on the Steelers 16-yard line. They sent out Nedney to win the game, setting up a wild finish. Nedney's first kick was good, but it was negated because the Steelers had called timeout. The fireworks operator at the stadium inadvertently set off the fireworks, delaying the game for several minutes. After the fireworks had fizzled, Nedney attempted to win the game again. His kick was wide right, but Washington was penalized for running into Nedney. After the five-yard penalty was assessed, Nedney was given a third try. This time he converted the kick, winning the game.

Wycheck finished the game with 10 receptions for 123 yards and a touchdown. McNair threw for a career postseason high 338 yards and two touchdowns, with two interceptions, while rushing for 29 yards and another score on the ground. Maddox threw for 266 yards, two touchdowns, and an interception. Ward caught seven passes for 82 yards and two touchdowns, while also rushing for 11 yards.

1/11/2003	Line/Total	1	2	3	4	OT	Final
Pittsburgh Steelers	{44.0}	0	13	7	11	0	31
Tennessee Titans	{-4.0}	14	0	14	3	3	34

Scoring

Team	
Titans	Steve McNair 8 yard rush (Joe Nedney kick)
Titans	Eddie George 1 yard rush (Joe Nedney kick)
Steelers	Hines Ward 8 yard pass from Tommy Maddox (Jeff Reed kick)
Steelers	Jeff Reed 30 yard field goal
Steelers	Jeff Reed 39 yard field goal
Steelers	Amos Zereoue 31 yard rush (Jeff Reed kick)
Titans	Frank Wycheck 7 yard pass from Steve McNair (Joe Nedney kick)
Titans	Erron Kinney 2 yard pass from Steve McNair (Joe Nedney kick)
Steelers	Hines Ward 21 yard pass from Tommy Maddox (Plaxico Burress pass from Hines Ward)
Steelers	Jeff Reed 40 yard field goal
Titans	Joe Nedney 42 yard field goal
Titans	Joe Nedney 26 yard field goal

2003 Pittsburgh Steelers

Their season began with the team trying to improve on their 10–5–1 record from 2002 in which they lost to the Tennessee Titans in the Divisional round of the playoffs. With the team suffering through injuries as well as less reliance on the running game than normal, the Steelers stumbled to a 6–10 record, going the entire season without winning consecutive games. Since moving to Heinz Field, this marked their first losing season as well as missing the playoffs along with the 2006, 2009, 2012, 2013, 2018 and 2019. The team's 6–10 finish matched their worst under Bill Cowher (1999). In his final season with the team, linebacker Jason Gildon became the franchise's career sack leader during a game against the Arizona Cardinals on November 9. **Antwan Randle-El tied a franchise record with 2 punt return touchdowns**.

Tommy Maddox led the team in passing with 3,414 yards and threw 18 touchdown passes. Jerome Bettis led the team in rushing with 811 yards and 7 rushing touchdowns. Hines Ward led the team in receiving with 95 receptions for 1,163 yards and 2 TD receptions. Brent Alexander led the team with 4 interceptions. **James Farrior set a franchise record with 141 tackles.**

PITTSBURGH			2003			6-10	Game Highlights
9/7/2003		vs	BALTIMORE	34	15	W	Maddox 260 pass yards-3 TD pass/Ward 2 TD catch
9/14/2003		@	Kansas City	20	41	L	**Scott INT return TD**/Maddox 336 pass yds-TD pass
9/21/2003		@	Cincinnati	17	10	W	Maddox 240 pass yards-TD pass to Ward/Bettis TD
9/28/2003		vs	TENNESSEE	13	30	L	Maddox 332 pass yards/Zereoue rush TD
10/5/2003	SNF	vs	CLEVELAND	13	33	L	Bettis rush TD/Reed 2 FGs/Steelers held 60 rush yds
10/12/2003		@	Denver	14	17	L	Bettis rush TD/Reed 2 FGs/Ward 8 catch-81 yards
10/26/2003		vs	ST. LOUIS RAMS	21	33	L	**Randle-El punt return TD**/Ward 2 TD catch
11/2/2003		@	Seattle	16	23	L	Maddox TD pass to Ward-Reed 3 FGs
11/9/2003		vs	ARIZONA	28	15	W	Maddox 159 pass yards-3 TD pass/Ward 2 TD catch
11/17/2003	MNF	@	San Francisco	14	30	L	Bettis rush TD/Randle-El TD catch/Maddox 327 yds
11/23/2003		@	Cleveland	13	6	W	Maddox TD pass to Breuner/Reed 2 FGs
11/30/2003		vs	CINCINNATI	20	24	L	Ward 13 catch-149 yards-TD catch/Bettis rush TD
12/7/2003		vs	OAKLAND RAIDERS	27	7	W	Bettis 106 rush yards-rush TD/Reed 2 FGs
12/14/2003		@	New York Jets	0	6	L	Maddox 137 pass yards/Bettis 68 rush yards
12/21/2003		vs	SAN DIEGO	40	24	W	**Townsend INT return TD**/Burress 2 TD catch
12/28/2003	SNF	@	Baltimore Ravens	10	13	L	**Miller 81 yd TD pass to Hope on fake punt**

Schedule courtesy of Steve's Football Bible LLC

2003 AFC Central	W	L	T	PCT	DIV	CONF	PF	PA
Baltimore Ravens	10	6	0	.625	4–2	7–5	391	281
Cincinnati Bengals	8	8	0	.500	3–3	6–6	346	384
Pittsburgh Steelers	**6**	**10**	**0**	**.375**	**3–3**	**5–7**	**300**	**327**
Cleveland Browns	5	11	0	.313	2–4	3–9	254	322

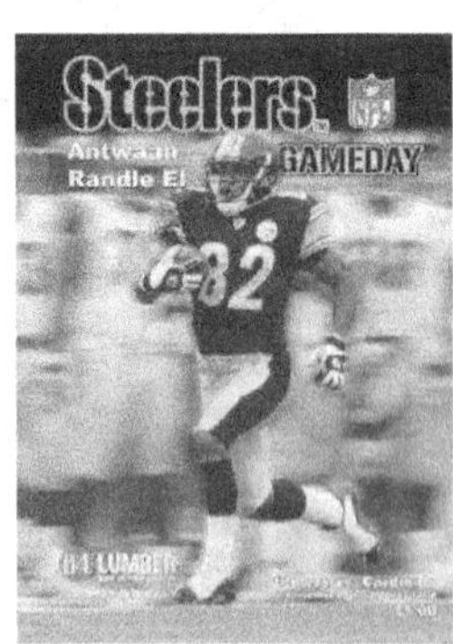

2003 NFL Draft

Round	Choice	Player	Position	School
1	16	Troy Polamalu	DB	USC
2	59	Alonzo Jackson	DE	Florida State
4	125	Ivan Taylor	DB	Louisiana-Lafayette
5	163	Brian St. Pierre	QB	Boston College
7	242	J.T. Wall	RB	Georgia

Oakland Raiders at Pittsburgh

The Raiders' collapse a season after playing in the Super Bowl reached new depths Sunday as Antwaan Randle El's playmaking led the Pittsburgh Steelers to a 27-7 victory in a matchup of disappointing teams. The Steelers outgained Oakland 399-161, with Jerome Bettis moving past Thurman Thomas into ninth place in NFL career rushing with 106 yards. Bettis' 11-yard touchdown run put Pittsburgh up 10-3 during the first 100-yard game by a Steelers runner this season. Randle El, the elusive receiver and kick returner who set NCAA records at Indiana for his versatility, enjoyed the best game of his two-season NFL career. He set up three scores with catches of 24 and 15 yards and a 51-yard punt return and had a 26-yard punt return and an 18-yard run.

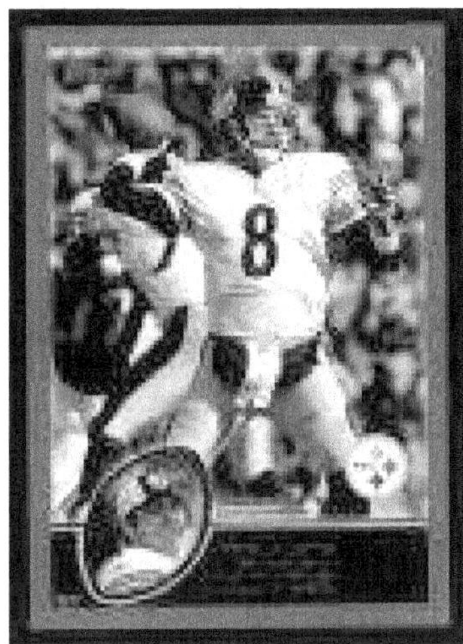

2004 Pittsburgh Steelers

It would be the first season the franchise would have under quarterback Ben Roethlisberger. The team looked to come back after a disappointing 6–10 season the year before, which saw the team go through the entire season without winning consecutive games. The team finished with a 15–1 record, topping the 14–2 team record from 1978 and joined the 1984 San Francisco 49ers, the 1985 Chicago Bears, and the 1998 Minnesota Vikings as the only teams in NFL history to that point since the league adopted a 16-game schedule in 1978 to finish with such a record. This also made the Steelers the first AFC team to achieve a 15–1 record, a conference-best at the time (the 2007 Patriots would surpass that by going a perfect 16–0); they are also the only AFC team to do so. Along the way, the Steelers ended the New England Patriots NFL-record 21-game winning streak in Week 8, then defeated their cross-state rival the Philadelphia Eagles the following week to hand the NFL's last two undefeated teams their first losses in back-to-back weeks, both at home. The season was highlighted by the surprising emergence of rookie quarterback Ben Roethlisberger, the team's top pick in that year's draft. Originally intended to sit behind veteran Tommy Maddox the entire season, plans abruptly changed when Maddox was hurt in the team's Week 2 loss to Baltimore. Surrounded by talent, "Big Ben" went an NFL-record 13–0 as a rookie starting quarterback before being rested for the final game of the season, shattering the old NFL record (and coincidentally, also the team record) of 6–0 to start an NFL career set by Mike Kruczek filling in for an injured Terry Bradshaw in 1976. The Steelers hosted the AFC Championship for the fifth time in eleven years. However, for the fourth time in that same span, the Steelers lost at home one game away from the Super Bowl, and like in 2001, lost to the Patriots in a rematch from Week 8. Alan Faneca {G}, Jeff Hartings {C} and James Farrior {LB} were selected to various first team All-Pro teams.

Ben Roethlisberger led the team in passing with 2,621 yards and threw 17 touchdown passes. Jerome Bettis led the team in rushing with 941 yards and 13 rushing touchdowns. Hines Ward led the team with 80 receptions for 1,004 receiving yards. Plaxico Burress led with 5 TD receptions. Troy Polamalu led the team with 5 interceptions.

PITTSBURGH			2004			16-2	Game Highlights
9/12/2004		vs	OAKLAND RAIDERS	24	21	W	Bettis 3 rush TDs/Reed GW FG with 7 seconds left
9/19/2004		@	Baltimore Ravens	13	30	L	Ward 6 catch-151 yds-TD catch/Big Ben 2 TD pass
9/26/2004	SNF	@	Miami	13	3	W	Ward 9 catch-96 yards-TD catch/Reed 2 FGs
10/3/2004		vs	CINCINNATI	28	17	W	**Polamalu INT return TD**/Haynes TD catch
10/10/2004		vs	CLEVELAND	34	23	W	Burress 6 catch-136 yards-TD catch/Staley 117 yds
10/17/2004		@	Dallas	24	20	W	Roethlisberger 176 pass yards-2 TD pass/Bettis TD
10/31/2004		vs	NEW ENGLAND	34	20	W	**Townsend INT return TD**/Burress 2 TD catch
11/7/2004		vs	PHILADELPHIA	27	3	W	Ward TD catch-rush TD/Reed 2 FGs
11/14/2004		@	Cleveland	24	10	W	**Stuvaints fumble return TD**/Bettis 103 yds-2 TDs
11/21/2004		@	Cincinnati	19	14	W	**Farrior INT return TD**/Big Ben TD pass to Kreider
11/28/2004		vs	WASHINGTON	16	7	W	Bettis 100 rush yards-rush TD/Reed 3 FGs
12/5/2004	SNF	@	Jacksonville	17	16	W	Bib Ben 2 TD pass/Reed GS FG with :18 left
12/12/2004		vs	NEW YORK JETS	17	6	W	Bettis rush TD/Tuman TD catch/Reed FG
12/18/2004	SAT	@	New York Giants	33	30	W	Ward 9 catch-134 yds/Randle-El 149 yds-TD catch
12/26/2004		vs	BALTIMORE RAVENS	20	7	W	Roethlisberger 221 pass yds-2 TD pass/Reed 2 FG
1/2/2005		@	Buffalo	29	24	W	**Harrison fumble return TD**/Reed 5 FGs
1/15/2005	**SAT**	**vs**	**NY JETS (OT)**	**20**	**17**	**W**	Bettis rush TD/Ward TD catch/Reed GS FG in OT
1/23/2005		**vs**	**NEW ENGLAND**	**27**	**41**	**L**	Ward 5 catch-109 yards-TD catch

Schedule courtesy of Steve's Football Bible LLC

2004 AFC North	W	L	T	PCT	DIV	CONF	PF	PA
Pittsburgh Steelers	**15**	**1**	**0**	**.938**	**5–1**	**11–1**	**372**	**251**
Baltimore Ravens	9	7	0	.563	3–3	6–6	317	268
Cincinnati Bengals	8	8	0	.500	4–2	4–8	374	372
Cleveland Browns	4	12	0	.250	1–5	3–9	276	390

2004 NFL Draft

Round	Pick	Player	Position	College
1	11	Ben Roethlisberger *	QB	Miami (OH)
2	38	Ricardo Colclough	CB	Tusculum
3	75	Max Starks	OT	Florida
5	145	Nathaniel Adibi	DE	Virginia Tech
6	177	Bo Lacy	OT	Arkansas
6	194	Matt Kranchick	TE	Penn State
6	197	Drew Caylor	C	Stanford
7	212	Eric Taylor	DT	Memphis

2004 AFC Divisional Playoffs

The Jets came out on the losing end of this overtime game when placekicker Doug Brien missed two consecutive field goals at the end of regulation, setting an NFL record of 3 missed game winning field goals in a single post-season. Despite a subpar performance by Steelers' rookie quarterback Ben Roethlisberger, the Steelers managed to win after Jeff Reed made a game-winning 33-yard field goal 11:04 into the extra period. Steelers running back Jerome Bettis finished the game with 101 rushing yards and a touchdown, along with a 21-yard reception. The Steelers opened up the scoring with a 43-yard field goal by Reed. Then after the ensuing kickoff, Steelers safety Troy Polamalu intercepted a pass from Chad Pennington and returned it 15 yards to the Jets 25-yard line, setting up a 3-yard touchdown run by Bettis. New York Responded with a 42-yard field goal from Brien on their next drive to cut their deficit to 10–3. Later in the second quarter, Jets receiver Santana Moss returned a punt 75 yards for a touchdown to tie the game.

Midway through the third quarter, Jets defensive back Reggie Tongue intercepted a pass from Roethlisberger and returned it 86 yards for a touchdown. On Pittsburgh's next drive, they drove all the way to New York's 23-yard line. But then Bettis fumbled, and New York's Erik Coleman recovered it. After forcing a punt, the Steelers drove into scoring range for the third consecutive drive, this time scoring with Roethlisbeger's 4-yard touchdown pass to Hines Ward to tie it at 17. The Jets responded with a drive inside the Steelers 30-yard line, but Brien missed a 47-yard field goal attempt with 2 minutes left in regulation. Two plays later, New York defensive back David Barrett gave his team another chance to score the winning points by intercepting a pass from Roethlisberger and returning it 25 yards to Pittsburgh's 36-yard line. But Brien missed another field goal, this one from 43 yards, as time expired in the fourth quarter, and the game went into overtime.

The Jets won the coin toss but were forced to punt. Pittsburgh then drove 72 yards in 14 plays and won the game with a 33-yard field goal from Reed.

1/15/2005	Line/Total	1	2	3	4	OT	Final
New York Jets	{35.0}	0	10	7	0	0	17
Pittsburgh Steelers	{-9.0}	10	0	0	7	3	20

Scoring

Team	
Steelers	Jeff Reed 45 yard field goal
Steelers	Jerome Bettis 3 yard rush (Jeff Reed kick)
Jets	Doug Brien 42 yard field goal
Jets	Santana Moss 75 yard punt return (Doug Brien kick)
Jets	Reggie Tongue 86 yard interception return (Doug Brien kick)
Steelers	Hines Ward 4 yard pass from Ben Roethlisberger (Jeff Reed kick)
Steelers	Jeff Reed 33 yard field goal

2004 AFC Championship Game

The game-time temperature of 11 °F made it the second-coldest game ever in Pittsburgh and the coldest ever in Steel City playoff annals. However, it was the Patriots that handed Ben Roethlisberger his first loss as a starter after a 14-game winning streak, the longest by a rookie quarterback in NFL history, as the Steelers became the second NFL team ever to record a 15–1 record and fail to reach the Super Bowl. The Patriots converted four Pittsburgh turnovers into 24 points, while committing no turnovers themselves. The Patriots' win also prevented an all-Pennsylvania Super Bowl from being played.

The Steelers never recovered from their poor performance in the first quarter. Patriots defensive back Eugene Wilson intercepted Roethlisberger's first pass of the game on his own 48-yard line, setting up Adam Vinatieri's 48-yard field goal to take a 3–0 lead. Pittsburgh responded with a drive to the Patriots 39-yard line. But then running back Jerome Bettis lost a fumble while being tackled by Rosevelt Colvin and linebacker Mike Vrabel recovered it. On the next play, Tom Brady threw a 60-yard touchdown pass to receiver Deion Branch. Later, the Steelers took advantage of Josh Miller's 27-yard punt that gave them the ball on their own 48-yard line. Roethlisberger completed a 19-yard pass to Hines Ward on the next play, setting up Jeff Reed's 43-yard field goal that cut the score to 10-3 with 1:26 left in the first quarter. But after an exchange of punts, Branch caught a 45-yard reception on Pittsburgh's 14-yard line. Two plays later, Brady threw a 9-yard touchdown pass to David Givens. Then on the Steelers ensuing drive, safety Rodney Harrison intercepted a pass from Roethlisberger and returned it 87 yards for a touchdown, giving the Patriots a 24–3 halftime lead.

In the second half, the teams scored three consecutive touchdowns. New England was forced to punt on the opening drive of the third quarter, and Antwaan Randle El returned the ball 9 yards to the Steelers 44-yard line. Then on the Steelers ensuing possession, he caught two passes for 46 yards as they drove 56 yards in five plays. Bettis finished the drive with a 5-yard touchdown run, cutting their deficit to 24–10. New England responded by moving the ball 69 yards in seven plays and scoring with Corey Dillon's 25-yard touchdown run. But Pittsburgh stormed right back, driving 60 yards in ten plays and scoring with Roethlisberger's 30-yard touchdown pass to Ward. Then after forcing a punt, Randle El returned the ball 22 yards to the Steelers 49-yard line. On their ensuing drive, Ward's 26-yard reception on the last play of the third quarter set up Reed's second field goal, making the score 31–20 with 13:32 left in the game. However, the Patriots took over the rest of the quarter. They responded with a 49-yard drive that took 5:26 off the clock and ended with Vinatieri's 31-yard field goal. Then two plays after the ensuing kickoff, Wilson intercepted another pass from Roethlisberger at New England's 45-yard line. The Patriots subsequently marched down the field on another long scoring drive, taking 5:06 off the clock. Branch capped it off with a 23-yard touchdown run on a reverse play, giving the Patriots a 41–20 lead. The

Steelers responded with Roethlisberger's 7-yard touchdown pass to Plaxico Burress on their next drive, but by then there was only 1:31 left in the game. Brady completed 14 of 21 passes for 207 yards and 2 touchdowns. Dillon rushed for 73 yards and a touchdown. Branch caught 4 passes for 116 yards, rushed for 37 yards, and scored two touchdowns. Roethlisberger threw for 226 yards and 2 touchdowns, and rushed for 45 yards, but was intercepted 3 times. Ward caught 5 passes for 109 yards and a touchdown.

1/23/2005	Line/Total	1	2	3	4	Final
New England Patriots	{-3.0}	10	14	7	10	41
Pittsburgh Steelers	{35.0}	3	0	14	10	27

Scoring

Team	
Patriots	Adam Vinatieri 48 yard field goal
Patriots	Deion Branch 60 yard pass from Tom Brady (Adam Vinatieri kick)
Steelers	Jeff Reed 43 yard field goal
Patriots	David Givens 9 yard pass from Tom Brady (Adam Vinatieri kick)
Patriots	Rodney Harrison 87 yard interception return (Adam Vinatieri kick)
Steelers	Jerome Bettis 5 yard rush (Jeff Reed kick)
Patriots	Corey Dillon 25 yard rush (Adam Vinatieri kick)
Steelers	Hines Ward 30 yard pass from Ben Roethlisberger (Jeff Reed kick)
Steelers	Jeff Reed 20 yard field goal
Patriots	Adam Vinatieri 31 yard field goal
Patriots	Deion Branch 23 yard rush (Adam Vinatieri kick)
Steelers	Plaxico Burress 7 yard pass from Ben Roethlisberger (Jeff Reed kick)

2005 Pittsburgh Steelers {Super Bowl XL Champions}

It was the 6th season under the leadership of general manager Kevin Colbert and the 14th under head coach Bill Cowher. The Steelers failed to improve upon their 15–1 record from 2004 and in 2005, the Steelers struggled. At one point, they were 7–5 and in danger of missing the playoffs but rose to defeat the Chicago Bears on December 11 and started a four-game win streak to finish the season at 11–5. The Steelers qualified for the playoffs as a wild-card team as the #6 seed and became just the second team ever (and the first in 20 years) to win three games on the road after they beat the #3 seed Cincinnati Bengals (11–5), the top-seeded Indianapolis Colts (14–2), and the #2 seed Denver Broncos (13–3) to become the American Football Conference representative in Super Bowl XL. They defeated the NFC champion Seattle Seahawks in Super Bowl XL to secure their league-tying fifth Super Bowl title. In doing so, they also became the only team at the time since the 1970 AFL-NFL merger to win a Super Bowl without playing a single home playoff game, though the New York Giants would repeat the feat two years later. Troy Polamalu {S}, Alan Faneca {G} and Antwan Randle-El {WR} were selected to various first team All-Pro teams. **Randle-El tied a franchise record with 2 punt returns for touchdowns.**

Ben Roethlisberger led the team in passing with 2,385 yards and threw 17 touchdown passes. Willie Parker led the team in rushing with 1,202 yards. Jerome Bettis led the team with 9 rushing touchdowns. Hines Ward led the team in receiving with 69 receptions for 975 yards and 11 TD receptions. Chris Hope led the team with 3 interceptions.

PITTSBURGH			2005			15-5	Game Highlights
9/11/2005		vs	TENNESSEE TITANS	34	7	W	Parker 161 rush yards-rush TD/Big Ben 2 TD pass
9/18/2005		@	Houston Texans	27	7	W	Roethlisberger 254 pass yards-2 TD pass to Ward
9/25/2005		vs	NEW ENGLAND	20	23	L	Ward 4 catch-110 yards-2 TD catch/Reed 2 FGs
10/10/2005	MNF	@	San Diego Chargers	24	22	W	Roethlisberger TD pass-rush TD/Reed GW FG
10/16/2005		vs	JACKSONVILLE (OT)	17	23	L	**Randle-El punt return TD**/Miller TD catch
10/23/2005		@	Cincinnati	27	13	W	Parker 131 rush yards-rush TD/Bib Ben 2 TD pass
10/31/2005	MNF	vs	BALTIMORE RAVENS	20	19	W	Roethlisberger 2 TD pass to Miller/Reed 2 FGs
11/6/2005		@	Green Bay	20	10	W	**Polamalu fumble return TD**/Staley TD/Reed 2 FGs
11/13/2005	SNF	vs	CLEVELAND	34	21	W	Ward 8 catch-124 yards-TD catch/Reed 2 FGs
11/20/2005		@	Baltimore Ravens (OT)	13	16	L	Maddox 230 pass yards-TD pass to Parker
11/28/2005	MNF	@	Indianapolis Colts	7	26	L	Steelers held to 197 total yards/Ward TD catch
12/4/2005		vs	CINCINNATI	31	38	L	Ward 9 catch-135 yards-2 TD catch/Bettis rush TD
12/11/2005		vs	CHICAGO	21	9	W	Bettis 101 rush yards-2 rush TD/Ward TD catch
12/18/2005		@	Minnesota	18	3	W	Parker 81 rush yards/Big Ben rush TD/Reed 3 FGs
12/24/2005	SAT	@	Cleveland	41	0	W	Parker 130 rush yards-rush TD/Ward 105 yards-TD
1/1/2006		vs	DETROIT	35	21	W	**Randle-El punt return TD**/Bettis 3 rush TD
1/8/2006		@	**Cincinnati**	**31**	**17**	**W**	Roethlisberger 208 pass yards-3 TD pass/Bettis TD
1/15/2006		@	**Indianapolis Colts**	**21**	**18**	**W**	Roethlisberger 2 TD pass/Bettis rush Td
1/22/2006		@	**Denver**	**34**	**17**	**W**	Roethlisberger 275 pass yards-2 TD pass-rush TD
2/5/2006		vs	**Seattle**	**21**	**10**	**W**	Ward 5 catch-123 yards-TD catch/Parker rush TD

Schedule courtesy of Steve's Football Bible LLC

2005 AFC North	W	L	T	PCT	DIV	CONF	PF	PA
Cincinnati Bengals	11	5	0	.688	5–1	7–5	421	350
Pittsburgh Steelers	**11**	**5**	**0**	**.688**	**4–2**	**7–5**	**389**	**258**
Baltimore Ravens	6	10	0	.375	2–4	4–8	265	299
Cleveland Browns	6	10	0	.375	1–5	4–8	232	301

2005 NFL Draft

Round	Pick	Player	Position	College
1	30	Heath Miller *	TE	Virginia
2	62	Bryant McFadden	CB	Florida State
3	93	Trai Essex	T	Northwestern
4	131	Fred Gibson	WR	Georgia
5	166	Rian Wallace	ILB	Temple
6	204	Chris Kemoeatu	G	Utah
7	207	Shaun Nua	NT	BYU
7	244	Noah Herron	RB	Northwestern

2005 AFC Wild Card

The Bengals' first playoff appearance in 15 years began when Pro Bowl quarterback Carson Palmer was knocked out of the game on their opening drive. They still managed to build an early 10-point lead but gave up 24 unanswered points later in the game while turning the ball over three times.

On the Bengals second offensive play of the game, Palmer suffered a season-ending knee injury after being hit by Pittsburgh's Kimo von Oelhoffen, but his 66-yard pass to wide receiver Chris Henry (who was also injured on the play) set up kicker Shayne Graham's 23-yard field goal. Then after forcing a punt, backup quarterback Jon Kitna completed three consecutive passes for 40 yards and rushed for 11, while running back Rudi Johnson finished the drive with a 20-yard touchdown run, increasing their lead to 10–0. Steelers defensive back Ike Taylor returned the ensuing kickoff 36 yards to the 40-yard line. Aided by a 15-yard penalty on cornerback Tory James, the Steelers subsequently drove 60 yards in eight plays and scored with Ben Roethlisberger's 19-yard touchdown pass to Willie Parker. The ensuing kickoff was returned by Tab Perry for 32 yards to his own 43-yard line, and then the Bengals drove 57 yards in 14 plays. Kitna completed the drive with a 7-yard touchdown pass to T. J. Houshmandzadeh, retaking their 10-point lead, 17–7. But on the Steelers ensuing drive, Roethlisberger's 54-yard completion to Cedrick Wilson set up his 5-yard touchdown pass to Hines Ward, cutting the score to 17–14 at halftime.

Cincinnati took the second half kickoff and advanced the ball 62 yards to the Steelers 15-yard line. Graham attempted a 34-yard field goal, but center Brad St. Louis' high snap sent the ball over holder Kyle Larson's head. Graham recovered the fumble, but the Steelers took over on the 34-yard line. On the seventh play of the drive, defensive back Kevin Kaesviharn committed a 40-yard pass interference penalty on the Bengals 5-yard line, and Jerome Bettis ran the ball into the end zone on the next play.

After Cincinnati was forced to punt, Pittsburgh receiver Antwaan Randle El took a direct snap, ran to his right, and threw the ball back to Roethlisberger — who then connected with Wilson for a 43-yard touchdown reception that increased their lead to 28–17. Then on the Bengals next drive, linebacker James Farrior intercepted a pass from Kitna and returned it 22 yards to the Bengals 40-yard line, setting up a 23-yard field goal by Jeff Reed. Later in the fourth quarter, the Bengals managed to drive to the Steelers 43-yard line, but safety Troy Polamalu ended the drive with an interception and the Steelers offense ran out the rest of the clock.

1/8/2006	Line/Total	1	2	3	4	Final
Pittsburgh Steelers	{-3.0}	0	14	14	3	31
Cincinnati Bengals	{46.5}	10	7	0	0	17

Scoring

Team	
Bengals	Shayne Graham 23 yard field goal
Bengals	Rudi Johnson 20 yard rush (Shayne Graham kick)
Steelers	Willie Parker 19 yard pass from Ben Roethlisberger (Jeff Reed kick)
Bengals	T.J. Houshmandzadeh 7 yard pass from Jon Kitna (Shayne Graham kick)
Steelers	Hines Ward 5 yard pass from Ben Roethlisberger (Jeff Reed kick)
Steelers	Jerome Bettis 5 yard rush (Jeff Reed kick)
Steelers	Cedrick Wilson 43 yard pass from Ben Roethlisberger (Jeff Reed kick)
Steelers	Jeff Reed 21 yard field goal

2005 AFC Divisional Playoffs {"The Immaculate Redemption"}

The Steelers became the first #6 playoff seed (since the league expanded to a 12-team playoff format in 1990) to defeat a #1 seed, and the first #6 seed to reach a conference championship game. Colts quarterback Peyton Manning threw for 290 passing yards and a touchdown, but it wasn't enough to win. The Steelers stunned the Colts home crowd at the RCA Dome by driving 84 yards and scoring on their opening possession. Pittsburgh quarterback Ben Roethlisberger completed six consecutive passes for 76 yards, including a 36-yard completion to tight end Heath Miller and a 6-yard touchdown pass to Antwaan Randle El. Later in the first quarter, Roethlisberger's 45-yard completion to Hines Ward moved the ball to the Colts 8-yard line, and they scored another touchdown with his 7-yard pass to Miller, increasing the Steelers' lead to 14–0. Five minutes into the second quarter, Indianapolis managed to get a good drive going, advancing the ball 96 yards to the Steelers 2-yard line and taking 9:39 off the clock, but were forced to settle for a field goal from Mike Vanderjagt, cutting their deficit to 14–3.

Late in the third quarter, Steelers linebacker James Farrior (who finished the game with eight tackles and 2.5 sacks) sacked Manning at the Colts 1-yard line on third down, and Randle El returned Hunter Smith's ensuing punt 20 yards to the Indianapolis 30. Five plays later, Jerome Bettis scored a 1-yard touchdown run, making the score 21–3. But this time, Indianapolis struck back, driving 72 yards in six plays and scoring with Manning's 50-yard touchdown pass to tight end Dallas Clark. The Steelers were forced to punt on their ensuing drive, but only after taking over seven minutes off the clock, leaving just 6:03 left in the game by the time Indianapolis got the ball back.

One play after the punt, an interception by Pittsburgh safety Troy Polamalu was overturned by instant replay (a reversal that the league would later admit was a mistake). Taking advantage of his second chance, Manning completed a 9-yard pass to Clark, a 20-yard pass to Marvin Harrison, and a 24-yard pass to Reggie Wayne, moving the ball to the Steelers 3-yard line. Running back Edgerrin James finished the drive with a 3-yard touchdown run, and then Manning threw a pass to Wayne for a successful 2-point conversion, cutting the Colts deficit to 21–18. The Steelers were forced to punt on their ensuing drive. But with 1:20 left in the game, Manning was sacked on fourth and 16 at the Colts' 2-yard line, and the ball was turned over to the Steelers on downs.

At this point, the game appeared to be over. However, the Steelers were forced to advance the ball towards another score instead of taking a quarterback kneel because the Colts still had three timeouts remaining. But on Pittsburgh's first play, in which Bettis tried to punch it in for an insurance touchdown, he fumbled for the first time all season when linebacker Gary Brackett popped it from Bettis' hands with his helmet. Indianapolis defensive back Nick Harper recovered the ball and

appeared to be on his way for an Indy touchdown that would have given the Colts the lead when Roethlisberger barely made a season saving tackle at the Colts' 42-yard line, recovering from getting spun around to grab Harper's ankle, which brought him down. Eventually, the Colts then advanced to the Pittsburgh 28-yard line, but Vanderjagt, who had been perfect at home in the playoffs, missed a 46-yard game-tying field goal attempt wide right with 17 seconds left, and the Steelers ran out the clock.

1/15/2006	Line/Total	1	2	3	4	Final
Pittsburgh Steelers	{47.5}	14	0	7	0	21
Indianapolis Colts	{-9.5}	0	3	0	15	18

Scoring

Team	
Steelers	Antwaan Randle El 6 yard pass from Ben Roethlisberger (Jeff Reed kick)
Steelers	Heath Miller 7 yard pass from Ben Roethlisberger (Jeff Reed kick)
Colts	Mike Vanderjagt 20 yard field goal
Steelers	Jerome Bettis 1 yard rush (Jeff Reed kick)
Colts	Dallas Clark 50 yard pass from Peyton Manning (Mike Vanderjagt kick)
Colts	Edgerrin James 3 yard rush (Reggie Wayne pass from Peyton Manning)

2005 AFC Championship Game

For the first time since 1984, the Steelers played on the road in the AFC Championship Game, but it hardly mattered as they forced four turnovers and went into halftime with a 24–3 lead en route to advancing to their sixth Super Bowl appearance in team history. In doing so, Pittsburgh became the first #6 playoff seed (since the league expanded to a 12-team playoff format in 1990) to advance to the Super Bowl. Second-year quarterback Ben Roethlisberger, already in his fifth career playoff game, completed 21 of 29 passes for 275 yards and two touchdowns (one each to Cedrick Wilson and Hines Ward) and ran for a third. Steelers running back Jerome Bettis rushed for the other touchdown.

Pittsburgh scored on their opening drive, moving the ball 62 yards in 12 plays and ending it with a Jeff Reed field goal. Three plays after the kickoff, Broncos quarterback Jake Plummer lost a fumble while being sacked by Joey Porter and Steelers lineman Casey Hampton recovered it at the Denver 39-yard line. Four plays later, Roethlisberger's 12-yard touchdown pass to Wilson increased the Steelers lead to 10–0 on the first play of the second quarter. The Broncos responded by driving 55 yards and scoring with a field goal from Jason Elam. But Pittsburgh stormed right back, marching 80 yards in 14 plays and scoring with Bettis' 3-yard touchdown run to take a 17–3 lead. Then on the first play after the ensuing kickoff, defensive back Ike Taylor intercepted a pass from Plummer on the Broncos 39-yard line. Four plays later, a Bettis touchdown run was called back because of a penalty on Ward. But Ward made up for his mistake by catching a touchdown pass on the next play, giving the Steelers a 24–3 lead with seven seconds left in the half.

In the third quarter, Plummer finally got the Broncos moving by completing four consecutive passes for 80 yards, the last one a 30-yard touchdown pass to Ashley Lelie. But Wilson caught two passes for 45 yards on Pittsburgh's next possession, setting up Reed's second field goal to make the score 27–10. In the fourth quarter, a 38-yard reception by Lelie and a 22-yard pass interference penalty on Taylor set up a 3-yard touchdown run by Mike Anderson, cutting Denver's deficit to 27–17. But after a Steelers punt, defensive end Brett Keisel forced a fumble on fourth down from Plummer and his teammate Travis Kirschke recovered it at the Broncos 17-yard line. Four plays later, Roethlisberger ended any chance of a Denver comeback with a 4-yard touchdown run. This would be the Broncos' last playoff game with Mike Shanahan as their head coach.

1/22/2006	Line/Total	1	2	3	4	Final
Pittsburgh Steelers	{41.0}	3	21	0	10	34
Denver Broncos	{-3.0}	0	3	7	7	17

Scoring

Team	
Steelers	Jeff Reed 47 yard field goal
Steelers	Cedrick Wilson 12 yard pass from Ben Roethlisberger (Jeff Reed kick)
Broncos	Jason Elam 23 yard field goal
Steelers	Jerome Bettis 3 yard rush (Jeff Reed kick)
Steelers	Hines Ward 17 yard pass from Ben Roethlisberger (Jeff Reed kick)
Broncos	Ashley Lelie 30 yard pass from Jake Plummer (Jason Elam kick)
Steelers	Jeff Reed 42 yard field goal
Broncos	Mike Anderson 3 yard rush (Jason Elam kick)
Steelers	Ben Roethlisberger 4 yard rush (Jeff Reed kick)

Super Bowl XL

The game was played on February 5, 2006, at Ford Field in Detroit, Michigan. It is currently the last Super Bowl broadcast on ABC and the first where all aspects of the game itself were aired in HD. With the win, the Steelers tied the San Francisco 49ers and the Dallas Cowboys with the then-record five Super Bowls. The Steelers' victory was their first Super Bowl victory since Super Bowl XIV. Pittsburgh, who finished the regular season with an 11–5 record, also became the fourth wild card team, the third in nine years, and the first ever number 6 seed in the NFL playoffs, to win a Super Bowl. The Seahawks, on the other hand, in their 30th season, were making their first ever Super Bowl appearance after posting an NFC-best 13–3 regular season record.

Pittsburgh capitalized on two big plays that were converted into touchdowns. The Steelers jumped to a 14–3 lead early in the third quarter with running back Willie Parker's Super Bowl record 75-yard touchdown run. Seahawks defensive back Kelly Herndon's Super Bowl record 76-yard interception return set up a Seattle touchdown to cut the lead 14–10. But Pittsburgh responded with Antwaan Randle El's 43-yard touchdown pass to Hines Ward, the first time a wide receiver threw a touchdown pass in a Super Bowl, to clinch the game in the fourth quarter. Ward, who caught 5 passes for 123 yards and a touchdown, while also rushing for 18 yards, was named Super Bowl MVP.

After the first four possessions of the Super Bowl XL ended with punts, Seahawks punt returner Peter Warrick gave his team good field position by returning Chris Gardocki's 37-yard punt 12 yards to Seattle's 49-yard line. Quarterback Matt Hasselbeck then started off the drive with a pair of completions to receivers Darrell Jackson and Joe Jurevicius for gains of 20 and 11 yards, respectively. On the third play of the drive, Jackson caught a pass in the end-zone, apparently for a touchdown, but the play was nullified as Jackson was called for pass interference. Running back Shaun Alexander ran the ball the next two plays but gained only three yards. Hasselbeck's third-down pass attempt fell incomplete, and the Seahawks were forced to settle for a 47-yard field goal by kicker Josh Brown, which was successful. By the end of the first quarter, the Steelers had failed to gain a first down, and quarterback Ben Roethlisberger had completed one of five pass attempts for one yard.

On their first second-quarter possession, Pittsburgh once more was forced to punt after three plays, but benefited from another Seahawks penalty, a holding call that nullified Warrick's 34-yard punt return. The Steelers forced a Seattle punt, but Seattle safety Michael Boulware intercepted a Roethlisberger pass at the Seattle 17-yard line on the ensuing drive. The Seahawks, though, were once more forced to punt after three plays, and Pittsburgh drove into Seattle territory on the following drive.

An offensive pass interference call against tight end Heath Miller and a sack for an eight-yard loss by Seahawks defensive end Grant Wistrom, though, backed the Steelers to the 40-yard line, and left the team facing a third-down-and-28. However, Roethlisberger hit receiver Hines Ward out of a scramble and extremely unorthodox, against the grain pass for a 37-yard gain to give the team the longest third down conversion in Super Bowl history. Jerome Bettis carried the ball on the next two plays, taking his team to the one-yard line but not into the end-zone. On the third-down play, after the two-minute warning, Roethlisberger faked a hand-off and dove into the end-zone himself. There was some confusion as to whether he had scored, since the referee hesitated for a bit after the play ended, but he eventually signaled a touchdown, and it was upheld after a replay challenge. On the strength of a 19-yard Jurevicius reception, Seattle advanced the ball to the Pittsburgh 36-yard line, but, after the drive stalled, Brown missed a 54-yard field goal attempt to the right and the Steelers ran out the clock to end the first half.

The Steelers took the ball to begin the second half, and just two plays in, running back Willie Parker broke through for a 75-yard touchdown run, giving his team a 14–3 lead and setting a record for the longest run in Super Bowl history, beating Marcus Allen's Super Bowl XVIII mark by one yard. The Seahawks drove into Pittsburgh territory on the next drive, sparked by a 21-yard run by Alexander, but Brown again missed a field-goal attempt, this one from 50 yards, as Seattle was unable to close the 11-point deficit.

Pittsburgh drove 54 yards to the Seattle six-yard line to put themselves in position to take a large lead, but Seahawks defensive back Kelly Herndon intercepted a pass from Roethlisberger and returned it a Super Bowl record 76 yards to the Steelers 20-yard line. From there, the Seahawks required just two plays to score on Hasselbeck's 16-yard touchdown pass to tight end Jerramy Stevens, cutting their deficit to 14–10. The teams exchanged punts (two from Pittsburgh, one from Seattle) to fill out most of the third quarter, but the Seahawks ended the quarter having driven from their own two-yard line to near midfield. The drive continued in the fourth quarter, as the Seahawks reached the Pittsburgh 19-yard line. An 18-yard pass to Stevens, though, was negated on a penalty call against Seattle tackle Sean Locklear for holding, denying the Seahawks an opportunity for a first-down-and-goal from the 1-yard-line. Three plays later, Pittsburgh defensive back Ike Taylor intercepted a Hasselbeck pass at the 5-yard line and returned it 24 yards. While tackling Taylor, Hasselbeck dove low and was flagged for blocking below the waist. The penalty added 15 yards to the return and gave the Steelers the ball on their own 44-yard line. Four plays later, Pittsburgh ran a wide receiver reverse, but the play turned out to be a pass play by wide receiver Antwaan Randle El, who played quarterback while in college. Parker took a pitch from Roethlisberger and handed off to Randle El, who was running in the opposite direction. Randle El then pulled up and threw a 43-yard touchdown pass to a wide-open Ward, giving the Steelers a 21–10 lead and also marking the first time a wide receiver threw a touchdown pass in a Super Bowl.

On the ensuing possession, Hasselbeck ran the ball for eighteen yards and was briefly touched by Steelers linebacker Larry Foote as the former fell to the ground. Though the play was initially ruled a fumble, with the ball recovered by the Steelers, a Seahawks challenge proved successful, as officials ruled Hasselbeck to have been down prior to his having lost the ball, Seattle, aided by a 13-yard Jurevicius reception, drove to the Pittsburgh 48-yard line but could go no further; a Tom Rouen punt entered the end zone, giving the Steelers possession on their own 20-yard line. Pittsburgh possessed the ball for nearly four-and-one-half minutes on the ensuing drive, as Bettis carried seven times, Seattle was forced to use all of its three timeouts to stop the clock, but nevertheless had only 1:51 left when it took the ball from its own 20-yard line following a Gardocki punt. A 35-yard reception by Jurevicius took the Seahawks into Pittsburgh territory, and a 13-yard Bobby Engram reception took the team to within field-goal range, but dubious clock-management and play-calling left the team with just 35 seconds remaining; an incompletion and a three-yard pass to Stevens over the middle of the field consumed 26 seconds, and Hasselbeck threw incomplete near Stevens on fourth down, giving the Steelers the ball on downs with just three seconds remaining, after which a Roethlisberger kneel-down ended the game.

2/5/2006	Line/Total	1	2	3	4	Final
Seattle Seahawks	{47.0}	3	0	7	0	10
Pittsburgh Steelers	{-4.0}	0	7	7	7	21

Scoring

Team	
Seahawks	Josh Brown 47 yard field goal
Steelers	Ben Roethlisberger 1 yard rush (Jeff Reed kick)
Steelers	Willie Parker 75 yard rush (Jeff Reed kick)
Seahawks	Jerramy Stevens 16 yard pass from Matt Hasselbeck (Josh Brown kick)
Steelers	Hines Ward 43 yard pass from Antwaan Randle El (Jeff Reed kick)

2006 Pittsburgh Steelers

It was the 7th season under the leadership of general manager Kevin Colbert and the 15th and last under head coach Bill Cowher, as he retired on January 5, 2007. The team failed to improve on their 11–5 record from 2005 and failed to defend their Super Bowl XL championship, Instead, they finished the season with an 8–8 record and missed the playoffs for the first time since 2003. Alan Faneca {G} was selected to various first team All-Pro teams. Prior to the season, backup quarterback Tommy Maddox and cornerback Willie Williams (a member of the Super Bowl XL Steelers team) were released for salary cap reasons. Later, the team lost wide receiver Antwaan Randle El, defensive end Kimo von Oelhoffen, and free safety Chris Hope to free agency, but picked up safety Ryan Clark from the Washington Redskins.

Ben Roethlisberger led the team in passing with 3,513 yards and threw 18 touchdown passes. Willie Parker led the team in rushing with 1,494 yards and 13 rushing touchdowns. Hines Ward led the team in receiving with 74 receptions for 875 yards and 6 TD receptions.

PITTSBURGH			2006			8-8		Game Highlights
9/7/2006	TH	vs	MIAMI	28	17	W		**Porter INT return TD**/Miller 3 catch-101 yds-TD
9/18/2006	MNF	@	Jacksonville	0	9	L		Steelers 153 total yards-commit 2 turnovers
9/24/2006		vs	CINCINNATI	20	28	L		Parker 133 rush yards-2 rush TD/Reed 2 FGs
10/8/2006	SNF	@	San Diego Chargers	13	23	L		Parker rush TD/Reed 2 FGs
10/15/2006		vs	KANSAS CITY	45	7	W		**Wallace INT return TD**/Parker 109 rush yards-2 TDs
10/22/2006		@	Atlanta (OT)	38	41	L		Ward 8 catch-171 yards-3 TD catch
10/29/2006		@	Oakland Raiders	13	20	L		Parker 111 total yards-TD/Reed 2 FGs
11/5/2006		vs	DENVER	20	31	L		Parker 137 total yards-rush TD-TD catch/Reed 2 FG
11/12/2006		vs	NEW ORLEANS	38	31	W		Parker 213 rush yards-2 rush TD/Big Ben 3 TD pass
11/19/2006		@	Cleveland	24	20	W		Parker TD catch-rush TD/Holmes TD catch
11/26/2006		@	Baltimore Ravens	0	27	L		Steelers held to 172 yards-commit 3 turnovers
12/3/2006		vs	TAMPA BAY	20	3	W		Roethlisberger 198 pass yards-2 TD pass/Reed 2 FGs
12/7/2006	TH	vs	CLEVELAND	27	7	W		Parker 223 rush yards-rush TD/Washington TD catch
12/17/2006		@	Carolina	37	3	W		**Holmes punt return TD**/Parker 132 yards-rush TD
12/24/2006		vs	BALTIMORE RAVENS	7	31	L		Steelers 63 rush yards/Miller TD catch
12/31/2006		@	Cincinnati (OT)	23	17	W		Parker 134 rush yards-2 rush TD/Homes GW TD

Schedule courtesy of Steve's Football Bible LLC

2006 AFC North	W	L	T	PCT	DIV	CONF	PF	PA
Baltimore Ravens	13	3	0	.813	5–1	10–2	353	201
Cincinnati Bengals	8	8	0	.500	4–2	6–6	373	331
Pittsburgh Steelers	**8**	**8**	**0**	**.500**	**3–3**	**5–7**	**353**	**315**
Cleveland Browns	4	12	0	.250	0–6	3–9	238	356

Pittsburgh at Cleveland Browns

After a scoreless first quarter, the Steelers trailed as DB Daven Holly returned an interception 57 yards for a touchdown. Afterwards, kicker Phil Dawson nailed a 23-yard field goal. In the third quarter, Pittsburgh finally scored as kicker Jeff Reed completed a 43-yard field goal for the only score of the quarter. In the fourth quarter, Dawson made a 35-yard field goal for the Browns, while the Steelers responded with QB Ben Roethlisberger completed a 20-yard TD pass to rookie WR Santonio Holmes. However, things looked grim as Browns WR Joshua Cribbs returned a kickoff 92 yards for a touchdown. RB Willie Parker answered with a 1-yard TD run and a 4-yard touchdown reception. Afterwards, the Pittsburgh managed to hold off a late drive by Cleveland.

2006 NFL Draft

Round	Pick	Player	Position	College
1	25	Santonio Holmes	WR	Ohio State
3	83	Anthony Smith	FS	Syracuse
3	95	Willie Reid	WR	Florida State
4	131	Willie Colon	T	Hofstra
4	133	Orien Harris	NT	Miami
5	164	Omar Jacobs	QB	Bowling Green
5	167	Charles Davis	FB	Purdue
6	201	Marvin Philip	G	California

Pittsburgh at Cincinnati Bengals

After a scoreless first quarter, Pittsburgh drew first blood in the second quarter with RB Willie Parker getting a 1-yard TD run. Afterwards, the Bengals managed to salvage a 34-yard field goal by kicker Shayne Graham. After a scoreless third quarter, Cincinnati took the lead by getting a Willie Parker fumble and ending it with QB Carson Palmer completing a 66-yard TD pass to WR Chris Henry. Parker managed to make amends with another 1-yard TD run. However, the Bengals went back into the lead with Palmer completing a 5-yard TD pass to TE Tony Stewart. The Steelers tied the game late with kicker Jeff Reed nailing a 35-yard field goal. Cincinnati quickly managed to get into field goal range, but Graham's 39-yard field goal went wide right. In overtime, Pittsburgh took advantage and won with QB Ben Roethlisberger's 67-yard TD pass to rookie WR Santonio Holmes.

2007 Pittsburgh Steelers

The 2007 Pittsburgh Steelers season was the franchise's 75th season as a member of the National Football League. It was the 8th season under leadership of general manager Kevin Colbert and the first under head coach Mike Tomlin, after going 8–8 last season. The Steelers finished the year at 10–6. However, they lost 31–29 at home to the Jacksonville Jaguars in the Wild Card round. Alan Faneca {G} was selected to various first team All-Pro teams.

Ben Roethlisberger led the team in passing with 3,154 yards and threw 32 touchdown passes. Willie Parker led the team in rushing with 1,316 yards. Najeh Davenport led with 5 rushing touchdowns. Hines Ward led the team with 71 receptions for 732 yards. Santonio Holmes led with 8 TD receptions.

PITTSBURGH			2007			10-7		Game Highlights
9/9/2007		@	Cleveland	34	7	W		Roethlisberger 161 pass yards-4 TD pass/Reed 2 FG
9/16/2007		vs	BUFFALO	26	3	W		Parker 126 rush yards-rush TD/Reed 4 FGs
9/23/2007		vs	SAN FRANCISCO	37	16	W		**Rossum kickoff return TD**/McFadden INT TD
9/30/2007		@	Arizona Cardinals	14	21	L		Holmes 6 catch-128 yards-2 TD catch
10/7/2007		vs	SEATTLE	21	0	W		Parker 102 rush yards/Davenport 2 rush TD
10/21/2007	SNF	@	Denver	28	31	L		Roethlisberger 290 pass yds-4 TD pass/Miller 2 TD
10/28/2007		@	Cincinnati	24	13	W		Ward 8 catch-88 yards-2 TD catch/Parker rush TD
11/5/2007	MNF	vs	BALTIMORE RAVENS	38	7	W		Holmes & Washington 2 TD catch each/Miller TD
11/11/2007		vs	CLEVELAND	31	28	W		Roethlisberger 278 pass yards-2 TD pass-rush TD
11/18/2007		@	New York Jets (OT)	16	19	L		Reed 3 FGs/Roethlisberger TD pass to Holmes
11/26/2007	MNF	vs	MIAMI	3	0	W		Ward 9 catch-88 yards/Redd GW FG with :17 left
12/2/2007	SNF	vs	CINCINNATI	24	10	W		Ward 11 catch-90 yds-2 TD catch/Big Ben rush TD
12/9/2007		@	New England Patriots	13	34	L		Parker 124 rush yards/Davenport TD catch
12/16/2007		vs	JACKSONVILLE	22	29	L		Roethlisberger 3 TD pass/Parker 100 rush yards
12/20/2007	TH	@	St. Louis Rams	41	24	W		**Taylor INT return TD**/Roethlisberger 3 TD pass
12/30/2007		@	Baltimore Ravens	21	27	L		Batch 218 pass yards-2 TD pass
1/5/2008	SAT	vs	**JACKSONVILLE**	29	31	L		Davenport 2 rush TD/Ward 10 catch-135 yards

Schedule courtesy of Steve's Football Bible LLC

2007 AFC North	W	L	T	PCT	DIV	CONF	PF	PA
Pittsburgh Steelers	**10**	**6**	**0**	**.625**	**5–1**	**7–5**	**393**	**269**
Cleveland Browns	10	6	0	.625	3–3	7–5	402	382
Cincinnati Bengals	7	9	0	.438	3–3	6–6	380	385
Baltimore Ravens	5	11	0	.313	1–5	2–10	275	384

Cleveland Browns at Pittsburgh

In the first quarter, Pittsburgh trailed early as Browns QB Derek Anderson completed a 4-yard TD pass to TE Kellen Winslow. The Steelers managed to get a 28-yard field goal from kicker Jeff Reed. In the second quarter, Cleveland increased its lead with Anderson completing a 2-yard TD pass to FB Lawrence Vickers, while Pittsburgh only managed to have Reed kick a 35-yard field goal. Afterwards, the Browns continued their fast start with Anderson completing a 16-yard TD pass to

WR Braylon Edwards. The Steelers drove into the red zone once again but settled for a 30-yard field goal from Reed. Both teams scored thrice in the first half; Cleveland led 21–9. In the third quarter, Pittsburgh began to come back as QB Ben Roethlisberger completed a 12-yard TD pass to WR Hines Ward for the only score of the period. In the fourth quarter, the Steelers took the lead with Roethlisberger getting a career-best 30-yard TD run. Cleveland WR/KR Joshua Cribbs returned the ensuing kickoff 100 yards for a touchdown. Pittsburgh on their next drive retook the lead with Roethlisberger completing a 2-yard TD pass to TE Heath Miller. The Browns tried to force overtime with a late field goal, but kicker Phil Dawson's 53-yard attempt came up short with 6 seconds left.

2007 NFL Draft

Round	Pick	Player	Position	College
1	15	Lawrence Timmons *	ILB	Florida State
2	46	LaMarr Woodley *	OLB	Michigan
3	77	Matt Spaeth	TE	Minnesota
4	112	Daniel Sepulveda	P	Baylor
4	132	Ryan McBean	NT	Oklahoma State
5	156	Cameron Stephenson	G	Rutgers
5	170	William Gay	CB	Louisville
7	227	Dallas Baker	WR	Florida

2007 AFC Wild Card

In a rematch of week 15, Jacksonville gained only 239 yards of offense, but still managed to win on Josh Scobee's 25-yard field goal with 37 seconds left. The Jaguars defense sacked Steelers quarterback Ben Roethlisberger six times, intercepted three of his passes, and forced him to lose a fumble on the final drive of the game. It was their first playoff win in eight years and their first playoff win on the road in ten years. For the Steelers, it marked the first time in franchise history they lost to one team at home two times in a season.

Pittsburgh opened the scoring by marching 80 yards in 10 plays on their first drive and finishing it off with Najeh Davenport's 1-yard touchdown run. But Jaguars running back Maurice Jones-Drew returned the ensuing kickoff 96 yards to the 1-yard line, and Fred Taylor scored a 1-yard touchdown run on the next play. Early in the second quarter, Jacksonville defensive back Rashean Mathis intercepted a pass from  Roethlisberger and returned it 63 yards for a touchdown. Then shortly after the kickoff, Mathis intercepted another pass at the Steelers 46-yard line, setting up David Garrard's 43-yard touchdown pass to Jones-Drew and making the score 21–7. Later in the second quarter, the Steelers took advantage of a missed Scobee field goal by driving all the way to the Jaguars 21-yard line. But defensive tackle Derek Landri intercepted a short pass from Roethlisberger, and the score remained 21–7 at halftime.

In the second half, the Steelers scored on their first four drives. Three plays after the opening kickoff, linebacker James Farrior's interception of a Garrard pass set up Jeff Reed's 28-yard field goal. Jacksonville responded by driving 82 yards in eight plays, with Garrard rushing for 15 yards and completing two passes to Ernest Wilford for 39, while Jones-Drew capped the drive with a 10-yard touchdown run, increasing their lead to 28–10. But the Steelers drove right back, and on the first play of the fourth quarter, facing fourth down and 12 on the Jags 37-yard line, Roethlisberger threw a 37-yard touchdown pass to Santonio Holmes. Then after a punt, Roethlisberger completed six passes for 65 yards on a 69-yard drive that ended with his 14-yard touchdown pass to Heath Miller. The Steelers attempted a two-point conversion to cut the lead to three points, and Roethlisberger initially completed a pass to Hines Ward, but the play was nullified by a holding penalty and Pittsburgh's second attempt was incomplete, keeping the score at 28–23. Three plays after the ensuing kickoff, Steelers defensive back Ike Taylor intercepted a pass from Garrard and returned it 31 yards to the Jacksonville 16-yard line.

Following a pass interference penalty against the Jaguars in the end zone on a fourth down play, Davenport scored his second 1-yard touchdown run of the day. The two-point conversion failed again, but the Steelers took the lead, 29–28. Jacksonville was unable to score on their next drive, but they forced the Steelers to punt after three plays and Dennis Northcutt returned the punt 16 yards, giving the Jaguars the ball at their own 49-yard line with one timeout remaining and 2:38 left to play. Three plays later on fourth down and 2, Garrard dropped back to pass, but then ran back to the line and took off for a 32-yard burst to the Steelers 11-yard line. After a few more running plays, Scobee kicked a 25-yard field goal, giving his team a 31–29 lead. The Steelers got the ball back with 37 seconds left, but Jaguars defensive end Bobby McCray sealed the victory by forcing a fumble from Roethlisberger which was recovered by Landri.

1/5/2008	Line/Total	1	2	3	4	Final
Jacksonville Jaguars	{-2.5}	7	14	7	3	31
Pittsburgh Steelers	{39.5}	7	0	3	19	29

Scoring

Team	
Steelers	Najeh Davenport 1 yard rush (Jeff Reed kick)
Jaguars	Fred Taylor 1 yard rush (Josh Scobee kick)
Jaguars	Rashean Mathis 63 yard interception return (Josh Scobee kick)
Jaguars	Maurice Jones-Drew 43 yard pass from David Garrard (Josh Scobee kick)
Steelers	Jeff Reed 28 yard field goal
Jaguars	Maurice Jones-Drew 10 yard rush (Josh Scobee kick)
Steelers	Santonio Holmes 37 yard pass from Ben Roethlisberger (Jeff Reed kick)
Steelers	Heath Miller 14 yard pass from Ben Roethlisberger
Steelers	Najeh Davenport 1 yard rush (pass failed)
Jaguars	Josh Scobee 25 yard field goal

2008 Pittsburgh Steelers {Super Bowl XLIII Champions}

The season concluded with the team winning Super Bowl XLIII to become the first franchise in the NFL with six Super Bowl titles. The Steelers entered the season as defending champions of the AFC North Division, coming off a 10–6 record in 2007. Based on the previous season's results, the team faced the most difficult schedule in over 30 years; however, they were called Super Bowl contenders by ESPN. The Steelers opened their regular season on September 7, with a win over the Houston Texans en route to a 12–4 record, and a second straight AFC North Division title. In his second season as head coach Mike Tomlin was selected in fan balloting as the Motorola Coach of the Year. Linebacker James Harrison was named the NFL's Defensive Player of the Year after leading a defense which set the standard for the league in nearly every defensive category, including total yardage allowed, points allowed, passing yardage allowed, first downs allowed, yards per play, and yards per pass, among others. The playoffs began on January 11, 2009, with a win over the San Diego Chargers. The following week saw the third victory of the season over the Baltimore Ravens in the AFC Championship game and the advancement to Super Bowl XLIII where the Steelers defeated the Arizona Cardinals on February 1, 2009. Prior to the season, the Steelers lost ten-year lineman Alan Faneca, after his contract expired, and he signed with the New York Jets. Allen Rossum, Jerame Tuman, and Clint Kriewaldt were released on February 22. The team also lost Dan Kreider, Verron Haynes, Brian St. Pierre, and eight-year veteran Clark Haggans to free agency. James Harrison {LB} and Troy Polamalu {S} were selected to various first team All-Pro teams.

Ben Roethlisberger led the team in passing with 3,301 yards and threw 17 touchdown passes. Willie Parker led the team in rushing with 795 yards and 5 rushing touchdowns. Hines Ward led the team with 81 receptions for 1,043 yards and 7 TD receptions.

PITTSBURGH			2008			15-4	Game Highlights
9/7/2008		vs	HOUSTON TEXANS	38	17	W	Parker 138 rush yards-3 rush TD/Ward 2 TD catch
9/14/2008	SNF	@	Cleveland	10	6	W	Parker 105 rush yards-Hines TD catch
9/21/2008		@	Philadelphia	6	15	L	Steelers held to 33 rush yards/Reed 2 FGs
9/29/2008	MNF	vs	BALTIMORE (OT)	23	20	W	**Woodley fumble return TD**/Reed 3 FGs
10/5/2008	SNF	@	Jacksonville	26	21	W	Roethlisberger 309 pass yards-3 TD pass/Reed 2 FG
10/19/2008		@	Cincinnati	38	10	W	Moore 120 rush yards-2 rush TD-TD catch
10/26/2008		vs	N.Y. GIANTS	14	21	L	Moore rush TD/Washington TD catch
11/3/2008	MNF	@	Washington Redskins	23	6	W	Parker-Roethlisberger rush TDs/Holmes TD catch
11/9/2008		vs	INDIANAPOLIS	20	24	L	Moore 2 rush TDs/Reed 2 FGs/Ward 8 catch-112 yds
11/16/2008		vs	SAN DIEGO	11	10	W	Reed 3 FGs/Roethlisberger 308 pass yards
11/20/2008	TH	vs	CINCINNATI	27	10	W	Roethlisberger 243 pass yards-TD pass to Miller
11/30/2008		@	New England Patriots	33	10	W	Roethlisberger 179 pass yards-2 TD pass/Reed 4 FGs
12/7/2008		vs	DALLAS	20	13	W	**Townsend INT return TD**/Reed 2 FGs/Miller TD
12/14/2008		@	Baltimore Ravens	13	9	W	Holmes TD catch/Reed 2 FGs/Ward 8 catch-107 yds
12/21/2008		@	Tennessee Titans	14	31	L	Roethlisberger 329 pass yards-2 TD pass/Ward 109 yds
12/28/2008		vs	CLEVELAND	31	0	W	**Carter INT return TD**/Leftwich-Parker-Russell TDs
1/11/2009		vs	**SAN DIEGO**	**35**	24	W	**Holmes punt return TD/Parker 146 rush yards-2 TDs**
1/18/2009		vs	**BALTIMORE**	23	14	W	**Polamalu INT return TD**/Reed 3 FGs/Holmes TD
2/1/2009		vs	**Arizona Cardinals**	27	23	W	**Harrison INT return TD**/Holmes GW TD catch

Schedule courtesy of Steve's Football Bible LLC

2008 AFC North	W	L	T	PCT	DIV	CONF	PF	PA
Pittsburgh Steelers	12	4	0	.750	6–0	10–2	347	223
Baltimore Ravens	11	5	0	.688	4–2	8–4	385	244
Cincinnati Bengals	4	11	1	.281	1–5	3–9	232	350
Cleveland Browns	4	12	0	.250	1–5	3–9	204	364

2008 NFL Draft

Round	Pick	Player	Position	College
1	23	Rashard Mendenhall	Running back	Illinois
2	53	Limas Sweed	Wide receiver	Texas
3	88	Bruce Davis	Linebacker	UCLA
4	130	Tony Hills	Offensive tackle	Texas
5	156	Dennis Dixon	Quarterback	Oregon
6	188	Mike Humpal	Linebacker	Iowa
6	194	Ryan Mundy	Safety	West Virginia

2008 AFC Divisional Playoffs

Pittsburgh gained 342 yards, did not commit any turnovers, held the ball for 36:30, and scored a touchdown in every quarter to defeat the Chargers. Willie Parker led the Steelers offense with 147 rushing yards and two touchdowns. However, the Chargers took the opening kickoff and scored with Philip Rivers' 48-yard touchdown pass to Vincent Jackson just two minutes into the game. Pittsburgh responded with a drive to the San Diego 34-yard line. On fourth down, rather than risk a long field goal attempt, they faked attempting to gain a first down and ran a surprise pooch punt with quarterback Ben Roethlisberger, who kicked the ball 25 yards to the San Diego 9-yard line. Following a three-and-out, Steelers receiver Santonio Holmes returned Mike Scifres' punt 65 yards for a touchdown to tie the game.

Late in the second quarter, Pittsburgh tried to fool the Chargers with another trick play, this one a fake punt with a direct snap to safety Ryan Clark. But the Chargers back-up linebacker Antwan Applewhite tackled Clark for a 4-yard loss on the Steelers 44-yard line. Several plays later, Nate Kaeding's 42-yard field goal gave San Diego a 10–7 lead on the first play after the two-minute warning. But with less than one minute left, Roethlisberger's 41-yard completion to Hines Ward moved the ball to the Chargers 3-yard line. On the next play, Parker's 3-yard touchdown run gave the Steelers a 14–10 halftime lead.

Pittsburgh dominated the third quarter, starting it out with a 77-yard drive that ended with Roethlisberger's 8-yard touchdown pass to tight end Heath Miller. Meanwhile, their defense limited San Diego to just one play in the entire quarter, an interception by linebacker Larry Foote that negated a 63-yard kickoff return by Darren Sproles.

In the fourth quarter, San Diego managed to make a goal line stand, tackling fullback Carey Davis for no gain on fourth down and 1 on the Chargers 1-yard line. After taking over at their own 1-yard line, the Chargers appeared to escape the shadow of their own end zone when Rivers hit Jacob Hester with a pass for an 11-yard gain. But a 10-yard sack by LaMarr Woodley and two incompletions forced San Diego to punt from their own 2, and Holmes returned the ball six yards to the 49-yard line. One play later, a 44-yard pass interference penalty on Eric Weddle in the end zone moved the ball to the 1-yard line and running back Gary Russell scored a 1-yard touchdown run on the next play, increasing Pittsburgh's lead to 28–10.

Rivers then led the Chargers 73 yards in 10 plays and finished the drive with a 4-yard touchdown pass to Legedu Naanee. But the Steelers stormed right back, with Parker rushing five times for 53 yards and finishing the drive with a 16-yard touchdown run. Following an exchange of punts, Rivers threw a 62-yard touchdown pass to Sproles, cutting the score to 35–24, but by then there was less than two minutes left in the game.

1/11/2009	Line/Total	1	2	3	4	Final
San Diego Chargers	{37.5}	7	3	0	14	24
Pittsburgh Steelers	{-6.0}	7	7	7	14	35

Scoring

Team	
Chargers	Vincent Jackson 41 yard pass from Philip Rivers (Nate Kaeding kick)
Steelers	Santonio Holmes 67 yard punt return (Jeff Reed kick)
Chargers	Nate Kaeding 42 yard field goal
Steelers	Willie Parker 3 yard rush (Jeff Reed kick)
Steelers	Heath Miller 8 yard pass from Ben Roethlisberger (Jeff Reed kick)
Steelers	Gary Russell 1 yard rush (Jeff Reed kick)
Chargers	Legedu Naanee 4 yard pass from Philip Rivers (Nate Kaeding kick)
Steelers	Willie Parker 16 yard rush (Jeff Reed kick)
Chargers	Darren Sproles 62 yard pass from Philip Rivers (Nate Kaeding kick)

2008 AFC Championship Game

Pittsburgh held the Ravens to 184 yards and forced five turnovers, including three in the last 3:13 of the game, en route to their seventh Super Bowl appearance in franchise history. Baltimore became the third consecutive road team (Pittsburgh was the last to win it), and the 11th out of 19 since the 1990 season, to lose the AFC title game and thus unable to duplicate their success in 2000 as a wild card team advancing to the Super Bowl.

On the first drive of the game, Ben Roethlisberger's 45-yard completion to Hines Ward set up a 34-yard field goal by Jeff Reed. Later in the first quarter, Steelers defensive back Deshea Townsend intercepted a pass from Joe Flacco and returned it to the Ravens 35-yard line. A few plays later, Santonio Holmes appeared to catch a 23-yard pass on the 1, but it was overruled by a Baltimore replay challenge, and they ended up settling for a 42-yard field goal to make the score 6–0. Later, the Ravens got a scoring opportunity when linebacker Ray Lewis forced a fumble from Pittsburgh running back Willie Parker and safety Jim Leonhard recovered it on the Steelers 43-yard line. But Baltimore turned the ball over on downs after failing to convert a first down on third and fourth down and 1.

Pittsburgh increased their lead to 13–0 on the second play of the second quarter with Roethlisberger's 65-yard touchdown pass to Holmes. But after several punts, a 45-yard punt return from Leonhard gave the Ravens a first down on the Pittsburgh 17-yard line. Two plays later, Willis McGahee scored a 3-yard touchdown run. Following an exchange of punts, Holmes returned a punt 25 yards to midfield. But the Steelers blew two chances to score before halftime. First, receiver Limas Sweed dropped a wide-open pass near the end zone and the team ended up punting. However, a roughing the punter penalty allowed the Steelers to retain possession. Heath Miller's 14-yard reception on the next play moved the ball to the Ravens 21-yard line with 23 seconds left in the half and no timeouts left. Pittsburgh decided to run a few more plays before attempting a field goal, but Mewelde Moore's 8-yard reception in the middle of the field took too much time off the clock, and Pittsburgh could not spike the ball before time in the half expired.

Midway through the third quarter, Pittsburgh drove 51 yards and scored with Reed's third field goal of the game, making the score 16–7. But in the fourth quarter, the Ravens took advantage of another key special teams play when Mitch Berger's punt went just 21 yards to the Baltimore 42-yard line. Flacco then led the Ravens 58 yards, completing all four of his passes for 44 yards on the way to a 1-yard touchdown run by McGahee, cutting their deficit to 16–14. Baltimore's defense subsequently forced a punt and got the ball back on their own 14-yard line with just over six minutes left in the game. But four plays later, safety Troy Polamalu intercepted a pass from Flacco, ran all the way across the field, and took off for a 40-yard touchdown return, making the score 23–14. Pittsburgh then put the game away by forcing two more turnovers on the Ravens next two drives. First, a hit by Ryan Clark on McGahee forced a fumble that was recovered by linebacker Lawrence Timmons; McGahee suffered a concussion and was removed from the field on a stretcher. Then after a punt, Tyrone Carter intercepted a pass from Flacco with less than a minute left in the game.

1/18/2009	Line/Total	1	2	3	4	Final
Baltimore Ravens	{37.5}	0	7	0	7	14
Pittsburgh Steelers	{-6.0}	6	7	3	7	23

Scoring

Steelers	Jeff Reed 34 yard field goal
Steelers	Jeff Reed 42 yard field goal
Steelers	Santonio Holmes 65 yard pass from Ben Roethlisberger (Jeff Reed kick)
Ravens	Willis McGahee 3 yard rush (Matt Stover kick)
Steelers	Jeff Reed 46 yard field goal
Ravens	Willis McGahee 1 yard rush (Matt Stover kick)
Steelers	Troy Polamalu 40 yard interception return (Jeff Reed kick)

Super Bowl XLIII {"The Best Ever"}

The game was played on February 1, 2009, at Raymond James Stadium in Tampa, Florida. With this victory, the Steelers became the first team to win six Super Bowl championships. The win was also Pittsburgh's second Super Bowl victory in four years, after winning Super Bowl XL at the end of the 2005 season. The Cardinals entered the game seeking their first NFL title since 1947, the longest championship drought in the league. The club became an unexpected winner during the regular season, compiling a 9–7 record, and the playoffs with the aid of head coach Ken Whisenhunt, who was the Steelers' offensive coordinator in Super Bowl XL, and the re-emergence of quarterback Kurt Warner, who was the Super Bowl MVP in Super Bowl XXXIV with his former team, the St. Louis Rams.

Pittsburgh jumped to a 17–7 halftime lead, aided by linebacker James Harrison's Super Bowl-record 100-yard interception return for a touchdown. Trailing 20–7 at the start of the fourth quarter, Arizona scored 16 consecutive points, including a safety by Pittsburgh that led to wide receiver Larry Fitzgerald's 64-yard touchdown reception, to take the first lead of the game with 2:37 remaining. But the Steelers marched 78 yards to score on wide receiver Santonio Holmes' 6-yard game-winning touchdown catch with 35 seconds left. Holmes, who caught nine passes for 131 yards and a touchdown, including four receptions for 73 yards on that final game-winning drive, was named Super Bowl MVP.

Pittsburgh took the opening kickoff and moved down the field on a 71-yard scoring drive, with quarterback Ben Roethlisberger completing a 38-yard pass to wide receiver Hines Ward and a 21-yard strike to Heath Miller, putting the ball at the Arizona 1-yard line. On third down, Roethlisberger appeared to score on a quarterback scramble, but it was overruled by a replay challenge, which determined that he was down before the ball crossed the goal line. Rather than make another attempt at a touchdown, Pittsburgh settled for a Jeff Reed 18-yard field goal to take the 3–0 lead. The Steelers quickly forced an Arizona punt and then drove back down the field for what would turn into more points. On the first play of their drive, Roethlisberger completed a 25-yard pass to Santonio Holmes. Following three more completions to Miller for 26 yards and another one to Holmes for 7, reserve running back Gary Russell went into the end zone for a 1-yard touchdown run to make the score 10–0 on the second play of the second quarter. They became the first team to score on its first two drives since the Denver Broncos in Super Bowl XXXII. On defense, Pittsburgh held Arizona to just one drive and one first down in the first quarter, while gaining 135 yards.

The Cardinals got going for the first time midway through the second quarter as a 45-yard completion from Kurt Warner to Anquan Boldin moved the ball to the Steelers' 1-yard line. On the next play, Warner nearly fell over after taking the snap, but he regained his balance and threw a 1-yard touchdown pass to tight end Ben Patrick. After an exchange of punts, Roethlisberger threw a pass that was tipped at the line of scrimmage and intercepted by linebacker Karlos Dansby at the Steelers 34-yard line with 2:46 left in the half. Seven plays later, the Cardinals drove to a first down on the Pittsburgh 1-yard line. But with 18 seconds left, Warner's pass intended for Boldin was intercepted at the goal line by linebacker James Harrison, who then took off down the sideline for the then-longest play in Super Bowl history (having since been passed by Jacoby Jones' 108-yard kickoff return in Super Bowl XLVII), a 100-yard return for a touchdown, increasing the Steelers' lead to 17–7 at halftime. Harrison faked a blitz and quietly moved into coverage to pick off Warner's pass. A booth review was called to verify that Harrison had broken the plane, as he was tackled at the goal line, and the ruling stood.

After forcing a punt, the Steelers started off the third quarter with another long scoring drive. Aided by three personal foul penalties against Arizona, they moved the ball 79 yards in 14 plays and took 8:39 off the clock. However, they were unable to get into the end zone, despite two first downs inside the Cardinals 10 (a penalty against Arizona on a Steelers field goal attempt gave them another chance), and they had to settle for another Reed field goal to give them a 13-point lead, 20–7.

After a few more punts, Warner led the Cardinals down the field on an eight-play, 87-yard scoring drive that took 3:57 off the clock, utilizing a no huddle offense. With 7:33 left in the game, Warner threw a fade pass to Fitzgerald, who made a leaping catch through tight coverage by Ike Taylor for a touchdown, making the score 20–14. Later, Ben Graham's 34-yard punt pinned the Steelers back at their own 1-yard line. Two plays later on third down and 10, Roethlisberger threw a 20-yard pass to Holmes, but center Justin Hartwig was called for holding in the end zone, which not only nullified the catch, but gave the  Cardinals a safety, raising the score to 20–16. Steelers coach Mike Tomlin later stated that losing the two points didn't faze him, as it did not change how the Steelers called plays for the rest of the game on either defense or offense. Taking over on their own 36 after the free kick, Arizona took two plays to score, as Warner threw a pass to Fitzgerald on a post route. Fitzgerald caught the ball without breaking stride and took off down the middle of the field past the Steelers secondary for a 64-yard touchdown reception, giving Arizona their first lead of the game, 23–20.

Pittsburgh got the ball back on their own 22-yard line with 2:37 left in the game and two timeouts remaining. On their first play, a holding penalty pushed them back 10 yards. Roethlisberger then completed a pass to Holmes for 14 yards. After an incompletion, Roethlisberger threw it to Holmes again for a first down. An 11-yard reception by Nate Washington followed, and a 4-yard run by Roethlisberger forced the Steelers to burn their first timeout. On the very next play, he completed a pass to Holmes, who took it 40  yards to the Cardinals' 6-yard line after safety Aaron Francisco fell. Two plays later, Roethlisberger found Mewelde Moore covered in the flat, then Ward covered. He looked and then threw to Holmes, who ran a flag route in the right corner. Holmes caught the pass in the back corner of the end zone for a touchdown, managing to land with his toes inbounds before falling out of bounds. "My feet never left the ground," said Holmes. "All I did was extend my arms and use my toes as an extension to catch up to the ball." After a booth review, the touchdown pass stood. Reed's ensuing extra point put the Steelers in front 27–23 with 35 seconds remaining. Following the ensuing kickoff, Warner completed a 20-yard pass to Fitzgerald and a 13-yarder to J. J. Arrington, moving the ball to the Steelers 44. With 15 seconds left, Warner prepared to attempt a Hail Mary pass, but linebacker LaMarr Woodley forced a fumble while sacking Warner. Defensive end Brett Keisel recovered the fumble, giving the ball back to Pittsburgh with five seconds left. Many viewers assumed that the play had not been reviewed for a possible incomplete pass, but NFL Head of Officiating Mike Pereira later explained that it was reviewed, unnoticed by the public: "We confirmed it was a fumble. The replay assistant in the replay booth saw it was clearly a fumble. The ball got knocked loose and was rolling in his hand before it started forward. He has to have total control."

2/1/2009	Line/Total	1	2	3	4	Final
Pittsburgh Steelers	{-7.0}	3	14	3	7	27
Arizona Cardinals	{46.5}	0	7	0	16	23

Scoring

Team	
Steelers	Jeff Reed 18 yard field goal
Steelers	Gary Russell 1 yard rush (Jeff Reed kick)

Team	
Cardinals	Ben Patrick 1 yard pass from Kurt Warner (Neil Rackers kick)
Steelers	James Harrison 100 yard interception return (Jeff Reed kick)
Steelers	Jeff Reed 21 yard field goal
Cardinals	Larry Fitzgerald 1 yard pass from Kurt Warner (Neil Rackers kick)
Cardinals	Safety, Justin Hartwig penalized for holding in the end zone.
Cardinals	Larry Fitzgerald 64 yard pass from Kurt Warner (Neil Rackers kick)
Steelers	Santonio Holmes 6 yard pass from Ben Roethlisberger (Jeff Reed kick)

2009 Pittsburgh Steelers

The Steelers were coming off a season in which they compiled a 12–4 regular season record and capped the season by winning the franchise's record sixth Super Bowl. The team's coaching staff remained the same for the third consecutive year. As the defending champions, the Steelers opened the season by hosting the NFL Kickoff Game on Thursday, September 10, 2009, which was an overtime victory against the Tennessee Titans. The team compiled a 6–2 record over the season's first half, but then began a five-game losing streak which included losses to all three division opponents. Three late wins led to a 9–7 record, but the team failed to qualify for the playoffs. This was the third straight time the team has missed the playoffs following a Super Bowl victory. LaMarr Woodley was selected to various first team All-Pro teams.

Ben Roethlisberger led the team in passing with 4,328 yards and threw 26 touchdown passes. Rashard Mendenhall led the team in rushing with 1,108 yards and 7 rushing touchdowns. Hines Ward led the team with 95 receptions. Santonio Holmes led the team with 1,248 receiving yards. Ward, Heath Miller and Mike Wallace led with 6 TD receptions each.

PITTSBURGH			2009			9-7	Game Highlights
9/10/2009	TH	vs	TENNESSEE (OT)	13	10	W	Holmes 9 catch-131 yards-TD catch/Reed 2 FGs
9/20/2009		@	Chicago	14	17	L	Roethlisberger 221 pass yards-TD pass to Spaeth
9/27/2009		@	Cincinnati	20	23	L	Roethlisberger 276 pass yards-TD pass-rush TD
10/4/2009	SNF	vs	SAN DIEGO CHARGERS	38	28	W	Roethlisberger 333 pass yards-2 TD pass
10/11/2009		@	Detroit	28	20	W	Roethlisberger 277 pass yards-3 TD pass
10/18/2009		vs	CLEVELAND	27	14	W	Roethlisberger 417 pass yds-2 TD pass/Reed 2 FG
10/25/2009		vs	MINNESOTA	27	17	W	**Woodley fumble return TD/Fox INT return TD**
11/9/2009	MNF	@	Denver	28	10	W	**Carter INT return TD**/Ward 2 TD catch
11/15/2009		vs	CINCINNATI	12	18	L	Ward 7 catch-88 yards/Reed 4 FGs
11/22/2009		@	Kansas City (OT)	24	27	L	Roethlisberger 398 pass yards-3 TD pass
11/29/2009	SNF	@	Baltimore Ravens (OT)	17	20	L	Holmes 6 catch-74 yards-TD catch
12/6/2009		vs	OAKLAND RAIDERS	24	27	L	Holmes 8 catch-149 yards-TD catch
12/10/2009	TH	@	Cleveland	6	13	L	Steelers 77 rush yards/Reed 2 FGs
12/20/2009		vs	GREEN BAY	37	36	W	Roethlisberger 503 pass yards-3 TD pass
12/27/2009		vs	BALTIMORE RAVENS	23	20	W	Roethlisberger 259 pass yards-TD pass/Reed 3 FG
1/3/2010		@	Miami	30	24	W	Roethlisberger 220 pass yds-3 TD pass/Reed 3 FG

Schedule courtesy of Steve's Football Bible LLC

2009 AFC North	W	L	T	PCT	DIV	CONF	PF	PA
Cincinnati Bengals	10	6	0	.625	6–0	7–5	305	291
Baltimore Ravens	9	7	0	.563	3–3	7–5	391	261
Pittsburgh Steelers	**9**	**7**	**0**	**.563**	**2–4**	**6–6**	**368**	**324**
Cleveland Browns	5	11	0	.313	1–5	5–7	245	375

2009 NFL Draft

Round	Pick #	Player	Position	College
1	32	Ziggy Hood	Defensive tackle	Missouri
3	79	Kraig Urbik	Offensive guard	Wisconsin
3	84	Mike Wallace	Wide Receiver	Mississippi
3	96	Keenan Lewis	Cornerback	Oregon State
5	168	Joe Burnett	Cornerback	Central Florida
5	169	Frank Summers	Running back	UNLV
6	205	Ra'Shon Harris	Defensive tackle	Oregon
7	226	A.Q. Shipley	Center	Penn State
7	241	David Johnson	Tight end	Arkansas State

Green Bay Packers at Pittsburgh

Pittsburgh would strike on their first play of the game when Ben Roethlisberger hit a wide-open Mike Wallace for a 60-yard TD pass. Green Bay would answer with an 83-yard strike from Aaron Rodgers to Greg Jennings for a TD. The Steelers would cap the 1st quarter with a 2-yard TD run by Rashard Mendenhall. In the 2nd quarter, QB Aaron Rodgers was able to scramble out of the pocket for a 14-yard TD run. Ben Roethlisberger would hit Mewelde Moore for a 10-yard TD pass in the final seconds of the 1st Half and the Steelers would take a 21–14 lead into halftime with them. The 2nd half got off to a slow start for both teams. Jeff Reed would kick a 37-yard field goal, the only scoring of the 3rd quarter. In the 4th quarter, it became a shootout between both quarterbacks. Aaron Rodgers would hit Jermichael Finley for an 11-yard TD pass. The Steelers answered with a 34-yard field goal but would lose the lead for the first time in the game when Ryan Grant rushed for a 24-yard score, putting Green Bay up 28–27. The Steelers would once again answer with a 43-yard field goal, but Aaron Rodgers would complete a 24-yard TD pass to James Jones and follow it with a successful 2-point conversion attempt. The Steelers, down 36–30, would get the ball back with just 2 minutes left in the game. With just 3 seconds remaining, Ben Roethlisberger would hit Mike Wallace in the left sideline of the endzone (in a TD pass that resembled the Super Bowl-winning catch by Santonio Holmes back in February) and the extra point was good, giving the Steelers a last-second 37–36 win over the Packers. **Ben Roethlisberger would finish with a record-setting game, going 29/46 for 503 yards and 3 TD passes. He would become the first quarterback in Steelers' franchise history to have a 500-yard game.**

2010 Pittsburgh Steelers

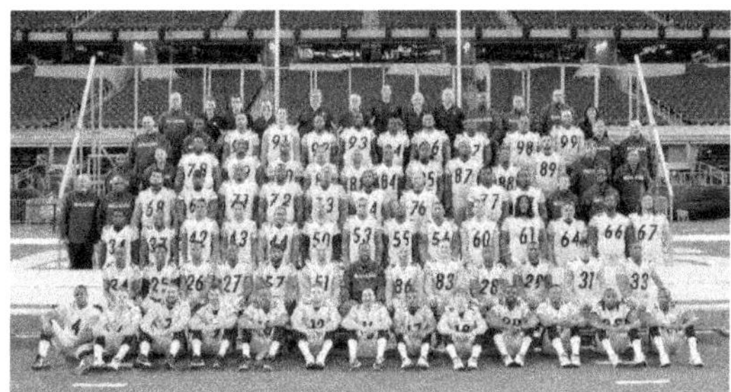

The 2010 Pittsburgh Steelers season was the eleventh season under the leadership of general manager Kevin Colbert, and the fourth under head coach Mike Tomlin. They reached Super Bowl XLV for the franchise's 8th Super Bowl appearance but lost to the Green Bay Packers 31–25. The Steelers allowed the fewest points in the NFL in 2010, with 232 (14.5 points per game). James Harrison {LB}, Troy Polamalu {S} and Lawrence Timmons {LB} were selected to various first team All-Pro teams.

Ben Roethlisberger led the team in passing with 3,200 yards and threw 17 touchdown passes. Rashard Mendenhall led the team in rushing with 1,273 yards and 13 rushing touchdowns. Mike Wallace led the team in receiving with 60 receptions for 1,257 yards and 10 TD receptions. Troy Polamalu led the team with 7 interceptions.

PITTSBURGH			2010			14-5	Game Highlights
9/12/2010		vs	ATLANTA {OT}	15	9	W	Mendenhall 120 rush yards-rush TD/Reed 3 FGs
9/19/2010		@	Tennessee Titans	19	11	W	**Brown kickoff return TD**/Reed 4 FGs
9/26/2010		@	Tampa Bay	38	13	W	**Keisel INT return TD**/Wallace 3-100 yds-2 TD
10/3/2010		vs	BALTIMORE RAVENS	14	17	L	Mendenhall 79 rush yards-2 rush TD
10/17/2010		vs	CLEVELAND	28	10	W	Roethlisberger 257 pass yards-3 TD pass
10/24/2010		@	Miami	23	22	W	Roethlisberger 302 pass yds-2 TD pass/Reed 3 FG
10/31/2010	SNF	@	New Orleans	10	20	L	Mendenhall 71 rush yards-rush TD/Reed FG
11/8/2010	MNF	@	Cincinnati	27	21	W	Wallace 5 catch-110 yards-TD catch/Reed 2 FGs
11/14/2010	SNF	vs	NEW ENGLAND	26	39	L	Wallace 8 catch-136 yards-2 TD catch/Reed FG
11/21/2010		vs	OAKLAND RAIDERS	35	3	W	Roethlisberger 275 pass yards-3 TD pass-rush TD
11/28/2010		@	Buffalo	19	16	W	Mendenhall 151 rush yards-rush TD/Shuisam 4 FG
12/5/2010	SNF	@	Baltimore Ravens	13	10	W	Roethlisberger 253 pass yds-TD pass/Shuisam FGs
12/12/2010		vs	CINCINNATI	23	7	W	**Polamalu & Woodley INT return TDs**
12/19/2010		vs	NEW YORK JETS	17	22	L	Wallace 7 catch-102 yards/Mendenhall rush TD
12/23/2010	TH	vs	CAROLINA	27	3	W	Wallace 4 catch-104 yards-TD catch/Shuisam 2 FG
1/2/2011		@	Cleveland	41	9	W	Wallace 3 catch-105 yards-TD catch/Shuisam 2 FG
1/15/2011	SAT	vs	**BALTIMORE**	31	24	W	Mendenhall 2 rush TD/Miller & Ward TD catch
1/23/2011		vs	**NEW YORK JETS**	24	19	W	**Gay fumble return TD**/Mendenhall 121 yds-TD
2/6/2011		vs	**Green Bay**	25	31	L	Wallace 9 catch-89 yds-TD/Ward 7 catch-78 yds-TD

Schedule courtesy of Steve's Football Bible LLC

2010 AFC North	W	L	T	PCT	DIV	CONF	PF	PA
Pittsburgh Steelers	12	4	0	.750	5–1	9–3	375	232
Baltimore Ravens	12	4	0	.750	4–2	9–3	357	270
Cleveland Browns	5	11	0	.313	1–5	3–9	271	332
Cincinnati Bengals	4	12	0	.250	2–4	3–9	322	395

2010 NFL Draft

Rd	Pick #	Player	Pos	College
1	18	Maurkice Pouncey	C / G	Florida
2	52	Jason Worilds	OLB	Virginia Tech
3	82	Emmanuel Sanders	WR	SMU
4	116	Thaddeus Gibson	OLB	Ohio State
5	151	Chris Scott	G	Tennessee
5	164	Crezdon Butler	CB	Clemson
5	166	Stevenson Sylvester	LB	Utah
6	188	Jonathan Dwyer	RB	Georgia Tech
6	195	Antonio Brown	WR	Central Michigan
7	242	Doug Worthington	DE	Ohio State

2010 AFC Divisional Playoffs

Steelers quarterback Ben Roethlisberger's 58-yard completion to Antonio Brown set up Rashard Mendenhall's game winning 2-yard touchdown run with 1:33 left in the game. Despite the game's high score, it was a defensive battle, with both teams combining for just 389 yards and scoring most of their points off turnovers. Roethlisberger was sacked six times, and Baltimore quarterback Joe Flacco was sacked 5. Meanwhile, the Ravens were held to just 126 yards and were buried under a mountain of turnovers, penalties, and dropped passes.

After forcing the Ravens to punt on the opening drive, Pittsburgh drove 80 yards on the way to Mendenhall's 1-yard touchdown run, assisted by a 37-yard pass interference penalty on Baltimore defensive back Josh Wilson. But the Ravens countered with a 68-yard scoring drive, aided by a 33-yard pass interference penalty on Pittsburgh's Anthony Madison. Ray Rice finished the drive with a 14-yard touchdown run to tie the game. Then two plays into the Steelers next drive, Roethlisberger was hit by Terrell Suggs as he pulled his arm back to throw a pass, resulting in a fumble. Nearly all the players on both teams thought it was an incomplete pass since the ball went forward and headed back to their huddles, but Ravens lineman Cory Redding realized the play was still ongoing and returned the ball 13 yards for a touchdown. In the second quarter, Ravens safety Ed Reed recovered a fumble from Mendenhall at the Steelers 16-yard line, setting up Flacco's 4-yard touchdown pass to Todd Heap that gave them a 21–7 lead. Pittsburgh responded with a drive to the Baltimore 25-yard line but came up empty when Shaun Suisham missed a 43-yard field goal attempt with 25 seconds left in the half.

However, the Steelers dominated the third quarter, forcing three turnovers and holding the Ravens to negative yardage. Less than five minutes into the quarter, Rice lost a fumble while being tackled by Ryan Clark, and linebacker LaMarr Woodley recovered it on the Baltimore 23-yard line. After a 14-yard run by Mendenhall, Roethlisberger threw a 9-yard touchdown pass to tight end Heath Miller. Then after an exchange of punts, Clark intercepted a pass from Flacco and returned it 17 yards to the Ravens 25-yard line. Mendenhall started the drive with a 13-yard screen, and Roethlisberger finished it with an 8-yard third down touchdown pass to Hines Ward, tying the game at 21. Just two plays after the ensuing kickoff, Flacco fumbled a snap and Steelers lineman Brett Keisel recovered it at the Baltimore 23. This time the Steelers were unable to get a touchdown, as Roethlisberger was sacked by Suggs on third down and six after driving inside the 10-yard line, but Suisham kicked a 35-yard field goal to give Pittsburgh their first lead with 12:15 left in regulation.

Later, Baltimore's Lardarius Webb returned a punt 55 yards for a touchdown, only to have it called back by a holding penalty on Marcus Smith. Still, his return gave them good field position on the Steelers 29-yard line. On the first play of the drive, Flacco completed a 21-yard pass to Heap. But over the next three plays, Baltimore rushers were stuffed twice and then receiver Anquan Boldin dropped a pass in the end zone, forcing them to settle for Billy Cundiff's field goal to tie the score with 3:54 remaining in the game. David Johnson returned the ensuing kickoff 16 yards to the 35-yard line, and Pittsburgh retook the lead with a 65-yard drive featuring three key third down conversions. After starting out with two incompletions, Roethlisberger threw a 12-yard pass to Ward on third down and ten. Then Roethlisberger was sacked for a 9-yard loss by Redding and Paul Kruger and threw another incompletion, bringing up third down and 19 with 2:07 to go. On the next play, Roethlisberger dropped back and launched a 58-yard bomb to Brown at the 4-yard line. After a defensive holding penalty moved the ball to the 1, the Ravens defense kept Mendenhall out of the end zone for two more plays. But on third down, he scored on a 2-yard touchdown run to give the Steelers a 31–24 lead with 1:33 remaining in regulation.

Le'Ron McClain returned Suisham's squib kick 12 yards to the Steelers 48-yard line, giving Baltimore a chance to drive for the tying touchdown. But their offense was unable to move the ball. After two incompletions and an 8-yard sack by Ziggy Hood, receiver T. J. Houshmandzadeh dropped a potential first down catch, ending any chance of a comeback. Roethlisberger completed 19 of 32 passes for 226 yards and two touchdowns. Steelers linebacker James Harrison recorded five tackles, two assists, and three sacks. Suggs finished with five tackles, three sacks, and a forced fumble.

1/15/2011	Line/Total	1	2	3	4	Final
Baltimore Ravens	{37.0}	14	7	0	3	24
Pittsburgh Steelers	{-3.5}	7	0	14	10	31

Scoring

Team	
Steelers	Rashard Mendenhall 1 yard rush (Shaun Suisham kick)
Ravens	Ray Rice 14 yard rush (Billy Cundiff kick)
Ravens	Cory Redding 13 yard defensive fumble return (Billy Cundiff kick)
Ravens	Todd Heap 4 yard pass from Joe Flacco (Billy Cundiff kick)
Steelers	Heath Miller 9 yard pass from Ben Roethlisberger (Shaun Suisham kick)
Steelers	Hines Ward 8 yard pass from Ben Roethlisberger (Shaun Suisham kick)
Steelers	Shaun Suisham 35 yard field goal
Ravens	Billy Cundiff 24 yard field goal
Steelers	Rashard Mendenhall 2 yard rush (Shaun Suisham kick)

2010 AFC Championship Game

Pittsburgh jumped to an early 24–0 lead and held off a desperate comeback rally to earn their third Super Bowl bid in the last six years.

Steelers running back Rashard Mendenhall rushed eight times for 28 yards on their opening drive, which took over nine minutes off the clock and ended with his 1-yard touchdown run. Then he rushed four times for 22 yards and caught an 18-yard pass on a drive to the Jets 32-yard line. Linebacker Bryan Thomas ended the drive with an interception, but the Steelers forced a punt and drove for another score, aided by Mendenhall's 35-yard burst. Shaun Suisham finished the drive with a 20-yard field goal to make the score 10–0. Following another punt, Ben Roethlisberger completed a 24-yard pass to tight end Heath Miller, a 20-yarder to Emmanuel Sanders, and a 14-yard throw to Mendenhall on the way to a 2-yard touchdown run. Two plays after the ensuing kickoff, Ike Taylor sacked Jets quarterback Mark Sanchez on a defensive back blitz and forced a fumble, which cornerback William Gay returned 19 yards for a touchdown, increasing their lead to 24–0 with just over a minute left in the half. This time New York managed to respond, with Sanchez completing four passes for 39 yards on a drive that ended with a 42-yard field goal by Nick Folk, cutting the score to 24–3 going into halftime.

New York took the second half kickoff and scored with just five plays. Shonn Greene started off the drive with a 23-yard run, while Sanchez finished it with a pair of completions to Santonio Holmes, the first for 16 yards, and the second a 45-yard touchdown completion. Pittsburgh responded with a drive to the Jets 37-yard line but turned the ball over when safety Brodney Pool intercepted a pass from Roethlisberger inside the 10. After an exchange of punts, the Jets converted two fourth downs on a 17-play drive to a first down on the Steelers 2-yard line. But Pittsburgh's defense made a key goal line stand. First Greene tried to run up the middle but was stuffed at the 1-yard line. Then Sanchez threw an incomplete pass and another that was batted down by linebacker LaMarr Woodley. On fourth down, LaDainian Tomlinson tried to run through the middle, but Brett Keisel and Casey Hampton tackled him for no gain, turning the ball over. On the next play, Roethlisberger fumbled a snap and was downed in the end zone for a safety. New York then drove 58 yards following the free kick and scored with Sanchez's 4-yard touchdown pass to Jerricho Cotchery, cutting their deficit to 24–19 with 3:06 left in the game. But the Steelers managed to pick up two key first downs on their next drive with a 14-yard reception by Miller and a 14-yard catch by Antonio Brown on third down and six with less than two minutes left, enabling them to run out the rest of the clock. Mendenhall rushed for 121 yards and a touchdown, while also catching two passes for 32. Sanchez threw for 233 yards and two touchdowns. Pool had six tackles and an interception.

1/23/2011	Line/Total	1	2	3	4	Final
New York Jets	{38.0}	0	3	7	9	19
Pittsburgh Steelers	{-3.5}	7	17	0	0	24

Scoring

Team	
Steelers	Rashard Mendenhall 1 yard rush (Shaun Suisham kick)
Steelers	Shaun Suisham 20 yard field goal
Steelers	Ben Roethlisberger 2 yard rush (Shaun Suisham kick)
Steelers	William Gay 19 yard defensive fumble return (Shaun Suisham kick)
Jets	Nick Folk 42 yard field goal
Jets	Santonio Holmes 45 yard pass from Mark Sanchez (Nick Folk kick)
Jets	Safety, Ben Roethlisberger tackled in end zone by Mike DeVito.
Jets	Jerricho Cotchery 4 yard pass from Mark Sanchez (Nick Folk kick)

Super Bowl XLV {"Leader of the Pack"}

The game was played on February 6, 2011, at Cowboys Stadium in Arlington, Texas, the first time the Super Bowl was played in the Dallas–Fort Worth area. Unlike most other Super Bowls, this game featured two title-abundant franchises: coming into the game, the Packers held the most NFL championships with 12 (9 league championships prior to the Super Bowl era and 3 Super Bowl championships), while the Steelers held the most Super Bowl championships with 6. The Packers entered their fifth Super Bowl in team history and became the first 6-seed team in the NFC to compete in the Super Bowl, after posting a 10–6 regular season record. The Steelers finished the regular season with a 12–4 record, and advanced to a league-tying 8th Super Bowl appearance.

After the first three drives of the game ended with punts, Green Bay opened the scoring with Aaron Rodgers's 29-yard touchdown pass to wide receiver Jordy Nelson, who managed to pull slightly ahead of cornerback William Gay enough to make a leaping catch and fall into the end zone. Then on the first play after the ensuing kickoff, quarterback Ben Roethlisberger was hit by Howard Green as he threw a pass, causing the ball to go well short of his intended target near the left sideline where it was intercepted by Nick Collins and returned 37 yards for a touchdown, giving Green Bay

a 14–0 lead. This score continued the unbeaten streak of Super Bowl victories recorded by teams scoring on an interception run-back, improving to 11–0 in such games. It was also the third consecutive Super Bowl with an interception return for a touchdown, as well as the eighth such score in the last ten Super Bowls. The Packers also tied the Miami Dolphins' record which still stands for the largest Super Bowl lead (14 points) at the end of the first quarter, set in Super Bowl VIII against the Minnesota Vikings and later tied by the Oakland Raiders against the Philadelphia Eagles in Super Bowl XV.

This time Pittsburgh managed to respond, driving 49 yards in 13 plays including Roethlisberger's 18-yard run on 3rd down and 9. Shaun Suisham finished the drive with a 33-yard field goal to cut the score to 14–3. Then after forcing a punt, the Steelers drove to midfield, but turned the ball over again when Roethlisberger's pass was intercepted by defensive back Jarrett Bush at the 47. After the interception, Rodgers led the Packers to another score, completing two passes for 20 yards before James Starks's 12-yard run moved the ball to the 21-yard line. On the next play, Green Bay increased their lead to 21–3 with Rodgers' 21-yard touchdown pass to Greg Jennings. Taking the ball back with 2:24 left in the second quarter, Roethlisberger made a 37-yard completion to Antwaan Randle El on their first play. After that, receiver Hines Ward caught three passes for 39 yards on the drive, the last one an 8-yard touchdown catch with 37 seconds left in the half, making the score 21–10 at halftime. This was the fourth time in their four 2011 postseason games that the Packers finished the first half with a lead of at least 11 points. The first half had taken a heavy toll on both teams. The Steelers lost wide receiver Emmanuel Sanders to injury, while the Packers lost receiver Donald Driver along with defensive backs Charles Woodson and Sam Shields. Shields would be the only player among them who would return.

Pittsburgh's defense forced Green Bay to punt on the first drive of the second half and got the ball at midfield after a facemask call on Tom Crabtree while tackling Antonio Brown on the punt return. The offense then scored in five plays (all runs). First, Rashard Mendenhall broke free along with right sideline for a 17-yard run, then Isaac Redman rushed for 3 yards, and Roethlisberger ran for 6, bringing up third down and 1. On the next play, Redman tried to run up the middle, but was held up at the line, so he backed away and ran to the outside for a 16-yard gain to the 8-yard line. Then Mendenhall scored an 8-yard touchdown run on the next play, making the score 21–17. After forcing a punt, Pittsburgh mounted a drive to the Packers 29-yard line, but Green Bay's defense made a stand. First Roethlisberger's pass was batted down behind the line by linebacker Clay Matthews, then Roethlisberger tried a screen pass to tight end Heath Miller, but Desmond Bishop tackled him for a 3-yard loss. Then on third down Frank Zombo sacked Roethlisberger on the 34, and Suisham's ensuing 52-yard field goal attempt sailed wide left.

On the first play of the fourth quarter, the Steelers lost their third turnover of the game when Mendenhall fumbled the ball while being tackled behind the line by Matthews and Ryan Pickett. Bishop recovered the ball and returned it 7 yards to the Packers 45. Five plays later on third down and 10, Rodgers completed a 38-yard pass to Nelson at the Steelers 2-yard line. Pittsburgh linebacker LaMarr Woodley sacked Rodgers for a 6-yard loss on the next play, but Rodgers threw an 8-yard touchdown pass to Jennings after that, increasing the Packers lead to 28–17. Roethlisberger led the Steelers right back with 6 of 7 completions. After a 9-yard pass to tight end Matt Spaeth, he threw three completions to receiver Mike Wallace for 27 yards to the Green Bay 40-yard line. Then after a 15-yard completion to Ward, he finished the drive with a 25-yard touchdown pass to Wallace. On the two-point conversion play, Roethlisberger faked a hand-off to Mendenhall and ran up to the line before pitching the ball to Randle El, who scored on an outside sweep, cutting the Steelers deficit to 3 points at 28–25.

Green Bay took the ball back with just over 7 minutes left and found themselves facing third down and 10 after two plays, but Rodgers kept the drive going with a 31-yard completion to Jennings over the middle. Starks then ran 14 yards to the Steelers 30. Two plays later, James Jones caught a 21-yard pass at the 8. The Steelers defense kept Green Bay out of the end zone, forcing the Packers to settle for a 23-yard field goal by Mason Crosby that gave Green Bay a 31–25 lead with 2:07 left in regulation. Pittsburgh got the ball back on their own 13-yard line following a penalty on the kickoff. On their first play,

Roethlisberger completed a 15-yard pass to Miller. But after a 5-yard reception by Ward, his next three passes were incomplete, turning the ball over and allowing the Packers to run out the rest of the clock.

2/6/2011	Line/Total	1	2	3	4	Final
Pittsburgh Steelers	{45.0}	0	10	7	8	25
Green Bay Packers	{-2.5}	14	7	0	10	31

Scoring

Team	
Packers	Jordy Nelson 29 yard pass from Aaron Rodgers (Mason Crosby kick)
Packers	Nick Collins 37 yard interception return (Mason Crosby kick)
Steelers	Shaun Suisham 33 yard field goal
Packers	Greg Jennings 21 yard pass from Aaron Rodgers (Mason Crosby kick)
Steelers	Hines Ward 8 yard pass from Ben Roethlisberger (Shaun Suisham kick)
Steelers	Rashard Mendenhall 8 yard rush (Shaun Suisham kick)
Packers	Greg Jennings 8 yard pass from Aaron Rodgers (Mason Crosby kick)
Steelers	Mike Wallace 25 yard pass from Ben Roethlisberger (Antwaan Randle El run)
Packers	Mason Crosby 23 yard field goal

2011 Pittsburgh Steelers

It was the twelfth season under the leadership of general manager Kevin Colbert and the fifth under head coach Mike Tomlin. The Steelers hoped to return to the Super Bowl and defend their AFC championship from 2010 but suffered a 29–23 overtime loss to the Denver Broncos in the Wild Card round of the playoffs. The Steelers played all their home games at Heinz Field in Pittsburgh, Pennsylvania. The Steelers' defense allowed the fewest points, passing yards, and total yards in the 2011 NFL season. Troy Polamalu {S} and Maurkice Pouncey {C} were selected to various first team All-Pro teams.

Ben Roethlisberger led the team in passing with 4,077 yards and threw 21 touchdown passes. Rashard Mendenhall led the team in rushing with 928 yards and 9 rushing touchdowns. Mike Wallace led the team in receiving with 72 receptions for 1,193 yards and 8 TD receptions.

PITTSBURGH			2011			12-5	Game Highlights
9/11/2011		@	Baltimore Ravens	7	35	L	Steelers 66 rush yards/Sanders TD catch
9/18/2011		vs	SEATTLE	24	0	W	Wallace 8 catch-126 yards-TD catch
9/25/2011	SNF	@	Indianapolis Colts	23	20	W	**Polamalu fumble return TD**/Wallace 144 yds-TD
10/2/2011		@	Houston Texans	10	17	L	Mendenhall rush TD/Shuisam FG
10/9/2011		vs	TENNESSEE TITANS	38	17	W	Roethlisberger 228 pass yds-5 TD pass/Ward 2 TD
10/16/2011		vs	JACKSONVILLE	17	13	W	Mendenhall 146 rush yards-rush TD/Shuisam FG
10/23/2011		@	Arizona Cardinals	32	20	W	Roethlisberger 361 pass yds-3 TD/Shuisam 3 FG
10/30/2011		vs	NEW ENGLAND	25	17	W	Roethlisberger 365 pass yds-2 TD/Shuisam 2 FG
11/6/2011	SNF	vs	BALTIMORE RAVENS	20	23	L	Brown 5 catch-109 yards/Wallace TD catch
11/13/2011		@	Cincinnati	24	17	W	Roethlisberger 245 pass yds-TD/Mendenhall 2 TD
11/27/2011	SNF	@	Kansas City	13	9	W	Saunders TD catch/Shuisam 2 FGs
12/4/2011		vs	CINCINNATI	35	7	W	Mendenhall 2 rush TD/Wallace 2 TD catch
12/8/2011	TH	vs	CLEVELAND	14	3	W	Brown 5 catch-151 yards-TD catch/Cotchery TD
12/19/2011	MNF	@	San Francisco	3	20	L	Steelers 84 rush yards/commit 4 turnovers
12/24/2011	SAT	vs	ST. LOUIS RAMS	27	0	W	Clay-Mendenhall-Redman rush TD each
1/1/2012		@	Cleveland	13	9	W	Redman 92 rush yards-rush TD/Shuisam 2 FGs
1/8/2012		@	**Denver {OT}**	**23**	**29**	L	Redman 121 rush yards/Shuisam 3 FGs

Schedule courtesy of Steve's Football Bible LLC

2011 AFC North	W	L	T	PCT	DIV	CONF	PF	PA
Baltimore Ravens	12	4	0	.750	6–0	9–3	378	266
Pittsburgh Steelers	**12**	**4**	**0**	**.750**	**4–2**	**9–3**	**325**	**227**
Cincinnati Bengals	9	7	0	.563	2–4	6–6	344	323
Cleveland Browns	4	12	0	.250	0–6	3–9	218	307

Pittsburgh at Indianapolis Colts

Pittsburgh scored first in the first quarter with a 48-yard field goal by kicker Shaun Suisham, followed by quarterback Ben Roethlisberger finding wide receiver Mike Wallace on an 81-yard touchdown pass. The Colts answered in the second quarter with kicker Adam Vinatieri getting a 21-yard field goal, followed by defensive end Jamaal Anderson returning a Roethlisberger fumble caused by Dwight Freeney 47 yards for a touchdown. Vinatieri got another 25-yard field goal before the end of the half. After a scoreless third quarter, the Steelers regained the lead in the fourth quarter with a 44-yard field goal from Suisham, followed by safety Troy Polamalu returning a fumble forced by James Harrison 16 yards for a touchdown. However, Indianapolis replied with running back Joseph Addai getting a 6-yard touchdown run. Pittsburgh prevailed, however, with Shuisham hitting a game-winning 38-yard field goal with 4 seconds remaining.

2011 NFL Draft

Round	Overall	Player Name	Position	College
1	31	Cameron Heyward	DE	Ohio State
2	63	Marcus Gilbert	T	Florida
3	95	Curtis Brown	CB	Texas
4	128	Cortez Allen	CB	The Citadel
5	162	Chris Carter	ILB	Fresno State University
6	196	Keith Williams	G	University of Nebraska
7	232	Baron Batch	RB	Texas Tech University

2011 AFC Wild Card {"Tebow's Playoff Win"}

This game was the first one ever played under the league's new overtime rules, in which winning would be more difficult for the team that won the coin toss because the game would not end on an opening field goal. It did not matter, as it took Denver just one play to win with Tim Tebow's 80-yard touchdown pass to Demaryius Thomas. Pittsburgh scored on their opening drive, with Ben Roethlisberger's 33-yard completion to tight end Heath Miller setting up a 45-yard field goal by Shaun Suisham. Later in the quarter, Steelers running back Isaac Redman rushed five times for 33 yards on a 47-yard drive that ended with Suisham's 38-yard field goal, increasing the score to 6–0.

But Denver, which gained just eight yards in the first quarter, suddenly exploded with offensive production in the second. On their first drive of the quarter, Tebow completed a 51-yard strike to Thomas. Then he followed it up with a 30-yard touchdown pass to Eddie Royal. Following a Pittsburgh punt, Tebow's 58-yard completion to Thomas set up his own touchdown on an 8-yard run, giving the Broncos a 14–6 lead. An interception by Denver defensive back Quinton Carter quickly led to a 20-yard field goal from Matt Prater, and before the end of the half, Prater added one more, the second set up by Tebow's 41-yard completion to tight end Daniel Fells. With time running out in the quarter, Roethlisberger completed a 25-yard pass to Antonio Brown and an 18-yarder to Emmanuel Sanders on a drive that advanced to the Broncos 32-yard line. But on third down, a fumbled snap resulted in a 23-yard loss, pushing the team out of field goal range.

Pittsburgh regrouped in the second half. After its defense forced a punt, Roethlisberger completed an 18-yard pass to Sanders and Redman broke off a 32-yard run on the way to a 1-yard touchdown run by receiver Mike Wallace on an end-around play, cutting the score to 20–13. Denver struck back with their third field goal from Prater, aided by a 32-yard pass interference penalty on Steelers defensive back Ike Taylor, but Pittsburgh responded with their own field goal-drive, featuring a 28-yard run by Redman, making it a one-score game at 23–16.

With 7:35 left in regulation, Denver running back Willis McGahee lost a fumble while being tackled by Ryan Mundy, and linebacker LaMarr Woodley recovered it at the Steelers 45-yard line. Though Roethlisberger was sacked on the first play, he recovered with a 15-yard completion to Sanders and a 6-yard run before tying the game with a 31-yard touchdown completion to Jerricho Cotchery. Both teams had one more drive to attempt a winning score, but Denver could go no further than their own 35-yard line, while Roethlisberger was sacked twice on his drive as time expired in the fourth quarter.

Following a touchback on the opening kickoff, Pittsburgh anticipated that Denver would take to the ground, so the Steelers defense put all 11 players within six yards of the line of scrimmage. But Tebow hit Thomas in stride on a slant pattern across the middle of the field, and he took the ball 80 yards to the end zone for the game-winning score.

      Tebow completed only 10 of 21 passes but threw for 316 yards and two touchdowns without any interceptions and added 50 yards and a touchdown on the ground and set a franchise record for passer rating in a playoff game, with 125.5. Thomas had 204 yards and a touchdown on just four receptions, an average of 51 yards per catch. Defensive end Robert Ayers had two sacks. For the Steelers, Redman finished with a career-high 121 rushing yards.

1/8/2012	Line/Total	1	2	3	4	OT	Final
Pittsburgh Steelers	{-7.5}	6	0	7	10	0	23
Denver Broncos	{34.0}	0	20	0	3	6	29

Scoring

Team	
Steelers	Shaun Suisham 45 yard field goal
Steelers	Shaun Suisham 38 yard field goal
Broncos	Eddie Royal 30 yard pass from Tim Tebow (Matt Prater kick)
Broncos	Tim Tebow 8 yard rush (Matt Prater kick)
Broncos	Matt Prater 20 yard field goal
Broncos	Matt Prater 28 yard field goal
Steelers	Mike Wallace 1 yard rush (Shaun Suisham kick)
Broncos	Matt Prater 35 yard field goal
Steelers	Shaun Suisham 37 yard field goal
Steelers	Jerricho Cotchery 31 yard pass from Ben Roethlisberger (Shaun Suisham kick)
Broncos	Demaryius Thomas 80 yard pass from Tim Tebow

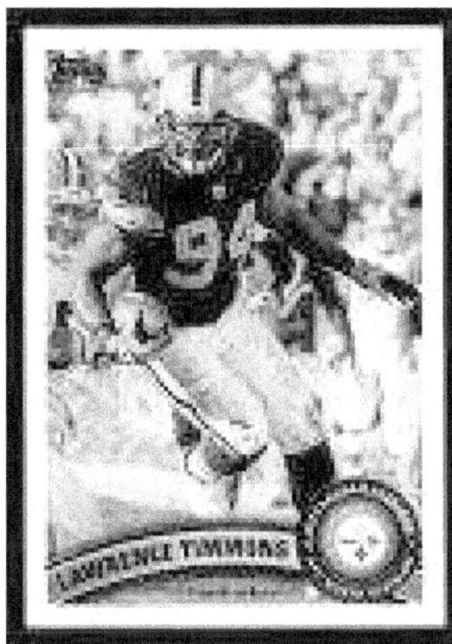

2012 Pittsburgh Steelers

It was the 13th season under the leadership of general manager Kevin Colbert and the 6th under head coach Mike Tomlin. The Steelers failed to improve on their 12–4 record from 2011 and did not reach the postseason for the first time since 2009. After a 6–3 start, the Steelers lost 5 of their last 7 games and finished the season with a record of 8–8, their first non-winning season since 2006. The 2012 Steelers set a new NFL record for the most games decided on the last play, with 6. For the first time since 1997, Hines Ward was not on the team's roster, as he was released in March 2012. Ward retired after he was cut. Maurkice Pouncey {C} was selected to various first team All-Pro teams.

Ben Roethlisberger led the team in passing with 3,265 yards and threw 26 touchdown passes. Jonathan Dwyer led the team in rushing with 623 yards. Heath Miller led the team in receptions with 71. Mike Wallace led with 836 receiving yards. Miller and Wallace each had 8 TD receptions.

PITTSBURGH			2012			8-8	Game Highlights
9/9/2012	SNF	@	Denver	19	31	L	Roethlisberger 245 pass yds-2 TD pass/Shuisam 2 FG
9/16/2012		vs	NEW YORK JETS	27	10	W	Roethlisberger 275 pass yds-2 TD pass/Shuisam 2 FG
9/23/2012		@	Oakland Raiders	31	34	L	Roethlisberger 384 pass yds-4 TD pass/Miller 2 TD
10/7/2012		vs	PHILADELPHIA	16	14	W	Mendenhall TD catch/Shuisam 3 FGs
10/14/2012	TH	@	Tennessee Titans	23	26	L	Roethlisberger 361 pass yds-TD pass/Shuisam 3 FGs
10/21/2012	SNF	@	Cincinnati	24	17	W	Dwyer 122 rush yds/Shuisam 3 FGs/Miller TD catch
10/28/2012		vs	WASHINGTON	27	12	W	Roethlisberger 222 pass yds-3 TD pass/Shuisam 3 FG
11/4/2012		@	New York Giants	24	20	W	Redman 147 rush yards-rush TD/Wallace TD catch
11/11/2012	MNF	vs	KANSAS CITY {OT}	16	13	W	Wallace TD catch/Shuisam 3 FGs
11/18/2012	SNF	vs	BALTIMORE RAVENS	10	13	L	Leftwich rush TD/Shuisam FG
11/25/2012		@	Cleveland	14	20	L	**Timmons INT return TD**/Steelers 49 rush yards
12/2/2012		@	Baltimore Ravens	23	20	W	Batch 276 pass yds-TD pass to Miller/Shuisam 3 FG
12/9/2012		vs	SAN DIEGO	24	34	L	Wallace 7 catch-112 yds-2 TD catch/Brown TD catch
12/16/2012		@	Dallas {OT}	24	27	L	Roethlisberger 339 pass yds-2 TD pass/Dwyer TD
12/23/2012		vs	CINCINNATI	10	13	L	Steelers 94 rush yards/Wallace TD catch/Shuisam FG
12/30/2012		vs	CLEVELAND	24	10	W	Roethlisberger 134 pass yds-3 TD pass/Shuisam FG

Schedule courtesy of Steve's Football Bible LLC

2012 AFC North	W	L	T	PCT	DIV	CONF	PF	PA
Baltimore Ravens	10	6	0	.625	4–2	8–4	398	344
Cincinnati Bengals	10	6	0	.625	3–3	7–5	391	320
Pittsburgh Steelers	**8**	**8**	**0**	**.500**	**3–3**	**5–7**	**336**	**314**
Cleveland Browns	5	11	0	.313	2–4	5–7	302	368

Philadelphia Eagles at Pittsburgh

After a scoreless first quarter, the Steelers drew first blood as Ben Roethlisberger connected with Rashard Mendenhall for a 13-yard catch for a TD to take a 7–0 lead. With 0:06 left in the first half, the Steelers increased their lead to 10–0 with a 20-yard field goal from Shaun Suisham going into halftime. In the 3rd quarter, the Eagles responded with Michael Vick's TD pass to WR LeSean McCoy to shorten the lead 10–7 for the only score of that quarter. The Steelers responded in the 4th quarter with Shaun Suisham kicking a 34-yard field goal to make the score 13–7. The Eagles however took the lead with Vick hooking up with Brent Celek for a 2-yard TD pass as the Eagles moved ahead 14–13. However, the Steelers were able to move down the field in the final seconds and capitalize their victory with another 34-yard field goal from Shaun Suisham as time expired as they went on to win the game 16–14.

<h2 align="center">2012 NFL Draft</h2>

Round	Selection	Player	Position	College
1	24	David DeCastro	Guard	Stanford
2	56	Mike Adams	Tackle	Ohio State
3	86	Sean Spence	Inside linebacker	Miami (Fl)
4	109	Alameda Ta'amu	Defensive Tackle	Washington
5	159	Chris Rainey	Running Back	Florida
7	231	Toney Clemons	Wide Receiver	Colorado
	240	David Paulson	Tight End	Oregon
	246	Terrence Frederick	Cornerback	Texas A&M
	248	Kelvin Beachum	Tackle	SMU

Pittsburgh at New York Giants

After a scoreless first quarter punt fest, the Steelers drew first blood with Ben Roethlisberger's 4-yard TD pass to Emmanuel Sanders for a 7–0 lead. The Giants however responded to tie the game with RB Andre Brown's 1-Yard Run to make it 7–7. After recovering a fumble, the Giants would take the lead as Michael Boley returned it 70 yards for a TD to move ahead 14–7. The Steelers would shorten the lead to 4 with Shaun Suisham's 30-yard field goal to make the score 14–10 at halftime. After the break, the Giants would increase their lead from 7 to 10 points with 2 Lawrence Tynes field goals from 50 and 23 yards out making the score at first 17–10 then 20–10. However, the Steelers responded in the 4th quarter with Roethlisberger finding Mike Wallace for a 51-yard catch and run pass to shorten the Giants' lead to 3 making it 20–17. After pressuring Eli and the Giants' offense, the Steelers then drove down the field and took the lead with Redman's 2-Yard Run with 4:02 left in the game to make it 24–20. Getting the ball back after the Giants' last 3 and out, Roethlisberger took a knee to end the game

2013 Pittsburgh Steelers

The 2013 Pittsburgh Steelers season marked the 14th season under leadership of general manager Kevin Colbert and the seventh under head coach Mike Tomlin. The Steelers finished the season 8–8, competing with the Baltimore Ravens, Miami Dolphins, and San Diego Chargers for the final AFC playoff spot going into Week 17. The Steelers tried to prevent their worst start since 1968 in Week 4, but the Minnesota Vikings would defeat them 34–27. Baltimore, Miami, and San Diego were all 8–7 going into Week 17, while Pittsburgh was 7–8. This meant that the Steelers had to win, and the Ravens, Dolphins, and Chargers all had to lose. Despite a win from the Steelers and losses from the Ravens and Dolphins, the Chargers went on to beat the Kansas City Chiefs 27–24 in overtime, taking the final playoff spot. It was the first season since the 1999 and 2000 seasons that the Steelers would miss back-to-back postseasons. Antonio Brown was selected to various first team All-Pro teams.

Ben Roethlisberger led the team in passing with 4,261 yards and threw 28 touchdown passes. Le'Veon Bell led the team in rushing with 860 yards and 8 rushing touchdowns. Antonio Brown led the team in receiving with 110 receptions for 1,499 yards. Jerricho Cotchery led with 10 TD receptions.

PITTSBURGH			2013			8-8	Game Highlights
9/8/2013		vs	TENNESSEE TITANS	9	16	L	Steelers 31 rush yards/Cotchery TD catch
9/16/2013	MNF	@	Cincinnati	10	20	L	Roethlisberger 251 pass yards-TD pass to Move
9/22/2013	SNF	vs	CHICAGO	23	40	L	Brown 9 catch-196 yards-2 TD catch/Shuisam 3 FG
9/29/2013		vs	Minnesota (London)	27	34	L	Bell 2 rush TD/Shuisam 2 FG/Cotchery TD catch
10/13/2013		@	New York Jets	19	6	W	Roethlisberger 264 pass yds-TD pass/Shuisam 4 FG
10/20/2013		vs	BALTIMORE RAVENS	19	16	W	Miller TD catch/Shuisam 4 FGs
10/27/2013		@	Oakland Raiders	18	21	L	Steelers 35 rush yards/Roethlisberger 275 pass yards
11/3/2013		@	New England Patriots	31	55	L	Cotchery 7 catch-96 yds-3 TD catch/Big Ben 4 TD
11/10/2013		vs	BUFFALO	23	10	W	Brown 6 catch-104 yards/Shuisam 3 FGs
11/17/2013		vs	DETROIT	37	27	W	Brown 7 catch-147 yards-2 TD catch/Shuisam 3 FG
11/24/2013		@	Cleveland	27	11	W	**Gay INT return TD**/Roethlisberger 2 TD pass
11/28/2013	TH	@	Baltimore Ravens	20	22	L	Roethlisberger 257 pass yards-2 TD pass
12/8/2013		vs	MIAMI	28	34	L	**Polamalu INT return TD**/Brown 5-138 yds-TD
12/15/2013	SNF	vs	CINCINNATI	30	20	W	Bell rush TD/Brown TD catch/Shuisam 3 FGs
12/22/2013		@	Green Bay	38	31	W	**Allen INT return TD**/Bell 124 rush yards-rush TD
12/29/2013		vs	CLEVELAND	20	7	W	Bell rush TD/Cotchery TD catch/Shuisam 2 FGs

Schedule courtesy of Steve's Football Bible LLC

2013 AFC North	W	L	T	PCT	DIV	CONF	PF	PA
Cincinnati Bengals	11	5	0	.688	3–3	8–4	430	305
Pittsburgh Steelers	**8**	**8**	**0**	**.500**	**4–2**	**6–6**	**379**	**370**
Baltimore Ravens	8	8	0	.500	3–3	6–6	320	352
Cleveland Browns	4	12	0	.250	2–4	3–9	308	406

2013 NFL Draft

Round	Pick	Player	Position	College
1	17	Jarvis Jones	OLB	Georgia
2	48	Le'Veon Bell	RB	Michigan State
3	79	Markus Wheaton	WR	Oregon State
4	111	Shamarko Thomas	SS	Syracuse
4	115	Landry Jones	QB	Oklahoma
5	150	Terry Hawthorne	CB	Illinois
6	186	Justin Brown	WR	Oklahoma
6	206	Vince Williams	ILB	Florida State
7	223	Nicholas Williams	DE	Samford

Baltimore Ravens at Pittsburgh

The Steelers scored first in the first quarter as Ben Roethlisberger hooked up with Heath Miller on a 3-yard touchdown pass making the score 7–0. Justin Tucker then got the Ravens on the board after nailing a 36-yard field goal shortening the lead to 7–3. In the 2nd quarter, the Steelers moved ahead by a touchdown as Shaun Suisham nailed a 34-yard field goal to make the score 10–3. The Ravens moved within 4 as Tucker nailed a 38-yard field goal for a 10–6 game at halftime with the Steelers leading. After the break, the Steelers went back to work in the 3rd quarter as Suisham kicked a 28-yard field goal for a 13–6 lead. The Ravens drew within 4 points again in the fourth quarter as Tucker kicked a 32-yard field goal for a 13–9 score. Again, the Steelers retaliated and moved ahead by 7 points as Suisham kicked a 38-yard field goal for a 16–9 lead. However, Joe Flacco was able to find Dallas Clark on a 1-yard touchdown pass tying the game at 16–16. The Steelers managed to drive down the field for the game-winning field goal as Suisham nailed it from 42 yards out as time expired for a final score of 19–16.

2014 Pittsburgh Steelers

The 2014 Pittsburgh Steelers season marked the 15th season under leadership of general manager Kevin Colbert and the eighth under head coach Mike Tomlin. The Steelers honored the 40th anniversary of their first Super Bowl winning team, Super Bowl IX, during their Week 13 game against the New Orleans Saints at Heinz Field on November 30. (The Steelers played the Super Bowl at Tulane Stadium that year.) The team wore a special patch and honored the players at halftime. Though it also serves as the team's annual alumni weekend, the team did not wear their alternate 1934 "Bumblebee" throwbacks for this game. Instead, the Steelers wore the "Bumblebee" jerseys vs. the Indianapolis Colts on October 26. They managed to improve from their 8–8 record from each of their previous two seasons with their week 15 victory against the Atlanta Falcons and ensured their first winning season since 2011. They also clinched a playoff berth for the first time since that same year with their week 16 victory over the Kansas City Chiefs. The Steelers won the AFC North division title but lost to the Baltimore Ravens in the Wild Card round of the playoffs by a score of 30–17. The Steelers became the first team in NFL history to have a 4,500-yard passer, 1,500-yard receiver and 1,300-yard rusher in the same season. This season holds the record for the most points the Steelers have ever scored with 436, which was possible in part by goring the Colts 51-34 and goring the Ravens 43-23 in back-to-back weeks. There were ten instances of the Steelers scoring 27 points or more. The Steelers went 9-1 in those games, with their only loss being by a field goal. Le'Veon Bell {RB}, Antonio Brown {WR} and Maurkice Pouncey {C} were selected to various first team All-Pro teams.

Ben Roethlisberger led the team in passing with 4,952 yards and threw 32 touchdown passes. Le'Veon Bell led the team in rushing with 1,361 yards and 8 rushing touchdowns. Antonio Brown led the team with 129 receptions for 1,698 yards. Brown led with 13 TD receptions.

PITTSBURGH			2014			11-6	Game Highlights
9/7/2014		vs	CLEVELAND	30	27	W	Bell 109 rush yds-rush TD/Brown 5-116 yds-TD
9/11/2014	TH	@	Baltimore Ravens	6	26	L	Steelers commit 3 turnovers/Shuisam 2 FGs
9/21/2014	SNF	@	Carolina	37	19	W	**Golden fumble return TD**/Bell 147 yds/Brown 2 TD
9/28/2014		vs	TAMPA BAY	24	27	L	Brown 7 catch-131 yds-2 TD catch/Miller TD catch
10/5/2014		@	Jacksonville	17	9	W	**McCain INT return TD**/Big Ben TD pass to Palmer
10/12/2014		@	Cleveland	10	31	L	Brown 7 catch-118 yards/Moore TD catch
10/20/2014	MNF	vs	HOUSTON TEXANS	30	23	W	Bell 145 total yards-TD catch/Brown TD pass
10/26/2014		vs	INDIANAPOLIS COLTS	51	34	W	**Gay INT return TD**/Big Ben 522 pass yds-6 TDs
11/2/2014	SNF	vs	BALTIMORE RAVENS	43	23	W	Brown 11 catch-144 yds-TD catch/Bryant 2 TDs
11/9/2014		@	New York Jets	13	20	L	Bryant 4 catch-143 yards-TD catch/Shuisam 2 FGs
11/17/2014	MNF	@	Tennessee Titans	27	24	W	**Gay INT return TD**/Bell 204 rush yds-rush TD
11/30/2014		vs	NEW ORLEANS	32	35	L	Bell 254 total yds-rush TD/Brown 2 TD catch
12/7/2014		@	Cincinnati	42	21	W	Bell 185 rush yards-2 rush TD-TD catch
12/14/2014		@	Atlanta	27	20	W	**Gay INT return TD**/Bell 2 rush TD/Shuisam 2 FG
12/21/2014		vs	KANSAS CITY	20	12	W	Bell rush TD/Brown TD catch/Shuisam 2 FGs
12/28/2014	SNF	vs	CINCINNATI	27	17	W	**Brown punt return TD**-7 catch-128 yards-TD catch
1/3/2015	SAT	vs	**BALTIMORE**	17	30	L	Roethlisberger 334 pass yards-TD pass to Bryant

Schedule courtesy of Steve's Football Bible LLC

Cleveland Browns at Pittsburgh

In the first quarter, the Steelers would score first when Shaun Suisham kicked a 36-yard field goal for a 3–0 lead. However, the Browns were able to tie it up when Billy Cundiff kicked a 39-yard field goal for a 3–3 game. The Steelers would score 24 unanswered points to end the first half with LaGarrette Blount running for a 7-yard TD to retake the lead 10–3. In the 2nd quarter, the Steelers continued their domination when Ben Roethlisberger found Antonio Brown on a 35-yard TD for a 17–3 lead followed by Le'Veon Bell running in for a TD from 38 yards out to increase their lead to 24–3 followed by Suisham nailing yet another field goal from 34 yards out as they led 27–3 at halftime. After the break, in the 3rd quarter, the Browns went to work as Isisah Crowell ran for 2 touchdowns: from 3 and 15 yards out for a 27–10 and 27–17 game. In the 4th quarter, the Browns managed to come within a TD as Cundiff nailed a 25-yard field goal for a 27–20 game. Later, Brian Hoyer hooked up with Travis Benjamein on a 9-yard TD pass to tie the game up 27–27. Regardless, Roethlisberger was able to move his team down the field and eventually, Suisham kicked the game-winning 41-yard field goal as time expired to win it 30–27 for the Steelers' only 3 points of the 2nd half.

2014 AFC North	W	L	T	PCT	DIV	CONF	PF	PA
Pittsburgh Steelers	**11**	**5**	**0**	**.688**	**4–2**	**9–3**	**436**	**368**
Cincinnati Bengals	10	5	1	.656	3–3	7–5	365	344
Baltimore Ravens	10	6	0	.625	3–3	6–6	409	302
Cleveland Browns	7	9	0	.438	2–4	4–8	299	337

2014 NFL Draft

Round	Pick	Player	Position	College
1	15	Ryan Shazier *	Inside linebacker	Ohio State
2	46	Stephon Tuitt	Defensive end	Notre Dame
3	97+	Dri Archer	Running back	Kent State
4	118	Martavis Bryant	Wide receiver	Clemson
5	157	Shaquille Richardson	Cornerback	Arizona
5	173+	Wesley Johnson	Offensive guard	Vanderbilt
6	192	Jordan Zumwalt	Inside linebacker	UCLA
7	215+	Daniel McCullers	Defensive tackle	Tennessee
7	230	Rob Blanchflower	Tight end	Massachusetts

2014 AFC Wild Card

Baltimore forced three turnovers and scored on 6-of-9 possessions to defeat Pittsburgh on the road for the first time in franchise playoff history. The Steelers scored first with a 43-yard drive, including a 22-yard completion from Ben Roethlisberger to Martavis Bryant that ended on a 45-yard Shaun Suisham field goal. Baltimore responded with a 9-play, 80-yard drive that gave them a 7–3 lead on Bernard Pierce's 5-yard touchdown run with 12:28 left in the second quarter. Roethlisberger struck back with an 18-yard completion to Antonio Brown and a 30-yarder to tight end Heath Miller that set up Suisham's 22-yard field goal. Baltimore quarterback Joe Flacco countered with a 23-yard pass to Steve Smith Sr. and a 19-yard completion to Owen Daniels on the way to a 28-yard field goal by Justin Tucker, making the score 10–6. With 42 seconds left in the half, Suisham kicked a 47-yard field goal that cut the score to 10–9 going into halftime.

On the Ravens' opening drive of the second half, Flacco completed a 17-yard pass to Torrey Smith on third and 12, allowing the team to hang onto the ball and drive to a 45-yard field goal by Tucker.

Then after a Steelers punt, Flacco hooked up with Smith Sr. for a 40-yard completion before throwing an 11-yard touchdown pass to Smith, increasing the team's lead to 20–9. Early in the fourth quarter, Pittsburgh defensive end Stephon Tuitt recovered a fumble from running back Justin Forsett on the Ravens' 45-yard line. Roethlisberger completed a 44-yard pass to Brown on the next play, and eventually got the ball into the end zone with a 6-yard toss to Bryant. Their two-point conversion attempt failed, but the Steelers had cut their deficit to one score at 20–15. However, they would get no closer. Baltimore responded with a 23-yard reception by Daniels that set up Tucker's 52-yard field goal. Then linebacker Terrell Suggs intercepted a pass from Roethlisberger, and Flacco increased the Ravens' lead to 30–15 with a 21-yard touchdown pass to tight end Crockett Gillmore on the next play. The Steelers responded with a drive to the Baltimore 14-yard line but came up empty when safety Darian Stewart picked off a pass from Roethlisberger in the end zone. Pittsburgh did manage two more points when lineman Shamarko Thomas blocked Sam Koch's punt, knocking the ball through the end zone for a safety. But after the free kick, Stewart put the game away by recovering a fumble from Miller. Roethlisberger finished the day 31-for-44 for 334 yards and a touchdown, with two interceptions. His top target was Brown, who caught nine passes for 117 yards. Flacco was 18-for-29 for 255 yards and two touchdowns, while Smith Sr. was the Ravens top receiver with five receptions for 101 yards.

1/3/2015	Line/Total	1	2	3	4	Final
Baltimore Ravens	{47.0}	0	10	10	10	30
Pittsburgh Steelers	{-3.0}	3	6	0	8	17

Scoring

Team	
Steelers	Shaun Suisham 45 yard field goal
Ravens	Bernard Pierce 5 yard rush (Justin Tucker kick)
Steelers	Shaun Suisham 22 yard field goal
Ravens	Justin Tucker 28 yard field goal
Steelers	Shaun Suisham 47 yard field goal
Ravens	Justin Tucker 45 yard field goal
Ravens	Torrey Smith 11 yard pass from Joe Flacco (Justin Tucker kick)
Steelers	Martavis Bryant 6 yard pass from Ben Roethlisberger (pass failed)
Ravens	Justin Tucker 52 yard field goal
Ravens	Crockett Gillmore 21 yard pass from Joe Flacco (Justin Tucker kick)
Steelers	Safety, Punt blocked by Shamarko Thomas out of bounds in end zone.

2015 Pittsburgh Steelers

The 2015 Pittsburgh Steelers season marked the 16th season under leadership of general manager Kevin Colbert and the ninth under head coach Mike Tomlin. For the first time since 2002, safety Troy Polamalu was not on the opening day roster, as he announced his retirement on April 9. The Steelers clinched the last AFC playoff spot, finishing tied with the New York Jets with a 10–6 record, but winning the tiebreaker over the Jets based on a better record vs. common opponents. The Steelers defeated the Cincinnati Bengals in the Wild Card round but lost to the eventual Super Bowl champion Denver Broncos in the Divisional round. 2015 marked a transition period for the Steelers defense, as longtime defensive coordinator Dick LeBeau resigned January 10. A member of the Pro Football Hall of Fame due to his 14-year playing career with the Detroit Lions, LeBeau served 13 seasons as the Steelers defensive coordinator under Tomlin and his predecessor Bill Cowher. Antonio Brown {WR} and David DeCastro {G} were selected to various first team All-Pro teams.

Ben Roethlisberger led the team in passing with 3,938 yards and threw 21 touchdown passes. DeAngelo Williams led the team in rushing with 907 yards and 11 rushing touchdowns. **Antonio Brown set franchise records with 136 receptions for 1,834 yards. Brown led with 10 TD receptions.**

PITTSBURGH			2015			11-7	Game Highlights
9/10/2015	TH	@	New England Patriots	21	28	L	Brown 9 catch-133 yards-TD catch/Scobee 2 FGs
9/20/2015		vs	SAN FRANCISCO	43	18	W	Brown 9 catch-195 yards-TD catch/Williams 3 TDs
9/27/2015		@	St. Louis Rams	12	6	W	Brown 11 catch-108 yards/Bell rush TD/Scobee 2 FG
10/1/2015	TH	vs	BALTIMORE {OT}	20	23	L	Bell 129 rush yards-rush TD/Scobee 2 FGs
10/12/2015	MNF	@	San Diego Chargers	24	20	W	**Blake INT return TD**/Bell 111 rush yards-rush TD
10/18/2015		vs	ARIZONA	25	13	W	Bryant 6 catch-137 yards-2 TD catch/Boswell 3 FGs
10/25/2015		@	Kansas City	13	23	L	Bell 121 yards/Brown 6 catch-124 yds/Boswell 2 FG
11/1/2015		vs	CINCINNATI	10	16	L	Miller 10 catch-105 yards/Brown TD catch
11/8/2015		vs	OAKLAND RAIDERS	38	35	W	Brown 17 catch-284 yds/Williams 170 rush yds-2 TD
11/15/2015		vs	CLEVELAND	30	9	W	Bryant 6 catch-178 yds-TD/Brown 10-139 yards-2 TD
11/29/2015		@	Seattle	30	39	L	Roethlisberger 456 pass yards-TD pass to Wheaton
12/6/2015	SNF	vs	INDIANAPOLIS	45	10	W	**Brown punt return TD**-8 catch-118 yrds-2 TD catch
12/13/2015		@	Cincinnati	33	20	W	**Gay INT return TD**/Boswell 4 FGs/Williams 2 TDs
12/20/2015		vs	DENVER	34	27	W	Brown 16 catch-189 yards-2 TD catch/Boswell 2 FG
12/27/2015		@	Baltimore Ravens	17	20	L	Williams 100 rush yards-2 rush TD/Boswell FG
1/3/2016		@	Cleveland	28	12	W	Roethlisberger 349 pass yds-3 TD pass/Boswell 2 FG
1/9/2016	SAT	@	**Cincinnati**	**18**	**16**	**W**	Brown 7 catch-119 yards/Boswell 4 FGs/Bryant TD
1/17/2016		@	**Denver**	**16**	**23**	**L**	Bryant 9 catch-154 yards/Boswell 3 FGs

Schedule courtesy of Steve's Football Bible LLC

2015 AFC North	W	L	T	PCT	DIV	CONF	PF	PA
Cincinnati Bengals	12	4	0	.750	5–1	9–3	419	279
Pittsburgh Steelers	**10**	**6**	**0**	**.625**	**3–3**	**7–5**	**423**	**319**
Baltimore Ravens	5	11	0	.313	3–3	4–8	328	401
Cleveland Browns	3	13	0	.188	1–5	2–10	278	432

Oakland Raiders at Pittsburgh

In the first quarter, the Raiders scored first as Derek Carr found Michael Crabtree on a 22-yard pass for a 7–0 lead. The Steelers got on the board later in the quarter when Chris Boswell kicked a 34-yard field goal for a 7–3 game. In the 2nd quarter, the Steelers took the lead when DeAngelo Williams ran for a TD from 3 yards out (with a successful 2-point conversion) for an 11–7 game. The Raiders, however, retook the lead when Carr found Amari Cooper on a 15-yard pass for a 14–11 lead. The Steelers closed the half when Williams ran for another 3-yard TD and Boswell kicked a 38-yard field goal for leads of 18–14 and then 21–14 at halftime. After the break, the Raiders went back to work tying the game up 21–21 when Carr found Clive Walford on a 1-yard pass for the only score of the third quarter. In the fourth quarter, the Steelers were able to retake the lead as Ben Roethlisberger found Martavis Bryant on a 14-yard pass for a 28–21 game. Roethlisberger then found Jesse James on a 4-yard pass for a 35–21 game. The Raiders would tie the game back up with 2 straight TDs of their own: First coming from Jamize Olawale who ran from 19 yards out for a 35–28 game and then Carr finding Crabtree again on a 38-yard pass to make it 35–35. Getting the ball back with seconds left, the Steelers had to depend on backup QB Landry Jones to help them get within field goal range. They would successfully do so and then Boswell kicked the game-winning 18-yard field goal with 2 seconds left in the game for a 38–35 final score.

2015 NFL Draft

Round	Pick	Player	Position	College
1	22	Bud Dupree	Outside linebacker	Kentucky
2	56	Senquez Golson	Cornerback	Ole Miss
3	87	Sammie Coates	Wide receiver	Auburn
4	121	Doran Grant	Cornerback	Ohio State
5	160	Jesse James	Tight end	Penn State
6	199	Leterrius Walton	Defensive tackle	Central Michigan
6	212+	Anthony Chickillo	Outside linebacker	Miami (FL)
7	239	Gerod Holliman	Free safety	Louisville

2015 AFC Wild Card

This game ended up being a rain-soaked vicious battle between two AFC North rivals, filled with injuries and personal fouls on both sides. After falling behind 15–0, the Bengals scored three times in the fourth quarter to take a 16–15 lead. But with less than a minute left in the game, two consecutive personal fouls against Cincinnati's defense got the Steelers close enough for Chris Boswell to make a 35-yard field goal with 18 seconds left on the clock. The game started off as a defensive battle with both teams punting at the end of its first eight drives. With less than six minutes left in the second quarter, Bengals linebacker Vontaze Burfict forced a fumble from Markus Wheaton that safety George Iloka recovered on the Cincinnati 47-yard line. But a few plays later, Bengals quarterback AJ McCarron threw an interception to Antwon Blake, who returned it 35 yards to the Bengals' 41-yard line. A 23-yard completion from Ben Roethlisberger to Antonio Brown on the ensuing drive set up Boswell's 39-yard field goal. Following a punt, Roethlisberger completed a 16-yard pass to running back Fitzgerald Toussaint and a 24-yard pass to Wheaton – with a personal foul penalty on safety Shawn Williams adding another 15 yards – to set up Boswell's 30-yard field goal just before halftime. Despite the Steelers' slim 6–0 lead, they had dominated the stat sheet, holding Cincinnati to just 56 yards and two first downs.

On the opening drive of the second half, the Bengals seemed primed to score when Jeremy Hill broke free for a 38-yard run to the Steelers' 29-yard line. But on the next play, McCarron lost a fumble due to a hit by linebacker Jarvis Jones. Defensive end Cam Thomas recovered the ball and ended up losing it while being tackled, then defensive back William Gay picked it up and returned it for a touchdown. However, replays showed that Thomas was down by contact before he lost the fumble, and a 15-yard penalty against Gay for excessive celebration moved the ball all the way back to Pittsburgh's 36-yard line. Receiver Martavis Bryant's 44-yard run on an end-around play then set up Boswell's 34-yard field goal that gave the Steelers a 9–0 lead. Following a punt, Roethlisberger completed a 60-yard pass to Brown on the Bengals' 10-yard line. Then he threw a pass in the back of the end zone to Bryant, who made a diving somersault catch and maintained possession for a touchdown by pinning the ball against one leg while falling to the ground. However, Pittsburgh's two-point conversion attempt failed, so the score remained 15–0. Cincinnati responded with a drive to the Steelers' 23-yard line but committed another turnover when running back Giovani Bernard lost a fumble that was forced and recovered by linebacker Ryan Shazier, who leveled Bernard with a devastating helmet leading hit that knocked the running back out of the game and out of consciousness. Shazier was not penalized for the hit, much to the dismay of the home crowd.

On the last play of the third quarter, Burfict sacked Roethlisberger for a 12-yard loss, forcing a punt from the Steelers' 5-yard line and temporarily knocking Roethlisberger out of the game with a shoulder injury. After Jordan Berry's 41-yard punt gave the Bengals a first down on the Pittsburgh 46-yard line, Steelers defensive back Will Allen committed a 42-yard pass interference penalty while trying to cover A. J. Green. Hill then got the ball into the end zone with consecutive carries, the second a 1-yard touchdown run that made the score 15–7. The Steelers, now led by Landry Jones, started off their next drive well, as Jordan Todman rushed for a 25-yard gain on the second play. But an 11-yard sack by Carlos Dunlap and Pat Sims ultimately forced the Steelers to punt. McCarron started the Bengals' drive off with two completions to Hill for 24 total yards. Later, he converted a 3rd-and-9 with an 18-yard completion to tight end Tyler Eifert, and eventually the Bengals got close enough for Mike Nugent to kick a 36-yard field goal, making the score 15–10 with 5:17 left. The Steelers had to punt after three plays on their ensuing possession, and Adam Jones' 24-yard return gave the Bengals the ball on the Pittsburgh 45-yard line. McCarron soon faced a 4th-and-2 situation but converted with a 9-yard completion to Marvin Jones. Then when faced with 3rd-and-7, he launched a 25-yard touchdown pass to Green. After their two-point conversion failed, the Bengals held a 16–15 lead with 1:45 left. On the first play after the kickoff, Landry Jones threw an interception to Burfict on the Steelers' 26-yard line. He celebrated by running all the way through the tunnel. But with the game now seemingly in the Bengals' control, they gave the ball right back on the next play when Shazier forced a fumble from Hill that was recovered by defensive back Ross Cockrell.

Now with the ball on his own 11-yard line with 1:23 left, Roethlisberger returned to lead his team 74 yards in nine plays for the game-winning score. After several short completions moved the ball to the 37-yard line, Pittsburgh faced a 4th-and-3, but overcame it on Brown's 12-yard reception. On the next play, with just 22 seconds left, Roethlisberger threw a pass intended for Brown. The pass was incomplete, but Burfict was flagged for a personal foul for contact with Brown's helmet. Brown was injured on the play, and as he was being attended and officials were dealing with both teams, Adam Jones was flagged for a personal foul after an altercation with Steelers linebackers coach Joey Porter, giving the Steelers another 15 yards and moving the ball to the Bengals' 17-yard line. On the next play, Boswell kicked a 35-yard field goal with 18 seconds left to win the game. Roethlisberger completed 18 of 31 passes for 221 yards and a touchdown, while Brown caught seven passes for 119 yards and Todman was the game's leading rusher with 65 yards. Shazier had 13 tackles – nine of which were solo tackles – a pair of forced fumbles, and a fumble recovery. McCarron completed 23 of 41 passes for 213 yards, with a touchdown and an interception. Hill rushed for 50 yards and a touchdown, while also catching three passes for 27 yards. Green caught five passes for 71 yards and a touchdown, while Burfict had six tackles, a sack, an interception, and a forced fumble.

1/9/2016	Line/Total	1	2	3	4	Final
Pittsburgh Steelers	{-2.5}	0	6	9	3	18
Cincinnati Bengals	{45.5}	0	0	0	16	16

Scoring

Team	
Steelers	Chris Boswell 39 yard field goal
Steelers	Chris Boswell 30 yard field goal
Steelers	Chris Boswell 34 yard field goal
Steelers	Martavis Bryant 10 yard pass from Ben Roethlisberger (pass failed)
Bengals	Jeremy Hill 1 yard rush (Mike Nugent kick)
Bengals	Mike Nugent 36 yard field goal
Bengals	A.J. Green 25 yard pass from A.J. McCarron (run failed)
Steelers	Chris Boswell 35 yard field goal

2015 AFC Divisional Playoffs

In a tough defensive struggle in which both teams could only get the ball into the end zone once, Denver pulled ahead by scoring 11 points in the final three minutes of the game. At the end of the game's opening possession, Broncos safety Omar Bolden returned a punt 42 yards to the Pittsburgh 30-yard line, setting up Brandon McManus' 28-yard field goal. Later in the first quarter, Britton Colquitt's 57-yard punt pinned the Steelers back at their own 3-yard line. Pittsburgh was unable to get a first down with their ensuing drive, and Jordan Berry's 27-yard punt gave Denver a first down on the Steelers 31. Despite their excellent starting position, Denver could not get into the end zone and ended up with another McManus field goal to take a 6–0 lead. Pittsburgh took the ball back and stormed 80 yards in just five plays. First, Ben Roethlisberger completed a 23-yard pass to receiver Martavis Bryant. Then Bryant took a handoff on a reverse and raced 40 yards to the Broncos 16-yard line. Fitzgerald Toussaint finished the drive with two carries; the first for 15 yards and the second a 1-yard score that gave Pittsburgh a 7–6 lead with less than two minutes left in the first quarter.

On Pittsburgh's next possession, Roethlisberger's 58-yard completion to Darrius Heyward-Bey set up a 43-yard Chris Boswell field goal that increased their lead to 10–6. Denver had a chance to respond with a drive to the Steelers 37-yard line, but they turned the ball over with an incomplete pass on 4th-and-3. Late in the second quarter, Berry booted a 50-yard punt that gave the Broncos the ball at their own 5-yard line. But a 34-yard burst by running back C. J. Anderson sparked a 62-yard drive then ended with McManus' 51-yard field goal, cutting the score to 10–9 on the last play of the first half.

After forcing Denver to punt of the first drive of the second half, Pittsburgh put together a 69-yard scoring drive featuring a 58-yard reception by Bryant. Boswell finished it with a 28-yard field goal, increasing the Steelers lead to 13–9. Denver had to punt again on their next drive, but Colquitt once again gave the team a big assist, this time with a 51-yard punt that put the ball on the Steelers 6-yard line. Pittsburgh could not get a first down, and Berry's 43-yard punt gave the ball back to Denver on their own 47-yard line. The Broncos were only able to move the ball 30 yards with their ensuing drive, but it was enough for McManus to make a 41-yard field goal, trimming their deficit to 13–12.

Pittsburgh took the ball back and drove to the Broncos 34-yard line but were halted there and decided to punt instead of trying a long field goal. The Broncos also ended up punting, and Pittsburgh drove back to the Denver 34-yard line with three consecutive Roethlisberger completions for 39 total yards. But on the next play, the first turnover of the game occurred when safety Bradley Roby forced a fumble from Toussaint that was recovered by linebacker DeMarcus Ware.

Now with 9:52 left in the game, 39-year-old Broncos quarterback Peyton Manning took to the field and led the team 65 yards in 13 plays for the go-ahead score. The key play of the drive was a 31-yard completion from Manning to rookie receiver Bennie Fowler on 3rd-and-12 from the Broncos 33-yard line. Running back Ronnie Hillman also made a big impact, with five carries for 18 yards. After Fowler's catch, the Broncos would not face another third down on the drive until the last play of the drive, when Anderson converted a 3rd-and-goal with a 1-yard touchdown run. Then Manning completed a pass to Demaryius Thomas for a 2-point conversion, giving the Broncos a 20–13 lead with three minutes left on the clock.

Pittsburgh started off their next drive with an 18-yard catch by Bryant but ended up facing 4th-and-5 on their own 43-yard line with less than two minutes left. They tried to pick up a first down, but Ware sacked Roethlisberger for a 13-yard loss. Taking over at the Steelers 30-yard line, Denver forced Pittsburgh to use up all their timeouts with three consecutive running plays. Then McManus kicked a 45-yard field goal that gave the Broncos a 23–13 lead with 53 seconds to go. A 20-yard pass interference penalty on safety T. J. Ward and a 22-yard reception by Bryant enabled Boswell to bring the deficit back to one score with a 47-yard field goal. But Anderson eliminated any chance of a comeback by recovering Boswell's ensuing onside kick. Manning completed 22 of 37 passes for 222 yards. Emmanuel Sanders caught five of them for 85 yards. Anderson was the top rusher of the game with 72 yards and a touchdown, while also catching two passes for 11 yards. Ware had three tackles, a sack, and a fumble recovery. McManus tied a playoff record with five field goals. Roethlisberger finished the game 24 of 37 for 339 yards. Bryant caught nine passes for 154 yards and had two carries for 40 yards. Linebacker James Harrison had seven tackles and a sack.

1/17/2016	Line/Total	1	2	3	4	Final
Pittsburgh Steelers	{41.5}	7	3	3	3	16
Denver Broncos	{-7.0}	6	3	3	11	23

Scoring

Team	
Broncos	Brandon McManus 28 yard field goal
Broncos	Brandon McManus 41 yard field goal
Steelers	Fitzgerald Toussaint 1 yard rush (Chris Boswell kick)
Steelers	Chris Boswell 43 yard field goal
Broncos	Brandon McManus 51 yard field goal
Steelers	Chris Boswell 28 yard field goal
Broncos	Brandon McManus 41 yard field goal
Broncos	C.J. Anderson 1 yard rush (Demaryius Thomas pass from Peyton Manning)
Broncos	Brandon McManus 45 yard field goal
Steelers	Chris Boswell 47 yard field goal

2016 Pittsburgh Steelers

The 2016 season was the 84th in the history of the Pittsburgh Steelers as a professional sports franchise and marked the 17th season under leadership of general manager Kevin Colbert and the 10th under head coach Mike Tomlin. For the first time since 2004, tight end Heath Miller was not on the opening day roster, as he announced his retirement on February 19, 2016. After going 4-5 in their first nine games, the Steelers ended their season on a high note, winning all of their last seven. The Steelers were the first team since the 2011 Green Bay Packers to play on both Thanksgiving and Christmas Day. The Steelers won the AFC North for the second time in three years and made the playoffs for the third straight year. The team also improved upon their 10–6 record from 2015. Le'Veon Bell made his career first playoff appearance with the Steelers in the 2016–17 playoffs. The Steelers went on to defeat the Miami Dolphins in the Wild Card round and the Kansas City Chiefs in the Divisional round before losing to the eventual Super Bowl champion New England Patriots 36–17 in the AFC Championship Game. This was the Steelers' first appearance in the AFC Championship Game since the 2010 NFL season. The team ranked 10th in both offense and defense. This was also the final season under the ownership of Dan Rooney, as he died on April 13, 2017. Antonio Brown {WR} was selected to various first team All-Pro teams.

Ben Roethlisberger led the team in passing with 3,819 yards and threw 29 touchdown passes. Le'Veon Bell led the team in rushing with 1,268 yards and 7 rushing touchdowns. Antonio Brown led the team in receiving with 106 receptions for 1,284 yards and 12 TD receptions.

PITTSBURGH			2016			13-6	Game Highlights
9/12/2016	MNF	@	Washington Redskins	38	16	W	Williams 143 rush yds-2 TD/Brown 8-126 yds-2 TD
9/18/2016		vs	CINCINNATI	24	16	W	Roethlisberger 259 pass yards-3 TD pass
9/25/2016		@	Philadelphia	3	34	L	Steelers 29 rush yards/Brown 12 catch-140 yards
10/2/2016	SNF	vs	KANSAS CITY	43	14	W	Roethlisberger 300 pass yds-5 TD pass/Bell 144 yds
10/9/2016		vs	NEW YORK JETS	31	13	W	Coates 6 catch-139 yards-2 TD catch/Big Ben 4 TDs
10/16/2016		@	Miami	15	30	L	Roethlisberger 189 pass yards-TD pass to Hamilton
10/23/2016		vs	NEW ENGLAND	16	27	L	Jones 281 pass yards-TD pass/Boswell 3 FGs
11/6/2016		@	Baltimore Ravens	14	21	L	Roethlisberger 264 pass yards-TD pass-rush TD
11/13/2016		vs	DALLAS	30	35	L	Roethlisberger 408 pass yards-3 TD pass-rush TD
11/20/2016		@	Cleveland	24	9	W	**Hargrave fumble return TD**/Boswell 3 FGs
11/24/2016	TH	@	Indianapolis Colts	28	7	W	Brown 5 catch-91 yards-3 TD catch/Bell 120 yards
12/4/2016		vs	NEW YORK GIANTS	24	14	W	Green 6 catch-110 yards-TD catch/Bullock 3 FGs
12/11/2016		@	Buffalo	27	20	W	Bell 236 rush yards-3 rush TD/Boswell 2 FGs
12/18/2016		@	Cincinnati	24	20	W	Rogers TD catch/Boswell 6 FGs
12/25/2016		vs	BALTIMORE RAVENS	31	27	W	Bell 122 rush yards-rush TD-TD catch
1/1/2017		vs	CLEVELAND {OT}	27	24	W	Jones 277 pass yards-3 TD pass/Williams 2 TDs
1/8/2017		vs	**MIAMI**	**30**	**12**	**W**	Brown 124 yds-2 TD catch/Bell 167 rush yds-2 TD
1/15/2017		@	**Kansas City**	**18**	**16**	**W**	Bell 170 rush yards/Boswell 6 FGs
1/22/2017		@	**New England**	**17**	**36**	**L**	Roethlisberger 314 pass yards-TD pass to Hamilton

Schedule courtesy of Steve's Football Bible LLC

Cleveland Browns at Pittsburgh

The Browns struck first in the first quarter when Seth DeValve ran for a 12-yard touchdown to make it 7–0 for the only score of the period. They made it 14–0 in the second quarter when RG3 found

Gary Barnidge on a 4-yard pass. The Steelers got on the board when backup QB Landry Jones found De'Angelo Williams on an 11-yard pass to make it 14–7 at halftime. After a scoreless third quarter, the Steelers continued their reign of scoring unanswered points in the fourth when Williams ran for a 1-yard touchdown to tie the game at 14–14 before taking the lead when Jones found Demarcus Ayers on an 11-yard pass to make it 21–14. Though, the Browns would close out regulation, tying the game at 21–21 when George Atkinson III ran for a 5-yard touchdown. In overtime, the Browns retook the lead when Cody Parkey nailed a 34-yard field goal to make it 24–21. The Steelers would eventually score the game-winning touchdown with just under 3 minutes left in overtime when Jones found Cobi Hamilton on a 26-yard pass to make the final score 27–24.

2016 AFC North	W	L	T	PCT	DIV	CONF	PF	PA
Pittsburgh Steelers	**11**	**5**	**0**	**.688**	**5–1**	**9–3**	**399**	**327**
Baltimore Ravens	8	8	0	.500	4–2	7–5	343	321
Cincinnati Bengals	6	9	1	.406	3–3	5–7	325	315
Cleveland Browns	1	15	0	.063	0–6	1–11	264	452

2016 NFL Draft

Round	Selection	Player	Position	College
1	25	Artie Burns	CB	Miami (Fla.)
2	58	Sean Davis	FS	Maryland
3	89	Javon Hargrave	NT	S.C. State
4	123	Jerald Hawkins	T	LSU
6	220	Travis Feeney	ILB	Washington
7	229	Demarcus Ayers	WR	Houston
7	246	Tyler Matakevich	ILB	Temple

2016 AFC Wild Card

In their regular season meeting, Miami racked up 474 yards as they defeated Pittsburgh 30–15, but this game would have a very different outcome. The Steelers gained 387 yards, forced three turnovers, recorded five sacks, and scored three touchdowns in the first half on the way to a dominant 18-point win. Pittsburgh took the opening kickoff and drove 85 yards in 5 plays, scoring on Ben Roethlisberger's pass to Antonio Brown, who hauled in the short screen and took it 50 yards to the end zone. Then after a punt, the Steelers moved the ball 90 yards in 6 plays on the way to a 62-yard touchdown completion from Roethlisberger to Brown. This time Miami managed to respond, aided by Kenyan Drake's 33-yard kickoff return to the 41-yard line. Faced with 3rd-and-13 after two plays, Matt Moore completed a 36-yard pass to receiver Kenny Stills, setting up Andrew Franks' 38-yard field goal that cut their deficit to 14–3. But after getting the ball back, Steelers running back Le'Veon Bell carried the ball 9 times for 79 yards on a 10–play, 83-yard drive that ended with his 1-yard touchdown run, giving the team a 20–3 lead after Chris Boswell missed the extra point.

Miami then drove 39 yards in 12 plays, scoring on Franks' 47-yard field goal with less than 5 minutes left in the second quarter. Pittsburgh responded with a drive to the Dolphins' 34-yard line, but with 1:12 left, Roethlisberger threw a pass that bounced off the outstretched hands of Brown and was intercepted by safety Michael Thomas, who returned it 16 yards to the Dolphins' 27-yard line. Miami subsequently moved the ball to the Steelers' 8-yard line, featuring a 37-yard completion from Moore to DeVante Parker. But on the next play, Moore lost a fumble while being sacked by James Harrison and Steelers defensive end Stephon Tuitt recovered the ball, allowing Pittsburgh to go into the half maintaining their 20–6 lead. Early in the third quarter, safety Mike Mitchell forced a fumble while sacking Moore that Leterrius Walton recovered for the Steelers at their 41-yard line. Bell then rushed 3 times for 49 yards on the way to a 34-yard Boswell field goal that increased their lead to 23–6. Then on the first play after the kickoff, linebacker Ryan Shazier intercepted a pass from Moore and returned it 10 yards to the Dolphins' 25-yard line. Miami's defense managed to force a 4th down, but a neutral zone infraction penalty against Dolphins defensive back Tony Lippett on the field goal attempt gave Pittsburgh a new set of downs. The Steelers took full advantage of the opportunity, scoring on Bell's 8-yard touchdown run that made the score 30–6 with 2 minutes left until the fourth quarter. Miami responded with a drive to the Steelers' 42-yard line but lost the ball when Tuitt tackled Moore for a 2-yard gain on 4th-and-4. Miami finally managed to get a touchdown in the fourth quarter – with 5:57 left – moving the ball 70 yards in 9 plays and scoring on Moore's 4-yard pass to running back Damien Williams. After a failed onside kick attempt, the Dolphins got one last chance to score when Xavien Howard intercepted Roethlisberger's pass and returned it 11 yards to the Miami 43-yard line. But the Steelers forced a turnover on downs at the Steelers' 33-yard line and ran out the clock to win the game. Bell rushed 29 times for 167 yards – surpassing the previous franchise playoff record of 158 yards set by Franco Harris in Super Bowl IX – and a touchdown. Linebacker Lawrence Timmons had 14 tackles (8 solo) and 2 sacks. James Harrison had 10 tackles (6 solo), 1.5 sacks and a forced fumble. Moore finished with 29 completions on 36 passing attempts for 298 yards and a touchdown, with one interception. His top receiver was Jarvis Landry, who caught 11 passes for 102 yards.

1/8/2017	Line/Total	1	2	3	4	Final
Miami Dolphins	{47.5}	3	3	0	6	12
Pittsburgh Steelers	{-11.0}	14	6	10	0	30

Scoring

Steelers	Antonio Brown 50 yard pass from Ben Roethlisberger (Chris Boswell kick)
Steelers	Antonio Brown 62 yard pass from Ben Roethlisberger (Chris Boswell kick)
Dolphins	Andrew Franks 38 yard field goal
Steelers	Le'Veon Bell 1 yard rush (Chris Boswell kick failed)
Dolphins	Andrew Franks 47 yard field goal
Steelers	Chris Boswell 34 yard field goal
Steelers	Le'Veon Bell 8 yard rush (Chris Boswell kick)
Dolphins	Damien Williams 4 yard pass from Matt Moore (pass failed)

2016 AFC Divisional Playoffs

This game was supposed to have started at 1:05 PM, EST, but was pushed back to 8:00 due to inclement weather, making this game the first ever divisional round playoff game in NFL history to premiere on Sunday Night Football. Although Pittsburgh was unable to get into the end zone, Chris Boswell's postseason record six field goals were enough for them to become the first team to win a playoff game without scoring a touchdown since the 2006 Indianapolis Colts on their run to a victory in Super Bowl XLI.

The Steelers scored on the game's opening drive, moving the ball 65 yards in 11 plays on the way to Boswell's 22-yard field goal. Kansas City quickly struck back after Demetrius Harris returned Boswell's short kickoff 25 yards to their 45-yard line. The Chiefs then drove 55 yards in six plays, including a 21-yard catch by Travis Kelce, to score on Alex Smith's 5-yard touchdown pass to Albert Wilson, giving them a 7–3 lead. Pittsburgh stormed right back, as Ben Roethlisberger's 52-yard completion to Antonio Brown led to another Boswell field goal that made the score 7–6. On their next drive, they went 53 yards in 14 plays, scoring on Boswell's third field goal, to give them a 9–7 lead with just over 9 minutes left in the half. The Steelers soon got another chance to score when linebacker Ryan Shazier intercepted a pass from Smith on the Chiefs' 44-yard line. Three plays later, Roethlisberger returned the favor with an interception to Eric Berry in the end zone. Kansas City ended up punting after three plays and Brown returned it 6 yards to the Chiefs' 45-yard line. Le'Veon Bell then carried the ball 5 times for 32 yards on a drive that ended with Boswell's 4th field goal, this one from 45 yards, that increased their lead to 12−7. Shortly before halftime, the Steelers had one last scoring chance when defensive back Artie Burns recovered a fumble from Charcandrick West on the Chiefs' 40-yard line. Roethlisberger then completed a 29-yard pass to Brown, but he was tackled on the 11-yard line as time expired.

On Pittsburgh's first possession of the second half, Bell carried the ball five times for 49 yards, including a 38-yard rush on the first play, as the team drove to a 43-yard Boswell field goal that put them up 15−7. Both teams had to punt on their next possessions and Jordan Berry's 35-yard kick gave Kansas City the ball with good field position on the Steelers' 46-yard line. Smith then completed a 20-yard pass to Jeremy Maclin that set up Cairo Santos' 48-yard field goal, cutting their deficit to 15−10 with 10 seconds left in the third quarter. Roethlisberger's completions to Eli Rogers and Jesse James for gains for 14 and 23 yards respectively on their next drive moved the team into position for Boswell to kick a record-setting sixth field goal of the game, which he made from 43 yards to give the team an 18−10 lead. For the Chiefs, Smith hit Kelce for a 24-yard gain on their first play and then Spencer Ware gained 11 yards on the ground. After a penalty pushed them into a 2nd-and-25, Smith completed a 17-yard pass to Kelce and a 12-yard completion to Chris Conley on 4th-and-8 allowed them to keep the ball. Several plays later, they faced 4th-and-2 on the Steelers' 4-yard line but converted again with Smith's 3-yard pass to fullback Anthony Sherman. Ware scored on a 1-yard touchdown run on the next play that cut the deficit to 18−16. Smith completed a pass to Harris on the two-point conversion play but was negated by a holding penalty on Eric Fisher as he tried to block an outside blitz from linebacker James Harrison. The second attempt was incomplete. With 2:43 left and one timeout remaining, Kansas City still had a chance to get the ball back, especially after Justin Gilbert was tackled on the 5-yard line during the kick return. However, Roethlisberger made completions to Rogers and Brown for gains of 5 and 7 yards respectively, picking up a first down allowing the Steelers to run out the clock. Roethlisberger completed 20-for-31 passes for 221 yards and an interception; Brown caught six passes for 108 yards and returned two punts for 9 yards, while Bell rushed 30 times for 170 yards, giving him the highest total of combined yards by any running back in history over his first two playoff games. Bell also joined Terrell Davis as the only two players to rush for at least 160 yards in consecutive postseason games. Smith finished the game 20-for-34 for 172 yards, a touchdown, an interception and nine rushing yards. This was the 5th consecutive home playoff loss for Kansas City, setting a new NFL record.

1/15/2017	Line/Total	1	2	3	4	Final
Pittsburgh Steelers	{45.5}	6	6	3	3	18
Kansas City Chiefs	{-2.5}	7	0	3	6	16

Scoring

Team	
Steelers	Chris Boswell 22 yard field goal
Chiefs	Albert Wilson 5 yard pass from Alex Smith (Cairo Santos kick)
Steelers	Chris Boswell 38 yard field goal
Steelers	Chris Boswell 36 yard field goal
Steelers	Chris Boswell 45 yard field goal
Steelers	Chris Boswell 43 yard field goal
Chiefs	Cairo Santos 48 yard field goal
Steelers	Chris Boswell 43 yard field goal
Chiefs	Spencer Ware 1 yard rush (pass failed)

2016 AFC Championship Game

New England advanced to their seventh Super Bowl in the last 16 seasons under quarterback Tom Brady and Coach Bill Belichick, racking up 431 yards and 26 first downs. Pittsburgh's offense had 368 yards, but could only score 17 points, eight of them on a touchdown late in the game with the outcome already decided. Meanwhile, the Steelers' rushing attack, that had been so critical to their earlier playoff wins, was crippled by an early injury to running back Le'Veon Bell, finishing the game with just 54 total yards on the ground.

On the game's opening drive, Brady's 41-yard completion to Julian Edelman set up Stephen Gostkowski's 31-yard field goal, giving New England a 3–0 lead less than two minutes into the game. Following several punts, the Patriots went on an 80-yard, 11-play drive, the longest gain being a 26-yard catch by receiver Chris Hogan. Brady finished it off with a 16-yard touchdown pass to Hogan, for a 10–0 lead. On the second play of Pittsburgh's next drive, Bell suffered a game-ending groin injury. However, his replacement DeAngelo Williams caught two passes for nine yards and rushed four times for 25 yards, the last carry a five-yard touchdown run to complete the 13-play, 84-yard drive early in the second quarter. Chris Boswell missed the extra point, with the score remaining 10–6.

New England stormed right back, driving 82 yards in nine plays and scoring on Brady's 34-yard touchdown pass to Hogan on a flea flicker play. Pittsburgh then moved the ball to the Patriots' 19-yard line, where Ben Roethlisberger threw a pass to tight end Jesse James that was initially ruled a touchdown, but a replay review determined James was down on the 1-yard line. On the next play, Williams was dropped for a one-yard loss by Dont'a Hightower and Patrick Chung. On second down, Williams was tackled for a three-yard loss by nose tackle Vincent Valentine. On third down, Roethlisberger's pass was incomplete, so the team settled for Boswell's field goal to make the score 17–9.

New England dominated the second half, burying the Steelers with four unanswered scores. After forcing them to punt, New England drove 55 yards in nine plays, 24 of them coming on a catch by Hogan. Gostkowski finished the drive with a 47-yard field goal that put the team up 20–9. Following another punt, Brady's 39-yard completion to Hogan led to a one-yard touchdown by LeGarrette Blount, giving the team a 27–9 lead with 2:44 left in the third quarter. On the first play after the kickoff, Kyle Van Noy forced a fumble from Eli Rogers that was recovered by linebacker Rob Ninkovich on the Steelers' 28-yard line. Brady completed an 18-yard pass to Edelman on the next play, and eventually found him in the end zone for a 10-yard touchdown pass. Gostkowski missed the extra point, but the Patriots had effectively put the game away with a 33–9 lead going into the fourth quarter.

In the final period, the Steelers drove to New England's 2-yard line but turned the ball over on downs. Then after a punt, Eric Rowe intercepted a pass from Roethlisberger and returned it 37 yards to the Steelers' 32-yard line, leading to a Gostkowski field goal that increased New England's lead to 36–9. All that remained from this point on was Roethlisberger's garbage-time 30-yard touchdown pass to Cobi Hamilton and subsequent 2-point conversion pass to Williams that made the final score 36–17. Brady completed 32 of his 42 passing attempts for 384 yards and three touchdowns. Hogan caught nine passes for 180 yards and two touchdowns, while Edelman had eight receptions for 118 yards and a touchdown. Roethlisberger threw for 314 yards, with a touchdown and an interception.

1/22/2017	Line/Total	1	2	3	4	Final
Pittsburgh Steelers	{49.5}	0	9	0	8	17
New England Patriots	{-5.5}	10	7	16	3	36

Scoring

Team	
Patriots	Stephen Gostkowski 31 yard field goal
Patriots	Chris Hogan 16 yard pass from Tom Brady (Stephen Gostkowski kick)

Team	
Steelers	DeAngelo Williams 5 yard rush (Chris Boswell kick failed)
Patriots	Chris Hogan 34 yard pass from Tom Brady (Stephen Gostkowski kick)
Steelers	Chris Boswell 23 yard field goal
Patriots	Stephen Gostkowski 47 yard field goal
Patriots	LeGarrette Blount 1 yard rush (Stephen Gostkowski kick)
Patriots	Julian Edelman 10 yard pass from Tom Brady (Stephen Gostkowski kick failed)
Patriots	Stephen Gostkowski 26 yard field goal
Steelers	Cobi Hamilton 30 yard pass from Ben Roethlisberger (DeAngelo Williams pass from Ben Roethlisberger)

2017 Pittsburgh Steelers

The 2017 Pittsburgh Steelers season was the 18th season under leadership of general manager Kevin Colbert and the eleventh under head coach Mike Tomlin. It was also the Steelers' first season since the death of Dan Rooney. The Steelers clinched the AFC North division title for the second consecutive season with a 39–38 win over the Baltimore Ravens in Week 14 and secured a first-round playoff bye for the first time since 2010 following a 34–6 win over the Houston Texans in Week 16. In the Divisional Round however, the Steelers suffered a loss to the Jacksonville Jaguars by a score of 45–42 after falling behind 28–14 at halftime. After their loss, the Steelers were criticized for looking past the Jaguars and anticipating a rematch with the New England Patriots. With a record of 13–3, the Steelers posted their best mark since 2004. Le'Veon Bell {RB}, Antonio Brown {WR}, David DeCastro {G} and Cameron Heyward {DT} were selected to various first team All-Pro teams.

Ben Roethlisberger led the team in passing with 4,251 yards and threw 28 touchdown passes. Le'Veon Bell led the team in rushing with 1,291 yards and 9 rushing touchdowns. Antonio Brown led the team in receiving with 101 receptions for 1,533 yards and 9 TD receptions. **JuJu Smith-Schuster set a franchise record with a 97 TD catch vs Detroit. Chris Boswell set a franchise record with 142 points.**

PITTSBURGH			2017			13-4	Game Highlights
9/10/2017		@	Cleveland	21	18	W	**Chickillo blocked punt return TD**/James 2 TD catch
9/17/2017		vs	MINNESOTA	26	9	W	Bryant & Smith-Schuster TD catch/Boswell 4 FGs
9/24/2017		@	Chicago {OT}	17	23	L	Brown 10 catch-110 yards-TD catch/Bell rush TD
10/1/2017		@	Baltimore Ravens	26	9	W	Bell 144 rush yards-2 rush TD/Boswell 2 FGs
10/8/2017		vs	JACKSONVILLE	9	30	L	Steelers held to 70 rush yards/Boswell 3 FGs
10/15/2017		@	Kansas City	19	13	W	Brown 8 catch-155 yards-TD catch/Bell rush TD
10/22/2017		vs	CINCINNATI	29	14	W	Bell 134 rush yds/Boswell 5 FGs/Big Ben 2 TD pass
10/29/2017	SNF	@	Detroit	20	15	W	Smith-Schuster 7 catch-193 yards-TD catch
11/12/2017		@	Indianapolis Colts	20	17	W	Roethlisberger 236 rush yards-2 TDs/Boswell 2 FGs
11/16/2017	TH	vs	TENNESSEE TITANS	40	17	W	Brown 10 catch-144 yds-3 TD catch/Boswell 4 FGs
11/26/2017	SNF	vs	GREEN BAY	31	28	W	Brown 10 catch-169 yards-2 TD catch/Boswell FG
12/4/2017	MNF	@	Cincinnati	23	20	W	Roethlisberger 290 pass yards-2 TDs/Boswell 3 FGs
12/10/2017	SNF	vs	BALTIMORE RAVENS	39	38	W	Roethlisberger 506 pass yards-2 TDs/Boswell 4 FGs
12/17/2017		vs	NEW ENGLAND	24	27	L	Roethlisberger 281 pass yards-2 TDs/Bell 165 yds
12/25/2017	MON	@	Houston Texans	34	6	W	Roethlisberger 226 pass yards-2 TDs/Bell rush TD
12/31/2017		vs	CLEVELAND	28	24	W	**Smith-Schuster kickoff return TD**/9c-143 yds-TD
1/7/2018		vs	JACKSONVILLE	42	45	L	Roethlisberger 469 pass yds-5 TD pass/Brown 2 TD

Schedule courtesy of Steve's Football Bible LLC

2017 AFC North	W	L	T	PCT	DIV	CONF	PF	PA
Pittsburgh Steelers	**13**	**3**	**0**	**.813**	**6–0**	**10–2**	**406**	**308**
Baltimore Ravens	9	7	0	.563	3–3	7–5	395	303
Cincinnati Bengals	7	9	0	.438	3–3	6–6	290	349
Cleveland Browns	0	16	0	.000	0–6	0–12	234	410

Pittsburgh at Cincinnati Bengals

On a 2nd and 5 early in the game, Steelers linebacker Ryan Shazier suffered a career-ending spinal cord injury while tackling Bengals wide receiver Josh Malone. Shazier was paralyzed from the waist down but later regained the ability to walk and run. The Bengals scored first in the first quarter when Randy Bullock kicked a 35-yard field goal to make it 3–0. They would then make it 10–0 when Andy Dalton found A.J. Green on an 8-yard pass. In the second quarter, Dalton and Green connected again on a 15-yard pass to make it 17–0. The Steelers managed to get on the board before halftime when Chris Boswell put a 30-yard field goal through to make the score 17–3. In the third quarter, the Steelers drew closer when Ben Roethlisberger found Le'Veon Bell on a 35-yard touchdown to make it 17–10. The Bengals moved back ahead by double digits when Randy Bullock kicked a 31-yard field goal to make it 20–10. In the fourth quarter, it was all Steelers when Boswell put up a 37-yard field goal to make it 20–13. Roethlisberger then found Antonio Brown on a 6-yard pass to tie the game up at 20–20 with 3:55 left. Finally, Boswell was able to seal the victory with a 38-yard field goal with 4 seconds left in the game to make the final score 23–20.

2017 NFL Draft

Round	Selection	Player	Position	College
1	30	T.J. Watt	OLB	Wisconsin
2	62	JuJu Smith-Schuster	WR	USC
3	94	Cameron Sutton	CB	Tennessee
3*	105*	James Conner	RB	Pittsburgh
4	135	Josh Dobbs	QB	Tennessee
5	173	Brian Allen	FS	Utah
6	213	Colin Holba	LS	Louisville
7	248	Keion Adams	OLB	Western Michigan

2017 AFC Divisional Playoffs

Jacksonville built up a 28–7 first-half lead and held off a second-half Steelers comeback to win the fourth highest scoring NFL playoff game. It was a week 5 game rematch between the 2 teams, which the Jags won 30-9 thanks to a defense that intercepted Steelers quarterback Ben Roethlisberger 5 times.

The Jaguars drove 66 yards in eight plays on their opening drive, with Blake Bortles completing passes to tight ends Ben Koyack and James O'Shaughnessy for gains of 21 and 19 yards on the way to a one-yard fourth-down touchdown run by Leonard Fournette. Later in the first quarter, linebacker Myles Jack intercepted a pass from Steelers quarterback Ben Roethlisberger on the Pittsburgh 18-yard line, and Fournette increased Jacksonville's lead to 14–0 with a touchdown run on the next play. The Steelers responded with a drive to the Jacksonville 21-yard line, but on fourth-and-1, running back Le'Veon Bell was tackled by Jalen Ramsey and Malik Jackson for a four-yard loss. The Jaguars then drove 75 yards in 11 plays and scored on T. J. Yeldon's 4-yard touchdown run, increasing their lead to 21–0 with just over 11 minutes left in the half.

This time, the Steelers responded with a 64-yard scoring drive, featuring a 21-yard run by Bell and ending on Roethlisberger's 23-yard touchdown pass to Antonio Brown. But the next time Pittsburgh got the ball, Roethlisberger lost a fumble while being sacked by Yannick Ngakoue. Linebacker Telvin Smith recovered the ball and returned it 50 yards for a touchdown, making the score 28–7 with less than two minutes left until halftime. However, the Jaguars were penalized 15 yards for excessive celebration, and then Cameron Sutton returned the ensuing kickoff 22 yards to the Jacksonville 49-yard line. Pittsburgh went on to drive 51 yards and cut their deficit to 28–14 on Roethlisberger's 36-yard touchdown completion to Martavis Bryant with 25 seconds remaining.

The Steelers drove 77 yards in 10 plays on their opening drive of the second half, cutting their deficit to 28–21 with Roethlisberger's 19-yard touchdown pass to Bell. Early in the final period, the Steelers got the ball on the Jaguars' 48-yard line due to a deflected punt but ended up turning the ball over with an incomplete pass on fourth-and-1. On the ensuing Jacksonville drive, Bortles' 45-yard completion to Keelan Cole put them on the Steelers' 3-yard line, and Fournette ran the ball in for a touchdown on the next play, giving the Jaguars a 35–21 lead. This was the start of a scoring run from both teams, cumulatively totaling 38 points in the fourth quarter. After Fournette's score, Roethlisberger started the next drive with a 21-yard completion to Brown, and eventually ended it with a 43-yard touchdown pass to Brown that cut the score to 35–28. Jacksonville stormed right back, moving the ball 75 yards in eight plays, one of them a 40-yard completion from Bortles to Yeldon on third-and-5. Fullback Tommy Bohanon caught a 14-yard touchdown pass from Bortles with 4:19 left, giving the Jaguars a 42–28 lead. The Steelers responded by moving the ball 75 yards in 12 plays, the longest a 22-yard reception from Bell. Bell finished the drive with an eight-yard touchdown run, reducing his team's deficit to 42–35 with 2:19 to play. However, Pittsburgh failed to recover their ensuing onside kick attempt, resulting in Jacksonville getting the ball back on the Steelers' 36-yard line and leading to a 45-yard Josh Lambo field goal that put the Jaguars up 45–35. Pittsburgh then drove 75 yards in 10 plays, including a 42-yard completion from Roethlisberger to Brown. He ended up throwing a four-yard touchdown pass to JuJu Smith-Schuster, but by then, one second remained.

Bortles completed 14 of 26 passes for 214 yards and a touchdown. Fournette was the top rusher of the game with 25 carries for 109 yards and three touchdowns, along with two receptions for 10 yards. Setting several franchise playoffs records, Roethlisberger completed 37 of 58 passes for 469 yards – the second highest total in NFL postseason history, behind Bernie Kosar's 489-yard tally, from January 1987 – with five touchdowns and an interception. Bell rushed for 67 yards and a touchdown, while also catching nine passes for 88 yards, while Brown caught seven passes for 132 yards and two touchdowns. Tight end Vance McDonald also went over 100 yards receiving, making 10 receptions for 112 yards. The Steelers lost despite gaining 545 yards of total offense, the most yards gained by a losing team in a playoff game (this record would later be surpassed by the Patriots in Super Bowl LII). Ben Roethlisberger became the first NFL quarterback in a playoff game to throw 5 touchdowns in a losing effort.

1/14/2018	Line/Total	1	2	3	4	Final
Jacksonville Jaguars	40.5	14	14	0	17	45
Pittsburgh Steelers	-7.0	0	14	7	21	42

Scoring

Team	
Jaguars	Leonard Fournette 1 yard rush (Josh Lambo kick)
Jaguars	Leonard Fournette 18 yard rush (Josh Lambo kick)
Jaguars	T.J. Yeldon 4 yard rush (Josh Lambo kick)
Steelers	Antonio Brown 23 yard pass from Ben Roethlisberger (Chris Boswell kick)
Jaguars	Telvin Smith 50 yard fumble return (Josh Lambo kick)
Steelers	Martavis Bryant 36 yard pass from Ben Roethlisberger (Chris Boswell kick)
Steelers	Le'Veon Bell 19 yard pass from Ben Roethlisberger (Chris Boswell kick)
Jaguars	Leonard Fournette 3 yard rush (Josh Lambo kick)
Steelers	Antonio Brown 43 yard pass from Ben Roethlisberger (Chris Boswell kick)
Jaguars	Tommy Bohanon 14 yard pass from Blake Bortles (Josh Lambo kick)
Steelers	Le'Veon Bell 8 yard rush (Chris Boswell kick)
Jaguars	Josh Lambo 45 yard field goal
Steelers	JuJu Smith-Schuster 4 yard pass from Ben Roethlisberger (Chris Boswell kick)

2018 Pittsburgh Steelers

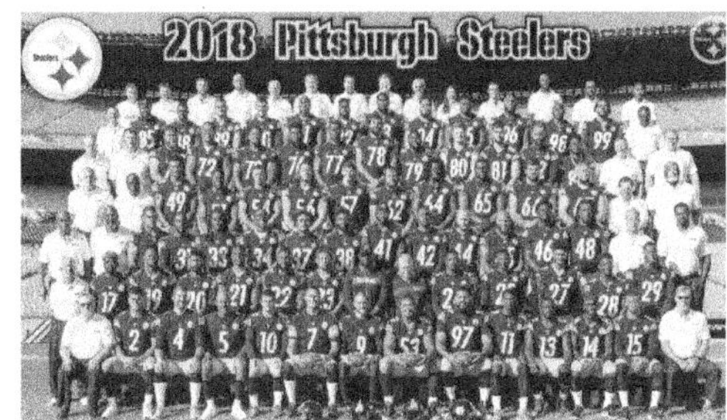

The 2018 season marked the 19th season under leadership of general manager Kevin Colbert and the 12th under head coach Mike Tomlin. After starting the season 7–2–1, the Steelers lost four of their last six games (including losing three straight to the AFC West), allowing the Ravens to clinch the AFC North on the last day of the season, and missing the playoffs for the first time since 2013. Star running back Le'Veon Bell refused to sign his franchise tag, holding out for a more permanent contract for what was first expected to be the first few weeks of the season, but later missing out on the entire season. Quarterback Ben Roethlisberger received criticism for openly calling out teammates during public interviews with the media, as well as for his initial reaction to the team drafting quarterback Mason Rudolph and wide receiver Antonio Brown was involved with a string of off-field incidents.

Ben Roethlisberger set franchise records in passing with 5,129 yards and threw 34 touchdown passes. Roethlisberger set records with 675 pass attempts and 452 completions. James Conner led the team in rushing with 973 yards and 12 rushing touchdowns. JuJu Smith-Schuster led the team with 111 receptions for 1,426 yards. **Antonio Brown set a franchise record with 15 TD receptions.**

PITTSBURGH			2018			9-6-1	Game Highlights
9/9/2018		@	Cleveland {OT}	21	21	T	Conner 135 rush yards-2 rush TD/Brown TD catch
9/16/2018		vs	KANSAS CITY	37	42	L	Roethlisberger 452 pass yards-3 TD pass-rush TD
9/24/2018	MNF	@	Tampa Bay	30	27	W	**Dupree INT return TD**/Roethlisberger 3 TD pass
9/30/2018	SNF	vs	BALTIMORE RAVENS	14	26	L	Roethlisberger 274 pass yds-TD pass/Bowell 2 FG
10/7/2018		vs	ATLANTA	41	17	W	**Fort fumble recovery TD**/Conner 110 yds-2 TDs
10/14/2018		@	Cincinnati	28	21	W	Conner 111 rush yards-2 rush TD/Boswell 2 FGs
10/28/2018		vs	CLEVELAND	33	18	W	Conner 146 rush yds-2 rush TD/Brown 2 TD catch
11/4/2018		@	Baltimore Ravens	23	16	W	Roethlisberger 270 pass yards-2 TD pass-rush TD
11/8/2018	TH	vs	CAROLINA	52	21	W	**Williams INT return TD**/Roethlisberger 5 TD pass
11/18/2018		@	Jacksonville	20	16	W	Roethlisberger 314 pass yards-2 TD pass-rush TD
11/25/2018		@	Denver	17	24	L	**Boswell TD pass to Villanueva**/Big Ben 462 pass yd
12/2/2018	SNF	vs	L.A. CHARGERS	30	33	L	Brown 10 catch-154 yards-TD catch/Conner 2 TD
12/9/2018		@	Oakland Raiders	21	24	L	Smith-Schuster 8 catch-130 yards-2 TD catch
12/16/2018		vs	NEW ENGLAND	17	10	W	Samuels 142 rush yards/Roethlisberger 2 TD pass
12/23/2018		@	New Orleans	28	31	L	Brown 14 catch-185 yards-TD catch/Samuels TD
12/30/2018		vs	CINCINNATI	16	13	W	Roethlisberger 287 pass yd-TD pass/McCrane 3 FG

Schedule courtesy of Steve's Football Bible LLC

2018 AFC North	W	L	T	PCT	DIV	CONF	PF	PA
Baltimore Ravens	10	6	0	.625	3–3	8–4	389	287
Pittsburgh Steelers	**9**	**6**	**1**	**.594**	**4–1–1**	**6–5–1**	**428**	**360**
Cleveland Browns	7	8	1	.469	3–2–1	5–6–1	359	392
Cincinnati Bengals	6	10	0	.375	1–5	4–8	368	455

2018 NFL Draft

Round	Selection	Player	Position	College
1	28	Terrell Edmunds	S	Virginia Tech
2	60	James Washington	WR	Oklahoma State
3	76	Mason Rudolph	QB	Oklahoma State
	92	Chukwuma Okorafor	OT	Western Michigan
5	148	Marcus Allen	S	Penn State
	165	Jaylen Samuels	RB	NC State
7	246	Joshua Frazier	DT	Alabama

Pittsburgh at Tampa Bay Buccaneers {Monday Night Football}

The Bucs scored first when Cameron Brate caught a 4-yard pass from Ryan Fitzpatrick to make it 7–0. The Steelers would answer when Ben Roethlisberger found Vance McDonald on a 75-yard pass to make it 7–6. The Steelers continued to score heading into the second quarter: they took the lead with Chris Boswell's 38-yard field goal to make it 9–7. This would be followed up by Roethlisberger finding Antonio Brown on a 27-yard pass to make it 16–7, and then Bud Dupree intercepted Fitzpatrick to return it 10 yards for a touchdown to make it 23–7. The Bucs came closer when Chandler Catanzaro kicked a 21-yard field goal to make it 23–10. The Steelers wrapped up the first half scoring when Roethlisberger found Ryan Switzer on a 1-yard pass to make it 30–10. In the second half, it was all Bucs as they would outscore the Steelers 17–0 heading into the fourth quarter when Catanzaro kicked a 28-yard field goal to make it 30–13 in the third. In the fourth, the Bucs ended up coming within 3 when Fitzpatrick threw 4-yard and 24-yard passes to Chris Godwin and Mike Evans to make it 30–20 and then 30–27. The Steelers' defense held them off at the last moment to win the game, sealing the win.

Pittsburgh at Jacksonville Jaguars

After a scoreless first quarter, the Jags put up 3 field goals in the second when Josh Lambo converted from 48, 38, and 43 yards out to make it 3–0, 6–0, and then 9–0 at halftime. In the third quarter, the Jaguars would make it 16–0 after Leonard Fournette ran for a 2-yard touchdown. From then on, it was all Steelers scoring when Ben Roethlisberger found Antonio Brown on a 78-yard pass to make it 16–6 heading into the fourth quarter. In the final quarter, Roethlisberger found Vance McDonald on an 11-yard touchdown pass to draw the Steelers within three points. On the Steelers' final offensive drive, Roethlisberger ran for a 1-yard touchdown to make it 20–16 with five seconds remaining in the game, completing the comeback victory.

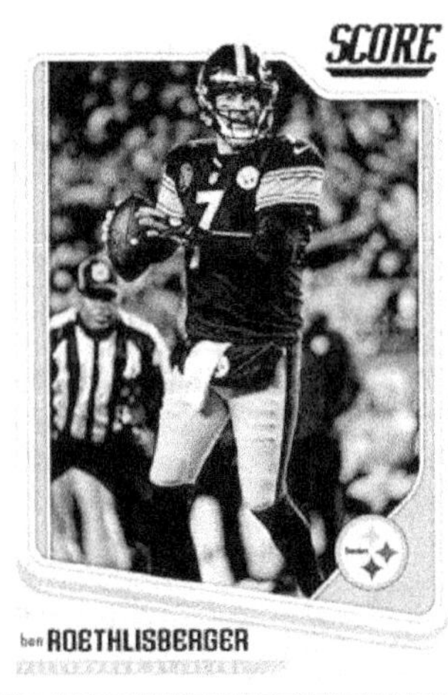

2019 Pittsburgh Steelers

  The 2019 season marked the 20th season under leadership of general manager Kevin Colbert and the 13th under head coach Mike Tomlin. The team failed to improve upon its 9–6–1 record from 2018 following a Week 16 loss to the New York Jets. For the first time since 2013, they started the season with a 1–4 record through Week 5, which included a 33–3 opening loss to the defending Super Bowl champion New England Patriots, and an injury to Ben Roethlisberger the very next game. However, they went on to win seven out of their next eight games to reach Week 14 of the season with an 8–5 record before losing three consecutive games to end the 2019 season with an 8–8 record and missed the playoffs for the second straight season. They also tied for their worst record (2006, 2012, 2013) since the 2003 season. For the first time since 2009, wide receiver Antonio Brown was not on the roster, as he was traded to the Oakland Raiders on March 9, 2019. Cameron Heyward {DT}, T.J. Watt {LB} and Minkah Fitzpatrick {S} were selected to various first team All-Pro teams. Longtime franchise QB Ben Roethlisberger was also ruled out for the season after suffering a non-contact elbow injury during the Seattle game.

  Mason Rudolph led the team in passing with 1,765 yards and threw 13 touchdown passes. James Connor led the team in rushing with 464 yards and 4 rushing touchdowns. Diontae Johnson led the team with 59 receptions and 5 TD receptions. James Washington led the team with 735 yards receiving.

PITTSBURGH			2019			8-8	Game Highlights
9/8/2019	SNF	@	New England Patriots	3	33	L	Steelers 32 rush yards/Boswell FG
9/15/2019		vs	*SEATTLE*	26	28	L	McDonald 2 TD catch/Boswell 2 FGs
9/22/2019		@	*San Francisco*	20	24	L	Rudolph 174 pass yards-2 pass TD/Boswell 2 FGs
9/30/2019	MNF	vs	CINCINNATI	27	3	W	Conner 125 total yards-TD catch/Boswell 2 FGs
10/6/2019		vs	BALTIMORE {OT}	23	26	L	Smith-Schuster 7 catch-75 yd-TD catch/Boswell 3 FG
10/13/2019	SNF	@	Los Angeles Chargers	24	17	W	**Bush fumble return TD**/Conner 119 total yds-2 TD
10/28/2019	MNF	vs	MIAMI	27	14	W	Conner 145 rush yards-rush TD/Boswell 2 FGs
11/3/2019		vs	INDIANAPOLIS	26	24	W	**Fitzpatrick INT return TD**/Boswell 4 FGs
11/10/2019		vs	*LOS ANGELES RAMS*	17	12	W	**Fitzpatrick fumble return TD**/Washington TD catch
11/14/2019	TH	@	Cleveland	7	21	L	Steelers 58 rush yards/commit 4 turnovers
11/24/2019		@	Cincinnati	16	10	W	Washington TD catch-Boswell 3 FGs
12/1/2019		vs	CLEVELAND	20	13	W	Washington 4 catch-111 yds-TD catch/Boswell 2 FG
12/8/2019		@	*Arizona Cardinals*	23	17	W	**Diaonta Johnson punt return TD**-TD catch
12/15/2019	SNF	vs	BUFFALO	10	17	L	Steelers 51 rush yards/Conner TD catch/Boswell FG
12/22/2019		@	New York Jets	10	16	L	Steelers 75 rush yards/Di. Johnson TD catch
12/29/2019		@	Baltimore Ravens	10	28	L	Steelers 91 rush yards/Snell rush TD/Boswell FG

Schedule courtesy of Steve's Football Bible LLC

2019 AFC North	W	L	T	PCT	DIV	CONF	PF	PA
Baltimore Ravens	14	2	0	.875	5–1	10–2	531	282
Pittsburgh Steelers	**8**	**8**	**0**	**.500**	**3–3**	**6–6**	**289**	**303**
Cleveland Browns	6	10	0	.375	3–3	6–6	335	393
Cincinnati Bengals	2	14	0	.125	1–5	2–10	279	420

2019 NFL Draft

Round	Selection	Player	Position	College
1	10	Devin Bush	ILB	Michigan
3	66	Diontae Johnson	WR	Toledo
	83	Justin Layne	CB	Michigan State
4	122	Benny Snell	RB	Kentucky
5	141	Zach Gentry	TE	Michigan
6	175	Sutton Smith	OLB	Northern Illinois
	192	Isaiah Buggs	DE	Alabama
	207	Ulysees Gilbert III	ILB	Akron
7	219	Derwin Gray	OT	Maryland

Pittsburgh at Los Angeles Chargers {Sunday Night Football}

The Steelers led 24–0 going into the fourth quarter, only for the Chargers to score 17 unanswered points, putting them a touchdown away from tying the game with less than 90 seconds remaining. Although they failed with their onside kick attempt, they forced the Steelers to go three-and-out on their ensuing possession, giving QB Philip Rivers the opportunity to attempt a 99-yard, game-winning drive; however, he was picked off by CB Cameron Sutton, allowing the Steelers to kneel out the clock for a 24–17 win.

Indianapolis Colts at Pittsburgh

In the first quarter, the Colts scored first when Adam Vinatieri kicked a 25-yard field goal to make it 3–0. The Steelers tied it up when Chris Boswell kicked a 21-yard field goal to make it 3–3. In the second quarter, the Colts moved back into the lead when Brian Hoyer found Jack Doyle on an 11-yard pass to make it 10–3. Though, the Steelers tied the game up again when Minkah Fitzpatrick returned an interception 96 yards for a touchdown to make it 10–10. The Colts regained the lead when Hoyer found Zach Pascal on a 14-yard pass (with a failed PAT) to make it 16–10. The Steelers drew closer when Boswell kicked a 51-yard field goal to make it 16–13 at halftime. In the third quarter, the Steelers took the lead when Mason Rudolph found Vance McDonald on a 7-yard pass to make it 20–16. The Colts then came with 2 when Alejandro Villanueva was sacked in the end zone for a safety by Justin Houston, making the score 20–18. The Steelers moved slightly further ahead in the fourth quarter when Boswell kicked a 33-yard field goal to make it 23–18. Though, the Colts regained the lead when Chester Rogers caught a 4-yard pass (with a failed 2-point conversion) from Brian Hoyer to make the score 24–23. Boswell then got the Steelers the lead back when he kicked a 26-yard field goal to make it 26–24. Getting the ball back with just under 90 seconds left, Vinatieri missed the potential game-winning field goal. This allowed the Steelers to kneel out for victory.

2020 Pittsburgh Steelers

The 2020 season is their 21st under general manager Kevin Colbert, and their 14th under head coach Mike Tomlin. The team vastly improved on their 8–8 record from 2019 beginning the season 11–0, a franchise-best. They became the first NFL team to do so since the Carolina Panthers in the 2015 season. However, that streak was broken after a Week 13 loss to the Washington Football Team. The Steelers clinched a playoff berth for the first time since 2017 after the Miami Dolphins' Week 14 loss to the Kansas City Chiefs and clinched their first AFC North title since 2017 with a Week 16 victory over the Indianapolis Colts. The season marked the return of Ben Roethlisberger, who was sidelined for 14 games the season prior. However, despite entering Week 13 at 11–0, the Steelers lost four of their last five games to finish 12–4 and join the 1969 Los Angeles Rams as the only teams in NFL history to go 11–0 and lose 3 consecutive games afterwards. In the playoffs, the Steelers faced the Cleveland Browns in the Wild Card round, where they were defeated 48–37. The Steelers swept the Ravens for the first time in three seasons. Their 11–0 start marked the longest the Steelers have gone before their first loss in a season in franchise history. They also went undefeated against the AFC South for the first time in six seasons. T.J. Watt {LB}, Craig Heyward {DT} and Minkah Fitzpatrick {S} were selected to various first team All-Pro teams.

Ben Roethlisberger led the team in passing with 3,803 yards and threw 33 touchdown passes. James Conner led the team in rushing with 721 yards and 6 rushing touchdowns. JuJu Smith-Schuster led the team with 97 receptions. Diaonte Johnson led the team with 923 yards receiving. Chase Claypool and Smith-Schuster each had 9 TD receptions. **Chris Boswell set a franchise record with a 59-yard field goal against Dallas.**

PITTSBURGH			2020			12-5	Game Highlights
9/14/2020	MNF	@	New York Giants	26	16	W	Roethlisberger 3 TD pass/Smith-Schuster 2 TD catch
9/20/2020		vs	DENVER	26	21	W	Roethlisberger 311 pass yds-2 TD pass/Conner TD
9/27/2020		vs	HOUSTON TEXANS	28	21	W	Roethlisberger 2 TD pass/Conner 109 rush yds-TD
10/11/2020		vs	PHILADELPHIA	38	29	W	Claypool 7 catch-1110 yards-3 TD catch-rush TD
10/18/2020		vs	CLEVELAND	38	7	W	**Fitzpatrick INT return TD**/Conner 101 rush yds-TD
10/25/2020		@	Tennessee Titans	27	24	W	Roethlisberger 268 pass yards-2 TD pass to Johnson
11/1/2020		@	Baltimore	28	24	W	**Spillane INT return TD**/ Roethlisberger 2 TD pass
11/8/2020		@	Dallas	24	19	W	Roethlisberger 306 pass yds-3 TD pass/Boswell 2 FG
11/15/2020		vs	CINCINNATI	36	10	W	Claypool 2 TD catch/Boswell 3 FG/Big Ben 4 TD pass
11/22/2020		@	Jacksonville	27	3	W	Roethlisberger 2 TD pass/Johnson 12 catch-111 yards
12/1/2020	WED	vs	BALTIMORE	19	14	W	**Haden INT return TD**/Boswell 2 FGs
12/7/2020	MON	vs	WASHINGTON	17	23	L	Roethlisberger 305 pass yards-2 TD pass
12/13/2020	SNF	@	Buffalo	15	26	L	Roethlisberger 187 pass yards-2 TD pass-2 INT
12/21/2020	MNF	@	Cincinnati	17	27	L	Johnson TD catch/Snell rush TD/Boswell FG
12/27/2020		vs	INDIANAPOLIS	28	24	W	Roethlisberger 341 yards-3 TD pass/Conner rush TD
1/3/2021		@	Cleveland	22	24	L	Rudolph 315 pass yards-2 TD pass/Wright 3 FGs
1/10/2021		vs	**CLEVELAND**	37	48	L	Roethlisberger 501 pass yards-4 TD pass-4 INT

Schedule courtesy of Steve's Football Bible LLC

2020 AFC North	W	L	T	PCT	DIV	CONF	PF	PA
Pittsburgh Steelers	**12**	**4**	**0**	**.750**	**4–2**	**9–3**	**416**	**312**
Baltimore Ravens	11	5	0	.688	4–2	7–5	468	303
Cleveland Browns	11	5	0	.688	3–3	7–5	408	419
Cincinnati Bengals	4	11	1	.281	1–5	4–8	311	424

2020 NFL Draft

Round	Selection	Player	Position	College
2	49	Chase Claypool	WR	Notre Dame
3	102	Alex Highsmith	OLB	Charlotte
4	124	Anthony McFarland Jr.	RB	Maryland
4	135	Kevin Dotson	G	Louisiana
6	198	Antoine Brooks	S	Maryland
7	232	Carlos Davis	DT	Nebraska

Pittsburgh at Dallas Cowboys

the Steelers traveled again to Arlington, Texas to take on the Cowboys. From the first into the second quarter, the Cowboys jumped to a 13–0 lead before the Steelers managed to score twice within the final two minutes of the half to make it a 13–9 game at halftime. In the third quarter, the Cowboys moved up by 10 with Greg Zuerlein's 45 and 39-yard field goals, making it 19–9. However, in the fourth quarter, it was all Steelers, who managed to come back with three straight scores: a Ben Roethlisberger to JuJu Smith-Schuster 31-yard TD pass (with a failed PAT); a Chris Boswell 43-yard field goal; and then finally a Roethlisberger to Eric Ebron 8-yard TD pass (with a failed 2-point conversion) to take a 24–19 lead with 2:14 left in the game. After forcing a turnover on downs, the Cowboys got the ball back to drive into Steelers territory with under a minute left in the game. However, Garrett Gilbert's pass fell incomplete in the end zone, sealing yet another Steelers win.

Indianapolis Colts

The Colts scored the only points of the first quarter when Jonathan Taylor ran for a 6-yard TD to make it 7–0. The Steelers would tie it up in the second quarter when James Conner ran for a 1-yard TD. The Colts would go up 21–7 at halftime after Taylor ran for another TD, followed up by Philip Rivers finding Zach Pascal on a 42-yard pass. In the third quarter, the Colts moved up by 17 after Rodrigo Blankenship kicked a 28-yard field goal for a 24–7 lead. Starting in the third quarter and info the fourth, the Steelers went on a 21–0 run, with Ben Roethlisberger finding 3 different receivers for TD passes: a 39-yard pass to Diontae Johnson late in the third; a 5-yard pass to Eric Ebron in the fourth; and then finally a 25-yard pass to JuJu Smith-Schuster to take a 28–24 lead. Getting the ball back with a little over two minutes in the game, the Colts were able to drive into Steelers' territory after a pass interference penalty on the defense. However, the Colts would eventually wind up with a turnover on downs, giving the ball and the game to the Steelers, snapping the team's losing streak.

2020 AFC Wild Card

The Browns dismantled the Pittsburgh Steelers 48-37 in the wild-card round Sunday night, picking up the franchise's first postseason victory in more than a quarter-century. Baker Mayfield threw for 263 yards and three touchdowns, including a screen pass that Nick Chubb turned into a 40-yard score that halted Pittsburgh's momentum after the Steelers pulled within 12. Kareem Hunt added 48 yards and two TDs on the ground while Cleveland's defense forced five turnovers to hand the Steelers (12-5) a staggering loss. Cleveland did it despite practicing just once over the last two weeks and having lost 17 straight at Heinz Field.

Pittsburgh's problems started on the first play from scrimmage when center Maurkice Pouncey's snap sailed by Roethlisberger into the end zone. Cleveland's Karl Joseph fell on it for a touchdown. Roethlisberger threw three first-half interceptions, two of which led directly to Browns scores. By the time the Steelers found their footing, they were down 28-0. Ben Roethlisberger ended his comeback season by throwing for 501 yards on an NFL-record 47 completions with four touchdowns and four interceptions.

1/10/2021	Line/Total	1	2	3	4	Final
Cleveland Browns	{47.0}	28	7	0	13	48
Pittsburgh Steelers	{-5.0}	0	10	13	14	37

Scoring

Team	
Browns	Karl Joseph fumble recovery in end zone (Cody Parkey kick)
Browns	Jarvis Landry 40 yard pass from Baker Mayfield (Cody Parkey kick)
Browns	Kareem Hunt 11 yard rush (Cody Parkey kick)
Browns	Kareem Hunt 8 yard rush (Cody Parkey kick)
Steelers	James Conner 1 yard rush (Chris Boswell kick)
Browns	Austin Hooper 7 yard pass from Baker Mayfield (Cody Parkey kick)
Steelers	Chris Boswell 49 yard field goal
Steelers	Eric Ebron 17 yard pass from Ben Roethlisberger (pass failed)
Steelers	JuJu Smith-Schuster 5 yard pass from Ben Roethlisberger (Chris Boswell kick)
Browns	Nick Chubb 40 yard pass from Baker Mayfield (Cody Parkey kick)
Steelers	Chase Claypool 29 yard pass from Ben Roethlisberger (pass failed)
Browns	Cody Parkey 24 yard field goal
Browns	37 yard field goal
Steelers	Chase Claypool 7 yard pass from Ben Roethlisberger (James Conner pass from Ben Roethlisberger)

2021 Pittsburgh Steelers

The 2021 season is their 22nd and final season under general manager Kevin Colbert and their 15th under head coach Mike Tomlin. They failed to improve upon their 12–4 record from 2020 and failed to win their division in back-to-back years for the first time since 2016–2017. However, they did make the playoffs in consecutive years for the first time since 2014–2017 after defeating the Baltimore Ravens, combined with the Las Vegas Raiders defeating the Los Angeles Chargers, and the Jacksonville Jaguars upsetting the Indianapolis Colts, all of which took place during the Sunday games of Week 18. However, the Steelers were defeated in the first round of the playoffs by the Kansas City Chiefs 42–21. For the first time since 2009, center Maurkice Pouncey was not on the roster, as he announced his retirement on February 12. Also, for the first time since 2011, guard David DeCastro was not on the roster, as he was released by the Steelers on June 24. It was also quarterback Ben Roethlisberger's final season after 18 seasons with the Steelers as he announced his retirement on January 27, 2022. A 6-time Pro Bowler, Roethlisberger led the Steelers to 12 playoff appearances and 3 Super Bowl appearances, winning 2 of them in 2006 and 2009 respectively. He also retired as 5th all-time in passing yards and was the last remaining active quarterback from the 2004 Draft class. Craig Heyward {DT} and T.J. Watt {LB} were selected to various first team All-Pro teams. **Watt set a franchise record with 22.5 quarterback sacks. Chris Boswell set a franchise record with 36 field goals.**

Ben Roethlisberger led the team in passing with 3,740 yards and threw 20 touchdown passes. Najee Harris led the team in rushing with 1,200 yards and 7 rushing touchdowns. Diaonte Johnson led the team in receiving with 107 receptions for 1,161 yards and 8 TD receptions.

PITTSBURGH			2021			9-8-1	Game Highlights
9/12/2021		@	Buffalo	23	16	W	**Gilbert blocked punt return TD**/Boswell 3 FGs
9/19/2021		vs	LAS VEGAS RAIDERS	17	26	L	Roethlisberger 295 pass yards-TD pass to Harris
9/26/2021		vs	CINCINNATI	10	24	L	Steelers 45 rush yards/ Roethlisberger 318 pass yds
10/3/2021		@	Green Bay	17	27	L	Johnson 9 catch-92 yards-TD catch/Boswell FG
10/10/2021		vs	DENVER	27	19	W	Harris 122 rush yards-rush TD/Claypool 130 yds
10/17/2021	SNF	vs	SEATTLE {OT}	23	20	W	Harris 127 total yards-TD catch/Boswell 3 FGs
10/31/2021		@	Cleveland	15	10	W	Harris 91 rush yards-rush TD/Freiermuth TD catch
11/8/2021	MNF	vs	CHICAGO	29	27	W	Freiermuth 2 TD catch/Boswell 3 FGs/Harris TD
11/14/2021		vs	DETROIT {OT}	16	16	T	Harris 105 rush yards/Boswell 3 FGs
11/21/2021	SNF	@	Los Angeles Chargers	37	41	L	Roethlisberger 273 pass yds-3 TD pass/Boswell 3 FG
11/28/2021		@	Cincinnati	10	41	L	Freiermuth TD catch/Boswell FG
12/5/2021		vs	BALTIMORE RAVENS	20	19	W	Johnson 8 catch-105 yds-2 TD catch/Boswell 2 FG
12/9/2021	TH	@	Minnesota	28	36	L	Roethlisberger 308 pass yds-3 TD pass/Harris 2 TD
12/19/2021		vs	TENNESSEE TITANS	19	13	W	Roethlisberger rush TD/Boswell 4 FGs
12/26/2021		@	Kansas City	10	36	L	Steelers fall behind 30-0/Johnson TD catch
1/3/2022	MNF	vs	CLEVELAND	26	14	W	Harris 188 rush yards-rush TD/Boswell 4 FGs
1/9/2022		@	Baltimore Ravens {OT}	16	13	W	Claypool TD catch/Boswell 3 FGs
1/16/2022	SNF	@	**Kansas City**	**21**	**42**	**L**	**Watt fumble return TD**/ Roethlisberger 2 TD pass

Schedule courtesy of Steve's Football Bible LLC

2021 AFC North	W	L	T	PCT	DIV	CONF	PF	PA
Cincinnati Bengals	10	7	0	.588	4–2	8–4	460	376
Pittsburgh Steelers	**9**	**7**	**1**	**.559**	**4–2**	**7–5**	**343**	**398**
Cleveland Browns	8	9	0	.471	3–3	5–7	349	371
Baltimore Ravens	8	9	0	.471	1–5	5–7	387	392

2021 NFL Draft

Round	Selection	Player	Position	College
1	24	Najee Harris	RB	Alabama
2	55	Pat Freiermuth	TE	Penn State
3	87	Kendrick Green	C	Illinois
4	128	Dan Moore Jr.	OT	Texas A&M
4	140	Buddy Johnson	ILB	Texas A&M
5	156	Isaiahh Loudermilk	DT	Wisconsin
6	216	Quincy Roche	OLB	Miami
7	245	Tre Norwood	CB	Oklahoma
7	254	Pressley Harvin III	P	Georgia Tech

Selected game(s) highlights

Seattle Seahawks at Pittsburgh {Sunday Night Football}

the Steelers stayed home for a Sunday Night duel against the Seahawks, who would be missing Russell Wilson after he suffered a finger injury the previous week. After a scoreless first quarter, the Steelers went up 14-0 at halftime in the second after Ben Roethlisberger found Najee Harris on a 5-yard touchdown pass, followed by Eric Ebron's 1-yard run for a touchdown. After the break, the Seahawks were able to get on the board in the third when Alex Collins ran for a 3-yard touchdown to make the score 14-7. Chris Boswell then increased the Steelers' lead when he kicked a 27-yard field goal to make it 17-7. The Seahawks came within 3 when Geno Smith found Will Dissly on a 1-yard touchdown pass to make the score 17-14. Then in the fourth quarter, they tied the game when Jason Myers kicked a 40-yard field goal at 17-17. The Steelers retook the lead when Boswell kicked a 52-yard field goal. However, with seconds left in regulation, Myers would kick a 43-yard field goal to tie the game at 20-20. In overtime, T. J. Watt forced a Geno Smith fumble recovered by Devin Bush that would lead to Boswell kicking the 37-yard game-winning field goal with 1:24 left in the game to make the final score 23-20.

Pittsburgh at Baltimore Ravens

In the first quarter, the Steelers scored the only points when Chris Boswell kicked a 28-yard field goal to make it 3–0. The Ravens tied it up at 3–3 in the second quarter when Justin Tucker kicked a 24-yard field goal. This would be the score at halftime. In the third quarter, the Ravens moved into the lead when Latavius Murray ran for a 46-yard touchdown to make it 10–3. The Steelers then came within 4 when Boswell kicked a 40-yard field goal, making the score 10–6. The Steelers retook the lead in the fourth quarter when Ben Roethlisberger found Chase Claypool on a 6-yard touchdown pass to make it 13–10. Tucker then tied the game up at 13–13 with a 46-yard field goal. In overtime, the Steelers were able to drive down the field and eventually Boswell was brought out to kick the game-winning 36-yard field goal with 1:56 left in ovetime to win the game 16–13. Head coach Mike Tomlin recorded his 162nd win with the Steelers, surpassing his predecessor, Bill Cowher's record of 161 wins to become the 2nd winningest head coach in franchise history, only behind Chuck Noll, who coached the team from 1969-1991. With the win, the Steelers finished the regular season at 9–7–1 and swept the Ravens for the second straight season.

2021 AFC Wild Card

Patrick Mahomes threw for 404 yards and five scores, leading Kansas City to the end zone on six straight possessions after the turnover, and the Chiefs cruised through the second half for a 42-21 wild-card victory. Byron Pringle caught touchdown passes from both Mahomes and Kelce, and Jerick McKinnon and Tyreek Hill also had scoring catches, while the Chiefs shut down the retiring Ben Roethlisberger and the Steelers offense. The 39-year-old quarterback was 29 of 44 for 215 yards with two meaningless TD passes late in the game. After the Steelers punted for a fifth straight time, the Chiefs inexplicably had Mecole Hardman take a snap rather than their four-time Pro Bowl quarterback. Darrel Williams bobbled the exchange and T.J. Watt grabbed the fumble and Pittsburgh had a 7-0 lead. Mahomes responded by completing his next six passes, capping a 76-yard drive with a nifty underhand flick to McKinnon that tied it. Then the brilliant young quarterback found Pringle in the corner of the end zone for a score, and he put an exclamation mark on the half by hitting Kelce with a 48-yard touchdown strike. In the span of less than six minutes, Mahomes and the Chiefs had turned a seven-point deficit into a 21-7 lead. Roethlisberger was 5 of 14 for 24 yards in the first half and Pittsburgh had 55 yards total offense.

1/15/2022	Line/Total	1	2	3	4	Final
Pittsburgh Steelers	46.5	0	7	7	7	21
Kansas City Chiefs	-12.0	0	21	14	7	42

Scoring

Team	
Steelers	T.J. Watt 26 yard fumble return (Chris Boswell kick)
Chiefs	Jerick McKinnon 4 yard pass from Patrick Mahomes (Harrison Butker kick)
Chiefs	Byron Pringle 12 yard pass from Patrick Mahomes (Harrison Butker kick)
Chiefs	Travis Kelce 48 yard pass from Patrick Mahomes (Harrison Butker kick)
Chiefs	Nick Allegretti 1 yard pass from Patrick Mahomes (Harrison Butker kick)
Chiefs	Tyreek Hill 31 yard pass from Patrick Mahomes (Harrison Butker kick)
Steelers	Diontae Johnson 13 yard pass from Ben Roethlisberger (Chris Boswell kick)
Chiefs	Byron Pringle 2 yard pass from Travis Kelce (Harrison Butker kick)
Steelers	James Washington 15 yard pass from Ben Roethlisberger (Chris Boswell kick)

2022 Pittsburgh Steelers

It was the Steelers' 90th season in the National Football League and their 16th under head coach Mike Tomlin. This is the first season since 2003 without long-time quarterback Ben Roethlisberger on the roster, as he announced his retirement on January 27, 2022. It is also the first season since 1999 without long-time general manager Kevin Colbert, as he announced on January 28, 2022 that after 22 years with the organization, he would step down following the 2022 NFL Draft. He was succeeded by Omar Khan as general manager and Andy Weidl as assistant general manager on May 25, 2022. The Steelers began their season with a 2–6 record, their worst start since 2003, failing to improve on their 9–7–1 record from 2021 following a loss to the Baltimore Ravens in Week 14, but despite the initial setback, the Steelers would stay in the playoff hunt in the following weeks by flipping those numbers. However, they narrowly missed the playoffs—the Steelers finished tied with the Miami Dolphins for the last Wild Card spot, but lost the tiebreaker based on the teams' Week 7 head-to-head meeting, won by the Dolphins. Following their 28–14 victory against the Cleveland Browns, they maintained their streak of having 19 consecutive non-losing seasons.

Kenny Pickett led the team in passing with 2,404 yards and threw 7 touchdown passes. Najee Harris led the team in rushing with 1,034 yards and 7 rushing touchdowns. Dontae Johnson led the team in receiving with 86 receptions for 882 yards. George Pickens led the team with 4 TD receptions. Minkah Fitzpatrick led the team with 6 interceptions. Chris Boswell led the team in scoring with 78 points.

PITTSBURGH			2022			9-8	Game Highlights
9/11/2022		@	Cincinnati {OT}	23	20	W	**Fitzpatrick INT return TD**/Boswell 3 FG's
9/18/2022		vs	NEW ENGLAND	14	17	L	Trubisky 168 pass yards/Johnson 6 catch-57 yards
9/22/2022	TH	@	Cleveland	17	29	L	Johnson 8 catch-84 yards/Trubisky TD pass
10/2/2022		vs	NEW YORK JETS	20	24	L	Pickett 2 rush TD/Boswell 2 FG's
10/9/2022		@	Buffalo	3	38	L	Steelers held to 54 rush yards/Boswell FG
10/16/2022		vs	TAMPA BAY	20	18	W	Claypool 7 catch-96 yards-TD catch/Boswell 2 FG
10/23/2022	SNF	@	Miami	13	16	L	Pickett 257 pass yards-TD pass-3 INT's
10/30/2022		@	Philadelphia	13	35	L	Pickett 191 pass yards/Sciba 2 FG's
11/13/2022		vs	NEW ORLEANS	20	10	W	Pickett 199 pass yards-rush TD/Wright 2 FG's
11/20/2022		vs	CINCINNATI	30	37	L	Pickett 265 pass yards-TD pass/Harris 2 rush TD
11/28/2022	MNF	@	Indianapolis	24	17	W	Wright 3 FG's/Snell & Harris rush TD's
12/4/2022		@	Atlanta	19	16	W	Wright 4 FG's/Heyward TD pass from Pickett
12/11/2022		vs	BALTIMORE	14	16	L	Trubisky 276 pass yards-Pass TD-3 INT's
12/18/2022		@	Carolina	24	16	W	Johnson 10 catch-98 yards/Harris & Warren rush TD
12/24/2022	SA	vs	LAS VEGAS	13	10	W	Pickett 244 Pass yards-TD pass to Pickens
1/1/2023	SNF	@	Baltimore	16	13	W	Boswell 3 FG's/Harris 111 rush yards-TD catch
1/8/2023		vs	CLEVELAND	28	14	W	Pickett 195 pass yards-TD pass to Pickens

Schedule courtesy of Steve's Football Bible LLC

2022 AFC North Division	W	L	T	PCT	DIV	CONF	PF	PA
Cincinnati Bengals	12	4	0	.750	3–3	8–3	418	322
Baltimore Ravens	10	7	0	.588	3–3	6–6	350	315
Pittsburgh Steelers	**9**	**8**	**0**	**.529**	**3–3**	**5–7**	**308**	**346**
Cleveland Browns	7	10	0	.412	3–3	4–8	361	381

2022 NFL Draft

Round	Selection	Player	Position	College
1	20	Kenny Pickett	QB	Pittsburgh
2	52	George Pickens	WR	Georgia
3	84	DeMarvin Leal	DT	Texas A&M
4	138	Calvin Austin III	WR	Memphis
6	208	Connor Heyward	FB/TE	Michigan State
7	225	Mark Robinson	LB	Ole Miss
7	241	Chris Oladokun	QB	South Dakota State

Selected game(s) highlights

Pittsburgh @ Cincinnati

The Steelers scored first in the first quarter when Minkah Fitzpatrick returned an interception 31 yards for a touchdown to make it 7–0. The Bengals made it 7–3 when Evan McPhearson made a 59-yard field goal. The Steelers then went ahead 10–3 after Chris Boswell kicked a 20-yard field goal. In the second quarter, the Steelers moved ahead 17–3 after Mitchell Trubisky found Najee Harris on a 1-yard touchdown pass. The Bengals drew closer at halftime when McPhearson made a 26-yard field goal to make it 17–6. After the break, the Bengals came within 3 in the third quarter when Joe Burrow found Tyler Boyd on a 2-yard touchdown pass (with a successful 2-point conversion) to make it 17–14. In the fourth quarter, the Steelers moved ahead by 6 when Boswell kicked a 48-yard field goal to make it 20–14. Later in the quarter, the Bengals tied the game when Burrow found Ja'Marr Chase on a 6-yard touchdown pass (with a blocked PAT) to send the game into overtime tied at 20–20. After going back and forth on possessions, the Steelers managed to win the game when Boswell kicked the game winning 53-yard field goal with seconds left to make the final score 23–20.

Tampa Bay @ PITTSBURGH

The Steelers returned home to face off against the Tom Brady-led Buccaneers. In the first quarter, the Steelers scored first when Najee Harris caught a 6-yard touchdown pass from Kenny Pickett to make the lead 7–0. The Bucs made it 7–3 when Ryan Succop kicked a 30-yard field goal. Succop got the Bucs closer in the second quarter when he kicked a 27-yard field goal to make it 7–6. Though, the Steelers pulled away when Chris Boswell kicked a 55-yard field goal to make it 10–6. As halftime approached, Succop got the Bucs within a point when he kicked a 54-yard field goal to make it 10–9. In the third quarter, the Steelers got back to work when Boswell kicked a 25-yard field goal to make it 13–9. Again, the Bucs came within a point when Succop kicked a 24-yard field goal to make it 13–12. Despite losing Pickett for the game, in the fourth quarter, Mitchell Trubisky came out and threw a 6-yard touchdown pass to Chase Claypool to make it 20–12. The Bucs would however score the remaining points of the game when Brady found Leonard Fournette on an 11-yard touchdown pass (with a failed 2-point conversion) to make the final score 20–18.

Pittsburgh @ Baltimore

The Steelers scored the only points of the first quarter when Chris Boswell kicked a 21-yard field goal to make it 3-0. However, the Ravens responded in the second quarter, taking a 10-3 lead at halftime by way of Justin Tucker's 30-yard field goal and then Tyler Huntley's 7-yard touchdown pass to Isaiah Likely. The Ravens went right back to work in the second half when Tucker kicked a 51-yard field goal to make it 13-3. The Steelers scored well into the fourth quarter by way of Boswell's 51-yard field goal, later in the third. In the fourth quarter, they followed up with Boswell kicking a 33-yard field goal and Kenny Pickett found Najee Harris on a 10-yard touchdown pass for the Steelers to make the final score 16-13.

2023 Pittsburgh Steelers

The 2023 season is the Pittsburgh Steelers' 91st season in the National Football League, their 2nd under general manager Omar Khan and their 17th under head coach Mike Tomlin. With their third win of the season against the Baltimore Ravens on October 8, they reached 700 wins in the club's history. The Steelers became the first team in AFC history to post 20 consecutive non-losing records.

T.J. Watt {LB}, Minkah Fitzpatrick {FS} and Miles Killebrew {Special teams} were selected to the AFC Pro Bowl team.

Date			Opponent				10-8	Game Highlights
9/10/2023		vs	SAN FRANCISCO	7	30	L		Pickett 232 pass yds-TD pass to Freiermuth-sacked 5 times
9/18/2023	MNF	vs	CLEVELAND	26	22	W		**Highsmith INT return TD/Watt fumble return TD**
9/24/2023	SNF	@	Las Vegas Raiders	23	18	W		Boswell 3 FG/Pickett 235 pass yds-2 TD pass/Wallace 2 INT
10/1/2023		@	Houston	6	30	L		Boswell 2 FG/Steelers held to 225 yards total offense
10/8/2023		vs	BALTIMORE RAVENS	17	10	W		Boswell 3 FG/Pickens 6 catch-130 yds-TD catch
10/15/2023			BYE					
10/22/2023		@	Los Angeles Rams	24	17	W		Pickett-Warren-Harris rush TDs/Pickens 5 catch-105 yds
10/29/2023		vs	JACKSONVILLE	10	20	L		Steelers held to 70 yds rushing/Pickens TD catch
11/2/2023	TH	vs	TENNESSEE	20	16	W		Boswell 2 FG/Harris rush TD/Pickett TD pass to Johnson
11/12/2023		vs	GREEN BAY	23	19	W		Boswell 3 FG/Warren 101 rush yds-rush TD/Harris rush TD
11/19/2023		@	Cleveland	10	13	L		Warren 129 rush yds-rush TD/Boswell FG
11/26/2023		@	Cincinnati	16	10	W		Boswell 3 FG/Freiermuth 9 catch-120 yds/Harris rush TD
12/3/2023		vs	ARIZONA	10	24	L		Trubisky TD pass to Johnson/Boswell FG
12/7/2023	TH	vs	NEW ENGLAND	18	21	L		Trubisky TD pass to Johnson-rush TD/Boswell FG
12/16/2023	SAT	@	Indianapolis	13	30	L		Steelers blow 13-0 lead/Trubisky TD pass to Johnson
12/23/2023	SAT	vs	CINCINNATI	34	11	W		Pickens 4 catch-195 yds-2 TD catch/Rudolph 290 pass yds
12/31/2023		@	Seattle	30	23	W		Boswell 3 FG/Harris 122 pass yds-2 rush TD
1/6/2024	SAT	@	Baltimore Ravens	17	10	W		Harris 112 rush yds-rush TD/Rudolph TD pass to Johnson
1/14/2024	**MON**	**@**	**Buffalo**	**17**	**31**	**L**		**AFC Wild Card**

Schedule courtesy of Steve's Football Bible LLC

2023 AFC North	W	L	T	PCT	DIV	CONF	PF	PA
Baltimore Ravens	13	4	0	.764	3–3	8–4	483	280
Cleveland Browns	11	6	0	.647	3–3	8–4	396	362
Pittsburgh Steelers	**10**	**7**	**0**	**.588**	**5–1**	**7–5**	**304**	**324**
Cincinnati Bengals	9	8	0	.529	1–5	4–8	366	380

Statistics

Team Leaders				
Passing Yds	Kenny Pickett	2070	TD Pass	Kenny Pickett	6
Rushing Yds	Najee Harris	1035	Rush TD	Najee Harris	8
Receptions	George Pickens	63	TD Rec.	Pickens-Johnson	5
Receiving Yds	George Pickens	1140	Points	Chirs Boswell	114
Interceptions	4 players tied	2	Sacks	T.J. Watt	19.0

2023 NFL Draft

Round	Selection	Player	Position	College
1	14	Broderick Jones	OT	Georgia
2	32	Joey Porter Jr.	CB	Penn State
2	49	Keeanu Benton	NT	Wisconsin
3	93	Darnell Washington	TE	Georgia
4	132	Nick Herbig	LB	Wisconsin
7	241	Cory Trice	CB	Purdue
7	251	Spencer Anderson	OL	Maryland

Selected game(s) highlights

Cleveland Browns @ Pittsburgh Steelers

Alex Highsmith opened the scoring 9 seconds in with a 30-yard pick-six. However, just over 6 minutes later, Dustin Hopkins kicked a 43-yard field goal to cut Pittsburgh's lead to 4 points. In the second quarter, the Steelers trailed for the first time when Browns quarterback Deshaun Watson hit Jerome Ford with a 4-yard touchdown pass followed by a two-point conversion to make the score 11–7 in favor of the Browns. Chris Boswell kicked a 52-yard field goal to bring Pittsburgh within one point. Kenny Pickett then hit George Pickens with a 71-yard touchdown pass to put the Steelers back up, 16–11. The Browns made it a 2-point game when Dustin Hopkins kicked a 55-yard field goal just before halftime. In the third quarter, Chris Boswell pushed the Steelers' lead back to five points by converting a 50-yard field goal. However, Pierre Strong, Jr. ran for a 1-yard touchdown, with a 2-point conversion, to put the Browns up, 22–19, 1 minute and 46 seconds later. In the fourth quarter, with 6:58 to go, T. J. Watt recorded a 16-yard fumble return for a touchdown, to reach the final score of 26–22 in favor of Pittsburgh.

Pittsburgh Steelers @ Los Angeles Rams

After a scoreless first quarter, the Steelers scored first when Chris Boswell kicked a 53-yard field goal to make it 3-0. Though, the Rams would take the lead before halftime when their kicker Brett Maher tied the game with a 41-yard field goal, followed by a 31-yard touchdown pass from Matthew Stafford to Tutu Atwell (with a failed PAT) to make it 9-3. In the third quarter, the Steelers retook the lead when Kenny Pickett ran for a 1-yard touchdown to make it 10-9. However, the Rams took the lead back when Darrell Henderson Jr. ran for a 1-yard touchdown (with a successful 2-point conversion) to make it 17-10. In the fourth quarter, it was all Steelers as they would win the game 24-17 with a pair of rushing touchdowns from Jaylen Warren from 13 yards out and Najee Harris from 3 yards out. The Steelers defeated the Rams for the fifth time in a row.

Pittsburgh Steelers @ Cincinnati Bengals

After a scoreless first quarter, the Steelers managed to take the lead in the second with Chris Boswell's 41-yard field goal to make it 3-0. The Bengals made it 7-3 at halftime when Jake Browning found Drew Sample on an 11-yard touchdown pass. The Steelers went back to work in the second half, scoring 3 straight times into the fourth quarter as they made it 16-7. The Bengals wrapped up the scoring of the game late in the quarter as Evan McPherson kicked a 47-yard field goal to make the final score 16-10.

2023 AFC Wild Card

This is the fourth playoff matchup between these two teams; Pittsburgh won two out of the first three. The game was originally scheduled to be played on January 14 at 1:05 p.m. EST but was delayed due to a state of emergency and travel ban declared in Western New York because of a massive snowstorm, marking the first time an NFL playoff game was postponed since the 2016–17 playoffs, a game that also featured the Steelers.

Josh Allen threw three touchdown passes and scored on a franchise playoff-record 52-yard touchdown run as Buffalo beat Pittsburgh 31-17 in a game that was postponed by 27 1/2 hours. Buffalo led 21-0 before Pittsburgh scored on three straight possessions to get within 24-17. Allen then sealed the win, throwing a 17-yard touchdown pass to Khalil Shakir with 6:27 remaining. Shakir caught the pass at the 10 over the middle, slipped Minkah Fitzpatrick's tackle attempt with a spin move, and outraced the rest of the Steelers defenders into the end zone. Allen finished 21 of 30 for 203 yards and ran for 74 yards on eight carries, becoming the first quarterback in NFL playoff history to throw three or more TD passes while rushing for 70 or more yards and a score. Mason Rudolph threw two touchdown passes with an interception in his first playoff start for the Steelers, but Pittsburgh was too inconsistent on either side of the ball to keep up with Allen and the Bills. The Steelers lost their fifth straight playoff game. Missed tackles, two turnovers that led to 14 points for Buffalo and the Bills' ability to bottle up the Steelers' running attack contributed to the loss.

Allen's 9-yard touchdown pass to Dawson Knox capped an 80-yard opening drive. After Buffalo linebacker Terrel Bernard recovered receiver George Pickens' fumble at the Pittsburgh 29, Allen threw a TD pass to Dalton Kincaid on the next play. Allen's touchdown run came after cornerback Kaiir Elam intercepted Rudolph's pass intended for Diontae Johnson in the end zone. The Steelers finally capitalized on one of the Bills' few errors of the half, when coach Sean McDermott elected to attempt a 49-yard field goal into the wind with a little more than two minutes left. Montravius Adams blocked Tyler Bass' low kick. The ball squirted some 20 yards into Bills territory and was recovered by Nick Herbig at Buffalo's 33. The Steelers scored five plays later on Rudolph's 10-yard TD pass to Johnson.

1/15/2024	Line	1	2	3	4	Final
Pittsburgh Steelers	39.0	0	7	3	7	17
Buffalo Bills	-10.0	14	7	3	7	31

Scoring

Team	
Buffalo	Dawson Knox 9-yard pass from Josh Allen (Tyler Bass kick)
Buffalo	Dalton Kincaid 29-yard pass from Josh Allen (Tyler Bass kick)
Buffalo	Josh Allen 52-yard run (Tyler Bass kick)
Pittsburgh	Diontae Johnson 10-yard pass from Mason Rudolph (Chris Boswell kick)
Pittsburgh	Chris Boswell 40-yard field goal
Buffalo	Tyler Bass 45-yard field goal
Pittsburgh	Calvin Austin 7-yard pass from Mason Rudolph (Chris Boswell kick)
Buffalo	Khalil Shakir 17-yard pass from Josh Allen (Tyler Bass kick)

2024 Pittsburgh Steelers

The 2024 season is the Pittsburgh Steelers' 92nd season in the NFL, their third under general manager Omar Khan and their 18th under head coach Mike Tomlin. Despite losing to the Philadelphia Eagles in Week 15, the Steelers made the playoffs for the second consecutive season after losses by the Indianapolis Colts and the Miami Dolphins that same day. Following a Week 13 victory against the division rival Cincinnati Bengals, the Steelers clinched their 21st consecutive non-losing season, tying the NFL record set by the Dallas Cowboys from 1965–85.

								10-8	Heinz Field
9/8/2024		@	Atlanta	18	10	W			Boswell 6 FGs/Pickens 6 catcvh-85 yds
9/15/2024		@	Denver	13	6	W			Boswell 2 FGs/Fields TD pass to Washington
9/22/2024		vs	LOS ANGELES CHARGERS	20	10	W			Boswell 2 FGs/Fields TD pass-TD run
9/29/2024		@	Indianapolis	24	27	L			Fields 312 pass yds-TD pass-2 TD runs
10/6/2024	SNF	vs	DALLAS	17	20	L			Heyward & Freiermuth TD pass from Fields
10/13/2024		@	Las Vegas	32	13	W			Boswell 4 FGs/Fields 2 rush TDs/Harris 106 yds
10/20/2024	SNF	vs	NEW YORK JETS	37	15	W			Wilson 264 pass yds-2 TD pass-rush TD
10/28/2024	MNF	vs	NEW YORK GIANTS	26	18	W			Boswell 4 FGs/**Austin 73 yd punt return TD**
11/3/2024			BYE						
11/10/2024		@	Washington	28	27	W			Wilson 195 pass yds-3 TD pass/Harris tush TD
11/17/2024		vs	BALTIMORE RAVENS	18	16	W			Boswell 6 FGs/Pickens 8 catch-89 yds
11/21/2024	TH	@	Cleveland	19	24	L			Wilson 270 pass yds-TD pass to Austin
12/1/2024		@	Cincinnati	44	38	W			**P. Wilson fumble return TD**/Wilson 414 yds
12/8/2024		vs	CLEVELAND	27	14	W			Freiermuth & Jefferson TD pass from Wilson
12/15/2024		@	Philadelphia	13	27	L			Boswell 2 FGs/Wilson TD pass to Freiermuth
12/21/2024	SAT	@	Baltimore Ravens	17	34	L			Patterson & Pruitt TD pass from Wilson
12/25/2024	Wed	vs	KANSAS CITY	10	29	L			Wilson rush TD/Boswell FG
1/4/2025	SAT	vs	CINCINNATI	17	19	L			Steelers held to 74 rush yds
1/11/2025	SAT	@	**Baltimore Ravens**	14	28	L			**AFC WILD CARD**

Schedule courtesy of Steve's Football Bible LLC

2024 AFC North	W	L	T	PCT	DIV	CONF	PF	PA
Baltimore Ravens	12	5	0	.706	4-2	8-4	518	361
Pittsburgh	**10**	**7**	**0**	**.588**	**3-3**	**7-5**	**380**	**347**
Cincinnati	9	8	0	.529	3-3	6-6	472	434
Cleveland	3	14	0	.176	2-4	3-9	258	435

Statistics

Team Leaders					
Passing Yds	Russell Wilson	2,482	TD Pass	Russell Wilson	16
Rushing Yds	Najee Harris	1,043	Rush TD	Najee Harris	6
Receptions	Pat Freiermuth	65	TD Rec.	Pat Freiermuth	7
Receiving Yds	George Pickens	900	Points	Chris Boswell	158
Interceptions	Donte Jackson	5	Sacks	T.J. Watt	11.5

2024 NFL Draft

Round	Selection	Player	Position	College
1	20	Troy Fautanu	OT	Washington
2	51	Zach Frazier	C	West Virginia
3	84	Roman Wilson	WR	Michigan
3	98	Payton Wilson	LB	NC State
4	119	Mason McCormick	G	South Dakota State
6	178	Logan Lee	DE	Iowa
6	195	Ryan Watts	CB	Texas

Selected game(s) highlights

Pittsburgh Steelers @ Washington Commanders

The Steelers traveled east to take on the Commanders. In the first quarter, they would score first, making it 7-0 by way of Russell Wilson connecting with George Pickens on a 16-yard touchdown pass. The Commanders then tied it up at 7-7 when Austin Ekeler ran for a 1-yard touchdown. The Steelers retook the lead in the second when Wilson connected with Pat Freiermuth on a 3-yard touchdown pass to make it 14-7. The Commanders however were able to take a 17-14 halftime lead by way of Zane Gonzalez's 48-yard field goal, followed by Ekeler running for another 1-yard touchdown. After the break, the Commanders went back to work in the third when Jeremy Nichols ran for a 1-yard touchdown to make the score 24-14. Though, the Steelers came within single digits again when Najee Harris ran for a 1-yard touchdown to make it 24-21. Gonzalez kicked his second field goal from 41 yards out to put the Commanders up 27-21. In the fourth quarter, the Steelers scored the only points when Wilson found Mike Williams on a 32-yard touchdown pass to make the score 28-27. They were then able to hold off the Commanders and eventually ran out the clock to seal the victory.

Pittsburgh Steelers @ Cincinnati Bengals

On the Steelers' first offensive possession, Russell Wilson threw a pick-6 to Bengals safety Cam Taylor-Britt, but they responded swiftly with a touchdown drive capped off by a George Pickens touchdown pass. The teams would go blow for blow, trading touchdowns until the Steelers decided to kick a field goal to take a 24-21 lead. The Bengals drove into Steelers' territory before Joe Burrow was strip stacked by T.J. Watt, leading to a Steelers fumble recovery. The ensuing Steelers drive set up Chris Boswell to make a 34-yard field goal as the half expired with the Steelers taking a 27-21 lead. The Bengals kicked a field goal to make the score 27-24 before the Steelers scored another touchdown on a pass to Pat Freiermuth near the end of the third quarter. Early in the 4th quarter, Joe Burrow was once again strip stacked by TJ Watt. This time, Payton Wilson recovered the loose football and ran it back for a touchdown to give the Steelers a 41-24 lead. The Bengals would attempt a comeback effort, scoring two touchdowns later in the fourth quarter, but it fell short. The Steelers held on to win 44-38. For the first time since October 2018, the Steelers scored 40 or more points in a football game. Russell Wilson also became the first Steelers quarterback to throw for 400 passing yards since Ben Roethlisberger in 2018.

2024 AFC Wild Card

Lamar Jackson threw for two touchdowns in a flawless first half, Derrick Henry scored twice while leading Baltimore's devastating running game, and the Ravens beat the Pittsburgh Steelers 28-14 on Saturday night to advance to the second round of the AFC playoffs. Jackson and Henry had the Steelers chasing shadows all night as Baltimore outrushed Pittsburgh 299-29. It was the most yards rushing allowed by Pittsburgh in a playoff game, breaking the mark of 232 set by the Oakland Raiders 51 years ago. Baltimore had a 19-2 advantage in first downs in the first half, when the Ravens produced touchdown drives of 95, 85 and 90 yards. Henry ran for 186 yards. Pittsburgh's season ends with five straight losses, two of which came in Baltimore. The ending was a familiar story for the Steelers, who have lost six consecutive playoff games. Henry made it 14-0 with an 8-yard run with 4:09 left in the half, and the Ravens didn't attempt a single pass on that 13-play drive. After a Pittsburgh punt, the Steelers called timeout on third-and-2 from the Baltimore 18, hoping to get the ball back, but the Ravens converted and then quickly moved into position to score. On second down from the Pittsburgh 5 with 11 seconds left, Jackson nearly used up the remaining time scrambling around, but he eventually dumped the ball off to an open Justice Hill, who went into the end zone with 2 seconds remaining. The Steelers drove 98 yards for a touchdown on their first second-half possession, with Russell Wilson throwing a 30-yard scoring pass to Van Jefferson. Baltimore quickly answered when Henry broke free up the middle for his 44-yard TD. Wilson answered with a 36-yard touchdown strike to George Pickens in the third, but that was it for the scoring. Wilson went 20 of 29 for 270 yards

1/11/2025	Line	1	2	3	4	Final
Pittsburgh Steelers	45.0	0	0	14	0	14
Baltimore Ravens	-9.5	7	14	7	0	28

Scoring

Team	
Ravens	Rashod Bateman 15 yard pass from Lamar Jackson (Justin Tucker kick)
Ravens	Derrick Henry 8 yard rush (Justin Tucker kick)
Ravens	Justice Hill 5 yard pass from Lamar Jackson (Justin Tucker kick)
Steelers	Van Jefferson 30 yard pass from Russell Wilson (Chris Boswell kick)
Ravens	Derrick Henry 44 yard rush (Justin Tucker kick)
Steelers	George Pickens 36 yard pass from Russell Wilson (Chris Boswell kick)

2025 Pittsburgh Steelers

The 2025 season was the Pittsburgh Steelers' 93rd in the National Football League, and their 19th and final season under head coach Mike Tomlin. They matched their 10–7 records from both 2023 and 2024 and made the playoffs for the third consecutive season and ended their four-year AFC North title drought with a win over the Baltimore Ravens during Week 18. With a Week 16 win over the Detroit Lions, head coach Mike Tomlin reached his 200th total career win, and the Steelers secured its 22nd consecutive non-losing season, breaking the record set by the 1965–1985 Dallas Cowboys.

The Steelers lost to the Houston Texans in the Wild Card round, and it extended their postseason losing streak to seven straight games dating back to the 2016–17 playoffs. On January 13, the day following the loss and the end of Pittsburgh's season, Tomlin announced that he stepped down as Steelers head coach. Tomlin compiled a 193–114–2 regular season record during his 19-year coaching tenure in Pittsburgh, tying him with Chuck Noll as the winningest head coach in franchise history. Tomlin also led Pittsburgh to 13 playoff appearances, 8 AFC North division titles, and the franchise's sixth Super Bowl title in Super Bowl XLIII. His win-loss record in the playoffs was 8–12.

Date			Opponent					10-8	Heinz Field
9/7/2025		@	New York Jets	A	34	32	W		Boswell 60 yd GW FG/Rodgers 4 TD pass
9/14/2025		vs	SEATTLE	G	17	31	L		Boswell 3 FG's/Warren 48 rush yds-86 yds rec.
9/21/2025		@	New England	A	21	14	W		Rodgers TD pass to Metcalf and Austin
9/28/2025		vs	MINNESOTA {@ Dublin}	G	24	21	W		Gainwell 2 rush TD/Metcalf 5 catch-126 yds-TD
10/5/2025			BYE						
10/12/2025		vs	CLEVELAND	G	23	9	W		Boswell 3 FG's/Rodgers 235 pass yds-2 TD pass
10/16/2025	TH	@	Cincinnati	A	31	33	L		Rodgers 249 pass yds-4 TD pass/Freiermuth 2 TD
10/26/2025	SNF	vs	GREEN BAY	G	25	35	L		Boswell 4 FG's/Rodgers TD pass to Wilson & Metcalf
11/2/2025		vs	INDIANAPOLIS	G	27	20	W		Warren 2 rush TD's/Boswell 2 FG's
11/9/2025	SNF	@	Los Angeles Chargers	A	10	25	L		Steelers held to 221 total yds/Wilson TD catch
11/16/2025		vs	CINCINNATI	G	34	12	W		**Dugger INT return TD/Pierre fumble return TD**
11/23/2025		@	Chicago	G	28	31	L		**Herbig fumble recovery TD**/Rudolph TD pass
11/30/2025		vs	BUFFALO	G	7	26	L		Warren rush TD/Steelers held to 166 total yds
12/7/2025		@	Baltimore	G	27	22	W		Rodgers 284 pass yds-pass TD-rush TD
12/15/2025	MNF	vs	MIAMI	G	28	15	W		Rodgers 224 pass yds-2 TD pass/Samuel INT
12/21/2025		@	Detroit	A	29	24	W		Rodgers 266 pass yds-TD pass/Warren 2 rush TD
12/28/2025		@	Cleveland	G	6	13	L		Boswell 2 FG's/Dugger & Swayer INT's
1/4/2026	SNF	vs	BALTIMORE	G	26	24	W		Rodgers 294 pass yds-TD pass to Austin
1/12/2026	MON	vs	HOUSTON	G	6	30	L		AFC WILD CARD

Schedule courtesy of Steve's Football Bible LLC

2025 AFC North	W	L	T	PCT	DIV	CONF	PF	PA	STK
Pittsburgh Steelers	10	7	0	.588	4–2	8–4	397	387	W1
Baltimore Ravens	8	9	0	.471	3–3	5–7	424	398	L1
Cincinnati Bengals	6	11	0	.353	3–3	5–7	414	492	L1
Cleveland Browns	5	12	0	.294	2–4	4–8	279	379	W2

Statistics

Team Leaders					
Passing Yds	Aaron Rodgers	3,322	TD Pass	Aaron Rodgers	24
Rushing Yds	Jaylen Warren	958	Rush TD	Jaylen Warren	6
Receptions	Kenneth Gainwell	73	TD Rec.	D.K. Metcalf	6
Receiving Yds	D.K. Metcalf	850	Points	Chris Boswell	123
Interceptions	Four players tied	2	Sacks	Alex Highsmith	9.5

2025 NFL Draft

Round	Selection	Player	Position	College
1	21	Derrick Harmon	DT	Oregon
3	83	Kaleb Johnson	RB	Iowa
4	123	Jack Sawyer	DE	Ohio State
5	164	Yahya Black	DT	Iowa
6	185	Will Howard	QB	Ohio State
7	226	Carson Bruener	LB	Washington
	229	Donte Kent	CB	Central Michigan

Selected game(s) highlights

Pittsburgh Steelers at Detroit Lions

The Pittsburgh Steelers survived a wild finish, pushing Detroit to the brink of playoff elimination and boosting their chances of winning their division for the first time in five years. Pittsburgh held on for 29-24 win over the Lions on Sunday. The game featured a controversial and memorable moment on its final play. On fourth down, Lions quarterback Jared Goff threw a pass to wide receiver Amon-Ra St. Brown that fell just short of the goal line. St. Brown pushed off Jalen Ramsey to create separation and, before being tackled by Steelers defenders, lateraled the ball back to Goff, who appeared to score a touchdown. However, multiple flags were thrown, and officials huddled for several minutes before announcing that the touchdown was nullified due to an offensive pass interference penalty on St. Brown, resulting in a final score of 29–24 in favor of Pittsburgh. With the win, the Steelers secured their 22nd consecutive non-losing season, breaking the NFL record they had previously shared with the Dallas Cowboys, who recorded 21 straight non-losing seasons from 1965 to 1985. Head coach Mike Tomlin has finished every one of his 19 seasons with the team at .500 or better and recorded his 200th total career win. During the game, Steelers receiver DK Metcalf got into an altercation with a Lions fan. Video footage from the game showed Metcalf grabbing a shirt and engaging in a verbal exchange with the fan before attempting to strike the individual.

Baltimore Ravens at Pittsburgh Steelers

Aaron Rodgers threw for 284 yards and a touchdown and even ran for a TD in perhaps his best game with the Steelers, and Pittsburgh took sole possession of first place in the AFC North, holding on for a 27-22 win over the Ravens when a Baltimore touchdown with 2:43 remaining was overturned by a replay review. The Ravens nearly rallied from an 11-point deficit in the final quarter, but a pair of big reviews went against them. With the Steelers up 27-22, a pass by Rodgers was batted into the air by C.J. Okoye before the ball disappeared into a mass of humanity, with Rodgers in the middle of it. The play was initially ruled an interception, but Rodgers very briefly had his hands on the ball before losing control, and after a review, officials determined Rodgers caught his own pass and was down by contact.
Later, Isaiah Likely secured a pass from Lamar Jackson with two hands in the end zone, and both his feet came down, but as he was about to complete another step with his right foot, Joey Porter Jr. of the Steelers knocked the ball free. It was initially called a touchdown then changed to incomplete. The Ravens eventually turned the ball over on downs. The Steelers led 17-9 at halftime, and as he did in the first half, Rodgers connected for a big gain to Metcalf to start the third quarter. That 41-yard pickup led to a field goal, but Keaton Mitchell raced free for a 56-yard run for the Ravens, who made it 20-16 on Jackson's 4-yard scoring pass to Likely. Rodgers answered with a 31-yard pass to Calvin Austin III on third down, then Jaylen Warren took a short pass 38 yards to the end zone — also on third down — for a 27-16 lead. The Ravens managed a couple of field goals but couldn't produce the late touchdown they needed.

2025 AFC Wild Card

The Steelers were unable to move the ball effectively as the Texans defense capitalized on a powerful performance, clamping the Steelers offense down to 175 total yards (112 passing, 63 rushing) as well as just two field goals before shutting them out in the second half. After three quarters of a defensive game, in the fourth quarter, the Texans scored two defensive touchdowns, one from Rodgers fumbling the ball that was recovered by defensive tackle Sheldon Rankins and returned for 33 yards, while the other was a pick six to safety Calen Bullock returned for 51 yards. With their first home loss to Houston since 2002, the Steelers secured their seventh postseason loss since 2016 and this would mark their final game under Mike Tomlin, as he would resign from the team and step down as head coach the following day. This also ended Pittsburgh's 23-game home winning streak on *Monday Night Football*.

1/12/2026	Line	1	2	3	4	Final
Houston Texans	-3.0	0	7	0	23	30
Pittsburgh Steelers	38.5	3	3	0	0	6

Scoring

Team	
Steelers	Chris Boswell 32 yard field goal
Texans	Christian Kirk 6 yard pass from C.J. Stroud (Ka'imi Fairbairn kick)
Steelers	Chris Boswell 35 yard field goal
Texans	Ka'imi Fairbairn 51 yard field goal
Texans	Sheldon Rankins 33 yard fumble return (Ka'imi Fairbairn kick)
Texans	Woody Marks 13 yard rush (Ka'imi Fairbairn kick)
Texans	Calen Bullock 50 yard interception return (Ka'imi Fairbairn kick failed)

Thursday Game Results

Date	TH		Opponent	2-6		13-22	Line	11-18-2	Total	13-17-1
10/16/2025	TH	@	Cincinnati	31	33	L	-5.5	L	45.0	O
11/21/2024	TH	@	Cleveland	19	24	L	-3.5	L	36.5	O
12/7/2023	TH	vs	NEW ENGLAND	18	21	L	-5.5	L	30.5	O
11/2/2023	TH	vs	TENNESSEE	20	16	W	-3.0	W	37.0	U
9/22/2022	TH	@	Cleveland	17	29	L	4.0	L	38.0	O
12/9/2021	TH	@	Minnesota	28	36	L	3.5	L	45.0	O
11/14/2019	TH	@	Cleveland	7	21	L	3.0	L	41.5	U
11/8/2018	TH	vs	**CAROLINA**	52	21	W	-3.5	W	51.0	O
11/16/2017	TH	vs	**TENNESSEE TITANS**	40	17	W	-7.0	W	44.5	O
11/24/2016	TH	@	Indianapolis Colts	28	7	W	-8.0	W	50.0	U
10/1/2015	TH	vs	**BALTIMORE RAVENS {OT}**	20	23	L	3.0	T	44.0	U
9/10/2015	TH	@	New England Patriots	21	28	L	7.0	T	51.0	U
9/11/2014	TH	@	Baltimore Ravens	6	26	L	2.5	L	44.0	U
11/28/2013	TH	@	Baltimore Ravens	20	22	L	3.0	W	40.5	O
10/14/2012	TH	@	Tennessee Titans	23	26	L	-5.5	L	42.5	O
12/8/2011	TH	vs	**CLEVELAND**	14	3	W	-14.5	L	39.5	U
12/23/2010	TH	vs	**CAROLINA**	27	3	W	-14.5	W	37.0	U
12/10/2009	TH	@	Cleveland	6	13	L	-10.0	L	33.5	U
9/10/2009	TH	vs	**TENNESSEE (OT)**	13	10	W	-6.0	L	35.5	U
11/20/2008	TH	vs	**CINCINNATI**	27	10	W	-11.0	W	34.5	O
12/20/2007	TH	@	St. Louis Rams	41	24	W	-8.0	W	43.0	O
12/7/2006	TH	vs	**CLEVELAND**	27	7	W	-7.0	W	34.0	T
9/7/2006	TH	vs	**MIAMI**	28	17	W	-1.0	W	35.5	O
12/2/1999	TH	@	Jacksonville	6	20	L	10.5	L	37.0	U
11/26/1998	TH	@	Detroit (OT)	16	19	L	-2.0	L	41.0	U
10/19/1995	TH	vs	CINCINNATI	9	27	L	-8.0	L	41.0	U
11/28/1991	TH	@	Dallas	10	20	L	6.5	L	39.5	U
9/6/1984	TH	@	New York Jets	23	17	W	-1.0	W	41.0	U
11/24/1983	TH	@	Detroit	3	45	L	-3.0	L	41.0	O
9/14/1981	TH	@	Miami	10	30	L	2.0	L	41.0	U
12/4/1980	TH	@	Houston Oilers	0	6	L	2.5	L	40.0	U
11/23/1950	TH	@	Chicago Cardinals	28	17	W				
11/28/1940	TH	@	Philadelphia	0	7	L				
11/23/1939	TH	@	Philadelphia	14	17	L				
9/14/1939	TH	@	Brooklyn Dodgers	7	12	L				

Thursday Football Highlights

9-2 S/U @ home on Thursday since 2006
11-4 S/U on Thursday as favorite since 2006
4-19 S/U on road on Thursday since 1939
2-6 S/U on Thanksgiving Day since 1939
vs Tennessee - HOME team 4-0 S/U on Thursday since 1980
0-3 S/U vs Baltimore on Thursday since 2013
Source: Steve's Football Bible LLC

Saturday Game Results

Date	Day		Opponent	Pitt	Opp	35-30	
1/11/2025	**SAT**	**@**	**Baltimore Ravens**	**14**	**28**	**L**	**AFC WILD CARD**
1/4/2025	SAT	vs	CINCINNATI	17	19	L	
12-21-2024	SAT	@	Baltimore Ravens	17	34	L	
12/23/2023	SAT	vs	CINCINNATI	34	11	W	
12/16/2023	SAT	@	Indianapolis	13	30	L	
12/24/2022	SAT	vs	LAS VEGAS	13	10	W	
1/9/2016	**SAT**	**@**	**Cincinnati**	**18**	**16**	**W**	**AFC WILD CARD**
1/3/2015	**SAT**	**vs**	**BALTIMORE RAVENS**	**17**	**30**	**L**	**AFC WILD CARD**
12/24/2011	SAT	vs	ST. LOUIS RAMS	27	0	W	
1/15/2011	**SAT**	**vs**	**BALTIMORE RAVENS**	**31**	**24**	**W**	**AFC Divisional Play-offs**
1/5/2008	**SAT**	**vs**	**JACKSONVILLE**	**29**	**31**	**L**	**AFC WILD CARD**
12/24/2005	SAT	@	Cleveland	41	0	W	
1/15/2005	**SAT**	**vs**	**NEW YORK JETS (OT)**	**20**	**17**	**W**	**AFC Divisional Play-offs**
12/18/2004	SAT	@	New York Giants	33	30	W	
1/11/2003	**SAT**	**@**	**Tennessee Titans (OT)**	**31**	**34**	**L**	**AFC Divisional Play-offs**
12/16/2000	SAT	vs	WASHINGTON REDSKINS	24	3	W	
12/18/1999	SAT	@	Kansas City	19	35	L	
1/3/1998	**SAT**	**vs**	**NEW ENGLAND PATRIOTS**	**7**	**6**	**W**	**AFC Divisional Play-offs**
12/13/1997	SAT	@	New England Patriots (OT)	24	21	W	
1/6/1996	**SAT**	**vs**	**BUFFALO**	**40**	**21**	**W**	**AFC Divisional Play-offs**
12/16/1995	SAT	vs	NEW ENGLAND PATRIOTS	41	27	W	
1/7/1995	**SAT**	**vs**	**CLEVELAND BROWNS**	**29**	**9**	**W**	**AFC Divisional Play-offs**
12/24/1994	SAT	@	San Diego Chargers	34	37	L	
1/8/1994	**SAT**	**@**	**Kansas City (OT)**	**24**	**27**	**L**	**AFC WILD CARD**
1/9/1993	**SAT**	**vs**	**BUFFALO**	**3**	**24**	**L**	**AFC Divisional Play-offs**
12/26/1987	SAT	vs	CLEVELAND BROWNS	13	19	L	
12/30/1978	**SAT**	**vs**	**DENVER**	**33**	**10**	**W**	**AFC Divisional Play-offs**
12/24/1977	**SAT**	**@**	**Denver**	**21**	**34**	**L**	**AFC Divisional Play-offs**
12/10/1977	SAT	@	Cincinnati	10	17	L	
12/11/1976	SAT	@	Houston Oilers	21	0	W	
12/27/1975	**SAT**	**vs**	**BALTIMORE COLTS**	**28**	**10**	**W**	**AFC Divisional Play-offs**
12/14/1974	SAT	vs	CINCINNATI	27	3	W	
12/22/1973	**SAT**	**@**	**Oakland Raiders**	**14**	**33**	**L**	**AFC Divisional Play-offs**
12/15/1973	SAT	@	San Francisco	37	14	W	
12/23/1972	**SAT**	**vs**	**OAKLAND RAIDERS**	**13**	**7**	**W**	**AFC Divisional Play-offs**
10/3/1970	SAT	@	Cleveland Browns	7	15	L	
10/18/1969	SAT	@	Cleveland Browns	31	42	L	
10/5/1968	SAT	@	Cleveland Browns	24	31	L	
10/7/1967	SAT	@	Cleveland Browns	10	21	L	

Date	Day		Opponent	Pitt	Opp		
10/8/1966	SAT	@	Cleveland Browns	10	41	L	
10/9/1965	SAT	@	Cleveland Browns	19	24	L	
10/10/1964	SAT	@	Cleveland Browns	23	7	W	
10/5/1963	SAT	@	Cleveland Browns	23	35	L	
10/6/1962	SAT	vs	PHILADELPHIA	13	7	W	
9/24/1960	SAT	@	Dallas	35	28	W	
9/26/1959	SAT	vs	CLEVELAND BROWNS	17	7	W	
12/13/1958	SAT	vs	CHICAGO CARDINALS	38	21	W	
12/7/1957	SAT	vs	NEW YORK GIANTS	21	10	W	
10/5/1957	SAT	vs	CLEVELAND BROWNS	12	23	L	
10/6/1956	SAT	vs	CLEVELAND BROWNS	10	14	L	
11/5/1955	SAT	@	Chicago Cardinals	13	27	L	
10/15/1955	SAT	vs	PHILADELPHIA	13	7	W	
11/20/1954	SAT	vs	SAN FRANCISCO	3	31	L	
10/23/1954	SAT	vs	PHILADELPHIA	17	7	W	
10/9/1954	SAT	@	Philadelphia	22	24	L	
10/2/1954	SAT	vs	WASHINGTON REDSKINS	37	7	W	
10/24/1953	SAT	vs	GREEN BAY	31	14	W	
10/17/1953	SAT	@	Philadelphia	7	23	L	
10/3/1953	SAT	vs	NEW YORK GIANTS	24	14	W	
10/4/1952	SAT	vs	CLEVELAND BROWNS	20	21	L	
10/7/1950	SAT	vs	CLEVELAND BROWNS	17	30	L	
10/8/1949	SAT	vs	DETROIT	14	7	W	
9/25/1949	SAT	vs	NEW YORK GIANTS	28	7	W	
10/9/1943	SAT	vs	NEW YORK GIANTS	28	14	W	Shibe Park
10/2/1943	SAT	vs	BROOKLYN DODGERS	17	10	W	Shibe Park

Saturday Football Highlights

17-5 S/U @ home on Saturday since 1958
9-1 O/U on road on Saturday since 1994
1-4 S/U on road on Saturday in Playoffs since 1973
5-0 S/U vs New York Giants on Saturday since 1943
0-7 S/U @ Baltimore on Saturday since 1965
3-0 S/U @ home vs Philadelphia on Saturday since 1954
3-0 S/U vs New England on Saturday since 1995

Source: Steve's Football Bible LLC

Sunday Night Football Game Results

			Pitt	Opp	34-30		29-33-2		32-31-1
1/4/2026	vs	BALTIMORE RAVENS	26	24	W	4.5	W	51.5	U
11/9/2025	@	Los Angeles Chargers	10	25	L	3.0	L	45.5	U
10/26/2025	vs	GREEN BAY	25	35	L	2.5	L	45.5	O
10/20/2024	vs	NEW YORK JETS	37	15	W	2.5	W	40.5	O
10/6/2024	vs	DALLAS	17	20	L	-2.5	L	43.5	U
9/24/2023	@	Las Vegas Raiders	23	18	W	3.0	W	43.5	U
1/1/2023	@	Baltimore Ravens	16	13	W	1.5	W	35.5	U
1/16/2022	@	**Kansas City**	**21**	**42**	**L**	**12.0**	**L**	**46.5**	**O**
11/21/2021	@	Los Angeles Chargers	37	41	L	6.0	W	47.5	O
10/17/2021	vs	SEATTLE {OT}	23	20	W	-5.5	L	43.0	T
12/13/2020	@	Buffalo	15	26	L	1.5	L	49.0	U
12/15/2019	vs	BUFFALO	10	17	L	-1.0	L	37.0	U
10/13/2019	@	Los Angeles Chargers	24	17	W	6.0	W	42.5	U
9/8/2019	@	New England Patriots	3	33	L	5.5	L	49.0	U
12/2/2018	vs	LOS ANGELES CHARGERS	30	33	L	-3.0	L	53.5	O
9/30/2018	vs	BALTIMORE RAVENS	14	26	L	-3.0	L	51.0	U
12/10/2017	vs	BALTIMORE RAVENS	39	38	W	-6.0	L	43.0	O
11/26/2017	vs	GREEN BAY	31	28	W	-14.0	L	43.0	O
10/29/2017	@	Detroit	20	15	W	-3.0	W	44.5	U
10/2/2016	vs	KANSAS CITY	43	14	W	-3.5	W	48.5	O
12/6/2015	vs	**INDIANAPOLIS COLTS**	45	10	W	-9.5	W	50.5	O
12/28/2014	vs	**CINCINNATI**	27	17	W	-3.0	W	48.5	U
11/2/2014	vs	BALTIMORE RAVENS	43	23	W	-2.0	W	47.5	O
9/21/2014	@	Carolina	37	19	W	3.0	W	42.5	O
12/15/2013	vs	**CINCINNATI**	30	20	W	2.5	W	43.5	O
9/22/2013	vs	CHICAGO	23	40	L	2.0	L	41.0	O
11/18/2012	vs	BALTIMORE RAVENS	10	13	L	3.0	T	41.0	U
10/21/2012	@	**Cincinnati**	24	17	W	-1.0	W	47.0	U
9/9/2012	@	Denver	19	31	L	3.0	L	45.5	O
11/27/2011	@	Kansas City	13	9	W	-10.5	L	41.0	U
11/6/2011	vs	BALTIMORE RAVENS	20	23	L	-3.5	L	42.0	O
9/25/2011	@	**Indianapolis Colts**	23	20	W	-10.5	L	39.5	O
12/5/2010	@	Baltimore Ravens	13	10	W	3.0	W	39.5	U
11/14/2010	vs	NEW ENGLAND PATRIOTS	26	39	L	-5.0	L	45.0	O
10/31/2010	@	New Orleans	10	20	L	1.5	L	44.5	U
11/29/2009	@	Baltimore Ravens (OT)	17	20	L	7.5	W	34.0	O
10/4/2009	vs	SAN DIEGO CHARGERS	38	28	W	-6.5	W	43.0	O
10/5/2008	@	Jacksonville	26	21	W	5.0	W	36.5	O
9/14/2008	@	Cleveland	10	6	W	-6.5	L	44.0	U

			Pitt	Opp					
12/2/2007	vs	**CINCINNATI**	24	10	W	-7.0	W	40.0	U
10/21/2007	@	Denver	28	31	L	-3.5	L	38.0	O
10/8/2006	@	San Diego Chargers	13	23	L	3.5	L	37.0	U
11/13/2005	vs	CLEVELAND	34	21	W	-7.5	W	34.5	O
12/5/2004	@	Jacksonville	17	16	W	-3.0	L	35.0	U
9/26/2004	@	Miami	13	3	W	2.0	W	31.5	U
12/28/2003	@	Baltimore Ravens	10	13	L	7.5	W	38.0	U
10/5/2003	vs	CLEVELAND	13	33	L	-7.0	L	42.0	O
9/15/2002	vs	OAKLAND RAIDERS	17	30	L	-3.5	L	40.0	O
12/16/2001	@	Baltimore Ravens	26	21	W	3.0	W	33.0	O
11/19/2000	vs	JACKSONVILLE	24	34	L	-3.5	L	37.0	O
9/12/1999	@	Cleveland	43	0	W	-6.0	W	37.0	O
11/9/1997	vs	BALTIMORE RAVENS	37	0	W	-7.0	W	44.0	U
10/12/1997	vs	**INDIANAPOLIS COLTS**	24	22	W	-11.0	L	41.5	O
10/30/1994	@	Arizona Cardinals (OT)	17	20	L	2.5	L	34.0	O
11/28/1993	@	Houston Oilers	3	23	L	3.0	L	40.0	U
10/25/1992	@	Kansas City	27	3	W	8.0	W	35.5	U
11/10/1991	@	Denver	13	20	L	-6.5	L	34.5	U
10/13/1991	@	**Indianapolis Colts**	21	3	W	-7.0	W	36.0	U
12/30/1990	@	Houston Oilers	14	34	L	-2.0	L	37.5	O
11/18/1990	@	Cincinnati	3	27	L	2.5	L	41.5	U
9/16/1990	vs	HOUSTON OILERS	20	9	W	-2.5	W	41.0	U
12/4/1988	@	Houston Oilers	37	34	W	11.0	W	46.5	O
12/8/1985	@	San Diego Chargers	44	54	L	6.0	L	49.5	O
11/12/1978	@	Los Angeles Rams	7	10	L	3.0	T		U

Sunday Night Football Highlights

2-8 ATS @ home on SNF since 2017
1-7 ATS on SNF as favorite since 2017
16-7-1 O/U @ home on SNF since 2000
3-1 S/U vs Kansas City on SNF since 1992
4-0 S/U vs Indianapolis on SNF since 1991
Game 3-0 O/U vs Indianapolis on SNF since 1997
4-0 S/U & ATS vs Cincinnati on SNF since 2007
Game 1-4 O/U vs Cincinnati on SNF since 1990
0-3 S/U & ATS @ Denver on SNF since 1991
4-0 ATS @ Baltimore on SNF since 2001

Source: Steve's Football Bible LLC

Monday Night Football Game Results

			MNF = (54-25)	Pitt	Opp	57-33		49-34-1		37-44-2
1/12/2026	MON	vs	**HOUSTON**	6	30	L	3.0	L	38.5	U
12/15/2025	MNF	vs	**MIAMI**	28	15	W	-3.0	W	43.0	T
10/28/2024	MNF	vs	**NEW YORK GIANTS**	26	18	W	-6.5	W	39.5	O
1/15/2024	MON	@	**Buffalo {AFC Wild Card}**	**17**	**31**	L	10.0	L	39.0	**O**
9/18/2023	MNF	vs	**CLEVELAND**	26	22	W	2.0	W	39.0	O
11/28/2022	MNF	@	Indianapolis	24	17	W	2.0	W	39.5	O
1/3/2022	MNF	vs	**CLEVELAND**	26	14	W	2.0	W	43.0	U
11/8/2021	MNF	vs	**CHICAGO**	29	27	W	-7.0	L	39.5	O
12/21/2020	MNF	@	Cincinnati	17	27	L	-14.0	L	44.5	U
12/7/2020	MON	vs	WASHINGTON REDSKINS	17	23	L	-5.5	L	43.5	U
9/14/2020	MNF	@	New York Giants	26	16	W	-6.0	W	43.5	U
10/28/2019	MNF	vs	**MIAMI**	27	14	W	-14.0	L	43.0	U
9/30/2019	MNF	vs	**CINCINNATI**	27	3	W	-3.5	W	45.0	U
9/24/2018	MNF	@	Tampa Bay	30	27	W	1.0	W	55.0	O
12/25/2017	MON	@	Houston Texans	34	6	W	-9.0	W	45.5	U
12/4/2017	MNF	@	Cincinnati	23	20	W	-4.5	L	42.5	O
9/12/2016	MNF	@	Washington Redskins	38	16	W	-2.5	W	49.5	O
10/12/2015	MNF	@	San Diego Chargers	24	20	W	4.0	W	45.5	U
11/17/2014	MNF	@	Tennessee Titans	27	24	W	-7.0	L	46.5	O
10/20/2014	MNF	vs	**HOUSTON TEXANS**	30	23	W	-3.0	W	44.0	O
9/16/2013	MNF	@	Cincinnati	10	20	L	6.0	L	40.5	U
11/12/2012	MNF	vs	**KANSAS CITY {OT}**	16	13	W	-12.5	L	39.5	U
12/19/2011	MNF	@	San Francisco	3	20	L	2.5	L	37.0	U
11/8/2010	MNF	@	Cincinnati	27	21	W	-4.5	W	41.5	O
11/9/2009	MNF	@	Denver	28	10	W	-3.0	W	39.5	U
11/3/2008	MNF	@	Washington Redskins	23	6	W	2.5	W	37.0	U
9/29/2008	MNF	vs	**BALTIMORE RAVENS (OT)**	23	20	W	-5.0	L	33.5	O
11/26/2007	MNF	vs	**MIAMI**	3	0	W	-16.0	L	39.0	U
11/5/2007	MNF	vs	**BALTIMORE RAVENS**	38	7	W	-9.0	W	36.0	O
9/18/2006	MNF	@	Jacksonville	0	9	L	-2.5	L	37.5	U
11/28/2005	MNF	@	Indianapolis Colts	7	26	L	8.5	L	47.0	U
10/31/2005	MNF	vs	**BALTIMORE RAVENS**	20	19	W	-11.0	L	33.5	O
10/10/2005	MNF	@	San Diego Chargers	24	22	W	3.0	W	46.0	T
11/17/2003	MNF	@	San Francisco	14	30	L	4.0	L	41.5	O
12/23/2002	MNF	@	Tampa Bay	17	7	W	4.5	W	39.0	U
10/21/2002	MNF	vs	**INDIANAPOLIS COLTS**	28	10	W	-4.0	W	46.0	U
9/9/2002	MNF	@	New England Patriots	14	30	L	-2.5	L	37.5	O
10/29/2001	MNF	vs	**TENNESSEE TITANS**	34	7	W	-3.0	W	36.5	O
10/25/1999	MNF	vs	**ATLANTA**	13	9	W	-5.5	L	37.0	U

				Pitt	Opp					
12/28/1998	MNF	@	Jacksonville	3	21	L	3.0	L	40.0	U
11/9/1998	MNF	vs	**GREEN BAY**	27	20	W	3.5	W	41.5	O
10/26/1998	MNF	@	Kansas City	20	13	W	6.0	W	36.5	U
11/3/1997	MNF	@	Kansas City	10	13	L	3.0	T	41.5	U
9/22/1997	MNF	@	Jacksonville	21	30	L	3.5	L	40.5	O
11/25/1996	MNF	@	Miami	24	17	W	2.5	W	42.0	U
10/7/1996	MNF	@	Kansas City	17	7	W	4.5	W	38.0	U
9/16/1996	MNF	vs	**BUFFALO**	24	6	W	-3.0	W	40.0	U
11/13/1995	MNF	vs	**CLEVELAND BROWNS**	20	3	W	-6.0	W	39.0	U
9/18/1995	MNF	@	Miami	10	23	L	7.5	L	40.5	U
11/14/1994	MNF	vs	**BUFFALO**	23	10	W	-2.5	W	36.5	U
10/3/1994	MNF	vs	**HOUSTON OILERS**	30	14	W	-8.0	W	39.5	O
12/13/1993	MNF	@	Miami	21	20	W	3.5	W	36.5	O
11/15/1993	MNF	vs	**BUFFALO**	23	0	W	-3.0	W	39.0	U
9/27/1993	MNF	@	Atlanta	45	17	W	3.0	W	43.0	O
10/19/1992	MNF	vs	**CINCINNATI**	20	0	W	-9.5	W	37.5	U
10/21/1991	MNF	vs	NEW YORK GIANTS	20	23	L	3.5	W	35.0	O
10/29/1990	MNF	vs	LOS ANGELES RAMS	41	10	W	Pk	W	44.0	O
10/13/1986	MNF	@	Cincinnati	22	24	L	8.5	W	44.0	O
9/15/1986	MNF	vs	DENVER	10	21	L	6.0	L	40.5	U
9/30/1985	MNF	vs	CINCINNATI	24	37	L	-6.5	L	46.5	O
9/16/1985	MNF	@	Cleveland Browns	7	17	L	-2.5	L	41.5	U
11/19/1984	MNF	@	New Orleans	24	27	L	-1.5	L	39.5	O
10/1/1984	MNF	vs	CINCINNATI	38	17	W	-4.5	W	41.0	O
10/10/1983	MNF	@	Cincinnati	24	14	W	-1.0	W	43.0	U
9/13/1982	MNF	@	Dallas	36	28	W	6.0	W	42.0	O
12/7/1981	MNF	@	Oakland Raiders	27	30	L	-4.0	L	44.0	O
10/26/1981	MNF	vs	HOUSTON OILERS	26	13	W	-5.5	W	40.0	U
12/22/1980	MNF	@	San Diego Chargers	17	26	L	5.0	L	44.0	O
10/20/1980	MNF	vs	OAKLAND RAIDERS	34	45	L	-10.0	L	45.0	O
12/10/1979	MNF	@	Houston Oilers	17	20	L	-3.5	L	42.5	U
10/22/1979	MNF	vs	DENVER	42	7	W	-9.0	W	37.0	O
9/3/1979	MNF	@	New England Patriots (OT)	16	13	W	-2.0	W	37.0	U
11/27/1978	MNF	@	San Francisco	24	7	W	-8.0	W		U
10/23/1978	MNF	vs	HOUSTON OILERS	17	24	L	-7.5	L		O
10/17/1977	MNF	vs	CINCINNATI	20	14	W	PK	W		U
9/19/1977	MNF	vs	SAN FRANCISCO	27	0	W	-14.0	W		U
10/4/1976	MNF	@	Minnesota	6	17	L	-4.5	L		U
11/24/1975	MNF	@	Houston Oilers	32	9	W	-3.5	W		O
11/25/1974	MNF	@	New Orleans	28	7	W	-8.0	W		U

Date				Pitt	Opp					
10/28/1974	MNF	vs	ATLANTA	24	17	W	-13.0	L		O
12/3/1973	MNF	@	Miami	26	30	L	8.0	W		O
11/5/1973	MNF	vs	WASHINGTON REDSKINS	21	16	W	1.0	W		U
10/18/1971	MNF	@	Kansas City	16	38	L	9.0	L		O
11/2/1970	MNF	vs	CINCINNATI	21	10	W	-5.0	W		U
9/26/1955	MON	vs	CHICAGO CARDINALS	14	7	W	PK	W		
10/3/1949	MON	vs	WASHINGTON REDSKINS	14	27	L				
9/29/1947	MON	vs	LOS ANGELES RAMS	7	48	L				
11/6/1939	MON	@	Brooklyn Dodgers	13	17	L				
10/2/1939	MON	vs	CHICAGO	0	32	L				
10/3/1938	MON	@	New York Giants	13	10	W				
10/4/1937	MON	vs	CHICAGO	0	7	L				

<u>Monday Night Football Highlights</u>

23-0 S/U @ home on MNF since 1992
20-0 S/U @ home on MNF as favorite since 1992
23-5 S/U on Monday since 2007
8-1 S/U on road on MNF since 2014
5-1 S/U @ home vs Cincinnati on MNF since 1970
4-0 S/U vs Tennessee on MNF since 1981
4-0 S/U @ home vs Baltimore on MNF since 1995
Game 0-3-1 O/U vs Miami on MNF since 1995
0-3 S/U & ATS @ Jacksonville on MNF since 1997
Game 0-3 O/U @ Kansas City on MNF since 1996
3-0 S/U @ home vs Buffalo on MNF since 1993
8-1 S/U @ home vs NFC on MNF since 1973
17-5 S/U vs NFC teams on MNF since 1973
3-0 S/U vs Atlanta on MNF since 1974
3-0 S/U vs Washington on MNF since 1973

Source: Steve's Football Bible LLC

Playoffs Game Results

				Pitt	Opp	36-31	
1/12/2026	**2025**	vs	HOUSTON	6	30	L	AFC WILD CARD
1/11/2025	**2024**	@	Baltimore Ravens	14	28	L	AFC WILD CARD
1/15/2024	**2023**	@	Buffalo	17	31	L	AFC WILD CARD
1/16/2022	**2021**	@	Kansas City	21	42	L	AFC WILD CARD
1/9/2021	**2020**	vs	CLEVELAND	37	48	L	AFC WILD CARD
1/7/2018	**2017**	vs	JACKSONVILLE	42	45	L	AFC Divisional Play-offs
1/22/2017	**2016**	@	New England Patriots	17	36	L	**AFC Championship**
1/15/2017	**2016**	@	Kansas City	18	16	W	AFC Divisional Play-offs
1/8/2017	**2016**	vs	MIAMI	30	12	W	AFC WILD CARD
1/17/2016	**2015**	@	Denver	16	23	L	AFC Divisional Play-offs
1/9/2016	**2015**	@	Cincinnati	18	16	W	AFC WILD CARD
1/3/2015	**2014**	vs	BALTIMORE RAVENS	17	30	L	AFC WILD CARD
1/8/2012	**2011**	@	Denver (OT)	23	29	L	AFC WILD CARD
2/6/2011	**2010**	vs	**Green Bay**	**25**	**31**	L	**Super Bowl XLV @ Dallas, TX**
1/23/2011	**2010**	vs	NEW YORK JETS	24	19	W	**AFC Championship**
1/15/2011	**2010**	vs	BALTIMORE RAVENS	31	24	W	AFC Divisional Play-offs
2/1/2009	**2008**	vs	**Arizona**	**27**	**23**	**W**	**Super Bowl XLIII @ Tampa, FL**
1/18/2009	**2008**	vs	BALTIMORE RAVENS	23	14	W	**AFC Championship**
1/11/2009	**2008**	vs	SAN DIEGO CHARGERS	35	24	W	AFC Divisional Play-offs
1/5/2008	**2007**	vs	JACKSONVILLE	29	31	L	AFC WILD CARD
2/5/2006	**2005**	vs	**Seattle**	**21**	**10**	**W**	**Super Bowl XL @ Detroit, MI**
1/22/2006	**2005**	@	Denver	34	17	W	**AFC Championship**
1/15/2006	**2005**	@	Indianapolis Colts	21	18	W	AFC Divisional Play-offs
1/8/2006	**2005**	@	Cincinnati	31	17	W	AFC WILD CARD
1/23/2005	**2004**	vs	NEW ENGLAND PATRIOTS	27	41	L	**AFC Championship**
1/15/2005	**2004**	vs	NEW YORK JETS (OT)	20	17	W	AFC Divisional Play-offs
1/11/2003	**2002**	@	Tennessee Titans (OT)	31	34	L	AFC Divisional Play-offs
1/5/2003	**2002**	vs	CLEVELAND	36	33	W	AFC WILD CARD
1/27/2002	**2001**	vs	NEW ENGLAND PATRIOTS	17	24	L	**AFC Championship**
1/20/2002	**2001**	vs	BALTIMORE RAVENS	27	10	W	AFC Divisional Play-offs
1/11/1998	**1997**	vs	DENVER	21	24	L	**AFC Championship**
1/3/1998	**1997**	vs	NEW ENGLAND PATRIOTS	7	6	W	AFC Divisional Play-offs
1/5/1997	**1996**	@	New England Patriots	3	28	L	AFC Divisional Play-offs
12/29/1996	**1996**	vs	INDIANAPOLIS COLTS	42	14	W	AFC WILD CARD
1/28/1996	**1995**	vs	**Dallas**	**17**	**27**	L	**Super Bowl XXX @ Phoenix, AZ**
1/14/1996	**1995**	vs	INDIANAPOLIS COLTS	20	16	W	**AFC Championship**
1/6/1996	**1995**	vs	BUFFALO	40	21	W	AFC Divisional Play-offs
1/15/1995	**1994**	vs	SAN DIEGO CHARGERS	13	17	L	**AFC Championship**
1/7/1995	**1994**	vs	CLEVELAND BROWNS	29	9	W	AFC Divisional Play-offs

Date	Season		Opponent	Pitt	Opp		Round
1/8/1994	**1993**	@	Kansas City (OT)	24	27	L	AFC WILD CARD
1/9/1993	**1992**	vs	BUFFALO	3	24	L	AFC Divisional Play-offs
1/7/1990	**1989**	@	Denver	23	24	L	AFC Divisional Play-offs
12/31/1989	**1989**	@	Houston Oilers	26	23	W	AFC WILD CARD
1/6/1985	**1984**	@	Miami	28	45	L	**AFC Championship**
12/30/1984	**1984**	@	Denver	24	17	W	AFC Divisional Play-offs
12/25/1983	**1983**	@	Los Angeles Raiders	10	38	L	AFC WILD CARD
1/9/1983	**1982**	vs	SAN DIEGO CHARGERS	28	31	L	AFC WILD CARD
1/21/1980	1979	vs	**Los Angeles Rams**	**31**	**19**	**W**	**Super Bowl XIV @ Pasadena, CA**
1/7/1980	**1979**	vs	HOUSTON OILERS	27	13	W	**AFC Championship**
12/30/1979	**1979**	vs	MIAMI	34	14	W	AFC Divisional Play-offs
1/21/1979	1978	vs	**Dallas**	**35**	**31**	**W**	**Super Bowl XIII @ Miami, FL**
1/7/1979	**1978**	vs	HOUSTON OILERS	34	5	W	**AFC Championship**
12/30/1978	**1978**	vs	DENVER	33	10	W	AFC Divisional Play-offs
12/24/1977	**1977**	@	Denver	21	34	L	AFC Divisional Play-offs
12/26/1976	**1976**	@	Oakland Raiders	7	24	L	**AFC Championship**
12/19/1976	**1976**	@	Baltimore Colts	40	14	W	AFC Divisional Play-offs
1/18/1976	1975	vs	**Dallas**	**21**	**17**	**W**	**Super Bowl X @ Miami, FL**
1/4/1976	**1975**	vs	OAKLAND RAIDERS	16	10	W	**AFC Championship**
12/27/1975	**1975**	vs	BALTIMORE COLTS	28	10	W	AFC Divisional Play-offs
1/12/1975	1974	vs	**Minnesota**	**16**	**6**	**W**	**Super Bowl IX @ New Orleans**
12/29/1974	**1974**	@	Oakland Raiders	24	13	W	**AFC Championship**
12/22/1974	**1974**	vs	BUFFALO	32	14	W	AFC Divisional Play-offs
12/22/1973	**1973**	@	Oakland Raiders	14	33	L	AFC Divisional Play-offs
12/31/1972	**1972**	vs	MIAMI	17	21	L	**AFC Championship**
12/23/1972	**1972**	vs	OAKLAND RAIDERS	13	7	W	AFC Divisional Play-offs
1/6/1963	*1962*	*vs*	*Detroit*	*10*	*17*	*L*	*NFL Play-off Bowl @ Miami, FL*
12/21/1947	**1947**	vs	PHILADELPHIA	0	21	L	NFL Divisional Play-offs

Playoffs Football Highlights

7-2 O/U on road in WILD Card since 1983
1-5 S/U on road on Saturday in Playoffs since 1973
12-2 S/U @ home in Divisional Play-offs since 1972
5-0 O/U @ home in Divisional Play-offs since 2002
5-1-1 ATS on road in Divisional Playoffs since 1984
5-0 S/U vs Indianapolis in Playoffs since 1975
7-0 O/U in AFC Championship since 1998
0-7 S/U & ATS in Playoffs since 2016
5-2 O/U in Playoffs since 2016

Source: Steve's Football Bible LLC

Pittsburgh Steelers Hall-of-Famers

Bill Dudley

Walt Kiesling

Ernie Stautner

John Henry Johnson

"Mean" Joe Greene

Jack Ham

Mel Blount

Terry Bradshaw

Franco Harris

Jack Lambert

Mike Webster

Lynn Swann

John Stallworth

Rod Woodson

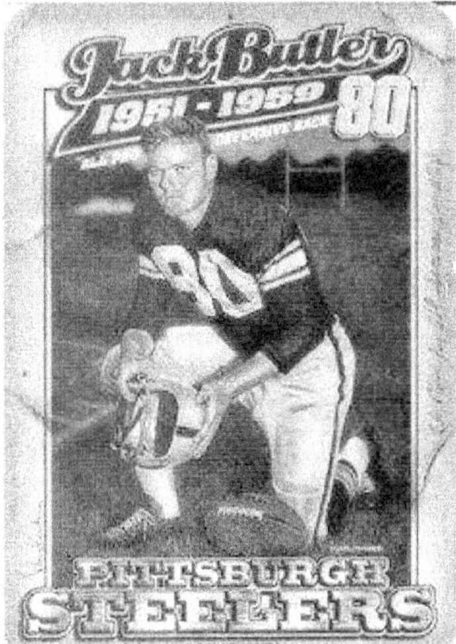

Jack Butler

Dermontti Dawson

Jerome Bettis

Kevin Greene

Troy Polamalu

Donnie Shell

Alan Faneca

www.ingramcontent.com/pod-product-compliance
Lightning Source LLC
Chambersburg PA
CBHW060558120726
48002CB00010B/2723